CLARENDON
AND HIS FRIENDS

CLARENDON
AND HIS FRIENDS

BY

RICHARD OLLARD

Atheneum · New York · 1988

Atheneum
Macmillan Publishing Company
866 Third Avenue, New York, N.Y. 10022

Originally published in Great Britain.

Library of Congress Cataloging-in-Publication Data

Ollard, Richard Lawrence.
Clarendon and his friends.

Bibliography: p.
1. Clarendon, Edward Hyde, Earl of, 1609–1674.
2. Clarendon, Edward Hyde, Earl of, 1609–1674—Friends
and associates.   3. Statesmen—Great Britain—Biography.
4. Historian—Great Britain—Biography.   5. Great Britain
—History—Stuarts, 1603–1714—Biography.   I. Title.
DA447.C6045   1988   941.06′092′4   87-19502
ISBN 0-689-11731-0

Macmillan books are available at special discounts for bulk
purchases for sales promotions, premiums, fund-raising, or
educational use. For details, contact:

Special Sales Director
Macmillan Publishing Company
866 Third Avenue
New York, N.Y. 10022

10 9 8 7 6 5 4 3 2 1

First American Edition

Printed in the United States of America

To

ROBERT LATHAM

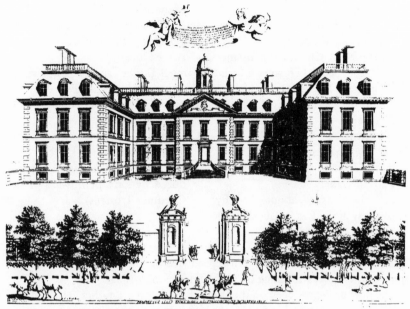

26. Prospect of Clarendon House, by William Skillman. c.1680. Engraving. 51 by 70.3 cm. (Department of Prints and Drawings, British Museum).

List of Illustrations

vii

Sir Alan Broderick (By courtesy of Christie's)

Paris in the 1650s (Trustees of the Ashmolean Museum)

An allegory of Charles II's alliance with the Scots (Trustees of the Ashmolean Museum)

William of Orange in childhood (Trustees of the Ashmolean Museum)

David Loggan's engraving of Clarendon (Trustees of the National Portrait Gallery)

Anne Hyde aged about 19 (By courtesy of the Earl of Clarendon)

Ormonde (By courtesy of Lord Home of the Hirsel)

James, Duke of York (Reproduced by gracious permission of Her Majesty the Queen)

Samuel Butler, author of *Hudibras* (By courtesy of Lane Fine Art)

Charles II (By courtesy of Lord Home of the Hirsel)

Catherine of Braganza (By courtesy of Lord Home of the Hirsel)

Lord Chancellor Clarendon (Reproduced by kind permission of the Chequers Trustees)

The portrait medal of Clarendon reproduced on the title page and on the spine of the jacket was struck by Abraham Simon in 1662.

The portrait reproduced on the front of the jacket is another version of the Hanneman portrait facing p. 176. A third version (not reproduced) hangs in the National Portrait Gallery.

A nineteenth-century drawing of the house in Rouen in which Clarendon died is reproduced on p. 339.

Acknowledgments

FRIENDSHIP is a principal theme of this book. The debts incurred in writing it have borne that pleasant interest. To the pioneers of modern Clarendonian scholarship, Dr Brian Wormald and Professor Trevor-Roper, I am under many obligations. Dr Paul Seaward and Dr Edward Chaney have also put me on the track of much that I would otherwise have missed. Sir Oliver Millar has spared neither pains nor time in finding out pictures and in arranging for me to see them, besides putting his own knowledge and understanding of the period at my disposal. To his initial and continued encouragement and to that of Robert Latham, who has crowned his kindnesses by reading through my typescript, I owe more than I can possibly say.

I had not gone far in setting down the names of the archivists, scholars and keepers of collections who have provided me with information or assistance before I began to feel like a speaker who is going on too long. I hope that they will believe my gratitude none the less for their being remembered *in pectore*. I wish however particularly to thank Sidney Ball for telling me of the memorial erected by Clarendon to his first wife.

The benefit conferred by my old friend Giles St Aubyn in presenting me with his set of the *Clarendon State Papers* can only be assessed by those who know the riches to be found there.

For their kindness in allowing me to see pictures in their possession and for permission to reproduce them I wish to thank Mrs Broughton-Adderley, the Earl of Clarendon, Lord Home of the Hirsel and Sir John Plumb.

For permission to quote from manuscripts in their possession I am grateful to the Curators of the Bodleian Library and to the Controller of H.M. Stationery Office, and to Viscount Middleton for permission to quote from the Brodrick MSS deposited in the Guildford Muniment Room. The staff of the Bodleian Library, the British Library, the

Clarendon

London Library, the National Portrait Gallery, the Ashmolean Museum, the Plymouth Museum and Art Gallery and of the Archives Diplomatiques have enhanced the pleasures of research.

The award of a bursary by the Literature Panel of the Arts Council and of a Research Fellowship by the Trustees of the Leverhulme Foundation have been of the greatest assistance. To them, and to everyone else who has helped me, my best thanks.

Richard Ollard
Norchard. November 1986.

Contents

Note

FOR THOSE not familiar with the process by which Clarendon's *History* and *Life* and *Continuation of the Life* came to assume their final form the following note may be useful for quick reference. A fuller exposition will be found in the text pp. 56–7.

Date	Place	Literary Activity
1646–8	Scilly and Jersey	Begins *History of the Rebellion* and carries it down to 1644.
1668–71	Montpellier	Writes his *Life* down to 1660.
1671–2	Moulins	Receives the original MS of the *History* and cannibalises the *Life* to compose the *History* as subsequently published.
1672–3	Moulins	Resumes work on the *Life* and extends it in the *Continuation*, from 1660 to 1668.

List of Abbreviations

Ath. Ox.	*Athenae Oxonienses*
BL	British Library
Bod.L	Bodleian Library
CJ	*Commons Journals*
CP	Correspondance Politique
CRO	County Record Office
Cal. Clar. SP	*Calendar of the Clarendon State Papers*
Clar. MSS	Clarendon Manuscripts
Clar. SP	*Clarendon State Papers*
Cont.	*Continuation of the Life*
DNB	*Dictionary of National Biography*
EHR	*English Historical Review*
HMC	Historical Manuscripts Commission
Hist.	*History of the Rebellion*
LJ	*Lords Journals*
PRO	Public Record Office
SP	State Papers
Tracts	*A collection of several Tracts of the Rt. Hon. Earl of Clarendon (1727)*
VCH	*Victoria County History*

I

Origins and Outlines

CLARENDON is so much a part of the landscape of English civilisation
that he is almost lost in it. Unlike his greatest opponent Cromwell he
presents no unfamiliar outline to arrest the curiosity or stir the emotions of his countrymen. The title that he chose for his earldom carries
the sound of church bells heard across the fields in summer; tranquil,
dignified, ordered, at home with itself. The Clarendon building at
Oxford, tall, firm, balanced and quietly magnificent, evokes responses
of the same order. Yet, if one thinks of him by the name he bore
throughout the conflict that gave him both his place in history and his
subject-matter as a historian, the associations of sound are very
different though not less true to the man. Mr Hyde (as he habitually
refers to himself in the *History* and the *Life*) or Sir Edward Hyde, as his
contemporaries knew him when he was forging the policy of constitutional Royalism, sounds as if he ought to be a more acerbic, quick-
witted, ambitious, amusing person than the ponderous figure,
swathed in his Lord Chancellor's robes, that gazes at us, not without an
inviting sparkle of intelligence, from the engraved frontispiece of the
History of the Rebellion.

To mention him in the same breath as Cromwell will seem to many
readers absurd. Certainly the great nineteenth-century historians who
drew the map of the period, particularly and especially S. R. Gardiner,
would have snorted with contempt. The two were, indeed, men of
utterly different temperament, capacity and type. Cromwell was a
leader of genius, in war and peace. No ruler in our history has shewn a
surer instinct for maintaining himself in power. What ideas he had,
what sense of history, what creative and constructive understanding of
politics is much less clear. Carlyle credits him with an intuitive grasp of
what was possible in politics hardly short of the divine authority
claimed by the Stuarts. Professor Trevor-Roper, with no less force and
much greater lucidity, depicts him as a woolly-minded, well-meaning,

1

political simpleton. In all these respects Clarendon is his direct antithesis. He was not a war leader, indeed was only present, and that in a
non-combatant capacity, at one of the battles of the Civil War. He was
not an effective leader in peace: he irritated and antagonised many
more than he conciliated or attracted. He had none of the antennae
that enabled Cromwell to sense a threat and to forestall it. When he
fell, he fell beyond the possibility of recovery. And the forces that over-
threw him were such as Cromwell would have dealt with before
breakfast.

On the other hand Clarendon's understanding of history and
politics was as vigorous as Cromwell's was weak. Few English statesmen
— and certainly not Cromwell — can claim to have acted so constructive and creative a part in the history of their country. To Clarendon
the only basis of political action was the rule of law. Against the incessant attacks of courtiers, soldiers, grandees and even the Queen, who of
all advisers had the firmest grip on Charles I's Protean character,
Clarendon insisted that the Royalist case rested, and must unyieldingly
rest, on the bedrock of the known and established laws of England. He
was more, far more, of a Parliament man than Cromwell, a speaker and
debater of outstanding quality, a Chairman of Committees whose services were more in demand than those of any other member making his
Parliamentary début in 1640. He had, it seems, been born for the
House of Commons. To him more than any other man belongs the
credit for the policy, derided and denounced through the long, hopeless, thankless years of exile, that brought about Charles II's Restoration with the whole-hearted acceptance of the country and without
foreign intervention. English politics flowed again through the old
channels. Development resumed from a historical past. The organic
view of society, the key to the English political tradition, triumphed
through the steadfast wisdom and integrity of a handful of men hardly
known to the great age of our history that they made possible. Everyone has heard of Cromwell and Charles I, of Pym and Strafford, of
Hampden and Prince Rupert, even perhaps of Clarendon himself. But
who except those who have more than a casual acquaintance with the
history of England in the seventeenth century have heard of Falkland
and Chillingworth and Morley and Earles, of Hopton and Capel, or
Ormonde and Nicholas? Yet these men were among the closest friends
and profoundest influences on a man who had, in Sir Charles Firth's
golden phrase, 'a genius for friendship' and whose wide curiosity and
questioning intelligence kept a naturally conservative temperament
open to experience and to argument.

Politicians are almost by definition intent on power. To achieve
office and to maintain themselves in it is assumed to be their chief
object in life. Clarendon is unusual in that he took, or appeared to

take, a subtler view. He was not, and did not pretend to be, without ambition. He loved not only the good things and the softnesses of life but its splendours and extravagances. In his years of power he built a house in Piccadilly of such magnificence that even his friends thought it far too grand, an opinion that he subsequently came to share. It was pulled down within a decade of his death. The great collection of pictures that it was to have housed survived for nearly a century at Cornbury, the handsome house he had built near Oxford, and a great part of it survives to this day.[1] Clarendon, convivial, sociable, cultivated, knew how pleasant it was to have money. But unlike so many to whom this insight has been granted he did not confuse the agreeable with the essential. He knew not only what it was to be perpetually hard up: he had experienced, what is bitterer, the transition to that state from a long and habitual prosperity. He had seen his wife and children living from hand to mouth. He had been cold and hungry for months together. He had had to endure the embarrassments of being shabby and down at heel in the smartest of courts and capitals where others had taken care to look after themselves better.

> Nil habet infelix paupertas durius in se
> Quam quod ridiculos homines facit.
>
> 'The worst of poverty, depressing as it is,
> is that it makes men look ridiculous.'

Yet he never fell into the error, so common in every age, that he observed in his friend, the Earl of Holland: 'He was a very well bred man, and a fine gentleman in good times; but too much desired to enjoy ease and plenty when the King could have neither, and did think poverty the most insupportable evil that could befall any man in this world.'[2] Easy sneers of sententiousness and hypocrisy fail before a man who had proved his right to postulate such principles by living up to them himself.

In the same way the facts of his political record clear him from seeking place and power. Twice he refused the office of Secretary of State when offered it by Charles I, contenting himself with the then much less important office of Chancellor of the Exchequer, a post in his time overshadowed by the high and mighty figure of the Lord Treasurer. In exile with Charles II he refused all honours and among the clamour of plaintive and grasping Cavaliers, each anxious to secure as it were a fistful of post-dated cheques, sought no reversion of profitable

---

[1] See on all this Robin Gibson *Catalogue of Portraits in the Collection of the Earl of Clarendon* (privately published 1977).
[2] *Rebellion* XI, 263.

sinecures. Although the Lord Keeper of the Great Seal, Sir Edward Herbert, had proved himself so incapable and untrustworthy that he had been forbidden the court, Clarendon refused the King's offer to dismiss him, preferring to wait until Herbert died in 1657 before accepting the Lord Chancellorship.

Does he then belong, like Cincinnatus or St Ambrose, to that rare category of historical figures who have been dragged to authority and eminence against personal preference or in spite of real humility? By no means. Clarendon, who confronted his own weaknesses as manfully as Pepys and has left almost as ample documentation, knew that he was a vain man. Was he then a dilettante, an aesthete of ideas who found the perfect symmetry of abstractions more satisfying than the world of affairs? This could, perhaps, be argued. Indeed to some extent it must be true of anyone with an open and speculative turn of mind and a distaste for intrigue. On the other hand Clarendon was a politician through and through. He held his beliefs passionately. He fought for them with all the energy and resource at his command. He was generous to his friends and not always just to his opponents. He worked for the advancement of those who shared his opinions and did his best to obstruct the careers of those who did not. He was a man of affairs, a successful barrister, a shrewd observer of men and women in and about the political world of his day. That he was also no less at home in a library or in the company of writers such as Ben Jonson or thinkers such as Selden or Hobbes, that he could enjoy a life of reading and writing, freed from the responsibilities and conflicts of high office, does not mean that he was not a politician. It means that he was many-sided and well-balanced to a degree that historians have been reluctant to admit.

Clarendon has been undervalued as well as misrepresented. As in his own day his firm refusal to substitute fashion for morality has counted against him. 'Clarendon, Charles II's stuffy Lord Chancellor' runs the caption to his portrait in the new and admirable *Oxford Illustrated History of England*. It reflects exactly the opinion of Lady Castlemaine, Charles II's principal and most expensive mistress, and her political hangers-on. Clarendon, the close friend of her father, had not concealed his detestation and disapproval of the gross and open licentiousness that she personified, had deplored her influence on the King and would, if he could, have sent her packing. No wonder that she and her associates thought as they did. 'Stuffiness' in that context means not condoning sexual laxity. But its real, central meaning is best understood in describing an atmosphere where fresh air and fresh ideas never penetrate, where laughter and cheerfulness are unthinkable, where formality and routine leave no room for spontaneity.

Clarendon's life presents so many formal designs that it resembles an act of imaginative creation. A novelist or a playwright would find his material mysteriously shaped for him, like so much of the landscape of the Wiltshire–Dorset borders, the countryside of Clarendon's childhood and youth, where it is often hard to judge from the skyline of a hill what is natural and what is man-made. Themes and characters re-enter his story with a strange symmetry. Take for instance the part of Wiltshire where he was born on February 18, 1609. The village of Dinton, where his father Henry Hyde had a small estate, lies about ten miles west of Salisbury in the high, wooded country of Cranborne Chase. Five miles south lies Broad Chalke, for so many years the home of his younger contemporary John Aubrey, whose vivid and racy evocation of the age of Charles II comes so much closer to our own than Clarendon's winding sentences. Nearer still, the next village in fact, is Compton Chamberlayne, the seat of the Penruddock family, whose kind and gentle head, Colonel Penruddock, was to be executed in 1655 for leading the only open Royalist rising against Cromwell's rule. Clarendon, who was on tenterhooks for a general rising proposed by the Royalist underground, thought him not bloody-minded enough to start such a conflagration.[3] Further south, another seven miles or so, is Wimborne St Giles, the great house, now sadly emptied of its pictures and documents, of Sir Anthony Ashley Cooper, first Earl of Shaftesbury. How artfully history entwined their lives. It was Clarendon who championed, in the Civil War, the right of the young Royalist territorial magnate to the governorship of Weymouth against the wishes of Prince Maurice, whose forces were then moving up to their successful siege of Lyme.[4] No doubt Charles I's grudging reluctance to deny the claims of his nephew disposed Ashley Cooper to throw in his lot with the Parliament and to serve the Cromwellian Protectorate. Returning, as so many Cromwellians did, to the royal service in 1660 he was among the ablest members of the administration over which Clarendon presided and was prominent among the group which finally displaced him. If Clarendon was the tutelary deity of the future Tory party, Shaftesbury was the historical founder of the Whigs. Few parts of England can have proved so politically fertile as Cranborne Chase.

Away to the north, still in Wiltshire, was Malmesbury, the home town of Clarendon's sometime friend and latterly most formidable intellectual opponent, Thomas Hobbes. When Clarendon was born Hobbes had just graduated at Oxford from Magdalen Hall, where thirteen years later he was to follow him. They were to meet in London when Clarendon, a rising barrister of scholarly and intellectual tastes, frequented the company of John Selden, the acknowledged leader and

[3] *ibid* XIV, 132.   [4] *ibid* VII, 199, 200.

patron of all learned inquiry. In the Interregnum they met again at Charles II's court in exile at Paris. There Hobbes shewed Clarendon the manuscript of *Leviathan* and watched with amusement the horrified reaction of a reader intelligent enough to understand the moral and religious devastation implicit in its arguments. Hobbes returned to make his peace with the Commonwealth government and, though Charles II welcomed him to his court at the Restoration because he found his sceptical wit sympathetic to his own, Clarendon would not condone the publication of opinions and arguments that he thought subversive of religion and society. They met for the last time as disputants when Clarendon's executors posthumously published his *Brief View and Survey of the Dangerous and Pernicious Errors to CHURCH and STATE in Mr Hobbes's Book entitled LEVIATHAN*.

All these people and events will be considered in their proper place. The point of the present survey is not to confuse the reader but to flush out the point perhaps indistinctly made that however far Clarendon travelled in life he seems always to be encountering persons who belong to his own earliest days. All his roads lead not to Rome, a destination of which he had a deep abhorrence, but to Wiltshire. Naturally enough his own relations were spread over the surrounding country and clustered in Salisbury. One uncle was Recorder and sat for the city in Parliament. There were cousins who held canonries in the Cathedral and one who briefly became Bishop. When King Charles II was a hunted man after the Battle of Worcester in 1651 it was the widow of one of his cousins who sheltered him at Heale House, a bare three miles north of Salisbury, as he made his way to the Channel coast. The two older men who worked most closely with Clarendon in the desperate period immediately after the execution of Charles I, Cottington and Sir Edward Nicholas, were Wiltshire neighbours. Cottington, who was the grander, owned the magnificent estate at Fonthill which is generally associated with its eighteenth-century occupant, William Beckford. But Sir Edward Nicholas was of much the same social and economic standing as Clarendon and had as a schoolboy at Salisbury lodged in the house of Clarendon's uncle Sir Laurence Hyde and shared a tutor with his sons. Salisbury runs through and through his life. It was to the Close that his father retired when he felt death approaching so that he might attend the daily offices in the Cathedral in which he had reserved a burial place. When the plague forced the Court out of London in 1665 it was to Salisbury they went after a brief sojourn at Hampton Court. The Bishops of Salisbury during Clarendon's administration were all three closely connected with him: Henchman, who had guided Charles II to Heale House in 1651: John Earles, his lifelong friend, of whom he wrote that 'he never had, or could have had, an enemy': and last of all Alexander Hyde,

6

Clarendon's first cousin. When he was offered an earldom it is surely probable that he would have taken the title of Salisbury if the Cecils had not already been in possession of it. As it was he did the next best thing and took that of the ancient royal manor of Clarendon that touches the city's eastern border.

Another possible projection of Clarendon's life would be along the meridian of his connexion with the Villiers family, who at length, generations after his death, were to inherit both his title (in the form of a second creation) and his great collection of portraits. But that will be evident enough from the story of his life. And what a story it is, what a plot. It is high time to embark on it.

The young Edward Hyde (it will be easier not to antedate his elevation to the peerage) has already been assigned a birthday and a local habitation. Something more must be said about his name. The Hydes were a Cheshire family who had been landowners there since at least the time of Henry III. (In the *Life* Clarendon claims, inaccurately, that they had owned the estate of Norbury since before the Norman conquest. In fact they acquired it by marriage in the thirteenth century.) They were still established there in Edward's day. His own cadet branch derived from his grandfather, an enterprising younger son who after a brief training in the Exchequer took service with Sir John Thynne, the builder of Longleat. This experience, according to his grandson, was short and unrewarding. But he displayed the family talent for marrying an heiress, herself a Westcountry woman, bought an estate at West Hatch, near Dinton, and settled down to raise a family. He owed his own start in life to his early education and he took care to breed his sons (there were four of them) at the University of Oxford, and the Inns of Court.

Henry, the third son, was Edward's father. The admiration and affection he aroused are bright on the pages of autobiography, written in 1668, when the father had been dead for thirty-four years and the son, prematurely aged and far from well, was contemplating the ruin of his career: '. . . not only . . . the best father, but the best friend and best companion he ever had or could have . . . the wisest man he had ever known; . . . though God Almighty had been very propitious to him, in raising him to great honours and preferments, he did not value any honour he had so much as being the son of such a father and mother, for whose sakes principally he thought God had conferred those blessings upon him.'[5] Although his mother is joined in this encomium it is about all that we are told of her, except the facts that she was married to his father for above forty years and 'never was in London in her life'. An odd omission since she lived to see her son's triumphant

[5] *Life* I, 17.

return in 1660 and was herself buried in Westminster Abbey the following year.[6]

That Henry Hyde was a great, probably the greatest, formative influence on his son seems clear. The outline of his life, as sketched in the *Life*, though shadowy is interesting. He was 'a very good scholar, having proceeded master of arts in Oxford' and fostered his son's inclination to the study of Latin literature. He had been entered at the Middle Temple but did not feel drawn to the law in which two of his brothers made highly successful careers. He had, his son tells us, 'long had an inclination to travel beyond the seas, which in that strict time of Queen Elizabeth was not usual, except by merchants, and such gentlemen as resolved to be soldiers'. To travel for mere curiosity in that age of plots, conspiracies and coups was to risk not only the suspicious glances of the government but the malicious attentions of the common informer. Henry Hyde however got his way. Supported by his widowed mother he travelled up the Rhine into Italy, spending some time in Florence and Siena and some months in Rome 'which was not only strictly inhibited to all the Queen's subjects, but was very dangerous to all the English nation who did not profess themselves Roman Catholic'. The authorities in England suspected such visitors of making subversive contacts while the English Roman Catholics feared they were spying on the priests being trained for the English mission where the rack and death by mutilation were the penalties of detection. None the less Henry Hyde, in spite of his robust Protestantism, struck up a warm friendship with Cardinal Allen, the last surviving English member of the Sacred College, and enjoyed privileges open to few loyal subjects of the Crown in that climate of cold war. His mother was relieved indeed when he came safe home. Anxious to prevent the repetition of such risky ventures she pressed him to marry and offered to settle a competence upon him if he did. Henry took a leaf out of his father's book and 'married Mary, one of the daughters and heirs of Edward Langford of Trowbridge, in the county of Wilts esquire, by whom . . . he had a good fortune, in the account of that age. From that time [i.e. the early 1590s] he lived a private life at Dinton aforesaid, with great cheerfulness and content . . .' His son emphasises the respect in which he was held by his neighbours, supporting the contention by the statement that 'he served as a burgess for some neighbour boroughs in many parliaments'. In fact he sat in two.[7] What if anything he did for them we do not know. The opportunities of private members in Tudor Parliaments were in any case limited in the extreme.

[6] J. L. Chester, *Westminster Abbey Registers*, 155.
[7] *History of Parliament. The House of Commons 1558–1603* ed. P. W. Hasler II, 361.

From one letter preserved in his son's papers[8] it is possible to form some idea of him. It is very long (the Hydes seem to have felt about letter-writing much as Falstaff did about potations) and, like father like son, not at all easy to read. It was written on April 20th from Dinton. Though no year is given the Parliament, to which the letter alludes, was opened on June 18, 1625. The recipient, his brother Sir Nicholas Hyde, was a member.

> I pray God prosper you all in the parlament and iff itt be possible I would greately wish that you might take away the uncharitableness and the inhospitality of the statute of the poore, that the earth might be free for men. And because I am entered into the parlament I wyll acquaint you with an earnest petition of certayne good and understanding husbandmen. They say the Rooke [is] the vildest and unprofitablest varmin that is, and in their opinion easiest destroyed. They wonder you have hetherto taken no order for them, they roote upp wheate in that abundance upon itt first sprouting out of the ground and breake whole eares off against harvest that they suppose they are a great occasion of the dearth. They say they might be utterly destroyed in two or three yeares if you would licence and compell men to kyll them in their owne grounde in breeding tyme only: compell them by penalty that whosoever lett a neste lye should forfeit 5d . . .

Henry Hyde goes on to consider the matter in all its aspects and implications, not forgetting the sport of rook shooting or the uselessness of 'your Rooke nett statute . . . they are so crafty that they will not come to the snare above once'. Softening the harshness of the Elizabethan Poor Law with its strict control over the mobility of labour and settling the methods of agricultural pest control are, in his view, the two things needful. Nothing is said of the reckless adventurism of Charles I's foreign policy which the parliament had been called to underwrite. It is odd that so travelled a man should take no interest in his country's involvement in European affairs. But he passes tranquilly on to a long and humorous account of his efforts to settle a boundary dispute at Trowbridge which apparently affected them both, as he ends his letter by promising to accept whatever arrangement his brother comes to.

And this, apart from his son's memorably affectionate description of him, is almost all the evidence we have about him. One letter, written late in life, is not much. But it does tell us something. Its tone and temper and subject-matter confirm the representation of a good-natured, neighbourly country gentleman, sure of his own position and more interested in the general well-being than in securing or advancing his own rights and privileges. In striking contrast to his son, who never in his voluminous writings takes the slightest notice of the

[8] Clar. MS 4 f.110.

condition of the poor, his first concern is with social justice. It is the letter of a deeply civilised man. Squire Western could not have written it. Filial piety seems in this case to have been justified.

The father adhered to the family tradition of setting a high value on education. Edward was sent to a school kept by the Vicar of Dinton, who had been a schoolmaster before becoming a parish priest, but his eminent pupil writes disparagingly of his abilities and attributes his early academic progress to his father's tuition. By the time he was thirteen he was thought to be ready for the university, not so unusual an age for entry in his time as in ours. His father and one of his uncles had been at Magdalen College Oxford and it was to that body that Henry Hyde wrote to ask that Edward might be admitted. He had previously obtained a letter from King James recommending the President to elect him to the first vacant demyship (a scholarship worth half the usual fees).

The application was received with a courtesy, indeed a warmth, very different from that shewn to Gibbon in the next century.

'That you would send your sonne to our Colledge I thank you, but that upon speciall affection you did it I must thank you much more: for the foundation is of men, not of stones; we are the object of your love and we interpret ourselves to be that Colledge whom you affect so faithfully . . .'[9] wrote John Oliver, the Fellow of Magdalen who was to become Edward's tutor. The relation was a happy one. Soon after term had begun he wrote again, in October 1622: '. . . his owne promising and forward ingenuity provokes my diligence. He hath at length a chamber warme and convenient to study in, and among so great a company as we are, at a reasonable price.'[10] Supported by the King, approved by his tutor, Edward should have been sure of his demyship. Yet it eluded him, and with it the membership of his father's College. Although his tutor was a Fellow, and in 1644 was elected President of Magdalen College Edward had only been admitted to Magdalen Hall. Halls were older than Colleges but far less conscious of their corporate identity and of their historical continuity. They were generally without much in the way of buildings or endowments. Forty-five years later this relegation to the academic proletariat still rankled. The President of Magdalen, in Hyde's view, had cheated over the election of demys, pretending that it had already taken place before the King's letter arrived. The President was reproved by the Secretary of State and humbly promised to elect the boy to the first vacancy. But for the first time in the history of the College no vacancy occurred throughout the whole of the following year.

By the next year Edward was no longer interested in demyships. The

9 *ibid* 3 f.143.   10 *ibid* f.154.

death of his elder brother made him heir to his father's estate. The career of a learned clergyman, which no doubt father and son had agreed on, was no longer appropriate. Instead he followed the family trail to the Inns of Court, the approved finishing school for landed gentry whose lifeblood was leases and marriage settlements. He was entered in the Middle Temple by his uncle Nicholas, then its Treasurer, shortly to be appointed Lord Chief Justice of the King's Bench. But the plague of 1625 which drove the new Parliament (of which as we have seen Nicholas was a member) from London to Oxford kept the young man from his new calling. He divided his time between his father's house and the university 'where he took the degree of bachelor of arts, and then left it, rather with the opinion of a young man of parts and pregnancy of wit, than that he had improved it much by industry, the discipline of that time being not so strict as it hath been since, and as it ought to be; and the custom of drinking being too much introduced and practised, his elder brother having been too much corrupted in that kind, and so having at his first coming having given him some liberty, at least some example towards that license, insomuch as he was often heard to say, "that it was a very good fortune to him that his father so soon removed him from the university," though he always reserved a high esteem of it.'[11]

This passage with its curiously Gaullist theatricality of expression (the third person extended even to self-quotation in direct speech) and its wholly Clarendonian clumsiness of syntax foreshadows much that is to come. At every stage of his life he was to complain, loudly and tirelessly, of his compatriots' habit of drinking too much. There is abundant confirmation from native and foreign witnesses that he was justified. The clear assertion, made by the ex-Chancellor of the University, that the discipline of the place was much improved since his time as an undergraduate, counts against the facile identification of him as a head-shaking custodian of the good old days. But of particular interest to the student of his mind and character is this, the first of many self-estimates. The Old Self appraises the Young Self: but the Young Self is not allowed, as in Max Beerbohm's cartoons, to answer back. How much should we believe him?

Perhaps not implicitly. This is not to deny his essential honesty, still less the seriousness of his moral purpose. Rather it is to acknowledge that these, in his scale of values, took precedence both of accuracy and of truthfulness. The medieval biographers of the saints like the paladins of Marxist historiography in our own time do not set out to mislead their readers. They see, or think they see, the essential pattern of underlying truth and they do not wish to distort it by an irrelevant

[11] *Life* I, 8.

enumeration of facts which may happen to be lying about on the surface of history. Clarendon shares this view. He lived and wrote with a
profound consciousness of moral responsibility. The writing of his own
life could least of all be false to such standards. If he was to demonstrate what he ardently believed to be true, namely that he had been
made a better man by the company and the friendship of the wise and
the good, that he had learnt from them to refer his thoughts and his
conduct to the will of God, it must follow that his youth was less virtuous than his age. To be regenerate one must first be unregenerate. The
Christian doctrine of Redemption, variously understood in the seventeenth century, produces similar effects in contemporaries of a very
different mentality. 'I was a chief, the chief of sinners,' exclaimed
Cromwell, borrowing the words of St Paul to describe his own undergraduate days at Sidney Sussex.

The point may seem hardly worth making, but Clarendon presents
much the same picture of himself during his early years at the bar:
gifted, pleasure-loving, idle; even, he half suggests, dissipated. It may
be true, but the small amount of independent evidence we have hardly
supports him. And in the case of Oxford we have his tutor's high commendation of his industry. Was the venerable statesman perhaps less
of a dog in his youth than he would have us believe? The reminiscences
of old age, especially of matters reflecting on their author, are pro-
verbially unsure ground. And can we believe that he was ever, by
choice, idle? He says himself that he could never bear to be '. . . being
idle is a great Vice and I thinke an intollerable paine'.[12] Every jot of
evidence about him confirms this.

---

[12] Clar. MS 29 ff.132–3. Letter to Lady Dalkeith February 26, 1647.

II

Young Mr Hyde

THE OXFORD from which young Mr Hyde graduated (at the age of sixteen) was less like a modern University and more like the public schools before Dr Arnold and other nineteenth-century reformers took them in hand. The real Universities of Elizabethan and Jacobean England were the Inns of Court.[1] The discipline and the teaching were better, the intellectual temper livelier; the students were recognisably young men, not overgrown children; tastes and friendships were formed there; the theatre and the court opened the eyes of young country squires; libraries such as those of John Selden or Sir Robert Cotton were superior to any to be found at Oxford or at Cambridge; the pulpit, that indispensable channel for the flow of ideas, of controversy, of propaganda, was far more richly and variously served in London than anywhere else in the country.

Except when overborne by grief or ill-health, of both of which he was to have his share, Hyde never lacked energy, curiosity or appetite for life. Indeed it was those qualities, forcing their way through whatever ruins might fall on them, that gave him his astonishing resilience. As a young man with no commitments, in easy circumstances and well connected in his future profession, he made the most of what London had to offer. The London he first knew was the London of Ben Jonson, raffish, drunken, swarming with unemployed officers of dubious antecedents. Ambitious above all of literary and intellectual acquaintance Hyde succeeded in striking up a friendship with the great man. Looking back in old age he singles him out as the dominant figure of his youth, uniting in his person so many leading roles. As poet and dramatist he was the acknowledged master. As a moralist, as a reformer of the English stage and of the English language Hyde accords him

---

[1] This point is admirably made in G. M. Young's lecture 'Shakespeare and the Termers' reprinted in his *Today and Yesterday* (1948).

equal eminence and in a learned age he does not forget to praise his learning. Those to whom Jonson's name suggests good talk in the convivial atmosphere of the Mermaid may be surprised by Hyde's admiration of 'the severity of his nature and manners'. He is more easily recognised perhaps in the account of how their friendship concluded: '. . . he had for many years an extraordinary kindness for Mr Hyde, till he found he betook himself to business, which he believed ought never to be preferred before his company.'

Here, as so often, the range of response, the multiplicity of vision and the actor's readiness to submerge his whole personality in the part he happens for the moment to be playing offer perhaps the best explanation of contradiction or at least discrepancy. Hyde, the writer, historian and autobiographer, has so many irons in the fire. It is not always possible for him to give an account that will serve his central purpose and yet satisfy all the evidence. His central purpose is to affirm that the England of Charles I was sound as a biscuit; happy, prosperous, tranquil and morally healthy. Rottenness set in with rebellion. It is the story of the Garden of Eden all over again.

So simple a view may well provoke a pitying smile. It is, of course, a gross oversimplification of what Hyde actually thought, but it is not a misrepresentation of what he believed to be the real meaning of the events, the terrible and shocking events, through which he had lived. His intelligence, his shrewdness, his intellectual energy and intellectual range opened hundreds of insights into the material he so industriously amassed as a historian and into his first-hand experience of nearly thirty years as a politician and statesman of the first rank. Of course he knew, and in his history demonstrated, that the régime of Charles I was feeble, corrupt, incompetent and unreliable. Of course he knew, and in his history demonstrated, that many of the men who opposed him and many of the causes they espoused were wise and good. But these were facts or incidents. What he was after was principle, the moral law, the will of God. History existed to teach its students morality. From this derived various other functions such as preserving the memory of those who had fought the good fight and exposing the wickedness of those who had brought disaster on their country. 'Nay, sir, if you jest upon sacred subjects, I do not jest with you.' Hyde's view of life was serious, like Dr Johnson's, though neither man could be thought deficient in either wit or humour. It is this seriousness that has to be remembered when considering his treatment of even such apparently frivolous or evanescent subjects as his friendship with Jonson or his life in London as a young man.

Even from what he does say it is clear that he took care to enjoy himself. He admits to spending 'too much of his time' during his first year in the company of unemployed officers, a dissipated set by his

account. But 'he was not sorry that he had some experience in the conversation of such men [no doubt it equipped him to deal with them
when he met them again at the King's headquarters during the Civil
War] and of the license of those times which was very exorbitant'. He
indicates discreetly that he sometimes shared their pleasures but
'without any signal debauchery, and not without some hours every
day, at least every night, spent among his books . . . to be able to
answer his uncle, who almost every night put a case to him in law . . .'
Yet in spite of this careful fostering of his career by the Lord Chief
Justice 'he could not bring himself to an industrious pursuit of the law
study, but rather loved polite learning and history, in which, especially
in the Roman, he had been always conversant'.

From first to last Hyde despised mere careerism. He valued application and ambition, but detachment and the duty of thinking out one's
own position, of deciding one's own priorities and of living one's life in
the light of them, took precedence. From those to whom much had
been given much would be required. What was good enough, even
praiseworthy, in a common labourer or a tradesman was not good
enough for a gentleman, a man of independent means and liberal
education. It is no use pretending that Hyde was ever in any way an
egalitarian. He was sure of his position in a stratified society and
accepted its obligations as well as its privileges. Indeed, with his adored
and admired father's example before him, was not the life of a cultivated country gentleman a high and honourable calling? Would not
the Roman authors he found so congenial have approved such a
choice?

The old self is candid in stating the dilemmas of youth. In the end he
reconciled a successful career at the bar with the life of a fashionable
intellectual. This called for rigorous self-discipline in the matter of
eating and drinking and in the hours allowed for sleep. In this form it
came easily to him. Method, efficiency, order, chimed with his temperament. Controlling his emotions, his prejudices and his tongue was
another matter. How far the young Mr Hyde was ever a man of pleasure
is not easy to judge. In his autobiography he admits, or at least half
admits, to having been a gourmet: 'He indulged his palate very much,
and took even some delight in eating and drinking well, but without
any approach to luxury; and, in truth, rather discoursed like an epicure
than was one . . .' What is given with one hand is taken away with the
other. And he draws our attention, at this as at later stages in his life, to
his resolute refusal to be beguiled into supper parties. He rose from the
dinner table, where the talk had ranged and sparkled as good talk
should, and returned to his chambers, to work far into the night. He
had taken his full part in the feast of reason and the flow of soul. He
had, he tells us, 'a fancy sharp and luxuriant' and there is good reason

15

to believe him. At every season of his life people found him good company. Whether or not he was an epicure he was convivial. He was gregarious, though not, as he often points out, indiscriminate in his choice of society. The pressure of his appetite for ideas and argument seems to have demanded instant release in speaking or writing. One cannot imagine him on a walking tour or a fishing holiday. He defined himself, he realised himself, by contact with other people. Hence his lifelong insistence on the importance of friendship and his genius for it.

The most profound, the most far-reaching was that formed with Lucius Cary, second Viscount Falkland. With the possible exception of Hyde's attachment to his father this did more to shape his mind and character than any other relation in his long and crowded life. So crucial is it to any understanding of him that it will be given a chapter to itself. It was in any case not until about 1630 that it began. As Clarendon himself puts it in his autobiography:

'Whilst he was only a student of the law, and stood at gaze, and irresolute what course of life to take, his chief acquaintance were Ben Johnson [*sic*], John Selden, Charles Cotton, John Vaughan, sir Kenelm Digby, Thomas May and Thomas Carew, and some others of eminent faculties in their several ways.'

He goes on to give a brief description of each. Literature and learning are the dominant notes of the list. Jonson has already been noticed. Both May and Carew were admired poets. Carew, who died before the Civil War, has even attained such immortality as is conferred by inclusion in the original *Oxford Book of English Verse* chosen by Sir Arthur Quiller Couch. Clarendon speaks respectfully of his '. . . many poems (especially in the amorous way) which for the sharpness of fancy and the elegancy of the language . . . were at least equal if not superior to any of that time' but reserves his real admiration for the Christianity of his death 'after fifty years of his life, spent with less severity or exactness than it ought to have been'. May, whom he clearly and justly thought the better writer, comes in for the thunderbolts reserved for those who had chosen the wrong side in the Civil War from ignoble motives. In the terrible words of his old friend he '. . . prostituted himself to the vile office of celebrating the infamous acts of those who were in rebellion against the King; which he did so meanly, that he seemed to all men to have lost his wits when he left his honesty; and so shortly after died miserable and neglected, and deserves to be forgotten'. Whether or no Clarendon is justified in his description of ingratitude and jealousy, there can be no doubting the partiality of this literary judgment. Thomas May's *History of the Parliament of England which began November 3rd 1640* (1647) is not only admirably written in an easy, lucid style that his greater rival might well envy; it is also good-tempered, fair, clear and above all unpretentious. '. . . I shall . . . intreat a Reader that in his Censure he would deal with the Writings of men, as with mankinde itselfe, to call that the best, which is least bad.' The tone of May's preface compels the goodwill of every fellow author.

Charles Cotton was the Raymond Asquith of his generation. 'His natural parts were very great, his wit flowing in all the parts of conversation . . . He had all those qualities which in youth raise men to the reputation of being fine gentlemen; such a pleasantness and gayety of humour, such a sweetness and gentleness of nature, and such a civility and delightfulness in conversation, that no man in the court, or out of it, appeared a more accomplished person; all these extraordinary qualifications being supported by as extraordinary a clearness of courage and fearlessness of spirit, of which he gave too often manifestation.' Cotton inherited a good estate and improved it by marrying an heiress. Hyde hints that great possessions and their entanglements damped the blaze of youth into the smoke of middle-aged self-pity. Cotton had no need to make his way in the world and could retire to the country. Both he and his son were close friends of Izaak Walton. The angler's contemplative temperament eluded the busy, questioning, ambitious Mr Hyde.

Sir Kenelm Digby by contrast was the most dashing of this early circle of friends. Romantic fiction pales beside the colour of his career. John Aubrey's inimitable account of his happy marriage to the most beautiful *poule de luxe* of his age has immortalized him. But as Clarendon points out there was a prodigality of gifts and an adventurousness of temperament remarkable even in that astonishing time. Tall, handsome, learned, rich, aristocratic, enchanting in conversation, he had enjoyed outstanding success as a semi-piratical commander in the Mediterranean. His mastery of languages and his skill as a courtier made him throughout his life a natural choice for diplomacy or secret intrigue. And all this was carried off against the background of having a father who had been executed for his part in the Gunpowder Plot. The son's own religious allegiance was at best equivocal. Twice at least he avowed his Catholicism, at other times categorically abjuring it. Clarendon's summing up is tinged with understandable amazement:

'In a word he had all the advantages that nature, and art, and an excellent education could give him; which, with a great confidence and presentness of mind, buoyed him up against all those prejudices and disadvantages . . . which would have suppressed and sunk any other man, but never clouded or eclipsed him, from appearing in the best places, and the best company, and with the best estimation and satisfaction.'

So far young Mr Hyde's friendships have reflected his love of literature, of polite learning and of well-bred society. The last two friends, Vaughan and Selden, take us back to the Inns of Court. Both of them indeed like Hyde himself were far from confining their intellectual range to their profession. John Selden became in his own lifetime a jurist of European reputation. In the whole history of English law there have been few minds more searching or better stocked than his. But law was only one department of that vast intellectual emporium. Clarendon's portrait of him, one of the most telling, is, for a major figure, one of the most brief:

'Mr Selden was a person whom no character can flatter, or transmit in any expressions equal to his merit and virtue. He was of so stupendous learning in all kinds and in all languages (as may appear in his excellent and transcendent writings) that a man would have thought he had been entirely conversant amongst books, and had never spent an hour but in reading and writing: yet his humanity, courtesy and affability was such, that he would have been thought to have been bred in the best courts, but that his good nature, charity and delight in doing good, and in communicating all he knew, exceeded that breeding. His style in all his writings seems harsh and sometimes obscure; which is not wholly to be imputed to the abstruse subjects of which he commonly treated, out of the paths trod by other men; but to a little undervaluing the beauty of a style, and too much propensity to the language of antiquity: but in his conversation he was the most clear discourser and had the best faculty of making hard things easy, and presenting them to the understanding, of any man that hath been known. Mr Hyde was wont to say that he valued himself upon nothing more than upon having had Mr Selden's acquaintance from the time he was very young; and held it with great delight as long as they were suffered to continue together in London . . .'

The allusion to their parting is of course an allusion to the Civil War. Selden stayed in London — he was, as Clarendon points out, an old man and could not have sustained life outside the natural habitat of his own magnificent library. He was, like Hyde himself, a moderate, good-tempered, rational, civilised man who deplored the resort to force. He emphatically opposed the trial and execution of the King. But on the other hand he had himself suffered imprisonment in the Tower for asserting the rights of the Commons against the pretensions of the Crown in the Parliament that had been so stormily dissolved in 1629. Elected to the Long Parliament as member for Oxford University in the autumn of 1640 he was the Grand Old Protagonist of constitutional liberty.

Selden comes so close to representing Clarendon's ideal, closer, perhaps, in political ideas than he was always ready to admit, that the severity with which he generally treats friends who adhered to the

Parliament is noticeably softened. And so loyal a son of Oxford could never forget the part that Selden played in preserving the Bodleian Library and the University in general from vandalism and vindictiveness when the city surrendered in 1646. As Chancellor of the University he knew how the bequest of Selden's books had enlarged its horizons.

What is especially revealing, however, is his frank admission of the impenetrable unreadability of the great man's 'excellent and transcendent writings'. Clarendon's appetite for the printed word enabled him to digest almost anything. But the contrast, so effectively made, between the lucidity, ease and wit that characterised Selden's conversation (happily preserved for posterity in his *Table Talk*) and the muscle-bound, lumbering gait of his prose was not lost on his young friend. A twentieth-century reader may find Clarendon himself an inhabitant of the glass house at which he is here throwing stones. But by comparison with the divines, lawyers, controversialists, historians whom he read his own writing is light and airy. Indeed his contemporaries, even his juniors such as Bishop Burnet, sometimes thought him not grave enough in his public utterances. If he sometimes strikes us as repetitious and long-winded, if his sentences appear to succumb to every random temptation to ramify into dependent clauses, if he seems to see in a full stop the image of death, we must remember the prose he was brought up to, the sermons, the debates, the legal opinions and arguments, the constitutional declarations, the official correspondence among which he passed his life. In all of these brevity, lucidity, wit were looked on as blemishes. A safe orotund sonority was the hallmark of sincerity and truth, of seriousness and competence.

The other lawyer, John Vaughan, derived his light from Selden's brilliance: '. . . so much cherished by Mr Selden, that he grew to be of entire trust and friendship with him, and to that owed the best part of his reputation.' Young Mr Hyde, it seems, did not really like him. '. . . Of so magisterial and supercilious a humour, so proud and insolent a behaviour, that all Mr Selden's instructions and authority, and example, could not file off that roughness of his nature.' Worse still: 'He looked most into those parts of the law which disposed him to least reverence to the crown, and most to popular authority.' None the less when the war came he did not remain in London with Selden, as might have been expected of a man with the leanings Clarendon suggests. He retired to his family estate in Wales and formally, though tepidly, adhered to the King. Towards the end of the war his house was pillaged by Parliamentary troops and he was subsequently fined for his allegiance. Clarendon thought he had got off lightly: '. . . he enjoyed a secure, and as near an innocent life, as the iniquity of that time would permit.' But he accepted, if grudgingly, his status as a Royalist who had preserved his political virtue and on his return as Lord Chancellor at the Restoration offered him a Judge's place on the bench. Vaughan refused. He had not practised for twenty years and perhaps felt rusty. But he lost no time in obtaining a seat in Parliament and in maintaining a temperate opposition to the Court party. At the time of Clarendon's fall he was one of the leaders of the hunt, a fact that his old friend (but were they ever friends?) misrepresents as a sudden, unexpected act of personal treachery.

Such were the young Mr Hyde's first friends. His circle reflects his literary and scholarly preferences, particularly if these could be combined with good breeding and good talk, and his disdain for the merely professional. Four professional friendships are separately mentioned but the autobiographer is careful to point out that they were 'all men of eminent parts, and great learning out of their professions' as well as being highly distinguished in it. The closest of these was with his fellow barrister, Bulstrode Whitelocke, who had come down from Oxford in 1622, three years earlier than Hyde, and had, like him, been entered at the Middle Temple. From the start both young men were high-flyers. Both were able, well-to-do and well connected in the law. (Whitelocke's father was a Judge of the King's Bench.) Both their fathers had sat in Parliament and it was to be expected that their sons would follow them. Whitelocke indeed succeeded in entering the House of Commons in the short-lived Parliament of 1626 when Edward Hyde was still too young to be a candidate. Both were men of fashion. Whitelocke had been chosen Master of the Revels by his Inn in 1628, and in 1634 he and the junior Edward Hyde were elected to represent the Middle Temple in a collaborative production with the other Inns of a Masque to be performed before the King and Queen. This was a very grand affair indeed. The total cost was over £21,000, say two million in our money. The greatest stage artist of the century, Inigo Jones, was employed to design the scenery and stage effects and William Lawes and Simon Ives to write the music.[2] Clarendon was not overstating matters when he wrote of himself in his autobiography that '. . . his condition of living . . . was with more splendour than young lawyers were accustomed to.'

By 1634 he was well established in his profession and could afford some extravagance. But from his early days at the bar he had managed a creditable appearance. 'I assure you, you may have greate joy of your son Nedd,' wrote his uncle, Sir Laurence Hyde, himself a highly successful lawyer, in November 1629. 'He studies hard, and is very orderly and frugall: making as handsome a show on his exhibicion (which is but forty pounds per annum as I heere) as my sonnes in the same place

---

[2] Ruth Spalding. *The Improbable Puritan. A life of Bulstrode Whitelocke* (1975). 47–50.

made of their several ninety pounds per annum.'[3] Nonetheless Sir Laurence advises his brother to consider increasing the young man's allowance to £90 and in any case to 'bestow on him a suite of Sattin for a Revelling' so that he can fittingly accompany the other 'fyne gentlemen that are students and yet revellers'.

Like his friend Whitelocke, Hyde successfully combined fine-gentlemanship with application to his career. Whitelocke had been advised by Selden to make it a rule always, however late he came back to his rooms, to read something before going to sleep. This was a lighter burden than being put through one's paces by a Lord Chief Justice, the examiner perhaps liverish, the pupil suffering from a hang-over, as the young Hyde was. But Whitelocke's grounding in the law was the broader and more thorough. He rode the circuits, no soft option once the English plain was left behind for the hill country of the north and west. This his friend was never to do, to his eloquent regret.

'He never did ride any country circuits with the judges, which he often repented afterwards, saying that besides the knowing the gentry, and people, and manners of England (which is best attained that way), there is a very good and necessary part of the learning in the law, which is not so easily got any other way as in riding those circuits; which as it seems to have much of drudgery, so is accompanied with much pleasure as well as profit; and it may be, the long lives of men of that profession (for the lawyers usually live to more years than any other profession) may very reasonably be imputed to the exercise they give themselves by their circuits, as well as to their other acts of temperance and sobriety. And as he had denied himself that satisfaction, purely to have that time to himself for other delight, so he did resolve, if the con-fusion of the time had not surprised him, for three or four years (longer he did not intend) to have improved himself by the experience of those journeys.'

No doubt it is largely true that Hyde sacrificed this exhilarating and educative experience to his preference for the social and intellectual pleasures of London. But not entirely. Accident, especially the acci-dent of ill health, played its part. He had hardly arrived in London before he went down with a fierce attack of fever. As soon as he was strong enough to travel he was carried down to his father's house at Purton near Swindon (the family moved there from Dinton in 1625) and it was a whole year before he could begin his career in earnest at Michaelmas 1626. In the summer of 1628 '. . . his father gave him leave to ride the [Norfolk] circuit with his uncle the chief justice . . . and indeed desired it, both that he might see those counties, and especially that he might be out of London in that season when the small pox

[3] Clar. MS 4 f.167.

raged very furiously . . .' The circuit then began at Cambridge. Young Mr Hyde arrived with his uncle on the Saturday night and was accommodated with him in Trinity College, presumably in the splendid rooms that still commemorate their assignment to the Judge's Clerk. The story of his arrival at the Middle Temple repeated itself. The very next day 'Mr Edward Hyde fell sick, which was imputed only to his journey the day before in very hot weather'. But it was the small pox all right, and a very severe attack that nearly killed him. He was moved out of college 'to the Sun inn, over against the college gate' and put under the best medical attention. It was however to God that he ascribed his preservation 'from that devouring disease, which was spread all over him very furiously'. Some five or six weeks later he was sufficiently recovered to pass 'in moderate journeys to his father's house at Pirton'.

There is nothing in this medical history to suggest a delicate constitution. Rather the reverse. Infectious diseases raged unchecked by medicine, public health regulations or adequate sanitation. To have recovered from two such attacks in so short a period is evidence of a physical resilience that matched his mind and his courage. Until the gout began to bother him in 1644, leading to fiercer and even prostrating attacks in the '50s and '60s, he enjoyed a robust health unearned by sedentary habits and incessant overwork. Unlike so many of those with whom he lived he was temperate in diet and in drink. Probably his metabolism would have worried him if he or anybody else had known what it was. Hostile or jocular comment on his girth seems to have been just as common in the lean years of exile as during his prosperity.

On February 4, 1632 Mr Hyde took a step that was to lead him far. He married '. . . with his father's consent and approbation a young lady very fair and beautiful, the daughter of Sir George Ayliffe, a gentleman of a good name and fortune in the county of Wilts, where his own expectations lay, and by her mother [a St John] nearly allied to many noble families in England'. It all sounds eminently suitable; perhaps rather too much so, for a temperament as passionate as young Mr Hyde's. Writing at forty years' distance, an exile for the second time in France, the old statesman's view of that far-off love affair has perhaps been distorted by the refractions of a failing memory. He imputes his own prime motive for the marriage to a desire to concentrate his energies on his profession 'to call home all straggling and wandering appetites, which naturally produce irresolution and inconstancy in the mind'. This desire, he explains, was reinforced by the death of his uncle, the Lord Chief Justice, from gaol fever caught on the summer circuit, an event which took place on August 25, 1631.[4] As to the cool dynastic calculations which, he implies, determined his choice of Anne

---

[4] Campbell. *Lives of the Lord Chief Justices*, i, 386.

Ayliffe we may reserve judgment. Certainly her father was a prominent Wiltshire landowner, being chosen High Sheriff for the county in 1636.[5] Certainly her mother's family connexions exerted a deep and far-reaching influence on the career not only of young Mr Hyde but of that remote figure Lord Chancellor Clarendon. But we should not neglect that measured phrase 'a young lady very fair and beautiful'. Within five months of the marriage she caught the small pox, miscarried and died two days later.

The young widower was inconsolable. 'He bore her loss with so great passion and confusion of spirit, that it struck all the frame of his resolutions, and nothing but his entire duty and reverence to his father kept him from giving over all thoughts of books, and transporting himself beyond the seas to enjoy his own melancholy; nor could any persuasion or importunity from his friends prevail with him in some years to think of another marriage.' It was in fact two years almost to the day, not 'near three' as he states in the *Life*, before he married again.[6]

The monument he erected to her memory bears a Latin epitaph :

> Vale anima candidissima Vale
> Mariti tui quem dolore et
> luctu conficis aeternum
> desiderium

> Farewell, most spotless of souls,
> Farewell, life of your husband
> bound to you forever
> by grief and yearning

> Vale feminarum decus et saeculi ornamentum.

> Farewell loveliest of women, adornment of your age.

Two days after Anne's death her aunt Barbara, Lady Villiers, wrote

---

[5] Fuller's *Worthies* Wilts, 163.
[6] For the history of the misdating of Clarendon's two marriages see my 'A Wedding in St Margaret's' in *For Veronica Wedgwood These* (1986). The wedding to Anne Ayliffe took place in Battersea Parish Church, where the St Johns had their London house (see the extract from the Parish Register printed in J. G. Taylor *Our Lady of Batersey* (1925) 213. Her monument is in Purley Parish Church near Reading, on the south wall of the Tower. Above the Latin epitaph is the inscription:

Here lyes the body of Ann, the wife of Edward Hyde of ye Middle Temple London Esq[r] and daughter of Sir George Ayliffe of Grittenham in the county of Wilts, Knt. who died on the 2nd day of July in ye yeare 1632 Aged 20.

Purley was another seat of the St John family at which the young couple had probably broken their journey to Wiltshire.

I am indebted to Mr Sidney Ball for his kindness in drawing these facts about the first marriage to my attention.

to commiserate and to counsel a Christian acceptance of suffering: '. . . but I pray you remember whoe hath done it: it is the Lord that gave her to you and I know you are so religious that you will submit all to him: and for my part I was so daly a witness of your affection to her that you may ever command me, if I may but beg thus much of you that you will be patient, for which I doe most hartely pray and will ever remane your most assured loveing Aunt.'[7]

The surname Villiers, that family whose beauty and allure enslaved three generations of Stuart kings, runs, as has been said, through and through the pattern of Clarendon's life. The connexion seems pre-figured in the stars of history. Sir Nicholas Hyde had been a protégé of the great Duke of Buckingham and had drafted his answer to the articles of impeachment presented by the Commons in 1626. It was this that had won him his knighthood and his elevation to the position of Lord Chief Justice. The young Edward Hyde's first prose work to have survived is his reply to Sir Henry Wotton's 'Parallel between Robert, late Earl of Essex and George, late Duke of Buckingham' in which he professed to see no point of comparison or similarity between the two men and their situations except that they were both Chancel-lors of Cambridge University. 'They were as distant, as unfit, as im-possible for Parallels, as any two vertuous and great persons (for so they were both) we can direct our discourse to.' In so far as a comparison can be made, the advantages lie decidedly with Buckingham, who had a much harder row to hoe. Of the Elizabethan age we are told: ''Twas an ingenuous, uninquisitive time, when all the passions and affections of the people were lapped up in such an innocent and humble obedience that there was never the least contestations, nor capitulations with the Queen.' Buckingham's lot was cast in a very different ground: ''Twas a busie querulous froward time, so much degenerated from the purity of the former . . . A general disorder throughout the whole body of the Commonwealth; nay, the vital part perishing, the Laws violated by the Judges, Religion prophaned by the Prelates . . .', etc. Whether things were really as bad as this or whether disaffected and difficult persons merely represented them to be so is not entirely clear from the sesqui-pedalian syntax. What is in no doubt is the beauty, charm and accom-plishment of the Duke, who so far from being effeminate was 'of so terrible a courage as would safely protect all his sweetnesses'.[8] No wonder that Charles I was so taken with the piece that he wished to encourage its author to attempt a full biography.

---

[7] Clar. MS 5 f.80 July 4, 1632.

[8] *Reliquiae Wottonianae* 3rd ed. (1672), 185, 189, 195. Sir John Bramston, who shared chambers with Hyde in the Middle Temple, explicitly connects the writing of this piece with the Ayliffe marriage of 1632. *Autobiography* (Camden Society 1845) p. 255.

But it was his marriage, not his as yet unwritten panegyric on Buckingham, that first introduced him to the world of the Court. His first wife's '. . . memory was very dear to him, and there always continued a firm friendship in him to all her alliance, which likewise ever manifested an equal affection to him'. Among them was a young man, William Villiers, Viscount Grandison, son of the Barbara Villiers whose letter has been quoted. Confusingly, at least to those who share the present writer's ineptitude for genealogy, he had inherited the peerage bestowed on Barbara's father, Sir John St John, with special remainder to provide for its descent through the female line. Thus the Grandison peerage originating in the St John family became almost at once, and has since remained, a Villiers title. William, Lord Grandison's portrait, still in the Clarendon collection, supports the description in the *Life* of 'a young man of extraordinary hope'. But this hope was cut short by the Civil War. He died of wounds received at the taking of Bristol in 1643, leaving a baby daughter who was to grow up into that most celebrated of Charles II's mistresses, Barbara, Duchess of Cleveland.

The immediate occasion of young Mr Hyde's entrée to Court circles was a famous scandal. Young Harry Jermyn, then in the first stages of a long and profitably dishonourable career as the most worthless of the many worthless courtiers for whom the Stuarts had so pronounced a taste, had made a hopeful beginning by seducing Grandison's sister, one of the Queen's maids-of-honour, under promise of marriage, and then going back on his word. Max Beerbohm once observed that it was strange how rarely one thought of Cromwell in the Cromwell Road. By contrast it would be hard to think of a more appropriate *genius loci* for Jermyn Street than the mercenary man of pleasure whose career intersected Clarendon's at so many points and who stood, more completely perhaps than any other contemporary, for everything he despised and detested.

Grandison at once issued a challenge or at any rate left no doubt that he was preparing to do so. The King, ever alert to reflections on royal dignity and decorum, clapped them both in the Tower. In the *Life* Clarendon praises the King's 'rigorous and just proceeding' and quotes with especial approval his uncompromising declaration that 'since he was satisfied that there was a promise of marriage in the case, the gentleman should make good his promise by marrying the lady; or be kept in prison and forever banished from all pretence and relation to the court'. In this account, written forty years afterwards, he takes elaborate care to name no names and explains that 'mention of this particular little story' is only made for two reasons. One was that his own concern in it introduced him for the first time 'into another way of conversation than he had formerly been accustomed to, and . . . by the friends and enemies he then made, had an influence upon the whole course of his life afterwards'. He instances particularly the intimacy it brought him with another connexion by marriage of the injured lady, the King's cousin and trusted adviser, the Marquis of Hamilton. He implies that Hamilton played false in the affair and perceived himself detected by Hyde. His second reason for mentioning it was that the affair gradually divided not only the court but even 'the very ministers of state'. There was a reversal of alliances among the favourites and the politicians which, he hints, in some sort laid the train leading to the explosion of civil war.

The key to all this is that Jermyn was, and consistently remained, the favourite of the Queen, Henrietta Maria. (It was widely rumoured that in her widowhood he became her lover, even perhaps her secret husband.) And Henrietta Maria had become, since the death of Buckingham in 1628, the regulator of the King's vacillations. Good judges of form would have put their money on the Queen's horse rather than the King's professions. Hamilton, it seems, was among them.

What did the young Mr Hyde think of it all at the time? Two letters that happen to have survived in an eighteenth-century manuscript give a very good idea: and the openness with which they reflect the liveliness of his affections and of the pain he still feels bring him at once before the reader. The first, dated July 10, 1633, is to his father.

'. . . My Lady Villiers [mother of the wronged girl] believes that I may be of some use there [at Greenwich where the King was expected in ten days' time] and therefore urges my tarriance in town till her unhappy affair have some end. So that I am not to wait at the assizes and by your good leave to defer my blessing of seeing you again longer than I expected.

'The King's abode at Greenwich is not purposed above ten days. If you are pleased that my horses be here the latter end of this month I shall as much hast home as possibly I may, professing piously that as I am capable of no earthly blessing that may be compared to your favour so I can propose no blessing so acceptable to my own disposition as the delight of being where you are.

'I have now endur'd the affliction of a Year's Widowhood and truly (though no Man hath been accompanied with sadder thoughts it is provided for pleasanter hopes) it hath pass'd nimbly. If the old adage *Vexatio dat Intellectum* [the trial of the spirit gives understanding] were universally true I might have made a fairer Growth than I can justify: but it is a melancholic Wisdom is gained by the experiment of Misery: and I can hardly think myself more wise when I feel myself less happy. I wear that about me will not suffer me to murmur: and yet I do not find those many blessings my Youth hath received have [? prepared] me for all my sufferance. My fortunes have hitherto not only satisfy'd my conveniences but my curiosity too is unrepented. I have many friends whereof many are learned and none burdened, and what crowns all my prayers I have the best father: and all these I mention not without infinite acknowledgment to my God. And yet I am not sufficiently provided to contemplate [? my losse] with a regular submission.

'Sir, I know not how this discourse may be forgiven by you: but it hath fallen from me in as great a Calm as my Mind hath long known and I cannot but be disturb'd to find so great an alteration in myself in so small a Revolution of time. You are the comfort of my life. Bless your most obedient son.'[9]

If the prose shows some traces of the elaborate ornament and antithesis then fashionable there is no mistaking the language of the heart. Another letter,[10] undated but evidently written after the King's expected return to Greenwich, tells us less about its writer's state of mind but throws a very different and much more characteristic light on Charles I's handling of the case than the account given in the *Life*. Too long to quote in full, it was addressed to a sister of Grandison's, Lady Dalkeith, with whom for many years, particularly in the years of exile after the Civil War, Hyde conducted a correspondence whose tone suggests an *amitié amoureuse*.

Hyde has, it seems, directed, or at least advised upon, the case ever since Grandison's confinement to the Tower. At the outset both parties were convinced that her sister was not with child. It only became plain that she was after six months had passed. Her case was originally heard at Whitehall before the Lord Treasurer (Portland), Arundel, Pembroke, Paulet and Secretary Windebanke. 'Her usage by the Lords was with much more civility than at first and truly with some favour. What she said in her own behalf was discreet and enough and seemed to find good acceptance from their Lordships. Mr Jermyn confessed he had no accusations to charge her withall.

'Whilst we waited in the Galleries he and I had much conference which methought on his side was broken and distracted as proceeding from a Man that had no Calm in his own thoughts. We all then thought her not with child, and on my conscience, then he would willingly have married her, for all that I could gather from his discusse was that if she proved with child it could not be by him. Which I conceive the conference with wicked persons contracted in him, rather than any jealousy of his own.'

Twenty-four weeks later pregnancy was unmistakably established. The King was away on progress.

'But on Friday last his Majesty called your brother to him and told him that he now intended to make an end of the unhappy business of

9 BL Add. MS 4187 ff.28–28v.   10 *ibid* ff.30–32v.

his sister and to banish Jermyn during pleasure and when my Lord offered to speak on behalf of his sister, the King replied "My Lord, you are mistaken in your information. Your sister hath been more to blame than you think. I know more in the business than you do, or than it is fit you should."'

Denied a hearing, Grandison, no doubt on Hyde's advice, proceeded by petition through the Lieutenant of the Tower, so that the evidence might be brought into the open and criticised. The King refused to accept the petition.

'. . . therefore as a last refuge we persuaded your mother to go to the King and lest her passions might make her unfit for the relation, she was pleased to take in writing a brief discourse . . . The King, who used her with good regard, having read the same told her in cold terms . . . he would do what he was able for her. The Queen stood by without any great sense of what had or could be said . . .'

The last sentence shows that it had not taken young Hyde long to take the King's measure. He ends his letter with a temperate but firm condemnation of his treatment of Lady Villiers: '. . . never poor Woman had less favour nor deserved more pity.'

No doubt his own staunchness in a distressing time bound him closer to Anne's family. When in 1637 his second marriage was blessed with a daughter she was christened Anne. Her daughter was to carry the name to the throne and her reign was to witness the publication of her grandfather's great *History of the Rebellion*.

III

Great Tew

No FRIENDSHIP in this life of friendships was richer or deeper than that formed in young manhood with Lucius Cary, second Viscount Falkland. It sprang from their love of literature, was nourished by their determination to make sense of their religion, and was consummated in a marriage of true minds. Clarendon's two portraits of his friend, one in the *History* and the second in the *Life*, are justly recognised as masterpieces. The nineteenth-century Whig historian Sir James Mackintosh was moved to tears by them. That in the *Life* supplies, appropriately, personal details, looks, tone of voice, money, circumstances, taste. That in the *History* is the fuller, more formal, characterisation. But the formality is animated by a love that, like the first kiss in the fairy tale, brings to the image the colour and beauty of life. 'In this unhappy battle was slain the lord viscount Falkland: a person of such prodigious parts of learning and knowledge, of that inimitable sweetness and delight in conversation, of so flowing and obliging a humanity and goodness to mankind, and of that primitive simplicity and integrity of life, that if there were no other brand upon this odious and accursed civil war than that single loss, it must be most infamous and execrable to all posterity.' The opening notes of the great threnody swell out from the description of the first battle of Newbury, fought in 1643, that his friend was writing in Jersey in the winter of 1647, the war lost, the King a prisoner, himself a proscribed exile anxious for the safety of the wife and children he had left behind in England. The likeness, intimate, affectionate, humorous, touched here and there with sympathetic criticism, is painted at full length. The passage closes in majesty: 'thus fell that incomparable young man, in the four and thirtieth year of his age, having so much despatched the business of life that the oldest rarely attain to that immense knowledge, and the youngest enter not into the world with more innocence: and whosoever leads such a life need not care upon how short warning it be taken from him.'

Falkland's breeding and education had little in common with Hyde's. His father was an ambitious aristocrat, with eyes only for the prizes of court and camp. He had, at first, achieved a record of success as a soldier that had carried him up to one of the highest posts under the Crown, the Lord Deputyship of Ireland. His eldest son and heir was brought over to Dublin and entered at Trinity College at about the same age that Edward Hyde became a member of Magdalen Hall. Intensively tutored, he had, according to his friend, a complete mastery of Latin and French by the time he was eighteen. Doubtless his father meant to found a political dynasty and was equipping his son for a career in the royal service. But at this point everything went wrong. Falkland *père*'s ineptitude as an administrator led, after a long series of squabbles, to a somewhat humiliating recall in 1629. A few years earlier the conversion of his wife, a rich and cultivated heiress, to Roman Catholicism had caused a breach between them. It had also caused her father to cut her out of the succession and to leave his splendid estates at Burford and Great Tew to his grandson Lucius. Lucius had for his part torpedoed his father's grand design by marrying a niece of Fynes Morison, the great traveller, who had not a penny to her name. The elder Falkland was so enraged that he refused to see or speak to his son for the rest of his life, even when the son, penitent for his want of filial obedience but unrepentant in his choice of a wife, offered to make over the whole inheritance from his grandfather and to subsist on his father's bounty. Disheartened by this strong rejection, the young man who had already had some military training in Ireland determined on making a career as a soldier. Like so many of his class who were all too soon to see service in their own country he went over to Holland to obtain a commission in the army of the Republic. But the plan fell through and the death of his father removed the last reason for staying abroad. He returned to England, threw up his military ambitions and decided to devote his time, energy and ample means to a life of reading and writing.

If Falkland had not enjoyed, as his friend had, the blessing of a happy and affectionate upbringing, he inherited from both parents high intellectual and literary connexions. Ben Jonson had addressed a poem to his father who in spite of his political preoccupations and unbalanced temper was a man of some learning. His mother's rigorous examination of her own theological position which had led her to the Church of Rome had made her acquainted with the ablest controversialists of the day. It was in her house that her son met William Chillingworth, the brilliant protégé of Archbishop Laud, who did more to form Falkland's mind and to direct his reading than any other member of the circle for ever associated with his house at Great Tew. Like Hyde, Falkland loved London, above all for its social and intellectual pleasures, Yet when, in his friend's phrase, he resolved 'to advance in letters' he forswore visiting it till he had mastered the Greek tongue 'and had read not only all the Greek historians, but Homer likewise, and such of the poets as were worthy to be perused'.

The friendship had been struck in London, where both men prized the society of poets. It was continued at Great Tew, the country house that the ageing Clarendon evokes with all its vanished magic. Great Tew is still beautiful, still secluded. The heather-honey stone and the thatched roofs of its barns and cottages look much as they must have done when young Mr Hyde, stiff and sore from a seventy-mile ride from London, dismounted at the great house. But the house he knew was faithfully dealt with by the Parliament troops in the Civil War and the present building shares nothing with it but the splendour of its site on the lip of its wooded valley. The Church that adjoins has the light, open, spacious quality that the scholars and thinkers whom Falkland gathered there in the 1630s would recognise as their own. It is an unapologetic, well-proportioned building, not disdaining, or conceal- ing its medieval origins nor aping the liturgical fashions of any party. It embodies the central, clear, tolerant tradition, so easily sneered at, so unsatisfying to the sergeant-majors of religion and politics, that Falkland and Clarendon stood and stand for.

Great Tew as Falkland maintained it (he had to sell the Great House at Burford, his grandfather's alternative seat, to pay off the debts that were all he inherited from his father) had something of a small, highly cultivated Renaissance court, say that of Federigo II at Urbino; some- thing of the Institute for Advanced Study at Princeton; something perhaps of All Souls College, Oxford, whose then Warden, Gilbert Sheldon, was a prominent though not a typical member of the circle. Sheldon as Warden of a College and later as Archbishop of Canterbury inclined to be a martinet. And that, in an age of political and theo- logical rigorism, was precisely what Great Tew set its face against. The house lay about sixteen miles north-west of Oxford. It looked, wrote Clarendon, 'like the university itself, by the company that was always found there. There were Dr Sheldon, Dr Morley, Dr Hammond, Dr Earles, Mr Chillingworth, and indeed all men of eminent parts and faculties in Oxford, besides those who resorted thither from London; who all found their lodgings there as ready as in the colleges; nor did the lord of the house know of their coming or going, nor who were in his house, till he came to dinner or supper, where all still met; other- wise there was no troublesome ceremony or constraint, to forbid men to come to the house, or to make them weary of staying there; so that many came there to study in a better air, finding all the books they could desire in his library, and all the persons together, whose com- pany they could wish, and not find in any other society. Here Mr

Chillingworth wrote, and formed, and modelled, his excellent book against the learned Jesuit Mr Nott [*The Religion of Protestants a Safe Way to Salvation*] after frequent debates upon the most important particulars; in many of which he suffered himself to be overruled by the judgment of his friends, though in others he still adhered to his own fancy, which was sceptical enough, even in the highest points.'

Apart from Clarendon and Falkland, all the people here mentioned were clergymen. Most of them will reappear in this book and need not be introduced before they do. But the whole passage defines the particular refreshment of spirit offered by the informal common life of learned men who took their religion seriously but welcomed debate and even scepticism. They were not dilettanti in religion: 'Here's a pretty thing and there's a pretty thing.' They tried to live it; and in so doing had found that the hard part of Christianity is the practice of it. Hard to achieve, not hard to understand. It was this that gave bone and sinew to their insistence on toleration of opposing views and charity towards opponents. Such an attitude was far from fashionable. Abroad, Europe was still drenched in the mindless, endless, bloodshed of the Thirty Years War. At home, the atmosphere was increasingly one of confrontation.

Laud on the one hand and the militant Puritans on the other had not much use for the values of Great Tew. How much these were the creation, the expression of Falkland's mind and character Clarendon makes plain. His friends' visits 'were so grateful to him that during their stay with him he looked upon no book, except their very conversation made an appeal to some book; and truly his whole conversation was one continued *convivium philosophicum*, or *convivium theologicum* [a feast of philosophy or theology], enlivened and refreshed with all the facetiousness of wit, and good humour, and pleasantness of discourse, which made the gravity of the argument itself (whatever it was) very delectable.'

Here was a lesson Clarendon never forgot. Pepys observed his technique at a meeting of the Tangier Committee thirty years later. 'And endeed, I am mad in love with my Lord Chancellor, for he doth comprehend and speak as well, and with the greatest easiness and authority, that ever I saw in my life. I did never observe how much easier a man doth speak, when he knows all the company to be below him, then in him; for though he spoke endeed excellent well, yet his manner and freedom of doing it, as if he played with and was informing only all the rest of the company, was mighty pretty.'[1] Clarendon never tires of telling us that if there was any good to be found in him it came from the company he kept as a young man. He could admit his

---

[1] *Diary* (ed. Latham and Matthews) 7/321.

own shortcomings and he could learn from observing and appreciating the superior qualities of other people. What he learned from Falkland was that serious subjects do not owe their seriousness to portentous treatment, and that strength of conviction need not imply intolerance. '. . . in all those controversies [of religion] he had so dispassioned a consideration, such a candour in his nature and so profound a charity in his conscience, that in those points in which he was in his own judgment most clear, he never thought the worse, or in any degree declined the familiarity of those who were of another mind; which, without question, is an excellent temper for the propagation and advancement of Christianity.'

Great Tew complements the rationality, the scholarship and the accessibility of the circle that revolved round Selden, who was certainly a friend of Falkland's and is sometimes reckoned among his learned guests. Both men inspired their friends by their determination to 'make hard things easy' without sparing themselves any effort of reading and research or without submitting their opinions to the test of argument. Clarendon's description of Selden already quoted has obvious points in common with his portrait of Falkland. These men stood, as Professor Trevor-Roper has pointed out in his tercentenary lecture, in a great if too rare tradition of Christianity. In the preceding century Erasmus had been its European champion and Richard Hooker its English interpreter. Reason, gentleness and charity distinguish it from the anger, violence and abuse so characteristic of sixteenth- and seventeenth-century religious disputation.

By far the most famous product of the reading and talk at Great Tew was Chillingworth's *The Religion of Protestants*. When Falkland dedicated himself to a life of retirement and learning Chillingworth was installed as his domestic chaplain and resident tutor. The history of his religious opinions is as interesting as that of any Oxford don, Cardinal Newman not excepted. The godson of Laud (not then Archbishop), he had won a glittering reputation as a disputant while still an undergraduate. Elected to a fellowship he was at once courted by the Laudian party as an ally in their controversies with the Church of Rome. Chillingworth accepted these overtures with enthusiasm. But the fearless honesty of his mind was such that on a full consideration of his opponents' arguments he felt obliged to accept them, resigned his orders and his fellowship and departed for the Benedictine seminary at Douai. Here history repeated itself. Asked by his superiors to write down the reasons for his change of position Chillingworth once again found weak links in the chain he was scrutinising. He abandoned the Church of Rome and returned to England but not, to his honour, to the preferments that the exultant Laudians were ready to shower on their prodigal son. Great Tew, not Lambeth or the Vatican, was his

spiritual home. Nothing could inhibit him from following the light of
rational argument and nothing could enlist him in the sectarian warfare of rival churches. *The Religion of Protestants* was written to assert
the right, the duty, of using one's reason as opposed to the acceptance,
against that reason, of authority, no matter whether the authority were
that claimed by the Pope, Archbishop Laud, the Calvinist party in the
Church of England or anyone else. And unlike all these otherwise
diverse partisans Chillingworth was not ready to damn anyone who
disagreed with him. He was in fact asserting that no one had the right
to damn anyone on grounds of belief or doctrine.

The Religion of Protestants was taken at the time to be as much the
expression of Falkland's views as Chillingworth's, a sort of Great Tew
manifesto. Those who disliked and feared its arguments, that is to say
the great majority of every school of religious opinion, were quick to
label the author and his friend Socinians, in other words that they
denied the divinity of Christ. In the lip-smacking language of a
contemporary,

> In the self-confounding ratiocination of his mind,
> and in what was consequent to it, the fluttering
> imbecility of his spirit, Mr Chillingworth slided
> down the precipice of Arianism into Socianism below.[2]

Modern champions of the Great Tew school, hospitably eager to
include them in the blessed company of all rational people, have accepted the description on behalf not only of Chillingworth and
Falkland but even of Clarendon himself. There is no historical warrant
for so doing. Clarendon emphatically and specifically denied the suggestion as an outrageous imputation on the two men.[3] His own vast
corpus of writings, public and private, are so manifestly those of a convinced Christian that evidence leaves no room for argument. What all
were agreed on was the relative unimportance of theology to the
teaching of Christ.

> It is very well worth our reflexion, how little pains our Saviour took (who
> well foresaw what disputations would arise concerning Religion to the end
> of the world) to explain any doctrinal points or indeed to institute anything
> of speculative doctrine in his Sermon upon the Mount, which com-
> prehends all Christianity, but to resolve all into practice . . .[4]

---

2 John Whitaker *The Origin of Arianism Disclosed* quot. Kurt Weber, *Lucius Cary, second Viscount Falkland* (N.Y. 1940) p. 200.
3 *Animadversions upon a Book . . . by* S[erenus] C[ressy] (1673), 184–7.
4 *ibid* 123–4.

In this sentence, written near the end of his life, Clarendon distils the essence of Great Tew.

For it was an essence, an atmosphere, an attitude of mind, not a party or a platform. Personally Clarendon thought that the very rapidity and force of Chillingworth's critical and dialectical powers '. . . contracted such an irresolution and habit of doubting, that by degrees he grew confident of nothing, and a sceptic, at least, in the greatest mysteries of faith'. Yet Chillingworth had returned to the ministry of the Church of England by 1640. Five years earlier he had written from Great Tew to Sheldon who was pressing him to subscribe the Thirty-Nine Articles and thus make himself eligible for a benefice.

'. . . I will never undervalue the happiness which God's love brings to mee with it, as to put it to the least adventure in the world, for the gaining of any worldly happinesse.'[5] This is not the language of scepticism. And everyone, friend or enemy, is agreed that Chillingworth was incapable of hypocrisy, pious or otherwise. Perhaps the phrase with which Clarendon concludes his catalogue of his virtues hits him off best: '. . . his only unhappiness proceeded from his sleeping too little, and thinking too much.'

Closely linked in Clarendon's mind as he looked back at that gentle, scholarly society was John Hales, sometime Professor of Greek at Oxford and for many years a Fellow of Eton where his charm and beauty of character as much as his distinction of mind earned him the title of 'ever memorable'. Like Falkland and Chillingworth he was a little man of great cheerfulness and affability — 'it was an age in which there were many great and wonderful men of that size.' As chaplain to the ambassador at The Hague he had attended the synod of Dort and had there, in his own phrase, 'said Good night to John Calvin'. Not that that led him towards the Church of Rome or even towards Laud, who was fond of him (they had known each other as young dons) and admired his remarkable scholarship. Clarendon thought him the best-read man he had ever met, with the possible exception of Falkland, and had no doubts that his library was the best private collection of books he had ever seen. His intellectual life ranged far and he recognized how much of its value lay in its independence: '. . . he would often say, his opinions he was sure did him no harm, but he was far from being confident that they might not do others harm . . . and therefore he was very reserved in communicating what he thought himself in those points in which he differed from what was received.' Like his old friend the Provost of Eton, Sir Henry Wotton, he detested above all 'the brawls which were grown from religion . . . and would

[5] Quot. Tulloch *Rational Theology and Christian Philosophy in Seventeenth Century England* (1872) i, 284–7.

often say that he would renounce the religion of the church of England to-morrow, if it obliged him to believe that any other Christians should be damned; and that nobody would conclude another man to be damned, who did not wish him so.' Refusing preferment, uninterested in money, he lived among his books until to his great grief his dispossession by the Commonwealth government forced him to sell them. 'He was one of the least men in the kingdom; and one of the greatest scholars in Europe.'

Not all the men that Clarendon lovingly lists, as he sees again from Montpellier in 1670 the Oxfordshire country house of the 1630s, were of this calibre. Sir Francis Wenman, a country neighbour whom Falkland particularly liked and respected, had no pretensions to scholarship but was highly literate and good company. Sidney Godolphin, over whose memory Clarendon was to quarrel with Thomas Hobbes, was a bookish charmer who when out riding with friends made no bones about turning his back on an east wind and making for a chair by the library fire. Again he was a little man. 'There was never so great a mind and spirit contained in so little room; so large an understanding and so unrestrained a fancy in so very small a body.' He had travelled widely in Europe and had served as a diplomat.

The nearest approach to worldliness — and it was very near indeed in Clarendon's view — was in the person of the poet Edmund Waller. The beauty of his verse and of his person was not the beauty of Great Tew. That is to say, it did not evidently arise from his character. He had added to great inherited wealth by carrying off a city heiress under the nose of the expensive young courtier who was, so to speak, the Government candidate for her fortune. In the Civil War he was to save his own skin by betraying friends and relations whom he had involved in the plot against Parliament that bears his name. At the Restoration, though still a rich man, he had jostled unsuccessfully for the Provostship of Eton. Revenge for Clarendon's coolness towards his candidacy may have fuelled the bitterness with which he turned on him in the House of Commons at the time of his fall. Surveying his career and his qualities his great contemporary damns him with inimitable serenity: 'There needs no more be said to extol the excellence and power of his wit and pleasantness of his conversation than that it was of magnitude enough to cover a world of very great faults; that is, so to cover them that they were not taken notice of to his reproach; viz. a narrowness in his nature to the lowest degree; an abjectness and want of courage to support him in any virtuous undertaking; an insinuation and servile flattery to the height the vainest and most imperious nature could be contented with; that it preserved and won his life from those who were most resolved to take it, and in an occasion in which he might to have been ambitious to have lost it . . .'

It is easy to see that Waller would have been good company any-where. But how and why did he find his way into that of Falkland? Through the introduction, it appears, of Dr Morley, one of the group of four or five Oxford divines that Clarendon saw as its nucleus. Morley had been applied to by Waller to guide his reading and form his taste in much the same way as Chillingworth had been by Falkland. Both young men of means, both ex-members though not graduates of another university (Waller had been a Fellow-Commoner of King's, Cambridge), they had chosen a course of self-directed study under the advice of a brilliant young Oxford don.

Of this set of cultivated and clever young clergymen George Morley and John Earles were to become Clarendon's close friends and com-panions until death or the final exile broke the link. Both men were witty and amusing without the least trace of uncharitableness. Neither sought fame or position. Morley indeed had gaily blocked his own prospects of preferment in the Church by a much-quoted repartee. The clergy of the Church of England had long been divided between the Calvinist theology, which had won hands down in Scotland and Holland, and its freewill opponents who were known as Arminians. Asked by some earnest seeker after truth, 'What do the Arminians hold?', Morley replied, 'All the best bishoprics and deaneries in England.' Archbishop Laud, the embattled chieftain of the party, was not amused. His disapproval, Clarendon tells us, was intensified by the respect in which Morley was held by John Hampden and Arthur Good-win. Politically Great Tew was well to the left of the Court and, had it been required to declare itself, hostile to the policies of Strafford and Laud. This was the position of both Clarendon and Falkland as they made very plain in the two Parliaments that met in 1640. Yet these clergymen, who never shifted their ground, became the favourite divines of Charles I in his time of trouble and seem to have compelled the respect, perhaps won the affection, of his notably less devout son and heir. Hammond, with whom Clarendon had least to do after the Great Tew days, became the King's favourite preacher and attended him as his chaplain in captivity until, in spite of Charles I's remon-strances, he was removed by order of Parliament.

George Morley's links with the first Charles were never so intimate, though he was made a Royal Chaplain and was chosen by the King as a delegate to the two conferences, at Uxbridge in 1645 and at Newport, Isle of Wight, in 1648, at which efforts were made, at least nominally, to compose the differences between the two sides. But he was chosen by Charles II to preach at his Coronation and made Bishop successively of Worcester and Winchester. Before that he had shared the hardships of exile and had passed that exacting test with flying colours. Few indeed are the Royalists who never grumbled, never said disobliging things about each other and never provoked a similar reaction. It was Morley's boast, perhaps his only one, that although he went abroad in 1649 with only £130 he came back in 1660 with very slightly more, having in the interval given away many times as much to others less fortunate than himself.[6] His own frugality was not then, or later, in the days of his prosperity, allowed to set the tone of his hospitality. Exile certainly bound him even closer to his old friend Hyde, in whose household at Antwerp he lived for nearly three years. For much of this time Hyde himself was absent, either as ambassador in Madrid or attending the King in Paris, but Morley was one of his most trusted and approved friends to whom was confided the early education and religious instruction of his children.

Morley's religion, like Clarendon's, seems to have altered little, if at all, during a long life. It was a simple but not naive Christianity, strong in practical and devotional piety, sceptical towards all claims of ecclesiastical authority whether they came from the Catholic or the Calvinist tradition, rejecting absolutely any idea of exclusive salvation. As a young man he was repelled, as Falkland was, by the aggressive character of Laud's churchmanship, the counterpart in religion of Strafford's authoritarian politics. He therefore defended — in conversation at least, for he published nothing until he was well over eighty — the old-fashioned moderate Calvinism represented by Laud's predecessor Archbishop Abbott. On the eve of the Restoration in 1660 he was sent over to England by Clarendon to negotiate with the leaders of the Presbyterian party in the hopes of framing a Church system that would comprehend and not insist. As we shall see the attempt failed, but Morley's approach seems to have been well received. He was by all accounts a very winning man.

In this quality he was matched if not surpassed by his own close friend John Earle or Earles as Clarendon usually calls him. 'He was amongst the few excellent men who never had nor ever could have an enemy, but such a one who was an enemy to all learning and virtue . . .' The tribute seems to have been no exaggeration. Even Bishop Burnet, who rarely misses the opportunity for a disparaging comment, says much the same thing, citing in evidence the opinion of Charles II. 'He was a man of all the clergy for whom the King had the greatest esteem. He had been his sub-tutor and followed him in all his exile with so clear a character that the King could never see or hear of any one thing amiss in him. So he, who had a secret pleasure in finding out anything that lessened a man esteemed eminent for piety, yet had a value for him beyond all the men of his order.'[7] What the King probably, and

[6] George Morley. *Several Treatises . . .* (1683), vii.
[7] Burnet. *History of my own Time* i, 402.

Clarendon certainly, valued in Earle next to his goodness and gentleness was his admirable wit. His *Microcosmographie* or Book of Characters published anonymously in 1628 went through edition after edition. The brief sketches of the differing types of don and cathedral dignitary, of shop-keepers, servants, courtiers, barmaids, under-graduates, show a keen edge, unblurred by the charity and kindness of heart, that their author brought to his dealings with his fellow men: '. . . a man of great piety and devotion; a most eloquent and powerful preacher; and of a conversation so pleasant and delightful, so very innocent and so very facetious* that no man's company was more desired and more loved.' With so many of Waller's gifts (he was much admired as a poet and though he suppressed many of his compositions enough have survived to justify his reputation) he was his antithesis in personality: slovenly and absent-minded in dress, contemptuous of ambition in a world he so easily understood. 'He was very dear to the Lord Falkland, with whom he spent as much time as he could make his own; and as that lord would impute the speedy progress he made in the Greek tongue to the information and assistance he had from Mr Earles, so Mr Earles would frequently profess that he had got more useful learning by his conversation at Tew . . . than he had at Oxford.'

So informal a society melts into its own background. These were the men that rose to Clarendon's mind when, forty years on and in another country, he sat down to recreate it. They, presumably, were those who had most influenced his own mind, his morals, his manners, his religion. Among others who may have taken their places at dinner there are Robert Sanderson, whom Clarendon knew too little and Thomas Hobbes, whom he knew too well. Among those who certainly did, but is omitted from his account, is another young Oxford don, Clarendon's contemporary and sometime friend, Hugh Cressy. We know from a controversy in which Clarendon engaged with him at the very end of their lives that he used to visit him in his rooms at Merton of which College Cressy, like Earles, was a Fellow.[8] It also seems probable that he had been for a time chaplain to Falkland, who secured him a canonry at Windsor in 1642.[9] But, by the time Clarendon came to write about Great Tew, Cressy had by his own acts expunged his name from that roll of honour. He had become a Roman Catholic. Worse still he had become a Benedictine monk and had publicly attacked the Church in which he had been bred. To pass him over in silence was best.

It was at this centre of all that was most learned, most liberal-

---

* In Johnson's *Dictionary* 'Gay, cheerful, lively'.
[8] *Animadversions upon a Book . . . By S. C.* 92–3.
[9] Wood *Athenae Oxonienses* (ed. Bliss) iii, 1011.

minded, in Caroline England that Falkland appeared to his friend as most characteristically himself. Of his influence — or is it safer to say of the interaction of their minds? — there will be much to say when to their common horror they saw the hands of light-headed favourites straying to the leash that held back the dogs of war. But it was not only in public matters and high questions that Falkland perhaps refined the stronger, coarser mentality of his friend. His latest biographer, Kurt Weber, prints a letter[10] from Hyde that not only illuminates their relationship but shows that Hyde meant what he said when he wrote 'The first and principal obligation [of friendship] is . . . to apply admonition and counsel and reprehension.'[11]

The occasion of the letter was this. The extravagant, learned but wildly indiscreet Bishop of Lincoln, John Williams, had laid himself open to a successful prosecution in the Court of Star Chamber by a worthless and unscrupulous informer who thus obtained the right to dispose of his sequestered goods. Amongst the Bishop's great possessions was a magnificent library. The informer, knowing Hyde to be a young man of literary tastes and ample means, offered him the first refusal of it. Here was temptation indeed. Such an opportunity, and on such favourable terms, was most unlikely to recur. Hyde's first, though evidently well-concealed, reaction was indignation. '. . . one thought the very proposition was an affront.' Though he did not believe the Bishop innocent of having said things he ought not to have said he thought the punishment monstrously severe, the informer unsavoury, and the Court of Star Chamber ripe for the abolition for which both he and Falkland were to vote in the Long Parliament in 1641. But . . . but . . . there were those books. If he didn't buy them someone else would.

'. . . I would imagine I might as innocently buy them now, as seven years hence, when they have changed three or four Owners more.

'I would very earnestly desire your Ldp's Opinion and Advice, under what Caution and Limitation I may become a purchaser in this sale: what Censure I must undergo from good Men; or what reproach I may from common persons. For I would avoid even unjust Imputations; neither shall it signify with me, that I can do it very secretly, if it be not fit to be done. If your Ldp like the traffic, you will lay some command on me for your own use; for no question there is much there fit even for your store. However I assure you, I am so unsatisfied and unstubborn in my doubts, that I promise to be wholly directed by your council, which can most exactly and will nobly help me upon it.

'If those Books were not to be sold, except I bought them, I would

---

[10] Weber, *op. cit.*, 70–1.
[11] In his essay 'Of Friendship' written at Montpellier in 1670.

think myself obliged to be no Chapman [i.e. not to trade in them]. But that it is a fault to buy them, because Mr Kilvert [the informer] is employed in the sale seemed to me no reason; as if I might not deal for Sr Robert Cotton's or Mr Selden's manuscripts, tho' upon my refusal my Lord Goring* should have them.'[12]

All of Hyde, past, present and future, is in this letter. The eager collector, the serious moralist, the lawyer who sees a colourable line of defence, but above all the friend who thinks that '. . . there can be no friendship but between good men, because friendship can never be severed from justice; and consequently can never be applied to corrupt ends'.[13]

Neither young Mr Hyde nor Lord Chancellor Clarendon is holier than we, but both of them square up to the question of right and wrong. That Lord Falkland helped him to clear his mind on this occasion seems probable; though no answering letter survives, no purchase was made.

---

* A dissipated young aristocrat who, turning soldier of fortune, had shewn considerable gifts for his profession. As a Royalist General he was to clash with Hyde in the closing stages of the Civil War. The character of him in the *Rebellion* tells us more about the incompatibility of temperament and character between them than it does about the actions and motives of the man it purports to describe.

12 Weber *loc. cit.*
13 'Of Friendship' printed in *A Collection of Tracts* . . . (1727).

IV

Marriage and Prosperity

ON JULY 10, 1634, Hyde had been partner to an act about which he had no doubts or second thoughts, and certainly no reason for them. He married, at St Margaret's, Westminster, Frances, daughter of Sir Thomas Aylesbury. It was, as subsequent writers have been quick to point out, a prudent marriage from the point of view of his profession. Sir Thomas as Master of the Court of Requests presided over the court in which most of Hyde's practice lay. He occupied a house in Dean's Yard, Westminster in which the young couple lodged.[1] Besides the Court of Requests Sir Thomas was also Master of the Mint and had a country house, Cranbourne Lodge, on the edge of Windsor Great Park, another mark of royal favour. From later correspondence between his son Will and his son-in-law Hyde it seems that some of the King's advisers pressed for him to be promoted to the Council when the failures of royal policy made change imperative. Nothing came of this. But it can hardly be doubted that his standing at Court improved that of his son-in-law.

What it certainly led to was a private introduction to Archbishop Laud.[2] Hyde had been retained by a group of merchants to draft a petition against the monopolistic practices of a wharfinger who had bought the lease of the Custom House quay, which, under pretence of ensuring the proper collection of duty, he was trying to compel them to use instead of their own. The monopolist had fortified a weak position by securing the countenance of the Lord Treasurer, doubtless by bribery, and it was in his capacity as a Commissioner of the Treasury that the Archbishop had been approached by one of the aggrieved merchants who happened to be his neighbour in the country. Anxious to discover the ins and outs of the business Laud

---

[1] See my 'A Wedding at St Margaret's', in *For Veronica Wedgwood These* (1986).
[2] *Life* I, 22.

was told that young Mr Hyde who had just married Sir Thomas Aylesbury's daughter was the man who could best explain it. Meeting Sir Thomas at Court immediately afterwards the Archbishop asked him to send his son-in-law to see him at Lambeth.

These circumstances have been described at length because, though accidental, they had decisive effects. It is as certain as anything can be that the rising young barrister with Parliamentary aspirations and the busybody Archbishop with a finger in every pie were bound to run across each other. And it is almost as certain that their encounter would have been an abrasive one. Hyde's friends were emphatically not the Archbishop's friends. The Great Tew Circle was in its quiet, scholarly way a movement of protest against his school of churchmanship and even more against his authoritarian tone in both religion and politics. When Falkland and Hyde were at last elected to Parliament in 1640 they were in the forefront of the attack on all the policies and institutions such as the Courts of Star Chamber and of High Commission with which Laud was identified. Politically they not only had nothing in common: they were, to all appearances, diametrically opposed.

Personally they had a great deal in common, and all of it likely to produce an explosion. Both men were at all times clear and positive as to their own position on any question at issue; both had quick minds, sharp tongues and strong prejudices. Both were fearless and high-minded. Both were too innocent, too uncalculating, to recognise that openness of manner may be resented as wanting in deference and that clear opinions vigorously expressed are much more likely to make enemies than to win friends. Both were by nature brusque and overbearing. Laud's manners were notoriously offensive: his complete lack of social or personal ambition gave him no motive to mend them. Hyde's evidently left something to be desired, but his anxiety to succeed, his readiness to learn and his power of recognising his own deficiencies put him in a different category. Nonetheless had the young Mr Hyde appeared for the aggrieved merchants in the ordinary way, before a court over which the red-faced choleric Archbishop was presiding, a meeting of minds would have seemed a most improbable outcome.

Yet this, evidently and crucially, appears to have taken place when Hyde went to see Laud in his garden at Lambeth in 1634. Their common qualities established an immediate rapport instead of exciting an instant antipathy. It was of immense professional advantage. The Archbishop '. . . ever afterwards used him very kindly and spoke well of him on all occasions, and took particular notice of him when he came of council in any causes depending at the council board as he did frequently'. As a result '. . . Mr Hyde (who well knew how to cultivate those advantages) was used with more countenance by all the judges in

43

Westminster Hall, and the eminent practisers, than was usually given to men of his years . . .' To someone as many-sided the friendship was of far more than professional value. All his life Clarendon was hostile to or at least suspicious of the Catholic tradition whether in the Church of England or under the allegiance of Rome. Laud enlarged his sympathetic understanding of a position he did not share by winning both his affection and his respect '. . . a man of the most exemplar virtue and piety of any of that age'. So close did their intimacy become that the young lawyer, perceiving that 'the greatest want the archbishop had was of a true friend, who would reasonably have told him of his infirmities, and what people spake of him', took the risk of undertaking this function and was not only not rebuffed but thanked and listened to. In old age when he had fallen from great place he recognised in himself the fault he had seen in Laud: 'he was too proud of a good conscience. He knew his own innocence and had no kind of apprehension of being publicly charged with any crime.'

The friendship with Laud gives the first inkling of Hyde's breadth of sympathy. Such a relationship would not have been possible with Strafford (for whose attainder Hyde may have voted in 1641). Strafford was not the man to accept correction from a young barrister. Unlike Laud he offended people because he meant to. Laud, a man of prayer, cultivated the Christian virtue of humility. The soil of his nature was, as has been indicated, a stony one, but the crop, if not rich, still struggled through. It was this, perhaps, that warmed Hyde to him. He, too, was a man of prayer: 'Prayer is a Habit of Devotion which good Men never put off, and inseparable from the whole Life of a Christian.'[3] And he knew, as those who have never made the experiment cannot know, the daunting difficulties of applying what he saw as an essentially simple, all too easily comprehensible code. Both Laud and Hyde took their religion seriously. No explanation of either life is worth much unless this point is taken as its centre. It was religion not politics that was to make Hyde a Royalist, and, having made him a Royalist, to make him the instrument of transforming that political creed.

Few people would have cast him for that role, had the drama been foreseeable, in 1634. As he tells us his friendships in politics were at least as much with those 'who were looked upon with reverence by all who had not reverence for the Court' as in the court itself. The phrase is the nearest that a man of his time could get to what would, much later, be called the Opposition. He mentions in particular two great noblemen, the Earl of Essex, later to be Parliamentary Commander-in-Chief, and his brother-in-law, the future Royalist commander in the

---

[3] *Reflections on the Psalms* Ps. lxxxvi.

west, the Marquis of Hertford. Even at this stage Hyde's instinct for the middle ground, for reconciliation as far as that were possible and beyond that for tolerance and good nature, reveals itself. He actually attempted to bring these two grandees into friendly relations with Laud, alienated as they were by public disparagement of the most gratuitous kind from the royal family whose natural supporters they should have been. With Essex he had no success but both Hertford and Laud allowed themselves to be drawn into a civil acquaintanceship. Here surely was an early shoot of what was ultimately to flower into the Parliamentary Monarchy for which Britain was so long admired. Here too perhaps is a flash of that connoisseurship of character and personality that led Boswell to engineer the meeting of Dr Johnson and John Wilkes:

'My desire of being acquainted with celebrated men of every description had made me, much about the same time, obtain an introduction to Dr Samuel Johnson and to John Wilkes, Esq. Two men more different could perhaps not be selected out of all mankind . . . yet I could fully relish the excellence of each; for I have ever delighted in that intellectual chymistry, which can separate good qualities from evil in the same person.'[4]

With Boswell, Clarendon is among the most vivid and the most convincing biographers in our literature. He gives us every reason to believe that he shared his ambitious curiosity.

Apart from their common achievement it was about all that they did share. Hyde ran his life with the discipline and efficiency of a taut ship. He looks back with approving pride at his economy of time. He enjoyed the London of his day as much as Boswell did his but he did not waste half the time in hang-overs or the even more dispiriting consequences of sexual indiscretion. He early became, and ever remained, a man of method as well as an aesthete and a lover of convivial conversation. His professional success was advanced by his two marriages, the first bringing him not only a useful addition to his Wiltshire connexions but an entry into the vast, sprawling interest of the St John family, the second the immediate and obvious benefits just described. But he did not let it run away with him. Indeed to his existing spheres of activity he added two more: family life and the management of the Purton estate.

That Clarendon was a devoted husband and a loved and loving father there is ample evidence. The decent reticence he shews in writing of his marriage in the *Life* is in marked contrast to the storm of tears, of shame, of rage he unflinchingly records in the scene when he heard of his daughter's secret marriage to James, Duke of York. There

[4] Boswell *Life of Johnson* (Oxford Standard Authors, 1961), 764.

is nothing there of the Old Roman sternly concealing his emotions. But the long, happy, affectionate marriage that sustained him in the years of exile and ruin, years when, rationally considered (and Clarendon was a highly rational man), the situation offered, as he frequently observed, no grounds for hope, is summed up in language that suggests the satisfied auditing of a prudent emotional investment:

> . . . by whom he had many children of both sexes, with whom he lived very comfortably in the most uncomfortable times, and very joyfully in those times when matter of joy was administered, for the space of five or six and thirty years; what befell him after her death will be recounted in its place.

And that, until he briefly mentions her illness and death thirty-three years later, hinting — but only hinting — at his own deep distress, is all. He cannot even remember accurately how long they were married.

These appearances are misleading. Clarendon is rarely to be trusted with dates, times, distances. Educated men of his generation had not been taught to multiply or divide. Even Pepys, a generation younger, was an important civil servant in a great spending department before he was introduced to these arts. What is, to our eyes, odd is the playing up of Clarendon's feeling for his father and the playing down of what he felt for his wife. If we had only the *Life* to go on, we should know nothing of the tenderness and strength of their love for each other. But fortunately some of the letters that he wrote to her during their long separation in 1650–1 have survived. 'The truth is, every letter from thee revives my hearte so much that I am the better for it for many dayes.' 'If it were possible, I would be very gladd . . . that thou mightest be without cause of the least melancholique thought to perplex thee, but since it were madnesse to expect such a degree of happynesse, ther is no reason it would make thee unwillinge to communicate the worst of it to me, for ther is some ease in the very communicating it, and thou and I together are likelier to finde some ease or remedy, then thou arte by thyselfe; at least it is a burthen fitt for us to beare togither.' If this is not the language of true love it would be hard to say what is.

Neither of Hyde's parents came to his wedding. He makes it a matter of pride, of the superiority of the old days over the degenerate age into which he had survived, that 'few gentlemen made journeys to London, or any other expensive journeys, but upon important business, and their wives never'. So when the courts rose for the long vacation the young couple went down to Wiltshire, to Purton, which Henry Hyde had already handed over to his son, and to Salisbury where he himself had moved so that he could attend the daily offices in the Cathedral and choose a place to be buried in. He had hardly time to settle the matter before he was carried off by a sudden attack of the angina to which he had been for some years subject. He was nearly seventy, a good age for those times. Nonetheless Clarendon remembered the shock: 'It cannot be expressed with what agony his son bore this loss . . . not only . . . the best father but the best friend and the best companion he ever had or could have.'

The death of Henry Hyde on September 29, 1634 left his son the undivided reponsibility for the Purton estate. A rising young barrister could hardly hope to do more than stay there for a few months in the summer and perhaps a week or two during the shorter vacations. But Hyde's local knowledge and family connexions made it easy to find a man of affairs, who could keep an eye on things as well as act as his agent. He chose the Archdeacon of Salisbury, Thomas Marler, a much older man whom he must have known all his life as Marler had been appointed to the living of Lydiard Tregoze, the St John estate that lay next to Purton, in 1612. In 1625 he had been made Archdeacon but evidently continued to hold Lydiard in plurality. Besides paying and receiving money on Hyde's behalf he comments on the activity or inactivity of the gardener at Purton, compares the merits of sitting and prospective tenants, presses the claims of bright young men to a clerkship in Hyde's office and tells him of the marriages and deaths among the Wiltshire gentry. In exchange he asks for news of the King's speech to Parliament and shakes his head over what he hears of the state of affairs.

The second half of the 1630s is the period of growth and of prosperity in every part of young Mr Hyde's many-sided life. A happy marriage did not curtail the social and intellectual pleasures of society in London or Great Tew. Assured professional success brought in plenty of money. Court connexions through both his first and second marriages opened the way to a career in public affairs if he were so minded. In any case they opened doors to the world of fashion, of political gossip. That he and his friend Bulstrode Whitelocke, a coming man if ever there was one, should have been chosen by the Middle Temple to manage the great affair of the Royal Masque shows how high his standing was. To this had now been added the wealth and status of a country gentleman by right of inheritance. Nothing short of ill-health or some unimaginable general catastrophe could stop Mr Hyde from making a figure in his country.

In the event it was that very catastrophe, unimagined in 1634 but perhaps just imaginable four or five years later, that at the cost of a smooth ascent gave his gifts of mind and character the fullest scope of which they were capable. The 1630s saw him successful in every relation of life. His marriage was blessed with a daughter, Anne, born on March 12, 1637 and with the first of several sons, Henry, born on

June 2, 1638. (The names were offered to the memory of his lost wife and father.) He had friends everywhere. His horn is anointed with oil. But in national affairs the scene darkens. In 1634 there has been no Parliament for five years. In that very year the first writs are issued for the collection of Ship Money. In the next two years they are extended to the inland counties, bringing John Hampden into their net. In 1637 William Prynne, an Oxford-bred lawyer of vast learning who had already been savagely punished by fine, imprisonment and mutilation, was again pilloried, again subjected to gross barbarities for publishing opinions offensive to, and remarks abusive of, Archbishop Laud and the Queen. At each step the growls of stirring public hostility became more audible, especially to a listener in London. In 1638 the King and the Archbishop attempted to impose their Prayer Book on Scotland, provoking the immediate response of the National Covenant. The train that led to the first and second Bishop's Wars of 1639 and 1640 and in direct sequence to the two Parliaments of 1640 was well alight.

Looking back, Hyde remembered the golden glow of his own happy and successful young manhood and discounted the rumblings and quakings at the foundation of things. Perhaps he was right. Perhaps that was what it felt like, especially if one was young and healthy, well-to-do and well-liked, a happy husband, a proud father. He, after all, was alive then and later historians who smile at his simplicities were not. The calm before the storm seems as much a historical as a natural phenomenon. The 1930s in England, for all the grimness of unemployment and poverty, seem in recollection to have something of the same trancelike quietude that Hyde experienced exactly three hundred years earlier. I have often heard men, some of them historians, who were young before 1914 emphasise that the war seemed to come out of a blue sky. Talleyrand recalling the *vrai douceur de vivre* of France before the Revolution was doubtless the victim of the same illusion, if illusion it be.

What line, in fact, was this young aspirant to a career in Parliament — could the King only be induced to call one — taking, as the monarchy drifted in its state barge, beautified by the genius of Rubens and Van Dyck and Inigo Jones, ever faster towards the rapids? The surest, most scholarly answer is, in the words of Mr Brian Wormald, that '. . . his attitude before the outbreak of civil war can hardly have been what he later implied it was'.[5] The wide spectrum of his political friendships has already been remarked: indeed he himself took care that we should notice it. But there is more than a suggestion that it is all part of the natural charm which enabled him to get on terms with so many people

---

[5] *Clarendon: Politics, History and Religion* (n.e. Chicago 1976), ix.

who would not, if they could help it, have been seen dead in each other's company. At the same time we are given to understand that the integrity of his principles was, thanks to the wisdom with which he chose his company, preserved unspotted from the world.

No doubt there is important truth in this. But even on his own showing, let alone on Mr Wormald's analysis, it is not the whole truth. When the Short Parliament met on April 3 what attitude did Mr Hyde, the new member for Wotton Basset, the next-door borough to Purton and Lydiard Tregoze, take? 'The next day after Mr Pym had recapitulated the whole series of the grievances and miscarriages which had been in the state, Mr Hyde told the house, that "that worthy gentleman had omitted one grievance, more heavy than (as he thought) many of the others; which was, the earl marshal's court: a court newly erected, without colour or shadow of law, which took upon it to fine and imprison the king's subjects, and to give great damages for matters which the law gave no damages for."' We may rub our eyes. Here, on the very first day, after the ceremonial formalities had been completed, of the first parliament that had been held for eleven years, Pym, the veteran general of those forces that Coke and Eliot had led against arbitrary power, is followed by the brilliant young lawyer, diner out, wit and intellectual, Edward Hyde. He even remembers, as he writes it all down at Montpellier nearly thirty years later, the droll stories of the Court's absurd pretensions with which he beguiled the House. As a Parliamentary début it must have been more successful than Disraeli's if less stunning than F. E. Smith's. The comparisons are not random. Clarendon shared their talent and temperamental inclination to amuse. As a change from the customary Parliamentary rhetoric of the time — the Old Testament ranting, the interminable citations of legal precedent and statutory authority or the abundant banalities of Seneca — how welcome his speeches must have been. Even three hundred years later the anecdotes of exchanges between watermen and tailors and their clients with which he regaled the House have not lost their power to please.

As an account of the opening proceedings of the Short Parliament this passage in the *Life* has been cuttingly dismissed by S. R. Gardiner as 'nearly worthless'.[6] From the point of view of the historian of events the judgment is just. Clarendon, writing without documents and with his usual contempt for dates, times and the paraphernalia of accurate measurement, has jumbled up their sequence. As Gardiner points out the first speaker was not Pym at all: but, as he also goes on to record, Pym did speak and very much in the sense that Clarendon describes.

---

[6] *History of England* ix, 99. Gardiner no doubt had the *History* particularly in mind but his dismissal of Clarendon as a witness is comprehensive.

Whether Gardiner accepts the fact, let alone the substance, of Clarendon's own speech his contemptuous silence leaves us to guess. That Clarendon should remember its details and the opening sentence by which he linked it to Pym's great philippic is warrant enough. Much more important is the fact that in his retrospective account of his political efforts he should so unselfconsciously assume a place in the front rank of those who were leading the attack on the King's government and associate himself so closely with its most formidable chieftain. Unlike so much in the *Life* he does not state this but leaves it to be perceived, or not perceived as the case may be. When he thought about the Short Parliament, that was how it rose to his mind. And the connexion with Pym that had impressed itself so deeply can hardly have been fortuitous. As Professor Hexter demonstrated forty years ago nothing that happened in the House of Commons with which Pym had anything to do happened by chance. If Clarendon spoke immediately after Pym that meant that they had concerted their tactics, and that they had a more than casual understanding.

This was the account he gave when he was telling the story of his own life. When he was describing the same events in his *History* a bare six years after they had taken place, he says nothing of his speech about the Earl Marshal's Court but plunges at once into the great question of supply. This after all was the crux of the struggle between the King and his subjects. If Charles I had not needed money to carry on his government he would never have called a Parliament in 1640. The Parliamentary leaders knew that their power to vote such taxes as were universally agreed to be legal was their one sanction against the King's readiness to exact payments of dubious legality, such as Ship Money. With this weapon they hoped to compel him not only to consult them about the methods and extent of taxation but also about the purposes and policies for which it was required and by the same token about the advisers and ministers who were to frame and execute them. To give the King what he asked without first securing a substantial quid pro quo would have been to throw away the trumps. To try to drive too hard a bargain with him might provoke him into yet more foolish and dangerous courses than he had already ventured on. Lurking in the background was Strafford, 'Black Tom Tyrant'. Was anyone safe until he had been dealt with, once and for all?

If, as seems overwhelmingly probable, Edward Hyde shared this view of the situation in the spring of 1640, both accounts, that written in the *History* in 1646 and that in the *Life* in 1668, cohere. The *History* of which S. R. Gardiner speaks so dismissively but which he nevertheless grudgingly draws on for a telling phrase or two, addresses itself, as we have seen, to the central question and is much ampler, even if characteristically inaccurate. In this version Mr Hyde plays a smaller but still by no means a minor part. In opposition to John Hampden, no less, who moved to divide the House on a government motion for supply that named an amount larger than members were likely to agree to, Mr Hyde ingeniously tried to take the thrust out of the question by dividing it into two. First, Whether the House would in principle agree to supply? Second, What should be the ways and means and amount by which they should do so? Thus the first vote, which he tells us would easily have been carried, would assure the King that if he behaved himself the Commons would do the same, and would effectively spike the guns of the Court hotheads who were urging the King to dissolve Parliament and forsake the paths of constitutional government. The second would enable the two sides to get down to real horse-trading. The device encapsulates Clarendon's whole approach to politics. Don't expect too much, or delude others into doing so. Don't imagine that anyone is going to get something for nothing. And don't, whatever you do, monkey about with the rules of the game or give anyone else a pretext for doing so. It does not sound very romantic; it is anything but revolutionary: but it could be argued that in both these aspects it is true to the political genius of the nation.

According to the *History* '. . . for a long time there was nothing said but a confused clamour and call "Mr Hampden's question" "Mr Hyde's question" the call appearing much stronger for the last than for the former'. But the hope of compromise was thwarted, deliberately Clarendon suggests, by Sir Henry Vane, the Secretary of State, rising to assert that the King would accept nothing less than the figure named in the original motion and that Hyde's motion was therefore beside the point. Gardiner rejects this interpretation with scorn: 'It is incredible that Vane should thus have acted without express authority from Charles'[7] but presumably could find no evidence since he cites none, preferring to expose the inaccuracy and selectivity of Clarendon's general account of the Short Parliament. Indeed the discrediting of Clarendon's whole estimate of that body and of its potentialities is fundamental to his case: 'It was impossible that such a body should long have escaped a dissolution.'[8] Such passionate assertion cites its own authority. If Clarendon was right and the whole Civil War and its consequences — the execution of the King, the military dictatorship of Cromwell — were unnecessary aberrations, the drama and the colour drain from Gardiner's view of these events. Clarendon's narrative constantly suggests that the Civil War *was* unnecessary in the sense that unlucky accidents, the mischief of this man, the folly of that, the sudden death of another, frustrated the overwhelming probability of a settlement. Of these accidents the dissolution of the Short Parliament

---

[7] *ibid* 115.   [8] *ibid* 118.

was one of the wickedest or most foolish depending on who it was who prevailed with the King and from what motive. That the Parliament was made up of men far readier than their immediate successors to achieve reform and a return to constitutional legality by steady pressure, of men who though not courtiers were well affected to the King, he leaves no doubt. Perhaps he was wrong. Perhaps, as so many schools of historical thought would have it, the causation of events is not to be crudely related to the actions and purposes of individuals but looked for in blind, impersonal forces as in the movement of the stars. But if we do not accept such explanations — and Gardiner certainly did not — we must, before rejecting Clarendon's interpretation, remember that he knew the people he was writing about and was present at the scenes he describes.

Gardiner's reason for rejecting it has been clearly identified by Conrad Russell. Writing in the age of Darwin, Gardiner saw the past in an evolutionary perspective. 'He thought that "the Parliament of England was the noblest monument ever reared by mortal man" and that the real cause of Charles's fall was his attempt to obstruct the inevitable development of the national will.'[9] This high, solemn vision was perhaps underpinned by Gardiner's undoubted pride in the fact of his own direct lineal descent from Oliver Cromwell. Yet Gardiner, great historian that he was, seems, perhaps subconsciously, to have felt that he had not disposed of Clarendon as completely or had not represented his position as fairly as he could have wished. Describing his activities in the next Parliament, to which we must shortly come, he wrote:

'Hyde was taking no mean part in the work of cutting away the extraordinary powers, which had been acquired by the Crown since the accession of the House of Tudor. He was zealous with more than ordinary zeal to establish the supremacy of the law. But with him the supremacy of the law was almost equivalent to the supremacy of lawyers. He fully shared in the contempt which is always felt by the members of a learned profession for those who are outside its pale . . . Being himself without strong passions, he never took account of the existence of strong passion in others. The Church of his ideal was one in which there would be no enthusiasm and no fanaticism, no zeal of any kind to break up the smooth ease of existence.'[10]

On the evidence to be found in the *Life* alone, Gardiner could hardly have concluded that Hyde was 'without strong passions' unless he had wanted to. More serious is the implication that a Christian cannot be whole-hearted in his profession unless he is a fanatic or at least

[9] *The Origins of the English Civil War* (1973), 5.
[10] Gardiner, *op. cit.* ix, 275–6.

unreasonable. Maybe this derives from Gardiner's personal sec-
tarianism — he was a member of the Plymouth Brethren. It is a sad
reflection on a lifetime's study of the seventeenth century that it should
have left so great an authority ready to dismiss the large-mindedness
and tolerance of Great Tew.

In the Short Parliament Clarendon saw those possibilities of compromise and the middle way that most Englishmen of any political
consciousness desired then and desire now. Whether they were on offer
no one can tell. Gardiner, and the great majority of historians with the
advantage of hindsight, thought that they weren't. Clarendon, certainly at the time and avowedly in his *History*, thought that they were.
Right or wrong, we should surely honour him for doing so. Consorting
as he evidently did with the opponents of the government his efforts,
through his contact with Archbishop Laud and others, to bring the
court to meet its critics half-way and to take into the administration the
Earl of Bedford and his lieutenant in the House of Commons, John
Pym were worth making. Can we doubt that his friends Selden and
Whitelocke, themselves also on excellent personal terms with Laud,
would have backed him for all they were worth?

> Oh Thou, that dear and happy Isle
> The Garden of the World ere while,
> What luckless Apple did we taste
> To make us Mortal, and Thee waste?

Thus Andrew Marvell in the early 1650s. Had not Mr Hyde, happily
married and the father of two very young children, every motive to act
and to encourage others to act on the assumption that catastrophe
could be avoided? He knew and liked and trusted so many of the men
against whom he was soon to find himself unwillingly ranged. That
these feelings were mutual is well instanced in Whitelocke himself who
in old age transcribed some of Hyde's letters into the journal he was
compiling for his children 'to lett you see the kindness and correspondence which was between this gentleman and me in these times'.[11] For
the constitutional historian the interest of the late 1630s consists in the
pressures that were building up against the régime. For the actual in-
habitants of the 1630s, even for those who interested themselves in
questions of law and government like these two politically minded
young barristers, the period was their share of the world, into which
they had to fit marriage and children and careers and friendships. This
is Hyde writing from Westminster in April 1636 to his friend enjoying
the vacation in the country:

---

[11] BL Add. MS 37343 ff 146v, 148v, 153, 162v, 198.

My good friend

I meant not you should have the advantage of calling on me first, and I will excuse myself not only to you but to your honest waterman whom I promised the last week a letter to you, but the truth is I was in the disorder of my remove to my new chamber and forgott it, for which I beate my boy, whom I commanded to remember me. Since thursday I have obeyed the Doctor in my chamber who hath eased me of a full pound of my blood, so that I looke like a pale girle, newly recovered of the green sickness.

Our best news is that we have good wine abundantly come over, and the worst that the Plague is in Towne and no Judges dye, the old absurd Barons out of mere frowardness resolving to live . . .

A year later he writes to congratulate him on the birth of a son and promises him a doe 'although this weather forbiddes you to looke for a fatt one. My pen is deepe in a Star Chamber Bill, and therefore I have only the leisure and the manners to tell you I am very prowde you are a friend to your most affectionate servant, Edward Hyde.'

In 1638, when the King's attempt to impose his Prayer Book on the Scots had brought them to the verge of rebellion, Hyde's letters are still taken up with the happiness and prosperity of their own lives. He is again writing to congratulate his friend on the birth of a child, this time a daughter.

. . . I will not so farre lessen my devotion to Fawley [Whitelocke's house near Henley] to tell you 'tis fitt I breathe the country aier. Indeed this belov'd Town is to me all health, yett I intend nothing more than to visit you this Lent and be so merry with you that you shall perceive you have much of my heart in your keeping . . . My little wench [Anne Hyde, scarcely a year old] desires you both to accept her humble service. Mine to my little friend.

Later in the year, thanking him for a present of cider, Hyde touches for a moment on the threatening state of affairs:

We talke of nothing but Lawe in the Hall and of warre in the Towne . . . my Lord Traquair brings nothing but dispayr from Scotland, so that even the Victory is like to prove melancholique enough.

In fact there was no victory. And the defeat left the King with no option but to summon a Parliament. Hyde wrote with the news, urging his friend to stand. Whitelocke, as Hyde well knew, had advised Hampden in his famous resistance to Ship Money. This was the sort of man he wanted to see in Parliament and with whom he was himself ready to act. Whitelocke was not returned, perhaps through corrupt electoral practices by his opponent: the Short Parliament was so short that there was not time to raise the matter. But the two friends were both successful at the elections later in the year that returned the most famous Parliament in history. How close they were in sympathy and situation is evident. Yet the one was to hold the Great Seal under Cromwell's Protectorate and the other under the restored Stuart monarchy. How many observers of the political scene in 1641 would have come near guessing as much?

V

Member of Parliament

THE PARLIAMENT that met on November 3, 1640 included friends from all the parts of Hyde's past life and friends that as yet he did not know. John Selden was returned for Oxford University, Whitelocke, after another disputed election, for the borough of Marlow. Most important of all, Hyde's closest, most admired friend, Lord Falkland, was for the second time that year elected for Newport, Isle of Wight. Among the members not of his old acquaintance with whom comradeship in war was to ripen into deep attachment was Sir Ralph Hopton, soon to be the victorious commander of the Royalist army in the south-west.

It was to be also a Parliament that divided friends from each other. Unlike modern Parliaments in which every member arrives already stamped and labelled, it had to discover its own identity and find as it went along its polarities of attraction and repulsion. To distinguish the figure of Edward Hyde in it is easy enough: to focus him difficult. It is not double but treble vision that troubles us. He is actor, historian and memoirist. The three roles are inextricably, or almost inextricably, entangled. And both the history and the autobiography that he wrote were written with distinct purposes that, in the case of the history at least, themselves changed in the course of their composition. The history was begun at the end of the First Civil War in 1646 with the blessing, even the direct and practical encouragement, of the King, then a prisoner. After the outbreak of the Second Civil War in 1648 it was laid aside, not to be resumed till its author was again an exile twenty years later. In the first period his aim was essentially practical. The King, if he were to retrieve the errors and disasters of his reign, must first of all be provided with a lucid and accurate account of what had gone wrong and why. Professor Trevor-Roper's description could hardly be bettered: 'It was a state paper by a faithful servant who took his duties seriously. It might be great literature too, or great history . . .'[1] When he resumed the work in his old age it was partly as an outgrowth of his autobiography but mainly as a moral and political exposition and analysis for the guidance of future kings.

Quite apart from the change in the conception there is also the change in the man who was thinking and writing. Sir Edward Hyde in Jersey was separated from the Earl of Clarendon in Montpellier by twenty years packed with reading and writing, with travel and business, with private reflection and prayer as well as with the framing and execution of policy. There were, there are, grand simplicities about his character and ideas but the story of their unfolding is neither straightforward nor easy.

That Hyde himself came to the new Parliament as an opponent of the Court seems clear even from that part of the *History* that he first wrote for the eyes of Charles I. 'Mr Hyde, who was returned for a borough in Cornwall [Saltash], met Mr Pimm in Westminster Hall some few days before the Parliament, and conferring together upon the state of affairs, the other told him . . . "that they must now be of another temper than they were the last Parliament; that they must not only sweep the house clean below, but must pull down all the cobwebs which hung in the top and corners, that they might not breed dust and so make a foul house hereafter; that they had now an opportunity to make their country happy, by removing all grievances and pulling up the causes of them by the roots, if all men would do their duties." '[2] Once again, as in the Short Parliament, it is in Pym's company that Hyde makes his entrance. The historian Hyde may deplore the alarming radicalism of the sentiments here voiced, but it by no means follows that Edward Hyde, M.P. for Saltash, did. In fact on his own showing he made mad work among the cobwebs. His efforts as Chairman of the Committee on the Council of the North were instrumental in its abolition. He was hardly less active in bringing down Star Chamber and the Court of High Commission. The Earl Marshal's Court, the first royal beast that he had stalked in the Short Parliament, fell victim to his marksmanship in 1641. There is not a line in any of his later writings to suggest that he subsequently disavowed or even regretted any of this. Why should he have, granted his own perspective and not Gardiner's? It was all part of a consistent programme of reform that included the destruction of Strafford and all his works, and his replacement by the Earl of Bedford as Lord Treasurer with John Pym as Chancellor of the Exchequer.

Both Bedford and Pym are portrayed by Clarendon, even in the

[1] *Clarendon and the Practice of History* (Los Angeles 1965) pp. 23–4.
[2] *Hist.* III, 3. This passage originally formed part of the *Life* written in Montpellier.

History, in a far more sympathetic light than any other of the Parliamentary leaders. It is obvious that he knew them, liked them and trusted them. Cromwell he did not know and violently disliked, to judge from the single personal recollection of him in the *Life*. St John he must have known both as a connexion by his first marriage and as a lawyer ten years his senior, eminent in his profession. Every reference shows that he detested him. The third member of that cousinhood, John Hampden, the general favourite of historians, is no favourite of Clarendon's. How well did he know him? Personally, it seems, hardly at all. Clarendon tells us in the *Life* that Hampden was one of those who kept a joint table at Pym's lodgings during the early days of the Long Parliament, at which he himself was a frequent guest. Want of sympathy is evident in all that he says about him. He does full justice to his charm of manner and to his persuasiveness as a speaker but sums him up as false and deceitful. 'No man had ever greater power over himself or was less the man that he seemed to be, which shortly after appeared to every body when he cared less to keep on the mask.' Clarendon impugns Hampden's fundamental sincerity as a man of good will, a quality that he never denies to Pym and expressly and repeatedly ascribes to Pym's patron, the Earl of Bedford.

How well trusted Hyde himself was by Bedford is shewn by a story he recollected nearly thirty years later. It was the end of April 1641 and Mr Hyde was at the height of his success as Chairman of the Committee investigating the illegalities of the Council of the North. Walking in the afternoon to the Bowling Green in Piccadilly he was met by Bedford who urged him to step down to the lower lawn where the Earl of Essex and his brother-in-law the Marquis of Hertford were playing. The case of Strafford had reached a crisis. The impeachment, led by Pym and St John, had failed. The only expedient left to Parliament was to proceed by Act of Attainder, that is by judicial murder. The King had promised Strafford that he should not suffer in life or estate, but was ready to expel him for ever from any part in government. This Bedford was ready to accept, but Essex (and no doubt Pym) were not. Would Hyde add his support? Hyde at once agreed and walked down the tree-shaded path. There was no one else but the two noblemen with both of whom he was on familiar terms. After exchanging courtesies, Hertford excused himself. Essex began at once to congratulate Hyde on his sterling work against the Council of the North: it had 'revived their indignation against the Earl of Strafford'. Hyde urged that 'there were crimes and misdemeanours evidently enough proved' against him to put a stop to his political career. Surely it was not necessary to attaint him of high treason? Essex shook his head, and answered, 'Stone-dead hath no fellow: that [if they let him live] . . . the King would presently grant him his pardon . . . and would likewise give him his liberty as soon as he had a mind to receive his service.'

Sir Charles Firth rejects the historical truth of this story, but its sharpness of detail is convincing. Why should Clarendon, at that distance from the event, bother to fabricate it? What is anyway incontestable is that by the fact of setting it down he is recording or purporting to record his own close relations with the leadership of the party that was soon to be out for his blood. For the man who devoted the best energies of his life to defending and restoring the royal power and to equipping it with a political and historical philosophy the only credible motive would seem to be truthfulness.

Two events that took place almost at once destroyed whatever chance there was for a coalition of Bedford and Pym with the King. Bedford died suddenly and prematurely — he was not yet fifty — and an army plot was discovered against the Parliament. Strafford's life, and the honour of the King who had pledged himself to defend it, were both forfeit. On May 12 he was beheaded.

When the Commons voted on the attainder the Ayes numbered 204, the Noes 59. These fifty-nine were placarded and abused as Straffordians, so that their names have been preserved. Hyde's is not among them. Very probably he voted with the majority. His silence on the point suggests this. After all at that point Bedford was still alive and co-ordinating policy with Pym and the others. The King's resentment at the forcing of his conscience — as he saw it — over Strafford, the Commons' alarm at the army plot, drove both sides rapidly further apart. The advocates of each hard line saw, and took, their advantage. Before the month was out Hyde for the first time spoke against a bill backed by those with whom he had hitherto acted. Its object was to take away the Bishops' votes in the House of Lords, thus depriving the King of something like a Trade Union block vote. Hyde opposed it on constitutional, not religious, grounds. The issue was after all strictly political. There was not as yet a proposal to abolish the Bishops as such. His greatest friend, Falkland, spoke in favour for reasons that were religious rather than political. He feared that if ground were not given the rising pressure would threaten not only episcopacy but the whole constitution of the Church. The House, Hyde tells us, was amused to see two such inseparable friends divided. Afterwards Falkland, according to Hyde, acknowledged that he had been deceived by promises from Hampden that the bill, if passed, would secure the Church from further Parliamentary attack. Its rejection by the Lords was rapidly followed by far more radical proposals. It was during the course of the debates on them that Falkland enunciated one of the great principles of our political tradition: 'Where it is not necessary to change, it is necessary not to change.'

Falkland like most of the Great Tew men was no enthusiast for episcopacy. Indeed of its most conspicuous and recent manifestations, fostered by Laud and the King, he was fiercely critical. But he thought the institution had practical and historical arguments on its side that justified its preservation. Hyde thought the same. It was their vigorous opposition to the so-called Root-and-Branch Bill for the utter extirpating of bishops that led the King to make secret approaches to them.

Thus began the most fateful and not the least tender of Clarendon's attachments — that to the King. It is useless to seek to explain the immediate mutual attraction of men whom those who knew them best, perhaps even the two men themselves, would confidently declare antipathetic. But it is wilful to deny it. Such an instant recognition of profound personal sympathy must have taken place between them. There seems no other explanation either of what in fact happened or of Clarendon's recollection of what was surely an unforgettable interview. It must be remembered that the King was shy, diffident and fastidious. As a child he had had to overcome severe physical handicaps. Up to his teens he had been overshadowed by a golden boy of an elder brother, Prince Henry, elegant, articulate and popular. His mother's open preference for Henry starved the younger brother of self-confidence. Pride and a proud insistence on formality were the only defences left to this physically puny, deeply sensitive, highly conscientious young man — in his middle twenties he had succeeded to the throne — called on to exercise the force of temporal power, wherein doth sit the dread and fear of kings. Anyone less like young Mr Hyde at the height of his prosperity, popularity, success and, it must be admitted, self-satisfaction can hardly be imagined.

In the *Life* Clarendon records his own incredulity at the approach. He told the Member who delivered the message to him in the House of Commons that 'he believed it was some mistake, for that he had not the honour to be known to the King; and that there was another of the same name, of the house.' When the meeting took place that very evening in Whitehall Palace it was tête-à-tête. Only a few phrases from that first conversation stuck in his mind when he came to write it down twenty-eight years later, but the tone of them is easy, almost humorous. Mr Hyde's clubbable, extrovert geniality had triumphed over the shying thoroughbred apprehensiveness that often made the King's manner so glacial. Charles I rarely made jokes but there are several, not very funny, but jokes nonetheless, in their subsequent conversations as reported by Clarendon. The gist of this first confabulation was that the King was especially grateful for Hyde's defence of the Church, to which Hyde for his part replied by reassurances that the Commons would not be able to carry anything very terrible against it before the Houses rose for the summer and the King left for Scotland.

It was not necessary, it would not have been tactful, for him to point out that he had defended the Church for political rather than theological reasons. And when he came to write the *Life* he perhaps felt it out of place to stress what is clear enough from the *History*, that he still believed, even after the death of Bedford, that Pym and Essex could be brought to work with the King. It was with Essex, less than a year later to be Lord General of the Parliamentary forces, and the Earl of Holland, a courtier who chopped and changed, that Hyde was walking and joking in Westminster Hall on the October morning on which the new session opened. They differed, as he records, in their interpretation of recent events in Scotland but they did not, quite clearly, feel themselves to be ranged on either side of a political chasm.[3]

Hyde had not in fact been in touch with the King since his departure for Edinburgh. It was not until early November that the King instructed Sir Edward Nicholas to convey his thanks to Hyde for the stand that he had found himself forced to take within a few days of the session opening. The Commons were alarmed by the news from Scotland. Had the King been up to his old tricks of attempting to suppress representative institutions by violence? If so, they themselves stood in immediate and grave danger, even though on the signing of the Scots Treaty his army had been disbanded. Hyde and Falkland argued that an English Parliament had no business to concern itself with the affairs of Scotland. Dissatisfaction with the King's supposed policies and with the advice on which they were based was every day evident. The bill to exclude the Bishops from Parliament was reintroduced. In these debates Hyde spoke in a sense of conservative constitutionalism that won the approval of the absent King and of Nicholas, soon to be Secretary of State, who kept him informed of what was passing in London.

Within a month Parliament's smouldering suspicion of the King burst into flame. At the end of October Pym reported the hatching of a second Army Plot: two days later news of the Irish rebellion reached Westminster. The stories of Papist massacres of unsuspecting defenceless Protestants were the red meat into which the strongest of all English prejudices could sink its teeth. The Queen was a Catholic and at the heart of an army plotting against Parliament. The King and Archbishop Laud with their re-introduction of ceremonial and their focusing of public worship on the altar rather than the pulpit were fellow-travellers on the road to Rome. All this buying of Italian pictures and statues was part of the same deadly infatuation. In a minute the fears and resentments of the whole reign leapt into one fierce incandescence, expressed in Parliamentary terms as the Grand

[3] *ibid* IV, 22. This passage again originally formed part of the *Life*.

Remonstrance. Reciting every grudge, imputing every motive that any Puritan might have felt disposed to lay at the door of the King or the Archbishop, it demanded powers for Parliament and abridgement of royal prerogative that went far beyond the substantial gains already registered by the King's assent to the abolition of the Star Chamber and the other courts that had operated outside the Common Law. Its champions appear not to have gauged how broad was the feeling among members who had hitherto acted with them that this was going too fast and too far. After a debate that went on to the unheard-of hour of midnight, the candles flickering on a scene of rising anxiety and anger, the Remonstrance passed by a bare eleven votes — 159 to 148. Hyde and Falkland were prominent in opposing it.

How crucial a point Hyde judged this in his own and his country's history can be seen from his account of Cromwell telling Falkland, as they were leaving the House after the division, that if the Remonstrance had not passed he would have sold all he had the next morning and never have seen England more '. . . so near was the poor kingdom to its deliverance'. From the speed at which his world was moving, so acute an observer must have found his own optimism of three months back — the Remonstrance was debated on November 22 — unimaginable. In a bare three weeks he had been swept from his first mild and modest dissent with Pym to vehement opposition. And yet, like the Red Queen, he had been running for all he was worth to stand still. He *had* stood still. It was the world before his eyes that was careering past him.

How did all this strike a contemporary, looking on from the position of a rising man in the government service? Philip Warwick was born in the same year as Hyde. After Charles II's Restoration in 1660 he was to be the chief Treasury official in the Clarendon administration, and as such the recipient of several notable encomia from that severe and expert critic of administrators, Samuel Pepys. Warwick wrote his memoirs just after Clarendon's death and left them unpublished so that he comes as near an impartial and well-informed witness as we are likely to find. Writing of this period between the Remonstrance and the outbreak of war he says:

> . . . the King had drawn over unto his Party three eminent Persons of the House of Commons, who had seemed very lukewarme in his interest: *viz* the Lord Viscount Faulkland, Sir John Culpepper, and Sir Edward Hyde. These for some time lay hid, and were not discerned; and their advices and pens were most used upon emergent and important disputes betwixt the King and the two Houses: and they most commonly framed such answers, as were fit for the King to give in that conjuncture; for they well knew the temper of the House of Commons, and were supposed to know that of the Nation . . .

Warwick was himself a member of the Long Parliament and, in spite of his dislike and distrust of Strafford, had been among the fifty-nine brave enough to vote against his attainder. His judgment that Hyde had, up to the end of 1641, been 'very lukewarme' in the King's interest is thus of exceptional value. So is his estimate of this new recruit to the royal cause:

> Sir Edward Hyde was of a cheerfull and agreeable conversation, of an extraordinary industry and activity, and of a great confidence: which made him soon at home at a Court. His naturall parts were very forward and sound; his learning was very good and competent; and he had a felicity both of tongue and pen; which made him willingly hearkened unto, and much approved; and having spent much of his studies in the Law, this made his discourse and writings the more significant; and his language and stile were very suitable to business, if not a little too redundant . . . Which for a time was very advantageous to his Majesty's service; for it drew the curtaine, and made plain the deceitfulness and unwarrantable designes of the Contrivers in Parliament, and the reasonableness of his Majestie's Propositions. But I remember a wise Lord, who had great influence on them all, would complain that their wit and elegancy, as it was very delightfull, so it would not long last usefull; since contests betwixt a King and his House of Parliament could not be separated from ill consequences and pressures upon the rest of his subjects in generall in their common course of life; and that would beget rather a frowardness in men to see such things treated of with elegancy and ironie, than any delight or complacence, and therefore he was wont to say, *Our good Pen will harm Us.*

Of the 'three eminent Persons of the House of Commons' described by Warwick only Culpepper, or Colepeper as Hyde called him, needs some introduction. From the time of the Remonstrance to the end of the First Civil War Hyde and he were close colleagues. In the years of exile while the Second Civil War was fought, the King tried and executed, his son the down-at-heel monarch of a court that had to beg its lodging from door to door through north-western Europe, they were regularly in touch but hardly ever in sympathy. What would have happened at the Restoration, when Hyde was in a position of apparently unchallengeable power, we do not know since Colepeper died three months after that event. It is perfectly clear that there was no love lost between them. Colepeper on all the evidence was not nourished by personal affections or exercised by questions of principle. Great Tew would have been an abomination to him. Pragmatic, shrewd, on the make, philistine, self-confident, the English ruling class in all ages has, and needs to have, a fair sprinkling of Colepepers. Clarendon's portrait of him is a masterly analysis of a social archetype as well as a convincing likeness of an individual.

Thrust and force are its keynotes, clear and immediate in the opening passage:

> Sir John Colepeper had spent some years of his youth in foreign parts, and especially in armies; where he had seen good service . . . and might have made a very good officer if he had intended it. He was of a rough nature, a hot head, and of great courage; which had engaged him in many quarrels and duels; wherein he still behaved himself very signally . . .

What he had to a quite exceptional degree was clearness of apprehension. Coming back to England, he married and settled down as a country gentleman of no great estate. But his quickness and penetration combined with unusual articulacy soon made him the obvious choice of his richer neighbours in affairs that involved stating a case before any government authority. He was returned as a borough member to the Short Parliament but in the Long Parliament he sat as a knight of the shire for the great county of Kent. His speeches made an instant impression on his fellow members. No question but he was a man to be reckoned with. And all this was achieved without any experience of business, any knowledge of the law, any acquaintance with the Court or any education, formal or otherwise. Clarendon was clearly interested by him as a natural phenomenon: '. . . a man of no very good breeding; having never sacrificed to the muses, or conversed in any polite company.' But his power of analysis he acknowledged to be formidable: 'He was warm and positive in debates, and of present fancy to object and find fault with what was proposed; and indeed would take any argument in pieces, and expose it excellently to a full view; and leave nothing to chance or accident, without making it foreseen.' But the speed and power of his critical and analytic faculty, in Clarendon's experience — and it was a long one — outran his constructive ideas and unsteadied his initiative. 'He . . . knew not so well what to judge and determine; and was so irresolute, and had a fancy so perpetually working, that, after a conclusion made, he would the next day, in the execution of it, and sometimes after, raise new doubts, and make new objections; which always occasioned trouble, and sometimes produced inconvenience.'

His private character was less remarkable. He had, unlike so many of his class, managed to live within a modest income, 'not being delighted with delicacies of any nature, or indeed ever acquainted with them'. But he 'was proud and ambitious, and very much disposed to improve his fortune, which he knew well how to do, by industry and thrift, without stooping to any corrupt ways, to which he was not inclined'. In some ways Sir John Colepeper appeared a more authentic representative than Hyde of the plain, bluff English country gentleman, untainted by the wickedness of the King's evil counsellors or the sophistication of the Court. Colepeper's most telling speech in Parliament had been his attack on Monopolies. Hyde was still acting for and advising the greatest, most execrated, monopolist of the century, Sir Giles Mompesson.[4] Mompesson, who had married a St John and was thus a connexion of Hyde's by his first marriage, was long out of the world of high finance. The concerns which he somewhat plaintively pressed on Hyde's attention were small beer, but the association would not have raised the standing of the member for Saltash if it had attracted any publicity.

The irony of this improbable triple alliance of Falkland, Hyde and Colepeper was that Colepeper had caught the King's notice by his vigorous defence of the Church and in particular the Prayer Book from Puritan attack. As his later differences with Hyde were to show he did not in fact care a fig for either. But with his piercing political understanding he saw at once their purely political significance. 'In matters of religion he was, in his judgment, very indifferent; but more inclined to what was established, to avoid the accidents which commonly attend a change, without any motives from his conscience; which yet he kept to himself; and was well content to have it believed that the activity proceeded from thence.'

The instigator of this transformation of the King's affairs was another friend of Hyde's, who drew and re-drew his character with a brilliance matching that of his sitter, yet, like that sitter, never quite achieving satisfaction or finality. The man was George, Lord Digby, son and heir of the Earl of Bristol, the most richly and variously gifted member of his generation. Three years Hyde's junior he had made his Parliamentary début at the age of twelve, appearing at the bar of the House of Commons to plead against the imprisonment of his father in the Tower of London. As a young man he had himself been imprisoned for duelling within the confines of the Royal Palace of Whitehall. Resenting what he considered unjust treatment he had taken an anti-Court line in both the Parliaments of 1640, to which he had been returned as a County member for Dorset. He had been one of the first to call for a Remonstrance and he had been one of the Committee that managed the impeachment of Strafford. During these proceedings his ideas changed with the violence and rapidity that still at three centuries' distance bemuse the historian as they bemused his contemporaries. Quite suddenly and unexpectedly he spoke against Strafford's attainder. His speech outraged the House of Commons and gratified the King who at once called him up to the House of Lords in the right of his father's barony of Digby. He was admitted to the

4 Clar. MS 20, f.5. *Cal. Clar. SP* i, 1444.

intimacy of both King and Queen, instant victims of his universally attested charm.

It was the passing of the Remonstrance, a brainchild whose paternity Digby had no doubt forgotten, that provided the occasion. '. . . Mr Hyde, only to give vent of his own indignation, and without the least purpose of communicating it, or that any use should be made of it, had drawn such a full answer to it, as the subject would have enabled any man to have done . . .' Digby 'who had much conversation and friendship with him' dropped in one day when he was alone in his room surrounded by his books and papers. They talked about what was happening in Parliament. The Remonstrance loomed so large in their discussion that Hyde read his friend the paper he had prepared. Digby was delighted. It was just what the King was looking for. Might he shew it to him? Hyde 'expressly and positively refused to give it to him, or that any use should be made of it; and reproached him for proposing a thing to him which might prove ruinous to him, if the house should have the least imagination that he exercised himself in such offices'. For the first time the note of fear, for himself, for his family, becomes audible. A few days later Digby returned to the attack, armed, this time, with the King's command and 'his royal word, that no person living should know that he had the least hand in it; so that no danger should accrue to him thereby'.

This left no alternative. Hyde felt some misgivings about Digby's involvement: not that he doubted his personal goodwill but he '. . . . did not like his over activity to which his restless fancy always disposed him'. But on reflection he had himself come to the conclusion that the paper might be useful to the King. He agreed, stipulating only that the document, if published, should bear the authority of the Council. It was so issued, and widely admired. The secret of the authorship was well kept.

So began Hyde's immensely successful if brief and clandestine career as the architect of Royalist defence works in the propaganda war. No doubt he did not see it like that at the time. He was still, at the end of 1641, sparing no effort to prevent the political conflict degenerating into the last resort of brute force. On January 1, 1642 the King applied the expedient that, as Clarendon the historian suggests, would six months earlier have defused the bomb. If Bedford and Pym had been taken into the government . . . Bedford was dead and in the intervening six months Pym's distrust of the King had solidified into a principle. Nonetheless he was offered the Chancellorship of the Exchequer. Whether he refused it instantly or whether Charles withdrew the offer as suddenly as he had made it is not known. But before the day was over the Exchequer had been offered to and accepted by Colepeper, and Falkland, under heavy pressure from Hyde, had become

Secretary of State. Hyde himself had been offered and had refused first the Solicitor-Generalship and then one other minor post which he does not specify. He knew that turning out St John, a lawyer senior to him and the cousin of Cromwell and Hampden, from the Solicitorship to which he had been appointed as a prelude to the projected Bedford–Pym manoeuvre would be the worst of tactics. In any case he was sure that he would retain far more influence in the House of Commons as a private member with no affiliation to the Court, indeed with the record of an anti-Straffordian reformer. That he would retain the function of chief draftsman of the King's political utterances and that he would co-ordinate policy and tactics with Colepeper and Falkland was understood.

Mr Hyde had not yet attained to the knowledge of the Stuarts that Lord Clarendon was to acquire by bitter experience.

> The truth is, it was the unhappy fate and constitution of that family, that they trusted naturally the judgments of those who were as much inferior to them in understanding as they were in quality, before their own, which was very good.[5]

Within forty-eight hours of these appointments, designed presumably to seize the middle ground of political opinion, Charles embarked on the worst judged, and worst executed, gamble of his career, the attempt on the five Members. There can be no question that the move was inspired by Digby, with the hysterical support of the Queen, terrified by reports that she was to be impeached of High Treason. Both the King's Gentleman of the Bedchamber, Will Murray, and the Queen's Lady in Waiting, Lady Carlisle, are credited with betraying intelligence of the operation to its intended victims. What is perfectly clear is that Hyde, Colepeper and Falkland heard nothing about it until it was a *fait accompli*, or rather *mésaccompli*. In one stroke of unimaginable idiocy the King had destroyed everything that they had been working for. He had made a present of the middle ground to his most implacable adversaries. '. . . They who formerly used to appear for all the rights and authority which belonged to the King not knowing what to say, between grief and anger that the violent party had by these late unskilful actions of the Court gotten great advantage and recovered new spirits: and the three persons before named [i.e. Falkland, Colepeper and Hyde], without whose privity the King had promised that he would enter upon no new counsel, were so much displeased and dejected that they were inclined never more to take upon them the care of anything to be transacted in the House: finding already that they could

5 *Continuation* 861.

not avoid being looked upon as the authors of those counsels to which they were so absolute strangers, and which they so perfectly detested.'[6]

The bitterest draught of politics is in that sentence. Honest failure, unfair dismissal, bad luck are nothing to the impotence and hopelessness of finding oneself the prisoner of loyalty and honour. If Hyde and Falkland and Colepeper had thrown in their hand and left the King to play his own game, the unbalancing of affairs would have been catastrophic. Colepeper anyhow was far too self-confident and ambitious to abandon office the moment he had got it. 'He was then (as was said before) very positive in his conclusions; as if he did not propose a thing that might come to pass, but what infallibly must be so.' Falkland's temperament as well as his political opinions made him at best a reluctant servant of the King with whom he certainly did not enjoy the *rapport* Hyde had so instantly established. The temptation to bow out must have been strong. Without Hyde's urging he would never have accepted office. We can hardly doubt that the same reason weighed with him in retaining it. What then of Hyde himself, the real controlling force of the King's new friends?

He has conveniently supplied us with a self-portrait taken at this very moment, though painted from memory twenty-seven years later, to form the third wing of a triptych whose other panels portrayed Falkland and Colepeper.

'Mr Hyde was, in his nature and disposition, different from both the other; which never begot the least disagreement between the lord Falkland and him. He was of a very cheerful and open nature, without any dissimulation; and delivered his opinion of things or persons, where it was convenient, without reserve or disguise; and was at least tenacious enough of his opinion, and never departed from it out of compliance with any man. He had a very particular devotion and passion for the person of the King; and did believe him the truest and the best Christian in the world. He had a most zealous esteem and reverence for the constitution of the government, and believed it so equally poised, that if the least branch of the prerogative was torn off, or parted with, the subject suffered by it, and that his right was impaired: and he was as much troubled when the crown exceeded its just limits and thought its prerogative hurt by it.'

The mind's eye of the portraitist has strayed from his sitter to the sitter's views. We are then regaled with an eloquent paragraph on his loyalty to the Church of England, a loyalty, we are reminded, that was anything but blind: 'He had taken more pains than such* men use to

---

* The antecedent of 'such' is not evident from the context. Perhaps he means those who shared his view of the constitution.

[6] *Hist.* IV, 158.

do, in the examination of religion; having always conversed with those of different opinions with all freedom and affection, and had very much kindness and esteem for many, who were in no degree of his own judgment.' This naturally leads on to his horror at the measure then being pressed on the King to take away the Bishops from the House of Lords, 'a violation of justice; the removing a landmark, and the shaking the very foundation of Government'.

King and Church, rather than Church and King, claimed his support, be the consequences what they would. In the shadow of a bungled *coup d'état* that had antagonised all moderate men he does not disguise his opinion that disaster and probable ruin lay ahead:

'Though he was of a complexion and humour very far from despair, yet he did believe the King would be oppressed by that party which then governed, and that they who followed and served him would be destroyed; so that it was not ambition of power or wealth, that engaged him to embark in so very hazardous an employment, but abstractedly the consideration of his duty.'

Neither Mr Hyde nor Lord Clarendon was ever slow to draw attention to his own disinterested integrity. He rounds off his account of himself in the spring of 1642 by suggesting rather than stating his closer understanding of the King:

'It is very probable, that if his access at that time had been as frequent to the King as sir John Colepeper's was, or the lord Falkland's might have been, some things might have been left undone, the doing whereof brought much prejudice to the king; for all his principles were much more agreeable to his majesty's own judgment, than those of either of the other; and what he said was of equal authority with him; and when any advice was given by either of the other, the king usually asked, "whether Ned Hyde were of that opinion;" and they always very ingenuously confessed that he was not: but his having no relation of service, and so no pretence to be seen often at court, and the great jealousy [i.e. suspicion] that was entertained towards him, made it necessary to him to repair only in the dark to the king, upon emergent occasions, and leave the rest to be imparted by the other two: and the differences in their natures and opinions never produced any disunion between them . . . the other two having always much deference to the lord Falkland, who allayed their passions; to which they were both enough inclined.'

A stronger compulsion to sink their differences of opinion and to rein in their tempers was the common danger they lived in. Arrests and imprisonments in London and Westminster were only to be made by the authority of Parliament or the Common Council of the City, now firmly under the control of Pym's friends. The thread by which the safety of the three men hung was the plausibility, daily wearing thinner, with which they could still claim that status. Hyde still enjoyed a high personal reputation with the northern M.P.s for his work in destroying the Council at York. But the political world of the 1640s was still a small one until the Civil War expanded it. A new hand in drafting the King's answers to the bills and messages with which Parliament bombarded him was evident. Hyde knew himself to be under suspicion: two unfortunate encounters, the first at Windsor with the Marquis of Hamilton, the second at Greenwich with the Earls of Essex and Holland, supplied possible evidence of the secret conferences with the King he had taken such care to protect. Even his meetings with Falkland and Colepeper took place after dark in his lodgings at his father-in-law's house in Dean's Yard. In unlit streets goings and comings were easier to conceal than in a modern capital, but after a time 'the resort of the other two every night to his lodging . . . satisfied them [the Parliamentary leaders] that he was the person'. Fortunately Colepeper's intelligence was as good as theirs, if not better. As Hyde explains: 'For though they managed these councils with the greatest secrecy, and by few persons . . . yet when any thing was to be transacted in public by the house, they were obliged not only to prepare those of whom they were themselves confident, but to allow those confidents to communicate it to others in whom they confided: and so men, who did not concur with them, came to know sometimes their intentions time enough to prevent the success they proposed to themselves.'

It thus happened that while Colepeper was making his way to the Commons one day he was informed that as soon as all three were in the chamber it was proposed to move for their immediate arrest and confinement in the Tower. With his usual presence of mind he turned back to his lodging 'not being able to give the same information to the other two; but [knowing] that his own being absent prevented the mischief'. As soon as they could meet they agreed never to be in the House together, and if possible not more than one at a time. Opinion in the House was still so fluid that the leaders would only dare to risk such a coup if they could make a clean sweep. Nonetheless their position was anything but secure, the more so because the King, against Hyde's advice, had himself left London. He had seen the Queen off from Dover to the safety of the Continent towards the end of February, returned to Greenwich to collect the Prince of Wales, against vigorous protests from the House of Commons, and had then crossed the Thames, moving north-westwards by easy stages, arriving at York at the end of March. His progress was punctuated by exchanges with Parliament, from Greenwich, from Theobalds, from Newmarket, in all of which Hyde's constitutional royalism was the note sounded on the King's side. His earliest surviving letter to the King, written in early March, contains the core of his position, then and later:

'. . . For your Majesty well knows that your greatest strength is in the hearts and affections of those persons who have been the severest asser- tors of the publick liberties, and so besides their duty and loyalty to your person, are in love with your inclinations to peace and justice, and value their own interests upon the reservation of your rights . . . neither can there be so cunning a way found out to assist those who wish not well to your Majesty (if any such there be) as by giving the least hint to your people that you rely on anything but the strength of your laws and their obedience.'[7]

Did his Majesty well know it? If he did, the promises he had made to Henrietta Maria that he would entertain no proposals and make no ap- pointments without her approval effectively nullified his knowledge. But Mr Hyde had, in the spring of 1642, not as yet been informed of this undertaking.

In those last weeks in London, before he received, towards the end of April, the King's command to join him at York, he had little time to think of his own wife and family. His second son, Laurence, was bap- tised at St Margaret's, Westminster on March 15, 1642.[8] Presumably Frances and the children must have left Dean's Yard very soon after that. His anxiety for them was always keen, as his later correspondence abundantly shows: and his knowledge of history combined with his logical readiness to pursue a political argument to its conclusion made him more apprehensive of revolutionary violence than matter-of-fact, unimaginative country gentlemen who did not believe that that sort of thing could ever happen here. Several letters from Archdeacon Marler about the affairs of the Purton estate written at this time show that they were not expected there. So the probable conclusion is that they were at her father's house near Windsor, Cranborne Lodge, out of harm's way. It was where they were to retire after Hyde had gone overseas with the Prince of Wales when the war was lost. Besides arranging for their welfare, clearing up his chambers in the Middle Temple, arranging with Marler for receipts and payments due at Purton, Hyde had to maintain both his nightly meetings with Falkland and Colepeper and his clandestine correspondence with the King. The summons to York must have been a relief.

---

[7] *Clar. SP* ii, 139.   [8] Chester, *op. cit.*, 272.

VI

The Outbreak of the Civil War

CLARENDON several times observed that he could not bear being idle. Yet though by nature and habit industrious he was aware that activity is a strong shield against uncomfortable self-questioning. He often recommended a pause for self-examination to his friends and associates. 'I am of your mind that it was happy that I staid in this Island,' he wrote to Lady Dalkeith from Jersey in February 1647, 'for in earnest I have had leisure to call my self to a stricter accôunt than these late yeares had given me leave to do, and though being idle is a great vice, and I thinke an intollerable paine, yet having too much to do commonly leaves somewhat undone that is of the greatest importance . . .'[1]

It is vacancy, not leisure, that Clarendon disapproves of and dislikes. Travel perhaps for him fell into that category. His experience of it was to be wide, and by no means generally agreeable. The journey from London to York in 1642 seems to have been exceptionally pleasant in spite of a touch, perhaps more than a touch, of danger. To leave London at all he had to get a doctor's certificate to satisfy the Speaker. A week or two earlier he had gone down to Purton in ignorance of this formality and had been immediately recalled by a messenger to attend the House. It was lucky for him that he had had this warning. He decided not to take a direct route and to avoid main roads. Because he knew nothing of the country and expected some hue and cry to be made after him he arranged for Chillingworth, then in residence at his college in Oxford, to join him at Ditchley and guide him through the Midlands. He paused some days at Ditchley until he heard from Falkland that there was a strong move to accuse him of high treason for his suspected complicity in the defection of the Lord Keeper, who had taken the Great Seal with him to the King at York. The intelligence had been given Falkland by another member of the Great Tew circle,

[1] Clar. MS 29, ff.132–3.

George Morley, and the messenger who brought Falkland's letter was 'John Ayliffe, whom he [Hyde] dearly loved'. Was he the brother of Anne? The links with his first wife's family remained close. Anne's cousin, Lord Grandison, had acted as his courier a month or two before when he wanted to forewarn the King at Theobalds of an imminent Parliamentary initiative that at all costs must not be answered before his advisers had had time to consider it. Hyde was still encompassed by those he loved and trusted. Too soon the war would take those he loved best: the new friendships it would bring would be some compensation.

In spite of his anxiety not to attract attention Hyde left Ditchley in style. He and Chillingworth sent their horses ahead to a farm near Coventry belonging to Chillingworth's brother. Next morning they bowled off in their hostess's coach and six, picking up their horses that evening and riding through the night across country to Lutterworth. The Rector was a friend of Chillingworth's and received them kindly. Although by now out of immediate danger of pursuit they took no risks, pursuing their journey through Derbyshire by back roads. Just across the Yorkshire border they reached Nostell Priory, the house of the great financier Sir John Wolstenholme, where their host though absent had left orders for their entertainment. Frances and the children soon joined him there, staying on when he removed to York.[2] Hyde sent word to the King of his whereabouts. He did not want to be seen in York, where the Parliamentary leaders had plenty of agents, until he had to. Correspondence with the King was easy. He resumed his drafting of Royalist manifestoes. Nostell was a delightful place, the more delightful, perhaps, for the total absence of the schemers and backbiters who thronged the court. All too soon they had brought the King to the verge of dismissing with ignominy the Lord Keeper whose arrival in York had been so heavy a blow to the Parliament. Hyde rushed over from Nostell and was just in time to avert this disaster. So many were hesitating whether to throw in their lot with Charles that such a precedent would have done incalculable damage. Hyde recognised the necessity of being on the spot and arranged to make his quarters at York.

Two echoes from his past as a Parliamentary leader, one comic, one serious, rebounded from this decision. The house in which he was billeted belonged to a man whose large income as an attorney with the Council of the North had been destroyed at a stroke by its abolition, for which he held Hyde responsible. Nothing would induce him to have him in his house. He would rather it were burnt down. Mr Hyde and his servant removed themselves to stay with one of the canons of the Minster.

[2] Sir John Bramston *Autobiography* (1845) p. 84.

The other was more threatening. A Parliamentary delegation, charged with a message to the King, heard that Hyde was walking with him in the garden of the King's Manor. They presented themselves and, with civil speeches, shewed him an instruction requiring them to inform any member of either house they might meet in York to attend the House forthwith, and to report the answer to this summons. It was the serving of a writ that he would defy at his peril. He had not long to wait for further proceedings. Out riding near Beverley he met the Earl of Holland, sent down by Parliament to dissuade the King from attempting Hull where the governor had refused him entry. Their greetings were genial enough: they were familiar acquaintances rather than friends and they felt free to say what they thought. Soon they were at high words. After they had parted in Beverley Hyde heard from others '. . . that the earl had, to many persons who resorted to him, repeated with some liberty and sharpness, what had passed between them; and not without some menaces what the parliament would do'. In August Hyde was expelled from the House of Commons; in September he was one of eleven excepted by name from pardon in any peace negotiations that might take place. This stipulation was repeated in all subsequent propositions for a negotiated settlement.

The Hull fiasco, which Hyde had advised against, marked the return of that comet which flamed through the Royalist sky whenever some masterstroke of folly was in contemplation, Hyde's old friend, George Digby. After the Five Members affair he had had to escape abroad. As soon as the King had moved his court from London to York Digby determined to rejoin him. Never one for the obvious or the humdrum he appeared at court so effectively disguised as a mysterious Frenchman that neither his own father nor the King recognised him. He set out again secretly for the Continent to raise money and buy arms but before his ship cleared the Humber she fell in with an inward-bound Royalist munition ship that was being chased by two Parliamentary frigates. Digby set off in the ship's boat but before he could get aboard the Royalist captain took his vessel up Paull Creek where the frigates drew too much water to follow. Frustrated, they seized on the boat's crew and her passenger and carried them prisoners to Hull.

Digby had no difficulty in maintaining his character as a Frenchman. But the opportunity for a single-handed *coup* that would transform the situation was irresistible. At great personal risk he convinced the astonished Governor of his real identity. Parliament was, he knew, out for his blood, and the Governor, Sir John Hotham, was, according to Clarendon, a personal enemy of Digby's and notably vindictive. Digby offered him the glorious opportunity of saving his country by opening the gates to the King. Hotham, whose loyalties were far from clear in his own mind, accepted and let Digby go. But when the King, acting on this information, appeared again before Hull with a respectable force he was humiliated by a second dismissal. Whether Hotham had changed his mind again, or whether his son had got wind of the arrangement and betrayed his father is not known. Both were shortly after sent prisoners to London and executed, largely on each other's evidence.

The whole story epitomises Digby's impact on the conduct of affairs, whether in peace or war: dazzling, dramatic and futile. To the King and Queen who so much preferred the allegories of a Court Masque to the tiresomeness of the real world his appeal is understandable. His style and his panache would have turned, did indeed later turn, steadier heads than theirs. What is much more surprising is that Hyde, seeing him for what he was, always admiring his gifts and almost always deploring his use of them, should have so long retained a kindness for him. Indeed at the end of the long road they travelled together it was Digby who broke with Hyde, not Hyde with Digby. This tolerant, even indulgent, attitude towards a man whom he judged wanting in principle and without a serious sense of religion is uncharacteristic. Hyde, it seems, was fond of Digby and could not help being amused by his antics.

In his last exile in 1669 he drew his character at full length.[3] The subtlety and brilliance of the portrait exhibit Clarendon's powers at their height. At the climax of the piece, he owns himself defeated by the subject's manifold self-contradictions. Any description of his life and actions, he says 'can only qualify a man to make a conjecture what his true constitution and nature was; and at best it will be but a conjecture, since it is not possible to make a positive conclusion or deduction from the whole or any part of it, but that another conclusion may be as reasonably made from some other action or discovery'. This was after thirty years of close observation and reflection. In 1642 he could hardly have attained to such penetration. Their standing in relation to each other was very different from what it later became. Digby was the scion of a noble house of vast wealth and territorial importance. His upbringing in Spain where his father had been ambassador had given him not only a mastery of that and other European languages but a style and a knowledge of the great world. His formal education, at home by private tutors, at Oxford and finally in France had been thorough. When he returned to England, 'he returned . . . the most accomplished person that that nation, or it may be that any other at that time could present to the world, to which the beauty, comeliness and gracefulness of his person gave no small lustre'. There is a strong family likeness to what Clarendon wrote in the *Life* about Digby's

[3] *Clar. SP* iii, Appendix, li–lxxiv. See below pp. 327–8 for a fuller discussion of this masterpiece.

cousin Sir Kenelm. Both portraits are touched with that wonder which, for all his experience of men and knowledge of the world, never altogether faded into the light of common day. The friendship of so glittering a creature could not but flatter the son of a Wiltshire squire. And it was to Digby that Hyde owed his introduction to the King.

Civil wars do not begin with a formal declaration. Some have taken the attempt on Hull — in which shots were fired in anger by the defenders — as the opening action. Certainly by then the lines were drawn and both sides were trying to forestall each other in seizing magazines, raising troops, and grabbing plate and cash with which to pay them. London had become too hot for any Member of Parliament who balked at professing his readiness to live and die with the Earl of Essex. Falkland and Colepeper had rejoined Hyde at York a few weeks after his arrival. But the necessities of the Royalists, beaten to it for control of the navy, the main ports and arsenals, were such as to drive everyone, from the King himself down, out to forage for arms, men and money. Hyde accompanied him, with the other two, on a sweep through the Midlands which culminated in the raising of the Royal Standard — the official recognition of an already existing state of civil war — at Nottingham on August 22. As so often at that season the weather was depressing. Clarendon has an unforgettable description of the scene and of the mood that it reflected. What lights it up for us is the intimate talk of friends. Sir Edmund Verney, the Knight-Marshal, compliments him on his retaining 'still his natural vivacity and cheerfulness . . . in so universal a damp', and goes on to confess that he is serving the King out of honour and loyalty, not out of conviction, and therefore hopes to lose a life that he cannot lead with an easy conscience. There is more than a foretaste here of Falkland's reckless charging to his death at the first battle of Newbury and more than an echo of Hyde's manful efforts to prevent the war. Verney, like both a man of peace, differed from Hyde in blaming the quarrel on the Bishops. 'It was not a time to dispute; and his affection to the church had never been suspected. He was as good as his word; and was killed in the battle of Edge-Hill, within two months after this discourse.'

It is a noble epitaph. The moral that Clarendon draws is one that he was never to tire of impressing on sceptical and impatient colleagues during the long years of defeated exile, namely that the doctrine of expediency and the taking of moral short cuts will never advance a good cause. An apparent advantage may be gained but the real objective, if it be itself in accordance with the will of God, must be made more remote. This is the lesson of Sir Edmund Verney's conduct:

> And if those who had the same and greater obligations had observed the same rules of gratitude and generosity, whatever their other affections had

been, that battle had never been fought, nor any of that mischief been brought to pass that succeeded it.

This shaft is aimed at those noblemen without whose support or collusion no armed force, military or naval, could at that time have been mustered against the King. The Earls of Essex, Warwick, Northumberland, Pembroke, Salisbury and Holland were the men he had in mind.

What, it may reasonably be asked, did Clarendon, looking back on it all, think would have happened if these men, subordinating with deep misgivings their convictions to their loyalty, had followed Verney's example? Would Charles I have seen the light and settled down to a happy marriage with his Parliaments? Would Henrietta Maria, in constitutional terms the threat to this vision of domestic bliss, have allowed this to happen or for a moment have abandoned her itch not just to interfere but to manage? It is impossible that Clarendon after so many years of trying to serve them can have believed anything of the kind. But what he did believe was that history was far too complex, too unpredictable, too awe-inspiring a process to be manipulated by mere cleverness or, far worse, by cheating over the rules or evading awkward questions of right and wrong. Verney's duty, as he frankly admitted to his friend, was clear and incontrovertible: his opinions on particular questions of policy or of historical causation were, as he again admitted, arguable — though in the circumstances the two friends did not argue them. If civilisation is to hold together and society is not to dissolve into a heap of jarring atoms this moral priority must be observed. Clarendon habitually states this position in theological terms but, whether or not one agrees with it, it seems intelligible without them.

In this desperate condition of affairs the time for drafting answers to Parliamentary manifestoes had passed. The propaganda war had been fought and by general consent of contemporaries and later historians Hyde had got the best of it. His pen was, indeed, once employed at Nottingham by the King in drafting a final message to both Houses which his Council, led by Colepeper, who had left Falkland behind at York, and the Earl of Southampton, talked him into sending much against his will. Hyde, not being a Privy Counsellor, was not present but he emphasises the King's obvious distress. The recollection of this was apparently more poignant than that of losing a son. He had heard the news only that morning, which, he told the King, 'did affect him, though it would not disturb him long'.[4]

This passage, one of those originally composed as part of the autobiography that Clarendon vivisected to give life to his history, was

---

[4] *Hist.* VI, 8.

written in 1669. This unnamed and otherwise unmentioned boy was his second son, Edward, who was baptised in St Margaret's, Westminster on April 9, 1640. The same Christian name was given to a younger brother, christened at Oxford in the chapel of All Souls on April 1, 1645. The high incidence of infant mortality in the seventeenth century made such sorrows commonplace. But that Hyde perhaps felt more than he here admits is suggested by his recollection of the incident in a letter of condolence written to his friend and fellow exile Sir Charles Cottrell on a similar loss in 1654.

The King's distress had certainly impressed itself on his mind since he tells us that Southampton, who had lain in his bechamber, 'told Mr Hyde the next morning that the King had been in so great an agony that whole night that he believed he had not slept two hours in the whole night, which was a discomposure his constitution was rarely liable to in the greatest misfortune of his life'. For a man who slept soundly for several hours the night before his execution, as Clarendon knew when he wrote, this marked profound disturbance. Yet to us it is carrying reverent sympathy a little far to find both the event and the memory of it more moving than the death of a son.

The message which Hyde drafted on this occasion had been prompted by the Council's alarm at the King's military weakness. To remedy this, and to remove the person of the King from the risk of a pre-emptive raid that might have ended the war before it had begun, the Court moved westward towards Shrewsbury. The town was strongly Royalist and covered the approaches to Wales, one of the King's best recruiting grounds, and to the north-western counties and ports. Hyde, somewhat to his surprise, was here entrusted with the task of raising money from the Roman Catholic gentry of Shropshire. He thought his outspoken antagonism to the Church of Rome too well known for him to have much hope of success. But by inducing them to compound for their recusancy fines for the next two or three years he quickly raised a substantial sum. How many years he was to spend, with ever-increasing urgency and ever-diminishing returns, in similar exertions, was mercifully hidden from him. Spirits in the Royalist camp began to rise. Prince Rupert, freshly arrived from the Continent, won an unexpected but psychologically important victory in a skirmish outside Worcester. Men and arms and money poured into Shrewsbury. Instead of resting on the defensive the King decided to march on London in spite of the fact that Essex with a larger Parliamentary force had established himself lower down the Severn at Worcester. Intelligence and reconnaissance on both sides was surprisingly amateurish considering the number of professional officers engaged. The armies blundered into each other near Banbury on the night of October 22 and next day fought the battle of Edgehill.

This is the only major action of the war at which Clarendon was present. For a man who hated and despised violence and whose talent for getting on with people rarely extended to military men, his descriptions of battles and campaigns are clear and vigorous, if not always accurate or fair. But that of Edgehill has the flavour of first-hand experience. The force and directness of his account gain from his personal knowledge of so many of the people involved, some of them his friends, some to burden his life with their squabbles and intrigues. Prince Rupert, whom he had met briefly at Nottingham, commanded the cavalry on the right, Wilmot, whom he knew as a court acquaintance, the left. Both men bulk large in his *History* and Wilmot in his correspondence. His dislike for each was mutual. Under Rupert was to charge that day his colleague Colepeper, and under Wilmot Falkland (who, like Hyde, resented Rupert's refusal to subordinate his command of the horse to that of the Earl of Lindsey as Commander-in-Chief). If it seems odd that the Chancellor of the Exchequer and the Secretary of State should lay aside their portfolios to ride as volunteers, it may seem odder that Mr Hyde, who held no office and was of military age, should not have joined them. Perhaps, as in the case of Mr Tupman in *Pickwick Papers*, his friends felt that he was too fat to do battle. Colepeper and Falkland had both been professional soldiers and had proved their physical courage. Perhaps it was felt that Hyde's political intellect was too valuable to expose to a chance knock on the head. He does not tell us; but we are told that he was in close attendance on the King throughout the battle and that it was the King who ordered him to take charge of the Prince of Wales and the Duke of York when it suddenly seemed they might be in danger from a force of Parliamentary cavalry that had been left unmarked by the prematurely triumphant Royalist left wing. Among those who had commanded regiments under Wilmot were Clarendon's particular friend Lord Grandison and the ubiquitous Lord Digby. When Sir Edmund Verney fell in the thickest of the fight and the Standard was taken, it was an officer of Grandison's regiment who galloped across the Parliamentary rear and snatched it back.

In Clarendon's account in which persons suddenly come sharply into focus before the camera of his mind travels, floats it seems, down a perspective of issues and causes, Edgehill epitomises the Civil War. The indulgent feebleness of the King, unwilling or unable to curb the insensitive arrogance of his nephew, a young man of twenty-three with no knowlege of English ideas and manners and no interest in them: the old, steady, tried supports of the Crown, the nobility and gentry, alienated by tactlessness and lack of recognition, let alone of gratitude: the young sparks and sprigs of that stock, Digby, Wilmot and the rest of them, looking on the war as a glorious scene for personal advancement and personal gallantry, not as the worst of evils. A battle is fought. Precious lives — that is, the lives of men of family and position — are thrown away. If through their courage and self-sacrifice the day is won, no constructive use will be made of the victory.

All these elements of the situation can be observed at Edgehill. The battle was indeed a near-run thing but the Royalists were left not only in possession of the field: much more important they were between the Parliamentary forces and London. If they marched on the capital there was nothing to stop them: the pressure on any government in so rich a city to treat with an advancing army before it got the smell of loot in its nostrils must have been overwhelming. Yet before marching on London the King turned aside to capture the neighbouring Parliamentary garrison of Banbury and then allowed himself the luxury of a triumphant entry into Oxford. By the time he was ready to take the initiative the opportunity had gone. Even so, Edgehill had discredited the war party at Westminster. Wavering supporters had been assured that the King could not possibly muster forces of any significance or arm them or keep them in pay.

Early in November the King advanced down the Thames Valley. After he had garrisoned Reading Parliament requested a safe conduct for a deputation. At Colnbrook he received the Earls of Northumberland and Pembroke together with three members of the House of Commons. Contemptuous of politicking, Rupert took the cavalry forward to Hounslow and asked his uncle to move up in support. This the King did. Rupert at once attacked the Parliamentary force holding Brentford and after a stiff fight beat them out of their positions, taking a number of prisoners. But the general alarm that a full-scale assault on the capital was being mounted brought the London train-bands, supported at last by the tardily arrived Essex, and there was nothing to do but withdraw. Clarendon strongly suggests in the *History*, and categorically asserts in the *Life* written twenty years later, that this mistimed and pointless display of force wrecked the best chance ever offered of nipping the war in the bud. To him Prince Rupert was the Sir Lucius O'Trigger who found the quarrel a very good quarrel and resented anyone trying to spoil it. Perhaps he was right. But perhaps Rupert had no alternative. Sir Philip Warwick, who had witnessed the impact of his arrival at Nottingham on 'a very thin and small army' and had charged under his command at Edgehill, says simply 'he put that spirit into the King's army, that all men seem'd resolved'. Without him there might well have been no respectful deputations from Westminster ready to treat. Warwick admits, in milder language than Clarendon's (he was a milder man), the charges that Clarendon brings against Rupert of arrogance and insolence towards the King's counsellors and ministers. 'And these great men often distrusted such downright soldiers as the Prince was . . . lest he should be too apt to prolong the warr; and to obtain that by a pure victory, which they wished to be got by a dutifull submission upon modest, speedy and peaceable terms . . .' This summarises Clarendon's own objectives perfectly. From start to finish he held a military solution to be no solution, and great was the odium he incurred thereby from the Swordmen. The conclusion Warwick draws was one from which Clarendon would not in his private correspondence have dissented:

And indeed had the Prince studied more to have removed this jealousy [i.e. the distrust of the Council], or the King more vigorously interposed therein, and bin Master of both parties, his armes had probably bin much more prosperous than they were; but neither of them stood in awe of him; and so the consequence was fatall.[5]

[5] *Memoires* 226–8.

VII

Royalist Oxford

ONLY the glummest student of history can deny the romance and colour of Royalist Oxford, so imaginatively recaptured in *John Inglesant*. Its realities, like those of other romantic scenes, were in many respects disagreeable. Seventeenth-century towns were at best insanitary places. When they were overcrowded, as Oxford was, contamination of the water supply with its resultant diseases was inevitable. And the cost of living where so many rich people were concentrated was very high. Seeking material for the *History* in 1647, Hyde wrote to his fellow exile Lord Hatton: 'If you write largely and kindly and like the man I used to feaste with at Oxford my volume will overwhelm you, and every week's correspondence will be as troublesome and almost as chargeable as a Dinner used to be.'[1]

From the autumn of 1642 to the spring of 1645 Hyde was based in Oxford. When he arrived he was plain Mr Hyde of the Middle Temple, without any official position though generally recognised as what would now be called the King's special adviser on public relations. When he left he was Sir Edward Hyde, Chancellor of the Exchequer, member of the Privy Council, charged by the King with responsibility for the safety and well-being of the heir apparent. He came a draftsman and controversialist; he went one of the most trusted advisers and executive ministers of the Crown.

It was at Oxford that he first acquired that experience of affairs which, he insisted, is essential to the historian: 'there was never yet a good History written but by Men conversant in Business . . . It is not a collection of Records, or an Admission to the View and Perusal of the most secret Letters and Acts of State . . . which can enable a Man to write a History if there be an Absence of that Genius and Spirit and Soul of an Historian, which is contracted by the Knowledge and

[1] Clar. MS 29 f.156.

82

Course and Method of Business, and by Conversation and Familiarity in the Inside of Courts and [with] the most active and eminent Persons in the Government . . .'[2] Since Oxford was also the headquarters of the Royalist army it gave him a close and continuous view of the generals and other officers who thronged the city. The portraitist William Dobson, who came there about the same time as Hyde and stayed on till the surrender in 1646, has represented them as they wished to be seen, not as so many of them appear in the pages of the *History* and the *Life*.

All these expensive and magnificent people brought with them a crowd of followers, wives, mistresses, servants, tradesmen and artificers who supplied the luxuries to which they were accustomed. Royalist Oxford was, by all accounts, raffish and dissolute. Even John Aubrey, an undergraduate at Trinity at the time, seems to have been mildly shocked as well as excited by the déshabille of the well-born if not well-behaved young women who were accommodated in his college. Of the high living and the abundance of victuals Clarendon writes enthusiastically in the *History*. In the hungry years of exile he reminds his favourite correspondent Secretary Nicholas of the venison pasties at Oriel where the Council used to meet at four o'clock on a Friday afternoon. He was himself accommodated at All Souls where Sheldon, his friend from Great Tew days, was Warden. They had renewed contact, most profitably for the Royalist cause, when Hyde had passed through Oxford in September on his way to Shrewsbury in advance of the King. He and Sheldon had together secured a large part of the plate from the various Colleges, virtually all of which was to be melted down for coining before the war was over.

Hyde's Oxford life began with the last flaring of the embers that Rupert had done his best to stamp out at Brentford. There was still a strong enough body of moderate, uncertain opinion in both houses of Parliament for the more forward party to think it politic at least to go through the motions of sending Commissioners to negotiate with the King. The peace party had been helped by a Royal Proclamation, drafted by Hyde, in terms that exposed the shakiness of the legal foundations on which Parliament was building, without closing the door to a negotiated settlement. The terms brought by the Commissioners were, as might be expected, unacceptable to the King. But the Commissioners themselves, particularly the Earl of Northumberland and Hyde's old friend Bulstrode Whitelocke, indicated unofficially but unmistakably that if the King would come a little way to meet them they would go the whole way to meet him. Northumberland, according to Hyde's account in the *Life*, even indicated

---

[2] *Tracts* 179.

that if the King would restore him to his post of Lord High Admiral he would engage his own credit to bring the navy back to his allegiance. Hyde specifies that he is here recording 'only what passed in secret, and was never communicated, nor can otherwise be known, since at this time, no man else is living who was privy to that negotiation' — a slight exaggeration since at the moment of writing Sir Edward Nicholas may just have been alive and Bulstrode Whitelocke certainly was.

Hyde, evidently, was central to the negotiation, probably because of all the three middle-of-the-road Royalists he was best at handling Charles. Secretary Nicholas, to whom the overture had been made, had found the King markedly unresponsive. Hyde took care to choose an auspicious moment and set out the enormous advantages of accepting such an unlooked-for opportunity, urging him 'to consider his own ill condition; and how unlike it was that it should be improved by the continuance of the war; and whether he could ever imagine a possibility of getting out of it upon more easy conditions than what was now proposed'.

Characteristically the King did not answer the point. He professed himself wounded by Northumberland's past behaviour after all the favours that had been showered upon him. 'And this discourse he continued with more commotion, and in a more pathetical style than ever he used upon any other argument.' Clearly, in recollection at least, Clarendon thought he was dissembling his real reason for 'this fatal rejection'. 'The true cause and ground thereof,' he explains in the *Life* ('this discourse which is never to see light, and so can reflect upon nobody's character with prejudice'), was the King's extraordinary devotion to the Queen 'insomuch as he saw with her eyes, and determined by her judgment; and did not only pay her this adoration, but desired that all men should know that he was swayed by her: which was not good for either of them'. The Queen, so long excluded from affairs by Buckingham, had developed an insatiable appetite for 'knowing all things and disposing all things'. When she went abroad in February 1642 'his majesty made a solemn promise to her at parting, that he would receive no person into any favour or trust, who had disserved him, without her privity and consent'. Charles had neither the self-confidence nor the strength of character to be flexible. He loved to dig himself in behind a stockade of pledges that denied any freedom of manoeuvre. It was an insurance against the awful dilemma of having to make up his mind.

This was farewell, a last farewell, to the hopes of Great Tew. There was to be no getting away from the war. The best plan now was to work on the King's undoubted intelligence and conscientiousness and to write a role for him in the great masque of English history that was consonant with its true spirit and not the invention of foreigners, favourites and adventurers.

Before the Parliamentary Commissioners had gone sadly back to London, recalled at the first possible moment by their justifiably suspicious masters, Hyde had accepted office at the King's renewed insistence. On February 22 he was knighted and admitted to the Privy Council and on March 3 made Chancellor of the Exchequer. The King had wanted to join him with Falkland in the Secretaryship, had indeed written a letter to the Queen, which had been intercepted and published by the Parliamentarians, saying, 'I must make Ned Hyde secretary of state, for the truth is, I can trust nobody else'. To do this the King proposed to move the recently appointed veteran of government service, Sir Edward Nicholas, to the post of Master of the Wards — a post avidly sought in peacetime but empty and useless in war. To Hyde this was intolerably embarrassing. Nicholas was a much older man with a far wider experience of administration and public business; he was also a very old family friend. As a boy he had been brought up in the household of Clarendon's uncle, Sir Laurence Hyde, and had gone to school in Salisbury with his first cousins. The King's proposal was impossible: he knew nothing of foreign affairs and had no languages: on the other hand 'he had great friendship for secretary Nicholas, who would be undone by the change'. The King was irritated by these objections. He would soon learn all he needed to know and as to Nicholas 'his change was by his desire'. Hyde had better go and speak to him about it.

The affectionate relations between the two men and their families, unbroken in their lifetime and echoing beyond, provide evidence as clear as it is attractive of the absence of pettiness or jealousy in their natures. 'When he came to the Secretary's lodging, he found him with a cheerful countenance, and embracing him, called him his son. Mr Hyde answered him that "it was not the part of a good son to undo his father".' With difficulty he persuaded Nicholas to have second thoughts. The timely death of the Master of the Rolls solved the problem. Colepeper had been promised the place as soon as it fell vacant. Falkland suggested to the King that Hyde should succeed him as Chancellor of the Exchequer. The King made the offer and Hyde with token protestations of his insufficiency accepted it. That, for once, should have pleased everybody concerned. But Colepeper was difficult: '. . . though he professed much friendship to the other, he had no mind he should be upon the same level with him; and believed he would have too much credit in the council.' Besides he was self-seeking and had secretly hoped to hold both posts. It was only when Falkland and Digby took him to task that he surrendered the office. But this passage left its mark and was noticed by others, including the King.

Colepeper no doubt feared that Hyde's articulacy, his knowledge of divinity and political philosophy, his wide acquaintance and his readiness to decline rather than to seek royal favours might predispose the King to solicit his advice at the Council board. But at least he was confined, unlike Falkland, Digby and Colepeper himself, to the Privy Council. He was not a member, as they were, of the War Council on which both the Royalist generals and the Privy Counsellors who could claim military experience sat together. It was this which made the Oxford period for Hyde one of apprenticeship to government rather than one of responsibility for the framing and execution of policy. The war made everything else peripheral. In 1643 the Royalists, at any rate up to their failure to take Gloucester in the early autumn, seemed to be winning it. What Sir Edward Hyde thought and did attracted less attention, naturally enough, than the exploits of Prince Rupert and Lord Wilmot, or the soldiers' battles by which Sir Ralph Hopton and Sir Bevil Grenville conquered the greater part of the South-West.

It was the immediate conseqeuence of these victories that took Clarendon out of Oxford in the summer of 1643. The storming of Bristol by Rupert at the end of July had been made possible by the virtual destruction of the Parliamentary forces in these hard-fought actions. As a reward the Marquis of Hertford, the titular Commander-in-Chief of the King's armies in the West, appointed Hopton, the effective fighting general, Governor of the captured city. This led to a damaging breach with Rupert, outraged at being done out of what he considered the lawful prize of war. Such a falling out could only be composed by the direct intervention of the King himself, who accordingly set out for Bristol accompanied by Hyde and many other Privy Counsellors and courtiers. On the way the King spent the first night at Malmesbury. Hyde seized the opportunity of spending the night at Purton where he entertained several of his colleagues including Falkland and Colepeper. He says nothing of the state of his property but no doubt it would have been vandalised by Parliamentary troops as his friend Whitelocke's house at Fawley had been by Rupert's men.

Charles settled the dispute over the Governorship substantially in Rupert's favour. At least that is what Clarendon evidently thought, though Rupert was, it seems, as resentful of the outcome as Hertford. The one person whose unselfishness made the compromise possible was Hopton, who accepted the post of Deputy to Rupert as Governor with the grace he brought to all the actions of his public life. Here was the beginning of another of Hyde's most fruitful friendships. But the consequences of the victory involved him in a jurisdictional quarrel of his own. As Chancellor of the Exchequer he had not had much to do in looking after the King's revenue because it had been effectively cut off. The capture of a major port put him in business. When he sent for the customs officers he found to his fury that Colepeper and Ashburnham, a groom of the King's bedchamber and one of Charles's most cherished favourites, had already induced the King to grant them an assignment. Falkland told them, and the King, what he thought of this usurpation 'with some warmth'. Colepeper and Ashburnham made excuses. The King, as usual, shuffled 'with many gracious expressions'. Hyde professed a lack of resentment which his readers may take leave to doubt.

This was one of Falkland's last acts of friendship. In the following month he was killed at the battle of Newbury. 'In this battle . . . the chancellor of the exchequer lost the joy and comfort of his life; which he lamented so passionately, that he could not in many days compose himself to any thoughts of business.' When Clarendon wrote that sentence a quarter of a century later, it was only two and half years since he had lost the partner of a long and happy marriage. Falkland, too, had been happily married. Yet in the single letter from him that survives among Clarendon's papers he addresses his friend as 'Dear Sweetheart'. Both men would have known by heart the words of David's lamentation

> Very pleasant hast thou been unto me:
> Thy love to me was wonderful,
> Passing the love of women.

Clarendon's essay on Friendship, written at Montpellier at the same time as he was at work on the *Life*, begins with a quotation from Cicero's essay on the same subject enjoining the preference of friendship over all human concerns. This pagan standard is still, in his eyes, valid for a Christian: 'Friendship is so much more a sacrament than marriage is . . .' The inequality of the sexes, axiomatic in the ancient world whether Jewish, Greek or Roman, was still all but axiomatic in the seventeenth century. Friendship was, as Clarendon defined it, a moral relation entered into by 'just and good men'. Equality of status is not stated but assumed as a fundamental requirement. It was only necessary to turn to St Paul to see that Christian marriage explicitly rejected any such conception of the relationship between man and wife. The sexual element in that relationship in any case relegates it to a lower category: '. . . the Temper and Composition of Friendship itself is so delicate and spiritual, that it admits no meer carnal Ingredients . . .'[3]

Clarendon who had returned to Oxford ahead of the army had written to Falkland, urging him that a Privy Counsellor and Secretary of State ought not to expose himself to unnecessary dangers. The day after the news of his death reached Oxford a letter came in reply,

[3] *Tracts* 132–4.

soothing his friend's anxieties but arguing 'that he was so much taken notice of for an impatient desire of peace, that it was necessary that he should likewise make it appear that it was not out of fear of the utmost hazard of war'. When the armies confronted each other at Newbury he had volunteered to charge at the head of Sir John Byron's regiment and had been killed in the first volley.

'Much hath been said of this excellent person before; but not so much, or so well, as his wonderful parts and virtues deserved. He died as much of the time as of the bullet; for, from the very beginning of the war, he contracted so deep a sadness and melancholy, that his life was not pleasant to him; and sure he was too weary of it.' He goes on to dispose of the story that John Aubrey was to seize on, namely that his melancholy was occasioned by an unhappy love affair. '. . . Neither of them was capable of an ill imagination. She was of the most unspotted, unblemished virtue; never married; of an extraordinary talent of mind, but of no alluring beauty . . .' It was yet another instance of the friendship that rising above 'meer carnality' touched human nature with the divine.

For a second time the King pressed Hyde to accept the Secretaryship now vacant by Falkland's death. For a second time he refused. Apart from the invidious distinction it would have conferred on a man regarded by many courtiers as a jumped-up intellectual, the pro-French influence of the Queen would have made the post impossible for anyone of Hyde's lifelong distrust and dislike of France. He had noted with satisfaction on being made Chancellor of the Exchequer the 'unusual circumstance . . . that it was without the interposition or privity of the queen'. When the King offered him Falkland's place, '. . . the queen did not oppose, though she rather wished that the lord Digby might have it', in which Hyde supported her. The two men were at this time fast friends: '. . . the confidence and friendship between them was mutual, and very notorious, until that lord changed his religion.' (Digby, or Bristol as he had then become, despairing of a Stuart restoration, became a Roman Catholic in 1659 in order to further his prospects of employment under the Spanish crown. This at any rate was Clarendon's interpretation of his motives.[4] Digby 'had so much kindness and friendship for the chancellor, (which was at that time and long after as sincere as could receive harbour in his breast) that he professed he would not have it, if the other would receive it . . .' There is no reason to doubt the value he set on Hyde's judgment. Once he became Secretary he consulted him and kept him informed. Almost certainly he encouraged the King, against the jealousy of many including Colepeper, to make Hyde a member of the inner committee or

---

[4] *Clar. SP* iii, supplement lxviii ff.

junto that was created about this time. The other members were the King's cousin and intimate friend, the Duke of Richmond, Lord Cottington, the two Secretaries (Digby and Nicholas), and Colepeper.

Living at close quarters with these people Clarendon had no occasion to correspond with them. We have therefore no exactly contemporary documentary evidence of what he thought of them and how they in turn influenced him. In view of his apparently compulsive need to express himself on paper it seems odd that he did not keep a journal. Nonetheless the early books of the *History* that he was to write in Jersey a mere four of five years later, and the correspondence he then conducted in the course of his researches, tell the reader a great deal about the Oxford years.

The friendships he either formed or deepened there were those with Digby and Nicholas and the King. That with Digby was perhaps more of an alliance of free spirits, men who read books and were accustomed to argue about politics and religion, against the swordmen who looked on such activities as subversive. Drinking, quarrelling and intrigue were, one gathers from the *History*, the swordmen's principal recreations. Apart from Rupert, whose temperance is particularly commended, the excessive conviviality, 'good fellowship' to use Clarendon's favourite term of scorn, of the Royalist officers was in his considered view the greatest single cause of their ultimate defeat. Not till Lloyd George in the First World War is there a statesman who takes the drink problem so seriously. No doubt it contributed to the quarrels and thus to the duels to which they gave rise. Both were symptoms of the almost complete lack of the idea of discipline which is the hallmark of a regular army officered by professionals with a career to think of. Even commanders of undoubted talent and experience such as Rupert, Wilmot or George Goring took themselves more seriously than they took their jobs, the mark of the amateur in any profession.

Digby was as ready to draw his sword in a duel as the best of them and was, indeed, as his friend came finally to recognise a supreme egoist. 'He doth not believe that anybody he loves so well can be unloved by anybody else.'[5] Clarendon had not seen enough of him in 1643 to make that judgment but he had seen quite enough, the attempt on the Five Members for instance, to know that caution and prudence were words not to be found in the vocabulary of his mind. Nonetheless his energy, intelligence, and resource made him a valuable counterpoise to the stupidity, arrogance and lack of imagination that characterised so many of the courtiers and the soldiers. And like Clarendon he had begun his political career as an opponent of the court.

[5] *ibid* lxxiii.

Nicholas was Digby's antithesis in every shade and tone of personality. Strict, shrewd, unselfseeking, unimaginative, he approached
every question with the habits and assumptions of a man who had
reached the summit of a successful career as a senior administrator. If
ever there was a born Wykehamist it was he. His parents indeed sent
him to Winchester at the unusually late age of fourteen but he was so
delicate that six months of it nearly killed him. It took him the best
part of a year to recover his health. A nervous and sensitive boy, even as
a man he was never robust. The pyschological damage inflicted by
exposing so tender a growth to the savage east winds of a seventeenth-
century public school may have something to do with the anxiety and
want of self-confidence so conspicuous in his private correspondence.
Well educated by private tutors he entered the Middle Temple in 1611
and in the same year went up to the Queen's College, Oxford. Like his
friend Hyde he took no degree but spent a couple of years there,
followed by another couple at the Middle Temple, rounding off his
education with a six months' stay in France. In the spring of 1616 he
returned to England and almost at once embarked on his bureaucratic
career by becoming secretary to the Chancellor of the Duchy of Lan-
caster. Like so many servants of the Crown in the seventeenth century
he graduated from one patron and one post to another till he succeeded Hyde's future father-in-law, Sir Thomas Aylesbury, as Secretary to the Admiralty under Buckingham in 1625. In 1635 he was sworn
Clerk to the Council and in 1641, after a few months as Clerk of the
Signet, he was promoted to the Secretaryship whose responsibilities he
had in fact already been discharging. It was during this period when
the King was away in Scotland that he had begun, secretly and as yet
unofficially, his long partnership in public affairs with the family
friend of old Wiltshire days, Edward Hyde.[6]

In Oxford their friendship ripened. Hyde was a compulsive com-
municator. After the death of Falkland Nicholas was the only Privy
Counsellor on whose absolute integrity and strict discretion he could
perfectly rely. It was from Nicholas that he must have learned — who
else could have taught him? — the remorseless discipline of efficient
bureaucracy against which his colleagues, most notably and wittily
Lord Cottington, were later to protest. 'I have more charity than *addere
afflictionem afflicto* [to add affliction to the afflicted]. Mr Chancellor
with his horrible volume hath given you sufficient vexacion.'[7] It was
from Nicholas that he imbibed what we should now call the doctrine of
Cabinet secrecy, whose violation he came to identify as a principal
cause of the King's downfall. Both men were, as Privy Counsellors,

[6] *Nicholas Papers* ed. Warner. vol i (1886). Donald Nicholas *Mr Secretary Nicholas* (1955).
[7] Cottington to Nicholas, March 18, 1650. *Nicholas Papers* i, 169.

granted the jealously restricted permission to accommodate their wives and children in Oxford. Affectionate intimacy between the two families strengthened the professional and political tie. The Nicholas children were of course much older than the little Hydes. The eldest son, John, the future recipient of some of Clarendon's most charming letters, had gone up to his father's old college before the war broke out. He left Oxford in February 1644 to continue his studies in France.

Above all Oxford was the place where Hyde got to know the King. Here, if anywhere, was the chance to convert him to the apparently vanquished values of Great Tew. Falkland had fallen at Newbury, but Sheldon, the Warden of All Souls, had impressed the King by his vigorous action in everything that might advance the Royalist cause and by the strength of his character. Hammond, whose sermons the King had previously admired, returned to Oxford in the summer of 1643 to escape arrest for Royalist activities in his Kentish parish. Both men were made Royal Chaplains and both were appointed to the delegation sent to meet the Parliamentary commissioners at Uxbridge in February 1645. Hammond published a devotional work in 1644 which the King treasured in his captivity: both were the chaplains whose services he later particularly requested as the shadows closed round him. In the surroundings of a university almost wholly clerical in character the King, by nature serious and devout, might be led to trust his own insights and to reflect on them. Perhaps if Henrietta Maria had stayed on the Continent, the King might have renounced what Hyde saw as a fatal readiness to take short cuts to evade principles and pledges, even quite simply to deceive. It is Hyde's argument constantly repeated, that if the King had backed his own judgments and stuck to them, he would soon have attracted the overwhelming support of the huge majority of the political nation who wanted peace and law. He was undone by his diffident, too humble, acceptance of other people's advice — though that is too weak a word for the Queen's fatuous certainties. It must have been at Oxford, where he saw the King often both at the Council board and in private audience, that he formed the estimate of his master that colours the history he was later to write. And it was certainly at Oxford that he had his first prolonged exposure to the personality of the Queen.

Clarendon's treatment of Henrietta Maria in his historical and autobiographical writings — which were composed for a strictly limited circulation — is a pattern of chivalrous restraint. What she stood for was, to him, the root of all evil and the ruin of his country. In personal terms she was, under both Kings he served so wholeheartedly, his most inveterate enemy. Yet the scorpions with which he chastises her favourites, the courtiers like Holland and Jermyn who from first to last were simply after money and the softnesses of life, are never employed against her. Perhaps the reason, beyond what was proper to her sex and to her position, is that they each recognised the other as persons of principle. Her disastrous and open policy of militant Catholicism, her no less disastrous refusal to admit that the interests of England might not always be identical with the requirements of French foreign policy, were genuinely and tenaciously established as articles of her faith, not detachable accessories of greed or self-interest. No doubt her evident dislike and personal hostility towards Clarendon sprang from her recognition that he was an opponent of the same quality. In fact she admitted as much to Lady Dalkeith, one of her ladies in waiting, in 1649.[8]

The Queen arrived in Oxford, riding in triumph with her husband and Prince Rupert who had gone out to escort the convoy of supplies she had brought from Holland, in July 1643. She was just in time to throw her weight against what Hyde considered a promising opportunity of whittling away the strength of their opponents offered by the defection of the Earls of Bedford, Holland and Clare. If they were well received and rewarded, others, in Hyde's view, would quickly follow, especially as this was the high water mark for the Royalists between the capture of Bristol and their failure to take Gloucester. Hyde was supported, unusually, by Rupert, a fact that he suggests may have swayed the Queen who was jealous of the Prince's influence on her husband. The King returned from the siege of Gloucester to hear her views and those of his Council. The peccant Earls were received but by no means with the welcome accorded to the Prodigal Son. They were allowed to join the army outside Gloucester and when that siege was raised they fought with some credit at Newbury. When Holland, who had always been on easy terms with Hyde, called on him in Oxford, Cottington and other unnamed Privy Counsellors who were there cut him dead and left the room. Hyde went out of his way to be pleasant. If the Hollands of this world, weathercocks of fortune, registered a breeze of Royalist success, the psychological gain was incalculable. But the coolness of the King and Queen checked the movement before it had begun. Two months later Holland returned to his earlier allegiance. The Parliamentary leaders might not think much of this accession to their strength but they knew how to exploit an opportunity for propaganda. It was exasperating to see it handed them on a plate. Propaganda and psychological warfare were, after all, what Hyde was there for. There were soldiers enough, professional and amateur; and though they quarrelled and disagreed about almost everything on one point they were united: the war could only be won in the field. This, if only he could bring it off, was the King's preferred solution. For all his

---

[8] *Life* V, 38. Lady Dalkeith is not named in the text.

gentleness to his servants and his tenderness of heart to those he loved the King seems to have felt neither compassion nor responsibility for the miseries of war. In every line Hyde writes about the war even at his most unfair there is a sense of outrage, of shame, even of sin. Charles certainly felt these emotions but in altogether different contexts. He would not have understood, as Hyde would, what the Duke of Wellington meant when he said that a victory was the greatest tragedy in the world except a defeat.

If the soldiers, Rupert, Maurice, Goring, Wilmot, old Lord Forth, get the rough edge of Clarendon's pen, something must be allowed for the two and a half years he spent in Oxford, powerless to restrain their follies and excesses, patronised if not insulted when he tried to recall the political and constitutional issues of the quarrel. His advice at such crucial moments as the Oxford discussions or the defection of the Earls was overridden, his initiatives frustrated. The most original of these was his idea of reconstituting a rival, Royalist, Parliament in Oxford. The King could count on a handsome majority in the Upper House even without the now disenfranchised Bishops. There were in the event a respectable number of members elected to the Long Parliament who answered the summons to Oxford at the end of 1643 — just over 100. The King performed the dignified part of his function with his usual felicity, welcoming them to Christ Church hall in a speech which made telling use of the alliance just concluded between the Westminster Parliament and the Scots. But as Dame Veronica Wedgwood makes clear in her masterly narrative, *The King's War*, his real hopes and intentions were concentrated in his underhand negotiations for the landing of Irish Catholic irregulars in Scotland, negotiations that were carefully concealed from Hyde and Nicholas. Hyde would have judged them then as he did when he found out about them two years later 'inexcusable to justice, piety, and prudence . . . Oh, Mr Secretary, those strategems have given me more sad hours than all the misfortunes in war, which have befallen the King, and look like the effects of God's anger towards us.'[9] What the King really thought about his faithful Lords and Commons assembled in Oxford was made brutally plain when his private correspondence, captured after his defeat at Naseby in April 1645, was published by the victors. A 'mongrel Parliament'. It was the long-suffering Secretary Nicholas who was blandly directed to explain away the phrase. Hyde had already taken leave of his master and embarked on his long housemastership of the son who was to succeed him.

9 *Clar. SP* ii, 337.

VIII

The Smell of Defeat

H<small>YDE'S</small> detestation of the War did not fluctuate with the military fortunes of Royalism. It was in the spring of 1643, when the King's hopes
were rising, that a Royal message to Parliament, surely of Hyde's drafting, urged that 'in a short time there will be so general a habit of uncharitableness and cruelty contracted through the whole kingdom that
even peace itself will not restore his people to their old temper and
security'.[1] In his last months in Oxford the outlook was much darker.
The Queen, pregnant for the last time, was so alarmed and depressed
that she left Oxford for the safety of the south-west as early as April
1644. She was delivered of a daughter, the future Henriette, at Exeter.
It was the King's solicitude for her health and nervous stability that, in
Clarendon's opinion, weighed most with him in choosing to follow
Essex,[2] who had marched somewhat aimlessly in that direction, instead of concentrating his forces on the central and northern sector
where everything was at stake and, at Marston Moor in July, everything
was lost. The King's march denuded Oxford of troops, thus giving
Hyde his one military opportunity of the war. He superintended the
repair of the fortifications and, by his own account, was much commended for 'his extraordinary diligence and industry' in obtaining
labour, materials and money from the surrounding country.[3]

The King returned in the autumn, perhaps too easily pleased with
his defeat of Essex in the far south-west and by bringing his army back
to Oxford without serious loss. The Queen had escaped to France, leaving her baby daughter safe in Exeter. The squabbles and insubordination in the Royalist command had led to the suspension and
exile of Wilmot. So far, from Hyde's point of view, perhaps so good.
But unlike his master he could tell a hawk from a handsaw. The loss of
the north was not to be offset by peripheral victories such as Lostwithiel

[1] *Hist.* VII, 50. [2] *ibid* VIII, 71. [3] *ibid* 73 fn 2.

94

or by tactical successes such as the second battle of Newbury against inept commanders. Parliament had got the upper hand: and inside Parliament it was Vane and Cromwell who were the rising men of power; Essex, Manchester, Sir William Waller, middle-ground men, who were discredited commanders. The King had offered to treat for peace after his victory over Essex. Parliament did not deign to take him up until after it had tried and executed Archbishop Laud, a calculated display of ruthlessness and of confidence in victory. It did not augur well for the negotiations at Uxbridge, less than three weeks later, at the end of January.

Hyde's chief recollection of the Treaty was of hopelessness and of physical exhaustion. Though not the senior in rank — the King's cousin, the Duke of Richmond, and noblemen such as Hertford and Southampton headed the Commission — he was effectively in charge. He was perhaps the only man who knew both the arguments and the fundamental necessities of Royalism in the three crucial fields of law, politics and religion. The barrister's training of appearing in court all day and mastering the next day's brief during the greater part of the night must have helped. But this was not the end of it. It was not only his own brief he had to prepare but that of his colleagues.[4] And when he had done that he had to prepare an account of the day's transactions together with questions and recommendations for instant dispatch to the King at Oxford.

The Royal Commissioners included old friends such as Secretary Nicholas and Geoffrey Palmer, old sparring partners such as Colepeper, and one at least who was to grow into close friendship, Lord Capel. On the Parliamentary side the one old friend was Bulstrode Whitelocke. But the terms in which Clarendon writes of him are colder than the grudging acknowledgment of his good intentions made at Oxford two years earlier: 'all his estate was in their quarters, and he had a nature that could not bear or submit to be undone.'[5] He is indeed accused of fundamental hypocrisy: 'who from the beginning had concurred with them without any inclination to their persons or principles . . . yet to his friends who were commissioners for the King he used his old openness and professed his detestation of all their proceedings, yet could not leave them.' Of his old associates in the House of Commons Denzil Holles is praised for his courage and integrity in owning his opposition to his militant colleagues. Granted their political principles and their readiness to avow them, Clarendon and he would appear natural allies. Yet though his political life began earlier and lasted longer he is never treated at the length and depth extended to figures of much less significance. Had the two men perhaps fallen foul of each

[4] *ibid* 221.　　　　　　　　[5] *ibid* 248.

other when Clarendon was retained for the other side in a Chancery case about Holles's wedding settlement in June 1638?[6]

From the start it was clear that the negotiations would not lead to anything. The middle ground had been washed away by the high tide of Parliamentary success. Northumberland, Pembroke, Salisbury and the rest of them were still there of course, and still actually present as Parliamentary Commissioners. But their day was over. What might have been on offer at Oxford in 1643 was no longer available at Uxbridge in 1645:

> The earls of Pembroke and Salisbury were so totally without credit or interest in the Parliament or country, that it was no matter which way their inclinations or affections disposed them; and their fear of the faction that prevailed was so much greater than their hatred towards them, that, though they wished they [i.e. the Militants] might rather be destroyed than the King, they had rather the King and his posterity should be destroyed than that Wilton should be taken from one of them or Hatfield from the other; the preservation of both which from any danger they both believed to be the highest point of prudence and politic circumspection.[7]

The sardonic contempt for people who put self-interest above duty is characteristic. Whatever Clarendon can be accused of, it is not that. With the disappearance of the centre and with the odds on the Royalists winning the war already long and growing daily longer, his standing changed. To the King he now appeared as the champion of positions in religion and politics that others regarded as negotiable. Here was a standard-bearer who would not be looking over his shoulder.

Such a man was needed for the plan now forming in contemplation of final military disaster. If the worst came to the worst and the King was captured or killed, the Prince of Wales must take his place. The danger that Oxford might be invested and starved into surrender was too apparent to risk delay. The Prince must be sent away to the southwest to establish, if possible, a Royalist redoubt. Should even that fail he would be well placed to escape to the Scillies, the Channel Islands, Ireland or the Continent. Since he was not yet quite fifteen, he would need sober, able and decisive ministers who might have to act on the most elastic instructions. By his performance at Uxbridge Hyde selected himself.

The Council was to have military as well as political responsibilities. The Prince had been appointed Commander-in-Chief in the West in the hope of reconciling the feuds and regulating the indiscipline of

---

[6] *Cal. Clar. SP* i, 1099. Wrongly endorsed. Hyde was retained by Lady Ashley, not by Holles.
[7] *Hist.* VIII, 245.

those quarrelsome and touchy officers, George Goring, Sir Richard Grenville and Sir John Berkeley. The Royalist troops under their command had behaved so badly that the four western counties had informed the King of their desire to petition Parliament for an immediate peace. The Council therefore included two of the best-liked, most widely respected, of all Royalist officers, Lord Capel and Lord Hopton. On the political side Colepeper and Hyde were to be joined with the Duke of Richmond and the Earl of Southampton. To Hyde's dismay these two noblemen at once excused themselves. He attempted to do the same. 'But the King told him positively, and with some warmth, that if he would not go he would not send his son.'[8] That settled the matter.

Clarendon saw the King for the last time on March 5, the day on which the little party was to set out. Charles expressed his lack of confidence in the Prince's governor, the Earl of Berkshire, who was to be of the company. Clarendon had no opinion of him and doubtless allowed the King to perceive this. Why in the serious strait of his affairs the King should have retained a nonentity in a post which was to carry new, possibly crucial, responsibilities is the kind of question which even so close a student of his character as Clarendon turns from as not worth putting. Perhaps, by raising the matter, the King thought that his minister's intelligence and resolution could be relied on to compensate for his own want of decision. Yet this inexplicable man concluded the interview by the far more difficult exercise of direct personal admonition. He warned Hyde against his tendency to quarrel with Colepeper, having apparently delivered the same reproof to the other earlier in the day. '. . . Any difference and unkindness between you two must be at my charge; and I must tell you the fear I have of it gives me much trouble.' The audience ended with an affectionate farewell. Hyde mounted his horse and set off, in driving rain, after the Prince and his fellow Counsellors. He could still feel the rain a quarter of a century later as he remembered that it had not stopped for an instant by the time they reached their first night's lodging at Faringdon. It was in this journey, he tells us, that he was first assaulted with the gout*, having never had the least apprehension of it before. By the time they

---

* Gout was to be so important a feature of his life that it may be pertinent to recall that from ancient times down to the nineteenth century this ailment was not distinguished from arthritis. The word 'arthritis' or 'arthrities' was used by doctors as the Latin name for the disease in preference to 'podagra', which accurately locates that pain in the foot, popularly associated with gout stools and vintage port. Johnson's *Dictionary*, a century later, still defines 'arthritical' as 'gouty, relating to the gout'.

8 *ibid* 254 fn. Although he says nothing about it Hyde himself had a better compassionate excuse to plead. His fourth son Edward, the second of that name (see Appendix II), was to be baptised in the chapel of All Souls on April 1. Frances can hardly have been out of childbed when he left her.

reached Bath he could not even stand and had to travel to Bristol by coach.[9]

We can shiver in sympathy at the wet and the cold. We can mark the onset of the painful affliction that for the rest of his life was liable to put him out of action for days, even weeks, together. Indeed when he was writing these recollections in his final exile he was, even when in health, unable to walk without the support of two men. But as so often he says nothing of what must have made everything harder to bear, the parting from his wife and children. Frances was left behind in Oxford[10] and they were not to see each other again for four years.[11] His domestic life for the immediate future was to be anything but tranquil as he found himself more or less responsible for the upbringing and the public and private conduct of a spoilt, rich and high-spirited adolescent. One of Charles I's aims in sending his son away was, in the King's phrase, 'to unboy him'. The process had its hazards. Even in Oxford the King had observed that his son's choice of friends was not all that could be desired. He had got rid of one particularly dreadful young man by sending him to Paris to attend on the Queen — an evasion that was later to claim its price. But hardly had the Prince and his little court arrived in the west before his father's worst fears were realised. The Prince fell under the influence of a woman who, in Clarendon's view, had nothing womanly about her but her body. That single asset she was not slow to exploit.

The lady in question, Christabel Wyndham, wife to the Governor of Bridgwater, had been the Prince's nurse when he was a child and she was a leading court beauty. What precisely her functions then were is not clear. Certainly they were of no menial kind: probably she amused him and played with him. These duties, to Clarendon's consternation, she now enthusiastically resumed. For the first, but by no means the last, time he felt compelled to combine the role of political adviser and executant with that of a housemaster attempting to restrain the excesses of a lecherous pupil who was too important to sack. It was not a part that he was well equipped to play. His own children were not old enough to have given him any experience of handling adolescents. His temper was warm, his manner direct, his sense of propriety and his moral convictions clear and strong. At the best of times such qualities would not have endeared him to the future Charles II. Their impact on him in the turbulence of calf love can hardly have got their relationship off to a good start.

It was not, as has been suggested by those who dislike Clarendon or thrill to the sexual athleticism of Charles II, simply the officious imposition of official morality. It was the public impropriety of Mrs

[9] *Life* III, 66–8.   [10] *Cal. Clar. SP* i, 1904.   [11] Clar. MS 37 f.38.

Wyndham's conduct and the private intrigues which she promoted. '. . . she valued herself much upon the power and familiarity which her neighbours might see she had with the Prince of Wales, and therefore upon all occasions in company, and when the concourse of people was greatest, would use great boldness towards him and sometimes in dancing would run the length of the room and kiss him.'[12] The image of monarchy, the foundation of its authority, could not survive this kind of thing. Worse still she spoke with open disrespect of the King and did all she could to undermine the authority of the Council. She diverted the Prince from attending it, pressed the private interests of herself, her children and her husband, and induced her young lover to promise important offices to her unsuitable friends. No wonder that Hyde had to put his foot down.

According to him it was the King's fear of the possible entanglements at Bridgwater that made him unwilling that his son should go farther west than Bristol. Nothing but the military and financial chaos they found would have led them to abandon so eligible a base. But without troops or money and with two Parliamentary armies in the offing, to say nothing of an outbreak of plague in Bristol, it seemed sensible to rally the divided and demoralised supporters of the Royalist cause where they were strongest and most secure.

To thread the maze of confusion and disorder, of conflicting commissions and overlapping commands, of jealousies and rivalries between the Cavaliers in the west would try the reader's patience. 'Well you Generalls are a strange kind of people', wrote Hyde to Lord Goring from Bristol on April 12, 1645.[13] The immediate occasion was Goring's placing his troops under the command of his rivals and withdrawing himself to take the waters at Bath. After recapitulating their discussions and Goring's apparent advocacy of the strategy from which he was now so emphatically distancing himself, the letter concludes: 'I am so much troubled I know not what to say . . . For God's sake let us not fall into ill-humour which may cost us dear. Get good thoughts about you.' Prince Rupert, Goring, Sir Richard Grenville and Sir John Berkeley were the *prime donne* who in a succession of scenes disputed the right to the principal role, Rupert admittedly at a distance but still jealous of his commission as Commander-in-Chief and of his particular title to the Governorship of Bristol. All of them bristled at the appearance of Capel and Hopton, more especially as Hopton for his early victories and for his excellent discipline commanded a personal standing in the West. No doubt their loyal support of their fellow Counsellor, Sir Edward Hyde, made them the more suspected and resented in the military snake pit of the south-west.

[12] *Hist.* IX, 19.   [13] Clar. MS 24 f.132.

Hyde's own opinion of them all may be fairly inferred from the letter to Goring. Their portraits are drawn, unflatteringly, in the *History* and, in the case of Berkeley, in an elaborate and subtle full-length printed as an appendix to the third volume of the Clarendon State Papers. In 1645, and for several years after, he looked on Berkeley as a friend. Hyde's letters to him when they were both in exile are written with an absence of reserve and an invocation of a long intimacy that the recipient seems to have found increasingly irritating as Hyde steadily declined to veer in his politics. Goring he found good company but distrusted and disliked to an extent that makes it unsafe to treat what he writes about him as anything but the evidence of a hostile witness. Grenville had so long a record of personal violence and barbarity that horror of him was generally shared.

Colouring all was the deep detestation of war, verging on Christian pacifism, that he expresses in an essay written in 1670:[14]

'It may be, upon a strict survey and disquisition into the elements and injunctions of Christian religion, no war will be found justifiable . . . All war hath much of the beast in it . . . very much of the man must be put off that there may be enough of the beast.' Above all he was disgusted, as most twentieth-century Englishmen are but few were in his day, by the idea of war as a trade to which one might be apprenticed by taking service in foreign armies: '. . . the guilt contracted by shedding the blood of one single innocent man is too dear a price to pay for all the skill that is to be learned in that devouring profession.' So much for Rupert, Goring, Wilmot, Grenville *et al*. But what about Falkland, who had tried to follow that career? What about Hopton, who had learned his soldiering in the same school of the Thirty Years War as Sir William Waller?

It could be argued that Hopton had originally volunteered to fight for what he and other loyal Protestant Englishmen regarded as the violated rights of Elizabeth of Bohemia, Charles I's sister, against the Popish Goliath. He was therefore covered by the saving clauses of patriotic duty and moral conviction that Clarendon allowed. Could not the same be pleaded in defence of Rupert (Elizabeth's son after all) and the rest of the swordmen? Yes, at least on the face of it. But it is here, perhaps, that the point lies. Clarendon, the thinker, cannot always square his conclusions and the judgments that depend from them with the observations and insights of Sir Edward Hyde who had long known these people, listened to them and watched their play of expression. Rupert might be allowed a high or rather a haughty sense of honour and family obligation: but to think of Wilmot or Goring or Sir Richard Grenville as acting from high-minded or disinterested

[14] *Tracts* 205–9.

motives was impossible. They enjoyed the war. That was what he had against them. The drinking and destructiveness expressed the disorder of their personalities.

The men whom Clarendon admired and loved, Falkland, old Sir Edmund Verney, Capel, Hopton and the rest, hated the war. Not to hate it was to show oneself inhumane, immoral and unpatriotic. 'That great God which is the searcher of my heart knows with what a sad sense I go upon this service, and with what a perfect hatred I detest this war without an enemy.' The words that Waller had written to Hopton across the lines of battle earlier in the war perfectly express Clarendon's own feeling. Like Waller he had to play the part assigned to him. For the moment that meant making the best of a bad job with military commanders he was not empowered to control, still less to remove, and in his capacity as Chancellor of the Exchequer to provide them as far as possible with the necessary means of carrying on the war.

Almost for the first time since the capture of Bristol he found himself, potentially at least, in a position to tap a flow of revenue that was still running. The Cornish tin mines were producing and exporting. Soon after he had left Bristol Hyde obtained the estimates of tin production 'in Slabbs and Spoonfulls' from the St Neot's Blowing House for the year ending at Midsummer 1645.[15] That he made effective use of the information obtained is evident from an angry letter, half hoity-toity, half seriously alarmed, from Jermyn, now comfortably established at St Germain as Henrietta Maria's *cavaliere servente*. He is outraged that the tin previously 'granted' to the Queen has been diverted to the Prince. The Queen would have arranged a sale in France on more advantageous terms. Her finances have been thrown into disorder by this sudden interruption. And so on. He wrote twice.[16] But Hyde had long ago taken the measure of Jermyn. Right up to the end of hostilities his papers show him arranging supplies of muskets and lead for bullets to reach Hopton, entrusted at last when all was lost with the command of a beaten rabble.[17] Jermyn, profuse in promises of French troops ready to embark, delivered in fact nothing.[18]

Yet even at this last gasp of the military struggle Hyde found himself undermined in the same way and by the same people as at Bristol. Through the agency of Ashburnham and Colepeper the King granted to a shady colonel (who was later in trouble for coining in Jersey) the right to set up a mint in Truro, from which the Crown dues were to be paid, not to the Chancellor of the Exchequer, but to Ashburnham.[19] In the torrent of disaster that was sweeping Royalism off the map this made no odds one way or the other. But as an instance of what a loyal

[15] Clar. MS 24 f.186.   [16] *Cal. Clar. SP* i, 1940 and 1947.   [17] Clar. MS 27 f.57 22 Feb 46.
[18] *Hist.* X, 2.   [19] Lister, iii, 44.

and disinterested servant of Charles I had to contend with it could hardly be more telling.

Hyde heard the news of Naseby when he was at Barnstaple in the last week of June. 'Indeed the tyde is turned shrewdly and unexpectedly, to finde ourselves soe fatally beaten, when wee had scarce apprehension of an enemy,' he wrote to Nicholas. '. . . I have not any doubt but that God will blesse the King still . . . and it may bee the western forces are not so contemptible as they have been reported.'[20] Barely a fortnight later they were ignominiously defeated at Langport. The safety of the Prince of Wales now became Hyde's chief preoccupation.

In the letter just quoted he had told Nicholas that the King had summoned Colepeper and himself to attend him at Hereford but that the Prince was unwilling to spare them both. To his regret he was to be kept in the west. Colepeper caught up with the King at Cardiff and returned early in August with a letter to the Prince dated from Brecknock on August 5 instructing him in case of danger to 'convey yourself into France, and there to be under your mother's care; who is to have the absolute full power of your education in all things, except religion, and in that not to meddle at all, but leave it entirely to the care of your tutor, the bishop of Salisbury [Brian Duppa, who had come with them from Oxford] . . .'

France was the last place that Hyde and his closest friends on the Prince's Council, Capel and Hopton, wanted. Hyde himself went so far as to say that he would rather see Charles in the hands of the rebels. It was however repeated in another letter written from Chirk Castle on September 29, after the surrender of Bristol had brought the King to as steady a sense of reality as he was capable of entertaining. It was something of a military feat for him to regain the temporary safety of Oxford. Once inside its walls he knew that his enemies had only to sit down outside it with the coming of spring. There was no Royalist army in the field to interfere with them. In the web of deceit and division, which was now his only expedient, keeping the Prince of Wales out of reach was of supreme importance. Influenced perhaps by Nicholas who reinforced the Francophobia voiced by the Council in the West he sent two letters, on November 7 and December 7, choosing Denmark, his mother's country, as the preferred refuge, but allowing France, Holland or indeed any country in case of emergency.

Denmark would not be easy to reach. The Prince could hardly risk sailing up the Channel, alive with Parliamentary frigates and with the main fleet ready to put to sea at short notice. Presumably he would have to sail out into the Atlantic, keeping to the west of Ireland and passing northabout to creep down the Scandinavian coast. Hyde did

20 *ibid* 20.

not think much of the idea. In any case he had no vessel at his disposal manned and victualled for such a voyage. The best he could do was to retain one of the privateers from Jersey or Dunkirk, fast, light craft well suited for inshore work such as a voyage to the Scillies or the Channel Islands which were in his view far more appropriate destinations. To put the heir apparent in the power of a foreign country was to diminish the sovereignty of England.

The ugliness of the situation played into Hyde's hands. The crumbling of Royalist resistance before the advance of Fairfax's army, the desertion of the troops, the disgraceful behaviour of a succession of commanders, culminating in Sir Richard Grenville's refusal to obey Hopton and his subsequent arrest for mutiny, warned the Council that it was later than they thought. There were alarming reports, highly probable in those circumstances of dishonour and demoralisation, of a plot among some of Grenville's officers to seize the person of the Prince of Wales and see what Parliament would give for him. He was then — it was late in February 1646 — in Pendennis Castle, a sea-girt stronghold dominating the entrance to Falmouth harbour, easily defensible against assault but equally easily convertible by treachery into a cage.

Hyde saw the need to act at once without waiting for further instructions or giving dubious people a chance to guess what was in the wind. Capel and Hopton were away with the remnants of the army in a gallant but hopeless attempt to relieve Exeter. In fact they had already been defeated at Torrington on February 16 and Hopton, game to the last, was trying, unsuccessfully, to re-form. That meant that Hyde's fellow Counsellors were reduced to Colepeper, the feeble Earl of Berkshire and the boozy, stone-deaf ex-Commander-in-Chief, Patrick Ruthven, Earl of Brentford. To console him for his dismissal from the position in November 1644 Charles had appointed him Chamberlain to the Prince of Wales. A more grotesque misfit could hardly be conceived. As so often the King's shifty aversion from clarity and openness left his best servants encumbered with all but impossible difficulties. Nothing but a unanimous, or near unanimous, decision of the Prince's Council could justify so important an action taken without direct royal authority. How to extract rapidity and decisiveness from two obstinate and suspicious old codgers was the problem. Hyde and Colepeper solved it by moving in Council that a messenger should be sent at once to ask Capel and Hopton for their advice. This was for the Prince's immediate departure. Supported by Hyde and Colepeper the old men adopted it, thus achieving the required unanimity. Hyde had already made his preparations. The Governor of Pendennis was informed and the Prince and his party went aboard the Dunkirk privateer that evening, March 2. Thirty-six hours later she arrived safely in the Scillies.

At least that is how Clarendon the historian puts it. The reality was far more unpleasant. His experiences of sea travel were never happy. In the first place he was always sick as a dog and the passage was very rough. In the second, the crew of a Dunkirker were not the shipmates one would have chosen. They plundered everyone unmercifully, breaking open trunks and scattering papers and possessions. Scilly, for all its bleakness, lack of accommodation and lack of provisions, at least was preferable. Short though his stay was — from March 4 to April 16 — it was a landmark in his life. For here, on March 18, he began his *History*. The date appears in the margin of the first page of the manuscript, written with a legibility he reserves for special occasions. He had, of course, no documents or printed sources with him. But he had what for the past five or six years he could never have imagined having — Time!

Suddenly there was nothing to do. From the day of their arrival the wind changed and blew steadily from the south-west. Nothing could reach them from England. But it was a fair wind for France. On the 6th Colepeper set off to tell Henrietta Maria the whereabouts of her eldest son. Hyde was thus left to himself, until the wind changed on April 11 bringing with it Hopton and Capel who had now negotiated the surrender of the forces under their command, together with a letter from Fairfax to the Prince requiring him to put himself in the hands of the Parliament. This was reinforced the next day by the appearance of a large Parliamentary fleet. Scilly was without means of defence . It looked as though it would prove the trap Hyde had feared at Pendennis.

Once again the weather obliged. A storm blew up during the night and raged for three days. When it abated there was not a sail in sight. The Prince and his party hurried aboard the *Proud Black Eagle*, a frigate that had escorted the Dunkirker to the Scillies and had sheltered in the harbour of St Mary's. They landed in Jersey next day. Once again their luck had been astonishing. Not only had the wind come right for them but approaching harbour without a pilot they had headed straight for a dangerous shoal. The watchers on shore waited for her to strike. But she sailed on, carried by the spring tide that gave her enough water under her keel to clear the rocks by inches. Clarendon's belief in the divine protection of the cause he served was not without its accidental evidences.

IX

Jersey

JERSEY, like Great Tew, is one of the oases in Clarendon's life where congenial company, agreeable quarters and, above all, leisure to read, to think and to write afforded him the highest happiness of which his nature was capable. It was here that he was to settle to his true vocation, the writing of history on the grand scale, that of high imaginative art that represents and interprets experience. Later, in his last exile, he was to write an essay, 'On an active and on a contemplative life and when and why the one ought to be preferr'd before the other', that distils his experience, then repeated, of passing from the conduct of affairs to the writing of history. He has no hesitation in claiming the one as the chief qualification for the other. Few men combine his zest for activity with his philosophical curiosity and readiness to reflect. The sheer energy of a man whose girth was the frequent gibe of contemporaries and whose goutiness is the constant subject of his own complaint never ceases to astonish.

Arriving in Jersey after the starkness and squalor of the Scilly interlude was like waking up after a nightmare. Sir George Carteret, the Deputy Governor who commanded the garrison, was a resolute and capable officer and an admirable host. Communication with France was easy and frequent: books and newspapers were to be had from Paris and Rouen: the privateers brought in plenty of money.

On the wider scene of politics the prospect was dark. When the Prince landed in Jersey the King was still, so far as anyone knew, in Oxford. Soon afterwards came the news that he had left with two attendants for an unknown destination: and two or three weeks later that he had surrendered at Southwell to the Scots, who had withdrawn with their prisoner to Newcastle. To establish communications with him was, at this crucial moment, impossible, whereas Henrietta Maria in Paris was too close for comfort. Categorical instructions that the Prince should at once join his mother where the French government would supply him with troops and money poured in by every post. Colepeper, who had been sent from Scilly to inform the Queen of the Prince's whereabouts, rejoined the little court in Jersey, not only bearing these orders in the most peremptory terms but, to Hyde's consternation, revealing himself a convert to the Queen's view. Hopton and Capel, however, were as vehement as Hyde himself in their opposition. To put the Prince in a state of vassalage to Cardinal Mazarin would be to inflict incalculable damage on the Royalist cause. The French government had every reason to rejoice in the discomfiture of Charles I. The memory of the expeditions against La Rochelle and St Martin was fresh and angry. They knew all about the Anglo-Spanish attempts at an entente in the later 1630s. An England reduced to diplomatic impotence by civil war was exactly what they wanted. If there was the least grain of sincerity in Mazarin's professions, why had France done nothing to help the King when he was in a fair way to winning the war?

The Prince was impressed by their arguments. But his mother's tone was not to be disregarded by a dutiful son. Hyde and his allies recognised that the only card that could overtrump her was a direct message from the King himself. Since this was, for the moment, unobtainable, Colepeper was sent back to Paris, this time accompanied by Capel, to represent to the Queen the Council's view that Jersey was safe against any force that was likely to be brought against it, and that if any unforeseen threat developed there would be ample time and means to whisk the Prince across to the mainland. Two days after they left news reached Jersey of the King's disappearance from Oxford. By the time they reached Paris it was known that he was a prisoner of the Scots.

Nothing was wanting to complete this tableau of Royalist futility but the presence of Lord Digby with some excitingly harebrained scheme. Sure enough into the harbour at this delicate moment sailed two frigates from Ireland under his command. After his débâcle as a field commander of the shattered Royalist forces in the North he had escaped first to the Isle of Man and thence had contrived to join Ormonde in Ireland. Hearing of the Prince of Wales's taking refuge in Scilly he suggested to Ormonde that Ireland was a far more suitable base from which he might lead a resurgence of Royalist power by reuniting the anti-Parliamentary forces so mischievously divided by foreign intrigue. Ormonde agreed and provided the frigates, which on finding the Prince gone from Scilly sailed on to Jersey.

The two friends, delighted to meet again, confided in each other without reserve. Hyde exploded about the wickedness of the French and the wilfulness of the Queen. Digby agreed wholeheartedly. Did not his plan for removing the Prince to Ireland solve the problem? Both Hyde and the Prince himself objected to taking so radical a decision on the spur of the moment. Digby could not have lived the life he had if such a state of mind had been imaginable to him. He told Hyde that he intended to invite the Prince to dine aboard and then cut the cable and hoist the sails. Hyde was outraged. Digby dejectedly accepted, if he did not understand, his friend's veto and began to think of other expedients. '. . . In the instant (as he had a most pregnant fancy) he entertained another with the same vigour, and resolved with all possible expedition to find himself at Paris, not making the least question but that he should convert the Queen from any farther thought of sending for the Prince into France, and as easily obtain her consent and approbation for his repairing into Ireland.'[1] The end is easily foretold. If Henrietta Maria was firm as a rock in her Francomania, Digby was clay in the hands of Mazarin. He returned to Jersey, bubbling with promises of French troops and money for Ireland, even of a possible French declaration of war, if only the Prince would join his mother in Paris where they could better settle the details. In the light of this *coup*, he expected Hyde to support the Queen's request. 'His friend, who in truth loved him very heartily, though no man better knew his infirmities, told him . . . he could not but wonder that the same artifices should again prevail with him.'[2]

On ne se moque que de ce qu'on aime. Digby is one of Clarendon's most skilful realisations of the comic in history. The achievement is the greater because so often the absurdity is perceived, as here, at a moment when Clarendon and all he held most dear were at the end of their tether. The reader cannot help laughing with him at Digby's gullibility, but the thought of the Queen and the French interest in the ascendant at a time of such danger was agony to him. The crisis was indeed upon him. Capel and Colepeper came back from Paris with a stay of execution until the King's whereabouts and condition were more certainly known: but the Queen reiterated that be they what they might she would still insist on the Prince's coming to Paris. Her tone became shriller when the King's favourite and companion on his travels, Ashburnham, arrived in Paris from Newcastle. As the last person to have had direct access to his master his views carried some aura of royal authority. He was clearly of the same opinion as Hyde and Capel: '. . . he thought it very pernicious to the King that the Prince should come into France in that conjuncture, and before it was known how the Scots would deal with him . . .'[3] Capel with characteristic courage volunteered to go to Newcastle to receive the King's instructions.

The Queen was not going to stand for that. A delegation of peers 'with their great train' was despatched from Paris to assert her demands. It was headed by Jermyn, who as Governor of Jersey, an

---

[1] *Hist.* X, 14.   [2] *ibid* 20.   [3] *ibid* 22.

office frivolously conferred on him in 1644, outranked Carteret, who had recaptured the island for the King and turned it into the most effective of Royalist privateering bases. Jermyn brought two cooks, one English and one French, and was supported by Hyde's old enemy, Lord Wilmot, who had been living in France since his disgrace in 1644, and Lord Wentworth, another cavalry commander whose career had ended somewhat ingloriously. Digby enthusiastically and Colepeper more guardedly took the Queen's line. The case against had been temperately but firmly stated by Capel. Hopton and Hyde were strongly of his opinion, but debate was stifled by the Prince's suddenly announcing that he was resolved to go to Paris and did not wish the point to be argued further. Hyde, Hopton and Capel, considering their commission to be ended by this flat rejection of their advice, respectfully asked to be excused from accompanying him. The language they used to, and received from, the others was much sharper.

The Prince sailed for France on June 25, followed by Colepeper and the Queen's champions. Two days later the Earl of Berkshire crossed to St Malo, en route for Holland and England. Hyde, Hopton and Capel were left to their own devices. Not, as they hastened to make plain to both the King and the Queen, that they considered themselves in any way released from their obligations of loyalty and devotion, but simply that 'we have rather chosen to wait a seasonable opportunity in this island to return to some condition and capacity of serving your Majesty than to attend his Highness into France'.[4] It was, nonetheless, a golden moment. All, all, were gone, the old familiar faces. And what a blessed relief. '. . . the chancellor of the exchequer remained there about two years after; where he presently betook himself to his study; and enjoyed, as he was wont to say, the greatest tranquillity of mind imaginable.'

It was at this time that he advertised, discreetly, his intention of setting up as historian by applying to friends and colleagues for original materials or simply by writing to ask them questions about transactions in which they had been involved. The King himself, for whom the work was particularly designed, gave his blessing and promised to send documents as soon as he should be in a position to do so. For the Parliamentary manoeuvres, the political skirmishing and the propaganda war Hyde's own memory was, for all its shortcomings and for all its owner's vigorous prejudices, an unrivalled source. For the military side of things, not altogether negligible when one is writing the history of a war whatever one may think of the morals and manners of certain commanders, he had Hopton and Capel at his entire disposal. Hopton indeed wrote an account of the war in the south-west from 1642–1644,

[4] *Clar. SP* ii, 240.

still preserved among the Clarendon manuscripts, on which his friend drew heavily in the *History*. In sea affairs, of which he was more superciliously ignorant and for which he had an even livelier distaste, he had in Carteret an expert whose good nature and good breeding almost made the subject tolerable.

Best of all he was now, at the height of his powers and in the best of health, suddenly, miraculously, emancipated from all official duties, from the opportunity of practising his profession, even from the ordinary obligations of family life. No burden of guilt was laid upon him by these disabilities. The situation in which he found himself was not in any degree of his own choosing, delectable as it might turn out to be. God had put him there. History had put him there. To him that was a tautology. For although the path of duty was also the path of purest pleasure it was in a profoundly religious sense that he set out on it. He would examine himself, take stock of the ideas and standards by which he had tried to live. He would springclean his mind and renew it by meditation and reading. It was in Jersey, on December 26, 1647, that he began to write the *Reflections on the Psalms* which he continued during his embassy to Madrid and then, as with the *History*, put aside until his second and final exile left him time to complete them. That, perhaps, was the culmination of a process frequently alluded to in his letters, such as that to Sir John Berkeley, written on July 12, 1646, less than three weeks after the Prince had left for Paris:

'. . . And truly, Jack . . . it will not be unseasonable or unuseful to a mind and spirit so wasted and weakened as mine, to refresh and strengthen itself with sitting still, and revolving past omissions or mistakes, and forming and making up a resolution and constancy (by principles that will be very pleasant in death, how unprofitable soever to live by) to bear cheerfully the worst that can happen by the malice or calumny or tyranny of the time.'[5]

It is in these years, long years, of ruin and defeat that the strength of Hyde's character, the depth of his historical analysis and the steadfastness of his principles shine their brightest. If history, that is in terms of present experience the actual course of events, reflected the Divine Will, there was for him no running away from the abundant evidence of God's displeasure with Royalism or Royalists or both. But it was as idiotic as it was blasphemous to think that one could haggle with Him over the terms on which His support might be enlisted. If the principles they were maintaining were right (a point to be established by rational criticism) and the means they employed were just (and every man's conscience must determine that) then, however dark the immediate prospect, ultimate triumph was certain because God had

[5] *ibid* 240–2.

made the world and had promised its inheritance to those who loved righteousness and hated iniquity. But God had never guaranteed them an easy passage, still less admitted his worshippers to such a knowledge of his mind or an understanding of his purposes as would take them out of the historical context in which, for the time of this mortal life, they had their being. 'For my thoughts are not your thoughts, neither are your ways my ways.' An infinite view of time and history could hardly be the same as a finite one. As Hyde had written to Nicholas on June 1, 1646 while he was still a member of the Prince's Council:

'It is ill logic to infer that because you cannot have it [peace] cheaper, therefore you must give whatsoever is asked. It may be, God hath resolved we shall perish; and then it becomes us all to perish with those decent and honest circumstances, that our good fame may procure a better peace to those who succeed us . . .'[6]

This was a cold and disquieting recognition for anyone in search of cosy reassurance or glib formulae for a settlement. But it was the secret of Hyde's strength. He had thought his position through, had faced its harsh consequences for himself and for those he loved. He had set his face like a flint and he was under no illusion as to what those who prided themselves on their realism would think of him.

'I know that all sober reliance upon God's providence is now called expecting of miracles, and the fixing upon honest principles . . . is reproached and laughed at as delighting in metaphysical notions and imaginary speculations,'[7] he wrote to Lady Dalkeith, his first wife's cousin, now again lady of the bedchamber to Henrietta Maria. She and Sir John Berkeley were at this time and for some four or five years among his most intimate correspondents. So many of his oldest, closest friends were scattered he knew not where, or were still in England where letters from him might draw unwelcome attentions on the recipient. The warmth of his letters to her often suggests an *amitié amoureuse*, to Berkeley that of a bosom friend. The few letters that survive from them to him are noticeably cooler.

Berkeley, it seems, was quick to show that leaning towards realism — or expediency as Hyde would have thought it — that steadily exacerbated their relationship. On August 14 Hyde wrote to him in his own defence:

'. . . I know your conversacion must now bee with those who thinke themselves (very unskilfully) concerned to infuse as ill an opinion into all Men of mee as they can, and therefore you are to keep your Justice steady and believe me I shall so demean myself as shall increase their envy and discreditt their malice . . . believe me, Jack, I will not come

[6] *ibid* 236–7.   [7] *ibid* 284–5, October 24, 1646.

into those ways till it appears that the rubbs and unsmoothness that are now in them towards me are but the tumors of passion and injustice, for I am so sure that I have performed my duty so exactly that if you knew the grounds and circumstances you would not differ from me in the least tittle, neither is it possible any inconvenience can ensue thereby to myself which I foresaw not and am well prepared for . . .'[8]

The point here at issue is still that of the Prince's joining his mother in Paris. Soon enough, as Hyde exactly forsaw, it would be the whole central question of the known laws and established religion of his country. Less than a month later, on September 28, the Queen, in a long and bitter letter to her unhappy husband, put the realist case with appropriate brutality:

'Presbitery, or something worse, will be forced upon you, whether you will or no. Com, the question in short is, whether you will chuse to be a King of Presbitery, or no King; and yet Presbitery or perfect Independancy to be.'[9] This was her answer to the King's letter from Newcastle of August 19 in which he showed how completely Hyde had understood and stated the fundamentals of Royalism:

'. . . how can I keep that innocency . . . if I should abandon the Church? Belive it, religion is the only firme foundation of all power: that cast loose, or depraved, no government can be stable.'[10]

The vehemence of Hyde's political conviction doubtless arose from the close and continuous examination to which he had been subjecting not only his own ideas and actions but the whole course of events that had led to the Civil War. He concludes the letter to Berkeley already quoted:

'I ought to give you an account of my own time that you may not believe I am only in love with sleep. As soon as I cam to Silley I began (as well as I could, without any papers, upon the stock of my own memory) to sett down a narrative of this prosperous Rebellion and have since I came hither continued it . . . so that I am now come to the King's leaving London, in which, though for want of informacion and assistances, I shall leave many truths unmentioned, upon my word there shall not be any untruth nor partiallity towards Persons or sydes, which though it will make the work unfitt in this Age for communicacion, yet may be fitt for the perusall and comfort of some men and being transmitted through good hands may tell Posterity that this whole nation was not soe badd as it will be then thought to have been.'

At this early stage the idea of what the *History* was to be had not defined itself as a confidential report to the King, though the freedom that the writer was claiming for himself obviously precluded publication in the foreseeable future. In the preparation of the ground there

[8] Clar. MS 28 f.178.   [9] *Clar. SP* ii, 263.   [10] *ibid* 248.

was no stinting. Letters, often sharp and amusing, sped off to ex-colleagues, friends, relations, acquaintances, asking for information on great matters and on the marginalia that so often touch the past into life. 'What was the meaning of your making so many Lords at Oxford, Brunkard, Bard, Ogle? What became of Ogle afterwards, and was he ever good for any thing?'[11] The soil was well mulched with the study of the best historians and political writers, ancient, medieval, Renaissance and contemporary. A year after the Prince's departure he could write to his old friend, Sheldon: 'I have read over Livy and Tacitus, and almost Tully's works . . . since I came into this blessed isle.'[12] This was, as his Commonplace Book[13] shows, only a small sample. On March 4, 1646 he started making an abstract of Speed's *Chronicle* beginning with William the Conqueror, skipping part of Edward III but resuming with Richard II. The 'Sundry and occasional compilations' that follow comprise eighty-three items from a wide variety of authors — post-classical, patristic, Renaissance. Particular attention is paid to the Papacy and to its latter-day shock troops, the Jesuits. No opportunity is lost, and some are contrived, of drawing analogies between papal claims or the arguments used by the Jesuits in their support and those advanced by his Parliamentary adversaries. Thucydides, Bacon, Macchiavelli, Philippe de Commines, Josephus, Plutarch — it is a rich and varied diet. Nor is it reverently consumed. Hyde interrupts these magisterial figures, to question, to argue, to dis-agree, to gloss. He criticises Macchiavelli's facile reliance on history as a guide to policy — 'wee rather know the misfortunes than the faults of our Ancestors' — and disagrees flatly that the people are best qualified to distribute 'degrees and dignityes . . . they are much fitter to judge of things than of persons, in which they have so rarely a good measure that they have seldom favoured any extraordinary person in any extra-ordinary degree'.[14]

As a historian he could be claimed as a forerunner by the champions of inter-disciplinary study. Law, divinity, philosophy, aesthetics are all represented in his reading. We learn something of his standards of historical criticism. Considering the evidence for the existence of pigmies he notes that an ecclesiastical author 'tells us of one in body no bigger than a partridge, yett endowed with reason and elocution, and Cardan [the great Italian Renaissance medical writer] that he saw a man at full Age in Italy, not above a cubitt high, carryed about in a Parrett's cage. This could have passed my beliefe, had I not been tolde by a gentleman of a cleere reputation, how he saw a man at Syena, about two yeare since, not exceeding the same stature . . . with a

11 *ibid* 347. Hyde to Nicholas, March 16, 1647.   12 *ibid* 374.
13 Clar. MS 126.   14 *ibid* 59v.

formall Bearde, who was also shown in a Cage for mony, at the end whereof was a little Hutch, into which he retyred and when the Assembly was full came forth and played on an instrument.'[15] .

The philosophical historian has time for natural curiosities. He also has time for conversation 'which is not only a greate ornament . . . but questionlesse hath a great influence upon businesse itself and by which . . . men so qualified . . . are less humbled by the captious humours and injustice of the tyme in which they live . . . men by it have a great inlett into the discovery of other men's natures, not without some insight into ther owne'.[16] It also satisfied, to some degree, the duty of wisdom to propagate itself: 'The gettinge of Children is the . . . vulgar work of nature, fooles can do it, and women can do it, but to begett men, to frame those moving lumpes into wise and good men is an exalted work . . .'

Here, as elsewhere, the Chancellor accepts a conventional view of the status of women that does not square with his letters to Lady Dalkeith and to his wife or with his affectionate pride in the clever daughter whose marriage was to cause him so much grief. But historical relativism was emphatically asserted: 'There is not a greater foundation for error than to conclude matter of right from matter of fact, Law from Precedents . . . There must be the Spirit of the tyme considered in all separate instances of Actions, as well as in expressions and wordes, many things being fitt in our tyme to be said or done, which in another would be justly censured or reprehended.'[17] Perhaps Clarendon's critics have sometimes fallen into an analogous error in gauging the subtlety and breadth of his understanding by the simplicity of his narrative.

The environment in which he worked was such that he 'enjoyed, as he was wont to say, the greatest tranquillity of mind imaginable. Whilst the lords Capel and Hopton stayed there, they lived and kept house together in St Hilary's, which is the chief town of the island: where, having a chaplain of their own, they had prayers every day in the church, at eleven of the clock in the morning; till which hour they enjoyed themselves in their chambers, according as they thought fitt: the chancellor betaking himself to the continuance of the *History*, which he had begun at Scilly, and spending most of his time at that exercise. The other two walked, or rode abroad, or read, as they were disposed; but at the hour of prayers they always met; and then dined together at the lord Hopton's lodgings, which was the best house; they being lodged at several houses with convenience enough. Their table was maintained at their joint expense only for dinners; they never using to sup; but met always upon the sand in the evening to walk,

[15] *ibid* 62.   [16] *ibid* 57.   [17] *ibid* 54v.

often going to the castle to Sir George Carteret; who treated them with extraordinary kindness and civility, and spent much time with them . . .'[18]

The order, tranquillity and fruitfulness of life in Jersey after the agitated futilities of the last stages of a losing war glow the brighter in recollection. So does the weather. An evening walk along the sands cannot have been very inviting in December or January. It was in fact summer that Clarendon, again an exile in a warm climate, was recalling. Capel left Jersey early in November 1646[19] and Hopton three or four months later. But Clarendon's close companionship with these two men, themselves brothers-in-law, at the time when he was revolving the mistakes and omissions of the King's party and reflecting on the causes and origins of the War, surely influenced his vision and perhaps lent it some of its nobility. By the testimony of both sides, of Fairfax and Cromwell as much as of any Royalist, here were two paladins, *sans peur et sans reproche*. Both were men whose friendship Clarendon owed entirely to the war. '. . . Till I had the happiness to know you as particularly as I do, (and in good faith I am the more charitable to this rebellion for bringing me to that good fortune) . . .'[20] he wrote to Hopton in May 1648. There is no full-length portrait of him in the *History*, perhaps because he died while still in exile in 1652 and there was no convenient point at which to sum up the achievements and character of a man who crops up so often in the narrative. Perhaps it was that his gentleness and generosity made him too easygoing, too unassertive for his friend to do him justice. '. . . All the errors of your life have proceeded from too great an excess of charity,' he wrote in the letter already quoted. In the *History* he is described as too indecisive and too apt to change his mind to be fit to command in chief.[21] Yet his universal acceptability — 'there was only one man in the council of whom nobody spoke ill, nor laid anything to his charge; and that was the lord Hopton'[22] — survived even the savage recriminations of the Second Civil War. On his death Hyde wrote to Nicholas of 'the irreparable loss in our good lord Hopton, who was as faultless a person, as full of courage, industry, integrity and religion as I ever knew man, and believe me, the sad consideration of that instance of God's displeasure to us in the taking away of such men from us makes my heart ready to break, and to despair of seeing better times . . .'[23]

Capel's death on the scaffold a few weeks after the execution of the King is one of the memorable set pieces of the *History*.[24] In simplicity and force of language Clarendon's epitome of his character has few

[18] *Life* i, 205–6.   [19] *Cal. Clar. SP* i, 342.   [20] *Clar. SP* ii, 401.
[21] VIII, 31.   [22] XI, 84.   [23] *Clar. SP* iii, 109.
[24] XI, 265–7.

superiors, even in his own pages: 'He was a man in whom the malice of his enemies could discover very few faults, and whom his friends could not wish better accomplished . . . In a word . . . whoever shall after him deserve best in that nation, shall never think himself undervalued, when he shall hear that his courage, virtue and fidelity is laid in the balance with, and compared to, that of the lord Capell.'

Both men were even farther removed from having any Court connexions than Hyde, who had himself married the daughter of a courtier and had ties of clientage with the great Duke of Buckingham. Capel was by inheritance and by marriage an immensely rich landowner who had been returned as a County member to both the Parliaments of 1640 and had there taken much the same line as Hyde, voting for the abolition of Star Chamber and the rest. 'And yet the King's honour was no sooner violated and his just power invaded, than he threw all those blessings behind him; and having no other obligations to the Crown than those which his own honour and conscience suggested to him, he frankly engaged his person and his fortune from the beginning of the troubles, as many others did, in all actions and enterprises of the greatest hazard and danger; and continued to the end, without ever making one false step, as few others did . . .'

These three men personified an attitude to politics which Clarendon articulated for his own day but which is still very much part of the English political tradition, a reverence for sticking to the rules, a respect for the rights of others and an acceptance that one's own enlightened self-interest is not a sufficient measure of the common good. What gave their creed its particular form and colour was their religion and its mediation through the latitudinarian rather than the Laudian modes of the Church of England. George Morley, pillar of Great Tew and later a member of Hyde's household in Antwerp, attended Capel to the steps of the scaffold (his friend forbade him to climb them), and Hopton's chaplain on his Civil War campaigns had been Thomas Fuller, the historian whose irony and amused discursiveness would have recommended him to Falkland and John Earles. What Capel, Hopton and Hyde had supremely in common was that they were mere Christians and mere English. None of them would have any truck with schemes for bringing in Irish Roman Catholics or Scotch presbyterians at the price of compromising the integrity of the Church of England, even if the King himself, disingenuously, were to appear to countenance such a thing. Still less would they do so if such a project emanated from the Queen and Lord Jermyn in Paris.

How far they were prepared to go was soon evident when they heard of Jermyn's plan for selling the Channel Islands to the French Crown in exchange for ready cash. Together with Carteret they signed Articles of Association binding them to seek immediate assistance from the

Parliamentary fleet (Northumberland was to be their honest broker) and the Dutch.[25] No more was heard of the scheme.

A fortnight later Capel left by a circuitous route that took in Paris and Holland to return to England to compound for his estates. These were so large that even the rescuing of a part of them would be a relief for his wife and children and no doubt a useful resource for other distressed Cavaliers. Clarendon intimates his entire approval of this step, as he does even more explicitly in the case of his friend Sir Charles Cavendish, brother of the Marquis of Newcastle. Indeed there he publicly takes the credit for persuading him to overcome his scruples and return.[26]

This is, to say the least, extremely odd. The arguments he was to use to Cavendish in 1650 were perfectly sensible and involved no hypocrisy. If, he says, Cavendish were to find himself confronted with taking an oath against his conscience such as accepting the Covenant or signing the Engagement to uphold the lawfulness of the existing government, he could always refuse. Imprisonment was most unlikely 'which was seldom used, but to persons under some notable prejudice'. And the value of what he could do for his friends and relations in exile was undoubtedly very great.

But if this were so, and known to Clarendon to be so, why does he fulminate, in letter after letter in both his private and semi-official correspondence, against the practice, time and again refusing even to consider the possibility for his own possessions? Why, if the authorities are in practice so lenient, does he write about them in terms that would nowadays not be inappropriate to a refugee from the limitless wickedness of Stalin or Hitler? What he says to his most intimate friends and colleagues must be presumed to be what he really thinks.

A few quotations may seem copious but are nothing to the torrents that flowed from his pen whenever he adverted to the subject.

'I hear no news from England or France, but of a multitude of men of honour running to compound,' he wrote to Lady Dalkeith on October 24, 1646. 'I neither envy nor censure them; though I confess I am not able to tell myself, how that comes to be lawful, which would have appeared 3 or 4 years since very odious to most men; or, that anything can be honest to recover an estate, which had not been so to have preserved it. And truly, though I must confess we have by our own gross folly and madness lost a game that might have been longer played, I do not know that any man doth now undergo a worse condition, than he had reason to expect, when upon such infinite disadvantage he first engaged himself in the King's good cause . . . I confess the straits men of all conditions are forced to submit to, are very

[25] *Clar. SP* ii, 279–82.   [26] *Life* i, 251–4.

unpleasant, and were not to be submitted to, if God Almighty had only forbid us to be impious, or sacrilegious, or rebellious as long as we could keep our estates, or to depart from good consciences till we are in danger to be banished or starved . . . Yet sure when men do a little consider either the being saved in the next world, or their being fairly mentioned after their deaths in this (which is the most glorious and desirable blessing after the other) they will find that this negligent treating with their consciences, is not the way to either. Oh my Lady Dalkeith, I pray God preserve poor England from being invaded by the Turks; for sure, men would give their Christianity and two years purchase for the preservation of their estates . . .'[27]

Two months later he wrote to Sir John Berkeley:

'I have told you how far I am from censuring those who compound; I wish heartily they may be as charitable to themselves upon second considerations, as I am to them; and yet your learned men tell you that . . . even they who had contracted and bargained for money with the state, to spare them from sacrificing to Idols (though this were done to redeem their vexation and trouble, and where they could no otherwise have avoided it) were separated from the holy Communion; so unindulgent were the Christians of those times to such convenient accomodations. Are you sure any have compounded without taking the Covenant and other oaths, and without confessing themselves guilty? Their ordinances are clear in the point, and no latitude for a dispensation. But if you mean they have avoided by some skill and craft, of having others take it for them, or of suborning people to say they have taken it, when in truth they have not; I take that to be altogether as bad, if not worse, than the stupid taking it themselves. Believe it, those subtleties will never save private men, much less a Kingdom.'[28]

In both these instances, though Clarendon professes not to censure, in fact he proceeds to do so, in terms both moral and religious. Until his fellow Royalists learn to accept God's will and stop thinking that they can always buy their way out of it he sees little hope of their cause prospering. But beyond moral and theological arguments lay a dispassionate hatred and fear of what we should now call totalitarianism. 'What would a man give for a lodging without a door to it in Bedlam, or for a fyne seat in a country inhabited by Canniballs? . . . the talke of settling Men's Estates is a Bugbear to fright children whilst they are above the Law and Justice.'[29] This outburst closes a long passage in which he has been inveighing against compounding to his closest political friend, Secretary Nicholas.

[27] *Clar. SP* ii, 284–5.   [28] *ibid* 315.
[29] Clar. MS 29 f.183. April 7, 1647.

Whatever advice he may have given to Capel in 1646 or to Sir
Charles Cavendish in 1650 the fact remains that he himself never for
one moment thought of compounding. Perhaps the decision took
itself. He had been excepted by name from any pardon that might
have resulted from any of the negotiations between King and Parliament. And even if the completeness of the Parliamentary victory had
brought, as it might have done, some relenting it is difficult to see how
Hyde, holding the views he held, could have availed himself of it. It
seems clear that he had access to some of his own funds in England. He
was to lament in September 1652 the death of his cousin Will Hyde
who had been managing his affairs and remitting him occasional
sums.[30] The death of the Earl of Essex, perhaps more unexpectedly,
was something of a blow to his personal finances: 'who had no contemptible sum of money in his hands of mine, and would surely have
paid me justly; how I shall now be dealt with I know not, and am afraid
to enquire.'[31] In the same letter he thanks Secretary Nicholas profusely
for the money he has advanced to Frances Hyde: 'I pray send me word,
whether I owe you 2 or 300 for though I am not ready to make you
present payment, I shall take care that it shall not be a desperate debt;
and hope by degrees to pay you some, though not all together.' As a
lawyer he must have been familiar with the mechanism of trusts and
other ways of concealing money. If he was no longer affluent he had yet
to discover what it was to be poor.

Hopton returned briefly to England to attend his wife's funeral early
in 1646. On March 16 Hyde wrote to him that he had only been to see
the Carterets once since he left, although he heard 'that the French
cooke performs his part admirably. The people here tell me (knowing
there can be no other cause for it) I am very melancholique since you
went . . . but I will comfort myself as you must do for your other loss;
you know I have always said I never yet knew sober, pertinent councell
given in that Argument and of all comforters mere divines are the most
unpleasant. When Pliny called for some upon a lesse losse than of a
wife (which sure are the best of friends) he forbade their dull, usual
Arguments. [In translation: 'Not this stuff: he was an old man, he was
ill, (I have long known that): but some new but large considerations
that have never been offered me . . . for what is now offered me gives
way under the weight of such a grief.'] Whatever the faults of Job's
comforters . . . I like their civility and method in comforting very well.
They sat down by him seven days and seven nights without speaking a
Word to him because they saw his Griefe was very great, and when all is

---

[30] *Clar. SP* iii, 96.
[31] *ibid* ii, 289–90 November 15, 1646. Oddly enough Essex's principal heir was the daring
Royalist Sir Robert Shirley, see below p. 165.

done, time can only allay the passion and not talking at all of it or talking of somewhat else is best . . . and therefore I will tell you 'tis hard for you to believe how neare your fort is finished, the Gunnes are already in and ye Ditch almost digged . . .

'. . . I need not tell you that all here long for you and ye Children cry for you . . .'[32]

Hopton never came back to Jersey but went to live with his uncle, Sir Arthur Hopton, at Rouen until the Second Civil War recalled him to action.[33] Left on his own, Hyde accepted the Carterets' hospitable invitation and moved into the castle. There he settled to his *History* in earnest, while still maintaining an enormous correspondence and still holding himself available for any service that might be required of him. In September 1646 he wrote to Ormonde, expressing his pleasure at the prospect of joining him in Ireland which he intended to do as soon as Digby could arrange a passage.[34]

Was there perhaps a chance that Frances and the children might have joined him there? A deeply unhappy letter from her, dated October 16 but endorsed 'received back from Ireland, November 28th', speaks reproachfully of 'doubting of your affection for not taking the advantage of the present opertunity which you will not find the like till next spring'. But it is unsafe to conclude anything from that brief, involved note beyond depth of affection and grief at indefinite separation.[35] A year later on August 30, 1647 he tells Secretary Nicholas that he is that very day setting out for Rouen and St Germain and hopes to be back in less than three weeks.[36] Fortunately for him nothing came of either of these plans. About Ireland he was optimistic but he feared that if he went to Paris the French might arrest him.

Meanwhile, nourished by a stream of materials, the *History* grew apace. A great part of his correspondence consisted of applications made to surviving sources of information. For those who were not his friends, who even disliked and disapproved of him, the support of the King could be invoked. Sir Edward Walker, Garter King of Arms, whose stiff-necked formalism was to exasperate and to amuse him through the long years of exile, had kept a journal of the Western campaign in 1644. This, and the even more valuable account of Prince Rupert's marches throughout the war, was put at the disposal of a historian whom both men regarded as no friend to their ideas. Secretary Nicholas could provide a wealth of information and could tell him about the procedure at the Council before the war and how far its records went back. Information confidentially obtained would be appropriately treated.[37] So completely had Hyde domesticated

[32] Clar. MS 27, ff.81–2.   [33] *Cal. Clar. SP* i, 363.   [34] *Clar. SP* ii, 258.
[35] Clar. MS 28 f.260.   [36] *ibid* 30 f.44.   [37] *ibid* 29 ff.83–4.

himself in his scholarly retreat that by the outbreak of the Second Civil War he had even become a gardener:

'. . . I that am busy about nothing but settinge Lettice, Onions and Carrots wish that you would send me some seedes for my garden, that you may be sure of sallats when you come,' he wrote to Cottington on March 18, 1648.[38] But the contemplative life that seemed to stretch so agreeably ahead was abruptly to be exchanged for the active.

[38] *ibid* 31 f.3.

X

Public Disasters and Private Affections

H<small>YDE</small> had been so isolated from the framing and execution of policies to which he was in any case opposed that the Second Civil War had all but come and gone before he was fully aware of it. In January 1647 the Scots had handed over the King to the English Parliament in exchange for the arrears of pay due to their army. The liberal conditions allowed by his new proprietors encouraged Charles to intrigue with his usual promiscuous duplicity. To trace that story is not the province of this book. When Clarendon came to do so in his *History* his vision was so inflamed by outrage at its ending that he concentrates his own, and his reader's, attention on the men responsible for what he thought an unheard-of atrocity and tiptoes past the shameless activities of the Royal victim. Amongst their consequences was the Second Civil War, an attempt to combine Royalist risings in various parts of the country with a Scottish invasion, fortuitously made more formidable by the sudden revolt of the greater part of the Parliamentary fleet.

Early in 1648 Hyde had been warned that he might be required at short notice to attend the Prince of Wales who was expected to leave France as soon as there was any sign of a revival in Royalist fortunes. In April the warning was repeated. Although Hyde did not yet know it the commander of a Parliamentary garrison in Wales had already declared for the King. At the end of the month Sir Marmaduke Langdale had surprised Berwick and Sir Philip Musgrave Carlisle. The two invasion routes were open to the Scots, whom the Duke of Hamilton was to lead to rescue his master and, more unlikely still, to impose the rule of the Kirk on Anglican and Independent alike. Hyde's distrust of Hamilton as a leader proved too well-founded. It was not until the beginning of July that the Scots army at last crossed the border. By that time there had been risings in Kent, in Surrey and in Essex, and the Fleet in the Downs had mutinied. But the failure to achieve synchronisation had enabled Cromwell and Fairfax to put nearly all the fires out before they had time to blaze up. Hyde in Jersey had no inkling of what was happening. In the middle of April he wrote to the Prince of Wales to thank him for procuring Rupert's war journal, an invaluable chronological aid, and to the Queen to clear himself of any imputation of factiousness towards her. At the beginning of May he wrote a letter of several thousand words to Hopton on the value of episcopacy.

It was not until the middle of June that an urgent summons from Jermyn, accompanied by a warrant on which he might raise money for his travelling expenses, jerked him into instant motion. '. . . You will easily believe that a man who hath not had a boot on these two years, nor in truth hath a boot to put on, cannot in a moment put himself into an equipage for such a journey.' His health too, was not good, probably, as he himself admits, because he had not been taking the exercise of which he was now to expect all too much.[1] But off he set to join the Prince at St Germain, making first for Caen where Secretary Nicholas was living. On his arrival there he found that the Prince had already left Paris for Calais and that Nicholas had joined Cottington at his house in Rouen. There Hyde was reunited with his old friends and colleagues who had received the same orders as he. But joining the Prince, who was never long in one place, over country that was infested by marauders or by sea that was alive with privateers (the war between France and Spain had still eleven years to run) was no easy matter. Hearing that he had gone to Holland to take command of the revolted fleet, Hyde and Cottington set off for Dieppe to find a ship, an act of heroism on Hyde's part 'who in good faith cannot look long to be a man of this watry world, three days at land not recovering the strength and spirit, which three hours sickness at sea takes from me, and this sickness being upon the matter the same, in fair and foul weather'.[2]

The horror of the weeks that followed was graven on Clarendon's memory. A French frigate took them to Dunkirk where the Governor offered them a vessel to carry them to the Prince who was at sea with the revolted fleet. They had not had time to sink the French coast before a pack of Ostend privateers was on them, plundering the passengers and taking them prisoner. Vigorous protests brought the smoothest of apologies and promises of redress from the Governor of Ostend, which, unsurprisingly, were not honoured as he was himself a shareholder in the freebooting business. They did, at length, get away in the clothes they stood up in, only to be embarked on more fruitless to-ing and fro-ing along the coast of Holland. By the time they actually met the Prince on his return from the cruise in September the war was over.

The promises that had promoted it were, however, still to be

[1] *Clar. SP* ii, 408.   [2] *ibid* 409.

honoured. If the past three months had brought Clarendon the acutest physical discomfort in his experience, the next three years were to be morally the most miserable. Not that he himself was to bow the knee in the house of Rimmon. But the price of alliance with the Scots, on which the Second Civil War and the subsequent policies depended, was the abandonment of the Church of England, whatever internal reservations Charles might deceive himself with. The Queen of course needed no such recourse. She hated the Church of England and would happily have danced on its grave. As early as September 22 Hyde drafted, but did not send, a letter to her explaining his position and regretting his inability to accompany the Prince to Scotland in the furtherance of a policy that he considered wrong in principle and disastrous in its prospects.[3]

For the moment Scotland was overshadowed in his mind by doubts and anxieties over the negotiations between the King and the Parliamentary Commissioners in the Isle of Wight. What was Hyde to do if his master obtained a settlement on terms that dishonoured the cause for which so many precious lives had been sacrificed? Distraction from such disquieting thoughts was provided by the need to get the fleet to sea before the sailors, disheartened and unpaid, changed sides again and before the ice, generally expected in December or January, froze it in. Here Prince Rupert proved a valuable ally, winning Hyde's unqualified praise. A further cause of friction with the Queen arose from the wild-cat scheme of her favourite agent and courier, Dr Stephen Goffe, for bringing 900 mercenaries, recruited by the Duke of Lorraine, from the island of Borkum to Jersey, to be used in an attack on Guernsey. Hyde steadily opposed what he knew to be a most dangerous gamble with the loyalty of the proud and independent Jerseymen.[4] The flinging of an untried rabble against a well-found, well-disciplined force in the most difficult of all military operations, an assault from sea, could hardly be considered sensible. The adventure was, happily, called off. But Hyde's opposition was resented and remembered.

Across the Channel the fever of Charles I's reign had entered its terminal stage. The vote for No More Addresses to the King was quickly followed by his trial, at which Dr Goffe's brother, a distinguished officer in Cromwell's New Model army, was one of the Judges who signed the death-warrant. The execution struck Clarendon to the soul. It violated religion, law and history, the three founts of humanity. The hysteria which sometimes breaks in on his shrewd, objective analysis, the defence of the indefensible which he sometimes advances, as, for instance, the assassination of opponents, seem to derive

[3] *ibid* 416–18.   [4] *ibid* 455–8.

from the overwhelming, unhingeing, horror he felt at this act. He kept the day with a solemnity that he did not extend to Good Friday. On the first anniversary, when he was serving as ambassador in Madrid, he set down his prayers and meditations at great length. His first concern is to restrain his own emotion:

'Frett not thyself because of him who prospereth in his way, because of the man who bringeth wicked desires to passe, was an antidote that David provyded against the poyson of successe which he saw was so apt to transporte the passyons and intoxicate the understandings of most men who were willinge to believe the prosperinge in what they went about to be an evidence of God's approovinge and likinge what they did.' Reading, experience and observation demonstrate that this is 'far from being a true or a reasonable conclusion'. The proper deduction for a Christian is that the nation is being punished for its sins. His first prayer is therefore for mercy on his country, his second for the young King then in Scotland.

'Gratious and Almighty God, take into thy Arms of immediate protection the sunn of that Blessed Martyr now with thee, the King's Majesty that now is, place him by thy power upon his father's Throne . . .

'Take the young yeares of the Kinge into thy Tutelage . . . as he growes in yeares, cause him to grow in virtue, piety, wisdome and courage . . . infuse into his harte and affections a love and value of good men, and a disyre only to be served by such and a disesteeme and hatred of prophane, licentious and wicked persons . . .'[5]

The cadences of the Prayer Book come naturally to his pen. So do his anxieties as to Charles II's choice of company.

The immediate consequences of the execution were a further diminution of Hyde's political influence and a sharp increase in his fear for the safety of his children. His brother-in-law Will was on easy terms with Algernon Sidney,[6] then Lieutenant-Governor of Dover, and it may have been through him that their passage was obtained.

'I have not had such content these many dayes as I had this eveninge in the reading of your letter without a date,' Hyde wrote to Will on March 18, 'for god's sake loose no time in getting them over, for which I have another reason, I meane for the speede of it, than I can yet impart to you . . .'[7] They left England on April 30, 1649 and were in their lodgings at Antwerp on May 6.[8]

---

[5] Clar. MS 39 f.49.

[6] *Clar. SP* ii, 421.

[7] Clar MS 37, foliation confused.

[8] BL Add. MS 15900. Both dates O.S. I am grateful to Dr Paul Seaward for drawing this unusual source (Anne Hyde's girlhood account book) to my attention.

The unexplained reason, no question, was Hyde's appointment as joint ambassador with Cottington to the court of Madrid. Cottington, with whom Hyde was sharing a lodging at The Hague, was disenchanted with his present life. The climate of Holland did not suit him. He was seventy-five, too old to contemplate accompanying the young King on a perilous and uncomfortable expedition to Ireland, which was then in prospect, or, worse still, to Scotland which the courtiers closest to Charles II were urging. He was unwilling to return to France, where he had not been well received because of his known attachment to Spain, dating from his service in the English embassy in James I's time. Spain was indeed the obvious choice, and friendly messages from Madrid suggested that some financial support might be obtained there, even perhaps some diplomatic assistance in controlling the antics of the Catholic Irish which were nullifying Ormonde's efforts to establish a firm base for Royalist recovery.

Cottington outlined this case to Hyde and suggested that in view of his own age and infirmity they should go together. Hyde at first smiled at so agreeable a fantasy. But the more he considered it the more sense it made. Although for the moment he and the Queen were agreed in urging the King to join Ormonde in Ireland he knew that she was working and talking against him. She had tried to prevent the King from retaining him in the Council. She complained that Hyde had maliciously obstructed Dr Goffe's brilliant scheme for the capture of Guernsey. She had always pressed for an alliance with the Scottish Covenanters and there was every reason to suppose that, under the skilful manipulation of Mazarin, she would revert to that policy. As at Jersey he was for the time hopelessly outgunned. He might as well retire from the scene of backbiting and frustration to employ himself in something that would certainly be interesting and might well be useful. Cottington and he found each other good company though each could be entertainingly waspish about the other.

The two friends kept the plan to themselves until the King approved it, enthusiastically, at the beginning of April. The Royalist hive buzzed with anger and with jubilation. Jubilation from Hyde's enemies and even from friends like Sir John Berkeley who were tired of being told that moral short cuts were no good: anger from friends like Secretary Nicholas who blamed Hyde for deserting the King and leaving him an easy prey to false counsel or from former allies such as Colepeper who would have liked the job themselves. Hyde more than half admits that pleasure and curiosity weighed heavily in his decision. Perhaps after two years out to grass it was hard to find himself back in harness, hauling a broken-down coach through a quagmire of malice. Anyway there was to be no time for second thoughts. After a brief reunion with his family, now safely established in Antwerp, the

ambassadors were to make their way overland, passing by Paris and
Bordeaux to the Spanish frontier at Irun.

Their instructions were drawn at The Hague on May 24.[9] Hyde was
detained there a little longer to assist with the drafting of letters to the
Dutch government, outraged by the assassination of the Commonwealth diplomatic representative, Dr Dorislaus, on May 3. At the
beginning of June he was looking forward to joining his wife in
Antwerp. 'My deere little Rogue . . . I do believe we shall be with thee
Wensday or Thursday at latest,' he wrote on Monday, June 7.[10] He
stayed for six weeks, partly occupied in preparing his own journey,
partly arranging for that of the King who was also going to Paris to see
his mother. He was to pass through Antwerp where Hyde had secured
him the best house in the town. 'I wish you had sent soberer officers to
take care of the accommodations,' he wrote to Secretary Long, 'for it is
no credit to us that when any thinge is to be done, though early in the
morning our people are in drinke.'[11] He and Cottington left Antwerp
on July 21. Their route took them through Brussels, Soignies, Mons,
Valenciennes, Cambrai, Péronne, Roye, Gournay and Senlis.[12] On
Saturday the 31st he wrote from Péronne: 'It will be Monday night at
soonest before we reach Paris . . . my shoulder . . . torments me exceedingly and therefor I will endure any remedy as soon as I come where Dr
Frozzar [Dr Frazier, Charles II's medical attendant] is, rather than
beare it. I have another vexation too, that I can get no flesh yesterday
nor this day, and the fish is so ill, and so ill dressed, that I am kept
hungry, which thou knowest I like not well.

'If thou desyrest I should prosper and have any happynesse in this
world, thou wilt remember all that I have said to thee concerning thy
selfe, and not suffer a melancholique thought to enter into thy hearte,
and I have no doubte but God will so blesse us, as to bringe us quickly
agayne to each other's company; which believe me I desyre as much as I
do to lyve, and the last only to enjoy the blessings of the first.'[13]

On August 4 he was entertained to dinner in Paris by John Evelyn
together with three old friends, Sir Edward Nicholas, Sir George
Carteret and Dr Earles.[14] Soon afterwards he joined the King at St
Germain where presumably Dr Frazier put his shoulder to rights since
in a letter of August 12 he tells Frances that his health is good and the
air of St Germain agreeable: '. . . but for all that I have yet seene, give
me old Englande, for meate, drinke and lodginge, and even for wyne
too.'[15] He was disturbed at not having heard from her. Both her

[9] *Clar. SP* ii, 481.
[10] *HMC Bath* MSS, ii, 80.
[11] *Cal. Clar. SP* ii, 15.
[12] Clar. MS 37 f.208.
[13] *Bath MSS* ii, 80.
[14] Evelyn's *Diary* ed. E. S. de Beer, ii 561.
[15] *Bath MSS* ii, 82.

nervous and her physical condition seem to have given him cause for alarm. 'My Lady Browne [Evelyn's mother-in-law], who was as leane as thou arte, and is now plumpe, sayes if thou will be cheerfull and drink soculate in the morninge, thou wilt be fatt.' When he did hear from her on September 11, 'I have at last, and just as I was beginning a grumbling letter to thee for so longe silence, receaved thyne of the 3rd', her letter evidently showed signs of distress. 'I conjure thee let me know the author of that prety news, that it is now declared that I am to stay in Spayne three yeares, and that I knew it when I was with thee.' If it were to be, so he assures her, 'I would not stir from this place till thou camest to mee, and wee would learn Spanish togither; and be confident if I find myself at any time fixed in one place for a third part of that time, I will not lyve without thee'.[16]

During the two months he was in Paris, cold water was continually poured on his forthcoming embassy. Nicholas could hardly contain himself. The Earl of Bristol, father of Hyde's volatile friend Lord Digby, himself a distinguished former occupant of the Madrid embassy, wrote to wish him prosperity and success in his mission: 'But to deal freely with you, I am not much satisfied with your present employment, knowing you were (in my opinion) the fittest man in the King's Dominions for another, and that of the most use.'[17] The Queen, with whom his relations had improved from the frigid to the cool, 'still expressed trouble that he was sent on that embassy, which, she said, would be fruitless, as to any advantage the King would receive from it; and, she said, she must confess, that though she was not confident of his affection and kindness towards her, yet she believed that he did wish that the King's carriage towards her should be always fair and respectful; and that she did desire that he should be always about his majesty's person'.[18] She thought, it seems, that 'he understood the business of England better than any body else' and that he would be a stabilizing influence on the young King, whose choice of friends fell below her standards. It was at this point that she told Lady Dalkeith of her confidence in his essential uprightness: '"if he thought her to be a whore, he would tell her of it" which when that lady told him he was not displeased with the testimony.' Whether such outspokenness was an ideal qualification for conducting diplomacy or for dealing with the house of Stuart might be a question. Perhaps it was an embarrassment in other relations of life. The letter he wrote to Lady Dalkeith (or Lady Morton as she had become by the death of her father-in-law) on leaving Paris is remarkably explicit for so long and intimate a friendship.

[16] *ibid.*   [17] *Clar. SP* ii, 490.   [18] *Life* i, 224–5.

Though no absence or distance ought to lessen or allay that virtuous habit of the mind which we call love or friendship, yet there is a passion and impatience which are not unnatural branches from that noble root, which sure time orders and corrects. How comes it else to pass, that I am worse prepared to bear, and more sensible of the pain of being deprived of your company now, than I was before I came last to you, when I had the same affection and value for you, which I have now?

Doubtless, as the same kindness and reverence to the memory of our friends continues a year after their death, that we were possessed with at the day of their funeral, though we were not transported with the same unruliness of passion and exclamation, so it is no wonder if after parting with those we entirely love (which is a civil death), we feel a sharper sense of the separation for a time, than we do after we have corrected our affections with thoughts of necessity and conveniency, and those other arguments which prevail over our understanding and judgment. And therefore, I am not afraid of bringing a scandal upon my affection to you, as if it were capable of diminution, when I tell you, I hope, and will endeavour to bear this absence from you, better than I yet find myself able to do. Nor do I think the worse of that passion I have for you, because it is without any mixture of that jealousy which your Court holds love to be compounded of, fear of rivals. It would be a great comfort to me to know you had any man with you (for he must be come since I left you) who loves you as well as I do. The greatest trouble I suffer is that you are left without a lover, without such a friend as you may safely receive advice from since the condition we are all in, and are like to be in, does exceedingly need a friend for our support and comfort in the difficulties we must struggle with. I would be glad Dr Morley were to come to you; who seriously I hope will do much good in your Court by his conversation. I am sure he will be of singular use to you, being of great ability and wisdom to advise you in whatsoever may concern you, and having a perfect value and esteem of you.

It is time to tell you, which is all I meant to say when I began to write, that we are, I thank God thus far well on our way. God of Heaven preserve you.[19]

What are we to make of this? There is, as its writer affirms, passion in this letter. But why should we not accept on the same authority the candour with which he disclaims the desire of sexual possession? Three months later he wrote to his wife from Madrid: 'I presume thou dost sometymes wryte to my Lady Mourton who is a very worthy woman, I am sure very kinde to thee.'[20] Is there a whiff of Tartuffe here? Some people, notably another intimate correspondent of these years, Sir John Berkeley, might have said so. He and Lady Morton had been

[19] *Clar. SP* ii, 492. The date of September 10 must be wrong since Hyde and Cottington did not leave Paris before September 29, see *Bath MSS* ii, 84.
[20] Add. MS 34727 f.78.

thrown together by the war. He had been in command of the Exeter
garrison when she had been there, first as lady in waiting to the Queen
and later, after the Queen had fled to France, as guardian and nurse to
the baby Henriette who had been born there. Berkeley had advanced
£500 to her for the Princess's support, an expense which Hyde later certified for repayment in the impoverishment of exile.[21] They had met
again in Paris, Berkeley in the household of James, Duke of York and
Lady Morton in that of the Queen, and in 1650 and 1651 he was
evidently anxious to marry her. (Her husband, from whom she was
estranged, died in Scotland early in 1650.)[22] Hyde seems to have advised her against accepting him, earning thereby his bitter and lasting
hostility. It is not clear from the correspondence how far his objection
was based on his anxiety not to prejudice either her or her children's
inheritance, how far on an old friend's judgment of personal compati-
bility, how far on his disapproval of, and alarm at, Berkeley's unscrupulous adoption of policies that, in Hyde's view, betrayed the cause for
which the war had been fought. In a long letter to Lady Morton written
on March 18, 1650 he professes himself '. . . hugely concerned for him
and troubled to see him carry'd away with a stream into opinions not
worthy of his discretion or his integrity. Alas he hath not wickedness
enough for that company and will at last find himself deceaved and be
more seveare to himself upon it than his Enimyes can be . . .'[23]

Again the letter begins with phrases that might be open to miscon-
struction from malicious persons or even, if she were ever to see them,
from Lady Hyde. '. . . As I am now even transported with the comfort
of your letters, soe seriously and as I hope ever to see you more (the
hope of which is one of the greatest cordialls I have) I have scarce in my
life felt a greater waight of trouble than the apprehension I began to
have that you might be unkinde . . .' He had not heard from her for
three months. By the third paragraph he is giving her expert professional guidance through the thicket of possible testamentary complica-
tions occasioned by the deaths, in fairly rapid succession, of her father-
in-law, her mother-in-law and her husband, a situation made more
difficult by her exile and by the fact that Scotland was still a theatre of
war. Much, much later the letter ends on a note of playful gallantry:
'You have lost a world of pritty Intelligence by soe absolutely discoun-
tenancing and contemning my Judgment of Beauty, which if you had
not done I would have sent you the History of a Masque at this court, to
which we were invited the Saturday before Shrovetide, and the excellence, order and Beautty of ye Ladyes, but you will againe tell me that
I am out of my Spheare when I talke of Ladyes, and therefore you shall
continue ignorant, for which I hope your Daughter will grive.'

[21] *Cal. Clar. SP* i.   [22] Clar. MS 39 f.111.   [23] *ibid.*

It was Hyde's unlucky concern in the daughter's rather than the mother's matrimonial negotiations that led, at last, to the breaking of this long friendship. The complexities of the story and the impenetrability of the evidence,[24] fragmentary, allusive and unreliable, deny a brief and coherent account. The withdrawal of the final candidate provoked from Lady Morton, who had returned to Scotland in 1651 and remained there till her death in December 1654, a letter that caused Hyde deep distress. On March 28, 1654 he wrote from Paris (where he had been for two years established as the King's chief minister) accepting her desire that he should break off all relations with her. He reminds her that in twenty years' conversation she has heard him speak ill of very few and has found him a man 'who never mynded doing a good office for any body of what condicion so ever if it were in his power. Doe not easily be persuaded that such a man is on the suddaine turned Hypocrite and a lyar and hath cloven feete . . . I pray suffer your Mother to continue in her old faith and to reteyne in her memory a favourable opinion of E.H.'[25] Such however was her fury that she wrote to the King himself:

'. . . I shall at this hasard ventur to aproch you, you were wons so far pleased to owne me and mine to take notis of my Lord Nuburgh's application to my Dau. which was verrie unworthie of her and though I did so much indulge to her as to aproove of what I could not helpe, yet the decline of his affection hath these manye months bin so vissible to her that to my great comfort she hath no more thought of him. I heare he is much in your Majesty's favor. I wish him no ill nor doe I thinke that upon my acounte he hath any part of your favor. I only humbly beg you will not think my Nane less steddie. I am sure she is most constant in those prinsepalls she hath of ever being with much humillitie and devotion yours, and though I do not desier to lessen that noble lord to you yet give me leave to saye he is a verrie ill lover . . .'[26]

Hyde drafted the King's soothing answer. He also wrote once more to her in his own person, 'not . . . without some debate with myself whether it were not a respect more agreeable to you not to write at all. I have so ill luck in my expression and I think that plainness and freedom become me in my letters which you have not been displeased with when we have walked in the gallery, and you now misinterpret all: besides I find my judgment exceedingly decays and that which appears to me reasonable seems to you quite contrary . . . and I do acknowledge

---

[24] *Cal. Clar. SP* ii, 65 and 176 and Clar. MS 45 f.20 and f.92 manifestly do not refer to the same aspirant to the hand of Lady Anne Douglas. Lord Hopton seems a most unlikely candidate. Was this perhaps a mistake for Lord Capel, Hopton's nephew by marriage, who became engaged to the Earl of Northumberland's daughter in 1654 *ibid* f.222v?

[25] Clar. MS 48 f.79.   [26] *ibid* f. 80.

to you I have that lowness of spirit in me that if it were possible I would not have an ill word spoken of me by the meanest person alive; and if we did enough consider the difficulty of repairing the wrong which every sharp word does to the reputacion, we would not think the peace to be only broken by the hands.

'With reference to myself I will tell you truly what I think of you. I do believe that you are so confident of my integrity, Affection and duty to you that you cannot really upon deliberacion and in cold blood entertain a doubt of it. But my grief and my complaint is that you write to all friends in such a manner, as they have cause to think you believe me to be unworthy and unfaithful to you: and let me tell you if you had once felt the pain of being unjustly and unreasonably suspected by one to whom you have been always very faultless, you would not think I ought to have a less sense of the smart of your Jealousy than I have expressed . . . But no more of these Arguments nor of anything that may displease you. Be as happy as I wish you and your fate will be a fair one . . .'[27]

This is the last of his letters to her. A few months later she was dead, having made no second marriage. But her daughter Anne, as her mother had implied in her letter to Charles II, had made an alliance suitable to her rank, with the seventh Earl Marischal.[28] Lord Newburgh continued in favour with the King and was given a place at Court at the Restoration. How deeply Hyde was disturbed by the affair may be gauged not only from the language he uses and from the volume of its flow but from the fact that these letters were written when he was working an eighteen-hour day, conducting often in his own hand an immense correspondence, all of which had to be copied and much of it encoded or decoded, with Royalist agents in England and Scotland and with representatives or sources of information all over central and western Europe.

His attachment, like that to her brother, Lord Grandison, perhaps drew its strength from his brief first marriage, so bright, so fresh in his recollection. Clarendon's loves and friendships, like wines of a great vintage, seem only to attain their full depth and character with the passing of time. Yet at the time he left Paris for Madrid in the autumn of 1649 he was preoccupied with anxiety for the wife, who, in his autobiography, melts into the background. Frances had evidently had a rough time of it looking after her ageing parents in addition to four very young children, as the party with which her husband and her father had been prominently identified went down to defeat. Her courage is praised in letters that Hyde wrote to others during their long separation. When they were, at last, reunited he was clearly shocked to

---

[27] *ibid* ff.97–8. [28] *Burke's Peerage* 99th edn. (1949) p. 1429.

see how thin and worn she was. No wonder that when she was almost immediately faced with the prospect of another parting, again of indefinite duration, she developed acute nervous depression. How alive her husband was to her condition, how tenderly he comforted her, is most eloquently expressed in a badly torn letter, now in the British Library, written just after he had set out for Paris at the end of June. The interruptions accidentally caused by the defects of the manuscript give the reader the illusion, almost, of overhearing a conversation at the distance of more than three centuries:

> . . . with what courage can I pursue my businesse which I know thou thinkest . . . to do, and which I am obliged by my duty, when thou tellest . . . one minute of content, till thou seest me agayne . . .
>
> . . . and really if by thy melancholique and trouble of . . . disquyett thy weake body with sicknesse, and shouldst [occasion] a disease thou couldst not agayne putt off, think what ruine thou bringst upon mee and thy children, for I protest to you, though thou accused me with want of fondnesse, though [*sic:* he means 'thou'] art so intirely all my joy, hope and comforte, and the hope of livinge hereafter happily togither, does so absolutely and solely supporte me in this affliction of our separation that if I should be so miserable as to loose thee I would never . . . of quyett houre in this world, but would make all haste after thee. The[refore as] thou lovest me and thy children, do not only resolve to be patient . . . be merry and preserve thy minde free from such thoughts and appreh[ensions] [as] much as it is in thy power to doe, and believe every indisposition or me[lancholy] inclination to be an enimy sent to do ill offices between thee and me . . .

He urges her to trust in God 'who hath reserved a portion of good fortune for us, even in this world' and confirms the plans he is making with her brother to bring over her father and mother 'wher ther will still be liberty and no feare of prysons', and concludes 'God of heaven blesse thee and thyne, in whome consistes all the happynesse of

> My Deare little Rogue
> Thy most affectionate Husband
> Bruxelles this Monday morninge 8 of the clocke.'[29]

This letter was the forerunner of others, written on the journey to Spain or from Madrid itself, which present a remarkably consistent, attractive and oddly unselfconscious self-portrait of Hyde in adversity. Central to it is the constancy of his affection and the gentleness of his care for his wife and children. It is lit by courage, cheerfulness and faith, as in the passage just quoted. It is one thing to accept that God's

[29] Add. MS 34727 f.75.

will may involve the overthrow of everything one loves best. It is another to go beyond that in the serene assurance of 'a portion of good fortune for us, even in this world'. How far this is to be derived from the teaching of Scripture, how far from the sanguine temperament of Sir Edward Hyde, is perhaps for a theologian to decide. But this was one of the periods at which his mind was much occupied with the study of the Psalms, a body of poetry whose recurrent theme is the triumph of hope over despair and of righteousness over apparently superior force. For this is the core of his public and private morality: the divine will has no use for clever tricks. God, by definition, must win in the end: God, by definition, cannot win by the cheating or even the gamesmanship of his servants.

It is in this dark passage of his life when the cause for which he had risked everything seemed, humanly speaking, lost; when his wife, on whom so much depended, needed comfort that he could only give from a distance; when he had neither money nor power; when friends on whom he had long relied, like Sir John Berkeley or Lady Morton, were turning away; when he had some grounds for thinking that every man's hand was against him, that his essential grandeur and magnanimity are seen at their clearest. The importance of the Spanish embassy in Clarendon's life was not public and political but moral and personal. He did not achieve much: but he became the man who was to achieve the Restoration.

XI

The Madrid Embassy

THE JOURNEY from Paris to Madrid, if not luxurious, was a considerable improvement on Hyde's recent experiences of European travel. The travellers put themselves into the hands of a contractor up to the French frontier 'for coach, horses, waggon and dyett, so that until we come into Bisquy, wee shall not be oblieged to spend one penny after wee are gone out of this towne'. The cost was 'above £100'.[1] The terms of the arrangement were such as to make the contractor's profit proportionate to the speed. At Blaye, near Bordeaux, he wrote to Frances on October 11: 'Havinge from the tyme wee left Paris to this minute, travelled as hard as I believe any people have done with so greate a trayne. Wee are up in the morning and in the coach as soone as it is light, wee stay about dynner tyme two houres by the way, as much for the horses sake as our owne, and come into our lodginge after night, so that never travellers saw lesse of a country to satisfy our curiosity than wee doe; and truly for ought I see of the country, I could be as well contented to lyve in poore Wiltshyre, as in any place I have seene.'[2] The conductor, he says, will not if he can help it allow them so much as a day's rest. As it happened he was in luck. Two days later he wrote from Bordeaux itself, normally a mere four hours further, that they had had a day's respite 'upon the fayling of our horses, which being no charge to us we are not sorry for'.[3]

Bordeaux reminded Hyde of England in 1640. 'Wee are in a place of the same temper and dispostion to rebellyon* as England was at the beginning of this Parliament only they doe it with lesse noise because all kinds of people are now agried in it and no person appears of a different opinion, so that though the whole towne be in as high

---

* The local discontents of Bordeaux had merged into the confused defiance of Mazarin's government known as the Fronde.
[1] *Bath MSS* ii, 84.   [2] *ibid* 85.   [3] Add. MS 34727 f.76.

rebellyon as can be imagined, and all day and all night shooting at the castle which holds out for the Kinge, yet saving the noyse of there gunnes all is quyett in the towne, the shoppes open and all imaginable quyett in the streetes, and they do really professe they are for the King and Parliament and only . . . [? refuse submission] to the Duke of Epernon [the unpopular hereditary governor of the province].' From the torn remainder of the letter it is clear that the young Anne Hyde, with the imitative instinct of a clever child, is daring to affect melancholy. 'By this tyme thy frends [i.e. her parents] are come to thee, and then Grandmother will whipp that humour out of her. Be sure you make her write me an account of herselfe, and if shee thinke fitt to discourse in the prayse of melancholique I will answer her.'[4]

On October 19 they at last reached the Spanish frontier at Irun.

'Wee are now come I thanke God safe to this towne and shall to-morrow be at St Sebastians where we shall refresh ourselves for 2 or 3 dayes, being then to begynn another journey in one respecte much worse than that we have past, for though it be not so longe a journey to Madrid (which we shall reach in 15 dayes continuall travell) yet it is much worse way, worse accomodation, and for ought I perceave we must travell on mules or horses, for there is no litter heare to be had, which I am sorry for for my companion's sake more than my owne, who I doubt will not so well beare that way of travell, though really it is not to be believed with what unwearyedness and cheerfulness he hath hitherto held out: and yett I assure you our journey hath been a sore one: wee havinge many morninges gone out 2 houres before day, and seldome come into our lodgings till it hath been darke, so that I looke it should make me leane, which I should be more gladd if thou couldst gett the fa[tter] . . .'[5]

Her health, her spirits and the children's education, especially the learning of French, are anxiously enquired after in this as in every letter. His forebodings about Spanish travel proved only too well founded. They had, indeed, to travel to San Sebastian on horseback. But he had reckoned without the weather. 'Wee thought to have stayed heare three or four dayes, for our refreshment after so long a journey, but God knowes now how longe we shall stay', he wrote despairingly on October 29, 'for the next morninge after we came, it begann to rayne in the extremest degree thou canst imagyne, and hath continued so ever since, with a continuall violent storme and tempest, which makes us very cold and weary of a place wher wee are very civilly treated.' They were accommodated in 'the best house in the towne, and as good one as ever thou sawest, without chimny or glasse window, which are thinges this people are not acquainted with'.[6] Throughout

[4] *ibid* f.76v.   [5] *ibid* f.77.   [6] *Bath MSS* ii, 85.

that bitter winter these defects were to be the subject of repeated, incredulous complaint.

They were still there on November 5, almost mad with impatience. It was not until November 28 that he could write from Madrid: 'Wee are at last I thanke God come safe to this towne, after so wearysome a journey as thou canst not imagyne, for it is not possible for thee to con- ceave such a country as this is to travellers. It is enough when thou knowest that the Inn at Pyrton is as much better then any one I mett with in the rydinge 400 myles, or indeede then any one in Spayne, as my house ther is better than that Inn . . .'[7]

The civility and ceremony with which they had been received at San Sebastian was conspicuously absent in Madrid. The delay, originally imposed by the weather, had been extended by the Spanish govern- ment. The house that was being prepared for them was not ready. Tired of waiting at a small town outside the capital they preferred to make their entry incognito and to put up at the house of a prominent English merchant. The feeble vacillations of the King and his Chief Minister, Don Luis de Haro, hardly seem worth recording. In prin- ciple, of course they favoured Royalism: but the warnings of the Spanish ambassador in London, Cardenas, of the power and energy of the English Republic weighed heavily against the impoverished repre- sentatives of an impotent émigré. Cardenas earned Clarendon's un- dying resentment and contempt: 'the parched stupidity of Don Alonso de Cardenas' is one of his best phrases.[8]

The first rise in Royalist stock was occasioned by the arrival of Rupert's semi-piratical squadron, formed out of the remnants of the revolted fleet, off Southern Spain. But it fell almost immediately with the appearance of a far superior Parliamentary force and the loss of half the Royalist ships outside Cartagena. Further damage, this time serious, was sustained by an outrage similar to the murder of Dorislaus at The Hague. Anthony Ascham, like Dorislaus a Cambridge don, had been sent by the Commonwealth as their first representative in Madrid. He was murdered in his inn by a gang of Royalist bravos, one of whom was actually on Clarendon and Cottington's staff. So gross a violation of the fundamentals of diplomacy could not be defended, even by Clarendon, convinced as he was that his country was virtually in a state of demoniac possession. The ambassadors disavowed the action and ate humble pie. It was indeed, as he wrote to Nicholas, a 'mad action'.[9] Don Luis accepted their innocence but the Spanish King did not forgive the disgrace. This was in May 1650. In June it became known that Charles II had sailed to Scotland. Once again Royalism soared, only to crash beyond hope of recovery when the news

---

[7] *ibid* 87.   [8] *Clar. SP* iii, Appendix lxv.   [9] *ibid* 21.

of the battle of Dunbar reached Madrid about the end of September. From then it was downhill all the way. In December the ambassadors were told, in pretty round terms, to be off. They stayed to haggle over the final instalment of the Spanish subsidy on which they had been living and closed with an improved offer in March, by which season the route northwards to France was just about tolerable.

It was a journey that Hyde took alone. Cottington had secured the grudging permission of the authorities to stay in Spain, though they would not let him live in Madrid. Cottington was never a close friend of Hyde's. He was too cool, sceptical, worldly-wise. If he had ever been invited to Great Tew he would have gone hunting or hawking — a sport in which he was expert — while the others were teasing out the principles of ecclesiastical authority. He laughed at Hyde's seriousness and shuddered at his long-windedness: but yet he had chosen him for his colleague and travelling-companion. Perhaps he was amused by him. Certainly he was too shrewd not to recognise integrity and ability when he saw them.

What Hyde thought of him is far easier to gauge. He admired his wit and his incomparable gift for settling a thorny issue by making everybody laugh. The best instance of this is his skilful torpedoing of Charles II's absurd intention of making Sir Edmund Wyndham his Secretary of State by gravely suggesting that he should by the same token make the late King's falconer one of his royal chaplains.[10] Hyde was ready to apprentice himself to a veteran diplomat who was the senior surviving professional member of Charles I's Council and to learn from him the principles and technique of conducting foreign affairs. Cottington also could teach him how to enjoy life in Spain. 'It is yett so hard frost, that wee spende the ice of our owne fountaynes in our guarden, which saves us two shillings a day, for how much soever I complayne of cold, my Lord Treasurer hath brought me to drinke all our wyne in ice,' Hyde wrote to his wife in February 1651.[11] What kept Cottington out of Hyde's high opinion was the frivolity of his religion. To have been received into the Roman Catholic Church while serving in Spain, to renounce Catholicism for Anglicanism on returning to a prosperous political career in England, and to settle again for Catholicism in his final retirement to Valladolid was to make higher things serve lesser. The Spanish Court, according to Clarendon, thought the same. He was, he told Nicholas, 'more contemned and hated here than you can imagine'.[12]

---

[10] This story is admirably told in *Hist.* xii, 64.　[11] *Bath MSS* ii, 94.
[12] Clar. MS 41 f.338. M. J. Havran in his *Caroline Courtier: The Life of Lord Cottington* (1973) points out that Cottington himself vehemently and repeatedly denied these reports of his earlier reception into the Roman communion.

All in all Madrid was neither so enjoyable nor so fruitful as Jersey but it had its points. The material circumstances of life, in spite of Hyde's frequent, and doubtless truthful, protestations to Nicholas that he could not put his hand on a single pistole*, were comfortable, even luxurious. The household accounts of the embassy when it was on the point of being wound up show that the establishment employed a coachman and his man, a gardener, a porter, a cook and undercook, a footman, a scullion, a French laundress and a kitchen laundress.[13] Presents of tobacco to Nicholas and Sir Thomas Aylesbury, of 'soculate' to Frances Hyde and Charles II and of sherry to these and other recipients are frequently alluded to. Some money was even dispatched both to Frances and to Nicholas, to repay a small part of his former loans to her. The parting present from the Spanish government for which the ambassadors held grimly on, enduring snubs and slights, was evidently regarded as their own perquisite. 'If I should not be with thee, by the end of Aprill, as I doubte not I shall, I have taken order that thou shalt receave £300 sterlinge, with which I hope all thy debtes will be payde, and that (as I have told thee before) I shall not heare the name of mony, in two or three moneths after I come to thee, and then I hope I shall be able to provyde for thee and all thy company [i.e. her father and mother as well as the children], for another whole yeere, and in that tyme I doubte not God Almighty will do somewhat for us, for in earnest (little Rogue) I cannot yett believe that wee are condemned to perish for want of breade. If we can but procure health (which I thanke God I have to heartes desyre) wee shall shift for the rest.'[14] In this letter written just as he was leaving Madrid on March 1, 1651 the financial reward of his mission sounds satisfactory. Indeed he seems to have been enabled to look forward to a life of scholarly amplitude: 'I have sent by sea, three trunkes, and one great cabinett . . . For thy comforte, ther is nothing in them but very good Spanish bookes, and therefore putt them into that roome thou dost destine for my study, which I expecte to finde handsomely provyded for that use.'

In his autobiography Clarendon's chief recollections of Madrid seem to have been the great occasions of public ceremonial, most notably a bullfight which he describes with a minuteness unusual to a man whose visual sense was not easily stimulated. It would be hard to say whether he was more offended by the inhumanity of the proceedings than by the waste of such expensive horseflesh. He there recalls too the diplomatic life of the capital and records the astonishing fact that apart from the Danish ambassador all his fellows were Italian and, except for one, all Florentines. By contrast his letters, both private and official,

---

* A Spanish gold coin usually reckoned at 80% to 90% of a sovereign.
[13] *Clar. SP* iii, 25.   [14] *Bath MSS* ii, 95.

say very little about the world he moved in. His view of Spaniards in general was that though honest and courteous they were feeble and supine — a favourite word — to the last degree. Spanish life he came by degrees almost to like. Madrid scored higher marks than most continental towns which were generally compared disobligingly with Wiltshire: '. . . the ayre of this place is so very delicate that if a dead dogg be throwen into the streete, it never stinkes and indeede the ayre had neede have that virtue.'[15] Backhanded, but still a compliment.

Clarendon spoke no Spanish. His want of an ear for languages was a common target of criticism in the years after the Restoration. But he set to work to master the grammar and the literature and above all the history, which he read with his own suspended work in mind. '. . . They are careful in writing their own histories, which I am studying diligently and out of them inform myself more of the state of England than I could do by my own Chronicles,' he wrote to Dr Morley.[16] The original work that occupied him was the *Contemplations and Reflections upon the Psalms* that he had begun in Jersey in 1647 and had put aside after Psalm 8. After Psalm 67 is written 'Thus far at Madrid'. He did a little work on the book after his return to Antwerp but very soon abandoned it. He did not return to it until the final exile that proved so rich in literary production.

The Madrid section of the work — one hundred and forty folio pages in the edition of 1727 — was thus composed at the height of his energies and from the depth of his experience. 'Adversity is the natural parent of Reformation in Understanding and Affections, it refines and purifies Mens Natures, and begets a warmth and Light of Piety and Religion, out of those Embers which lay scattered and almost extinguished in Pleasures and Incogitancy,' he wrote of Psalm 63. It is this positive, even creative, reaction to the frustrating of all his purposes that is the secret of his strength. The book sparkles with epigram. 'Not to feel pain is a much worse Sign than any Impatience to bear it' (p. 407). And every heart must surely return an echo to '. . . the cold, and unnourishing Comfort of being Honest, and in the Right . . .' (p. 408). There is, too, the gusto of the born controversialist: '. . . there must go Wit, and Parts, and Knowledge, and Industry to make such Fools; meer Nature cannot do it.' (p. 507)

The essentials of Clarendon's religion and politics, that is to say his understanding of life, are here marshalled into the force that was to carry through the Restoration and to shape a tradition. At the foundation lay the notion of acceptance: 'We are not Judges what is to be preserved, nor which is the Way of preserving. It may be, God thinks it fit that our Estates, our Liberties and our Lives should be sacrificed to

---

[15] Add. MS 34727 f.80.   [16] *Clar. SP* ii, 516.

his Truth, and for the Defence of it . . .' (p. 499). Deriving directly from it is the distrust of instant remedies and impatient meddling: 'there is no Misery so strong and grievous . . . as can bring God to Article for the time of his deliverance: if we will not wait he will not come' (p. 442). But acceptance and submission does not imply inertia; on the contrary: 'We must . . . know there is a Religion of the Hand, as well as a Religion of the Heart, and look to what we do, as well as what we believe' (p. 421); '. . . we must not look upon this Life as consisting in Length of Days, but Integrity of Actions; not in living long, but living well' (p. 460). In a striking metaphor drawn from, of all things, the conventions of seventeenth-century duelling he writes: 'God is a Second, who never fails if we call upon him as we ought; and knows well how to grapple with our fair-speaking Adversaries' (p. 517). Above all the notion of time and of waiting on God should preserve the Christian from 'that bold and blasphemous Impudence, as to challenge the Almighty Providence to be the Patron . . . of those monstruous and unparalleled Wickednesses . . . and make their Success an Argument of their having done that which pleases him' (p. 499).

For the rest his Christianity is still the Christianity of Great Tew: 'There need little else to make us good Christians, than this thorough exercise of that Consideration of the continual Presence of Almighty God, and of our doing all that we do, and suffering all that we suffer in his sight . . .

'Let us not perplex ourselves with hard words of Justification and Merit, which signify no more, or less, than they who use them intend they should . . . God will find out a name for the Good we do' (p. 414). In the very last Psalm on which he commented before closing the embassy he affirmed his liberal creed: 'that any man should be punished meerly for Error in Opinion, seems to be not only against the uncontrollable Liberty of the Soul of Man, which cannot be restrained or constrained to other thoughts than what result from the natural Faculties of the Understanding, but against the Elements of Justice' (p. 539). Falkland and Chillingworth would have applauded.

XII

The Call to Paris

W<small>HEN</small> Hyde parted from Cottington outside Madrid he was looking forward to an indefinite period of scholarly and domestic retirement. He would be reunited with his wife and children and be able to look after her health and their education. He would be within easy distance of his old friend Secretary Nicholas at The Hague. He would once again have in Dr Morley the services of a domestic chaplain, a lack he had felt since the death in October 1650 of Dean Beale whom he had brought with him to Madrid. He would have his books. He would even have a little money.

Liberality where there is plenty is no more than decency. What is consistently admirable about Hyde is his entire freedom from meanness; even there is a generosity that grows bolder as the future grows blacker. While he was in Madrid there was trouble over his in-laws. It seems that the old Aylesburys did not settle down easily to émigré life and thought of going back to England. Were they not also a burden to their already hard-pressed son-in-law? Clarendon would have none of it. If they went back to 'that cursed country of ther owne . . . to the want of [bread] may be added want of liberty, besydes all other reproches . . .' As to his own impoverished state:

'If wee have any thinge, it will be ther dew to have parte of it, and if we are putt to begg, let us all begg . . . and devyde our begginge amongst us all. And whereas thou supposest that some may be willinge to helpe us who will not do it, whilst we are so many; in good earnest no necessity shall make me take any thinge of a man who makes a scruple of givings because wee would give parte of it to our Father and Mother. To conclude if they finde example and encouragement to goe, I cannot hinder them . . . by the grace of god, they shall not want, whilst I can make any shift, and thou shalt thyselfe wante at the same minute: for the meane tyme let us comforte ourselves with a hope that God Almighty hath a blessinge in store for us.'[1]

[1] BL Add. MS 34727 f.85 Hyde to his wife. December 5, 1650.

What makes this staunchness even nobler is that Frances's brother Will had betrayed their trust by decamping with the remittance that Hyde had with such a world of difficulty arranged for her support and had compounded his offence by taking service with the Commonwealth government. Hyde says nothing about this in his letters to her. There are one or two anxious inquiries as to why he never hears from Will but after the dreadful news not a word of reproach or recrimination. It is not from him that we know about it but from a brief though circumstantial account in a letter from Morley, then chaplain to the household, written in November 1650.[2] Will had, it appears, also sold his father's books and appropriated the proceeds.

Morley, who had been acting as chaplain to Lady Ormonde at Caen, had arrived at the moment when his support was most needed. 'In this condicion I found her . . . in March last, that is to say at least £200 in debt — an old father & mother, an aunt, a sister, 4 children & as many more as come in all to 19, to find clothes & provide for, without anything in present or any probability for the future, to support this great charge, which cannot with any possible thrift be maintained or defrayed in this very dear place, under £500 p.a. sterling, for I find the weekly charge of what belongs to the belly only to come *communibus septimanis* [taking one week with another] to £6, besides paying house-rent, clothing & physic, which last only hath cost her at least £30 for herself & family.'

Morley, kindest of men, gave her all he could 'viz. £20' and obtained a promise of £200 from one of Hyde's friends who in the end went away 'without effecting any part of his undertaking . . . Besides this she had at several times £50 from her husband's sister in England & £40 from an unknown friend there.'

It is rare indeed to find such a lucid, convincing and detailed statement of émigré finances. It is clear enough that the Hydes knew what it was to be poor and to live under the perpetual anxiety of commitments which seemed always to exceed the most optimistic estimate of future resources. Yet, somehow, they managed. They even bought books and had their portraits painted. Living beyond one's means seems to have been in the seventeenth century the rule of life, both public and private. In the Spain of Philip IV, the England of Charles I, the Commonwealth, Cromwell, Charles II, how often one finds the spending ministers bewailing the mountains of debt and the total absence of cash or credit to keep the show on the road. Yet the curtain always went up. Perhaps Clarendon's serene faith in the blessings held in store owed something to the financial optimism of his age.

The return journey, so eagerly begun, proved long and exhausting.

[2] Printed in *Theologian & Ecclesiastic* ed. W. Nelson Clarke, vii (1849), 125.

It began well with a visit of a whole day to the great university at Alcala 'where the college and other buildings made by the cardinal Ximenes are well worth seeing'[3]; two days were passed in civil entertainment by the Viceroy of Navarre in the palace at Pamplona and then the gout struck. No litter was available for crossing the Pyrenees, so it was mule-back again. 'The truth is,' he admitted to Frances a month before setting out, 'I am too old, and it may be too fatt, to ryde post.'[4] Gout made it painful to ride at all. On arriving at Bayonne he took to his bed for '. . . ten days under the Phisicion's hands and was then put in a litter more like a dead than a living man for Bourdeaux, where I again committed myself to the care of a Phisicion, & stayd another ten days there, when I considered myself to be very fitt for the continuance of my journey & I must confess I endured it very well & mended every day in it'.[5] So he wrote from Paris on April 29, a week after his arrival there. But the good effects of his treatment at Bordeaux by 'Dr Lopez, a very learned Jew'[6] were undone by an hour's interview with Henrietta Maria. The gout returned with such violence that a week later he was still 'stretched out upon my Bed, not able to sett either foote to the grounde'. A week later it was still too bad for him to do more than scrawl 'my deere little rogue, thy owne E.H.' at the end of a long dictated letter to Frances. But he was getting better. In a day or two he hoped 'to be able with the helpe of my fyne new crutches to walke up & downe the chamber, & then it will not be long before I have strength to goe abroad, which God willing shall quickly bring me to thee: God knows with what impatience I desire that happynesse'.[7] Already he had Lady Browne, the ambassador's wife, 'at worke in bespeaking bands & handkerchers, though under your favour your instructions are conceived very obscure & imperfect'. Would she send the hat-sizes of the boys 'and . . . likewise the size of thy father's hat'? Suggestions for presents for her mother and her aunt would also be welcome.

By late June the family were happily reunited. On leaving Madrid Hyde had succeeded in obtaining letters from the King of Spain and Don Luis de Haro granting him not only freedom of movement and residence in any Spanish possession but also the privileges due to an ambassador. On his way to Antwerp he called on the Archduke, Governor of the Netherlands, in Brussels and secured the right, not easily obtained in the dominions of his most Catholic Majesty, to the public ministrations of a clergyman of the Church of England. His chapel at Antwerp was frequented by a number of Royalist exiles including the Marquis of Newcastle and his brother Sir Charles Cavendish, whose combination of intellectual distinction and charm of character with a

3 *Life* VI, 7.   4 *Bath MSS* ii, 95.   5 Clar. MS 42 f.52.
6 *Life* VI, 7.   7 *Bath MSS* ii, 96.

143

puny physique recalls, in Clarendon's description, his old friends Falkland and Godolphin. 'The chancellor was now at a little rest again with his own family in Antwerp; and had time to be vacant to his own thoughts and books; and in the interval to enjoy the conversation of many worthy persons of his own nation, who had chosen that place to spend the time of their banishment in.'[8] This is the nearest that he can bring himself to the pure, unashamed idleness that Fox and Disraeli were to find so refreshing. He resumed briefly his *Reflections on the Psalms* though he did not return to the manuscript of the *History*. But it seems a fair inference that the *History* was in the forefront of his thoughts. The presence of Newcastle and other prominent Royalists was doubtless put to good use (he had, in fact, no high opinion of that nobleman's abilities, remarking in a letter to Nicholas that he was as fitted to be a bishop as a military commander). Above all he was anxious to extract the priceless ore from that mine of information, Secretary Nicholas. He had written to him when he knew he was leaving Madrid, suggesting that Nicholas should move to Antwerp so that they could see each other every day.[9] Nicholas countered that Antwerp was too expensive and suggested Wesel in North Germany.

Before Hyde could settle down to writing history he had, however, one important and delicate mission to discharge. Henrietta Maria was alarmed and distressed by the headstrong conduct of her second son, James, Duke of York, who had been flattered by his own courtiers into assuming the independence befitting the heir to the throne, and had left Paris, first for Brussels and then for The Hague. 'Never little family was torn into so many pieces and factions.' Charles II and his mother were not on good terms; but before leaving for Scotland he had told his brother to stay with her and obey her instructions in everything except religion. The Queen antagonised him, as she had his elder brother, by using his financial dependence on her to keep him on too tight a rein. In the confusion of war the Duke and his Governor, Lord Byron, had been separated. Hyde's old but far from easy-going friend Sir John Berkeley had been appointed as his substitute after the Duke's escape from England. As soon as Byron was known to be on his way to Paris Berkeley's interest in encouraging his young master to strike out on his own became urgent. He had, according to Clarendon, already done his best to lessen the Duke's esteem of him. Off they went, in spite of Henrietta Maria's entreaties and commands, and in no time at all Berkeley had involved James in a grotesquely unsuitable marriage negotiation with the illegitimate daughter of the Duke of Lorraine. Whatever Hyde might think of Henrietta Maria's judgment it could hardly be as erratic as that. He therefore undertook to use his best

---

[8] *Life* VI, 29.   [9] *Clar. SP* iii, 27.

efforts to persuade James to return to Paris. To this end he prepared for a journey to The Hague, where James had gone to stay with his sister, the Princess of Orange, only to be forestalled by the news that James had moved, conveniently but for no discernible purpose, to Breda. There the Chancellor visited him and seems easily to have persuaded him to return to Paris.

Clarendon's account of all this,[10] written when James had been his own son-in-law for ten years, is of interest in view of this very fact. The sketch of the young Duke is drawn with more sharpness than affection. 'The Duke himself was so young, that he was rather delighted with the journeys he had made, than sensible that he had not entered on them with reason enough; and they had fortified him with a firm resolution, never to acknowledge that he had committed any error . . . he was not above fourteen years of age, and backward enough for that age.' The judgment is very likely true but the mathematics, as usual, are wrong. James was within a month or two of his eighteenth birthday. On his way to Paris he accompanied Hyde to Antwerp. Anne, his future wife, was then fourteen and a half, an age at which many of her contemporaries were married, or at least betrothed. Her vivacity and good looks were soon to attract notice. In May 1653, when she was appointed a maid of honour to the Princess of Orange, her aunt Barbara Aylesbury wrote to Hyde that 'the unkind gerle hath robed me of all my Galants'.[11] Three months later he received, through a third party, a request 'to address the fair young lady, his daughter in marriage' from a young Shropshire squire, whose widowed mother had recently married the notorious Parliamentarian Serjeant Glynne, 'yet much beter affected, as he sayth, than her husband to the King and his cause . . . Mr Thomas Lawley is not yet 19 yeares of age but a proper handsome gent well mined and well inclined for ought I perceive'. His mother 'had placed him upon trial with Mr Shaw of Antwerp [the merchant on whose advances so many exiles depended], intending if he liked that profession to bind him for 8 yeares, but his spirits will not stoop to it and since this passion of love hath possessed him he dislikes all there'.[12] His overtures were indignantly rejected.

By the middle of September 1651 it was known that Royalist arms had been irretrievably defeated at Worcester and that the King was a fugitive. For two months nobody knew where he was or even whether he were alive or dead. Even Hyde was not philosopher enough to detach himself from present anxieties and uncertainties in the solitude of authorship. He still behaved as though he were preparing to retire to a life of study. He wrote to Nicholas à propos of their joint retreat: 'I have been over at Leyden, & though the town be not unpleasant &

10 *Life* VI, 16.   11 Clar. MS 45 f.367.   12 *ibid* 46 f.187.

some walks about it very good I have always taken it to be the most unhealthy place in those parts besydes some unquietness by reason of the Schollers: the Hague is much better sure than Leyden, though not to be compared with Antwerp.'[13] Just over a fortnight later, on November 7, he heard of the King's safe arrival in Paris with Lord Wilmot. Next day he heard that the King had sent for him and Nicholas to join him at once. The contemplative life was once again to be abandoned for the active.

For the next fifteen years Hyde was to be Charles II's chief minister. The duration and the vicissitudes of the experience call to mind the vows of the marriage service: 'in sickness and in health, for richer, for poorer.' Bad as things were when Hyde took over they were to get a great deal worse before the triumph of 1660. Why, at this juncture, was he summoned? What were the strengths, and what the weaknesses, of his position at the end of 1651?

The reason for his recall can only have been the young King's recognition that this verbose old moraliser had got it right when everyone else had got it wrong. Hyde had foretold the consequences of the Scottish venture, undertaken in bad faith by both contracting parties, and had warned that English Royalism, the one political force indispensable to the regaining of the throne, would never rally to so tainted a cause. His predictions had proved true in every particular. As to his discretion and his efficiency in the conduct of affairs, Charles had seen Hyde at work and was, as a later minister of his observed, a shrewd judge of men. Two other recommendations perhaps carried weight: he would neither ask nor accept honours or post-dated grants of places in the royal gift and he was not, emphatically not, likely to give an inch under the incessant pressure of Henrietta Maria.

For his part Hyde had the strength that comes from knowing one's own mind and from the consciousness of an integrity that had been tested by unpopularity and rejection. He had the good opinion of those whose opinion he valued. 'I have for these many years observed in no Minister of State that hath been employed in his Majesty's or his blessed father's time greater integrity and ability, nor that hath gone on better maxims of religion and policy,' wrote Nicholas to Ormonde on December 13, 1651.[14] Ormonde himself had only lately arrived in France and had just missed meeting Hyde when he passed through Paris on his way from Madrid to Antwerp. In spite of Clarendon's claim in the *History*[15] that 'there had been a great acquaintance' between them as young men 'so that when they now met at Paris, they met as old friends', it is perfectly clear from Ormonde's letters to Nicholas and

[13] *ibid* 42 f.167 October 21, 1651.   [14] *Nicholas Papers* i, 281.
[15] XIII, 121.

to Hyde himself that he had never met him and was keenly anxious to do so.[16] His views and the theological grounds from which he derived them exactly correspond to Hyde's.

'. . . All imaginable trials for the recovery of the royal interest have been made and failed . . . but Hee that for our sins hath covered us with this confusion is able in a moment to bring greater things by lesse probable means to passe, & his not blessing all our endevours in soe just a cause I would fain understand to bee a command to stand still & see the salvation Hee will work for us . . .'[17] There were friends to whom Clarendon was closer in affection but during the whole course of his life it may be doubted whether there was any man to whom he was closer in sympathy.

James Butler, twelfth Earl, first Marquis and first Duke (as he later became) of Ormonde, had travelled a very different road from Hyde's. Born to a great name and estates that enabled him to contribute nearly a million pounds (the computer flickers in incredulity at modern conversion) to the Royalist cause in Ireland between 1641 and 1660,[18] he was a year his junior. To the end of a long life a pattern of elegance in manners and dress and a notable horseman, his youth had been spent in the world of sport and fashion. When young Mr Hyde was building up his practice at the bar and cultivating the acquaintance of literary London, young Lord Thurles (as he then was) impressed his contemporaries by riding from Edinburgh to Ware in three days — it was said he could easily have completed the journey to London had he so wished.[19] Like Hyde's friend Falkland, he inherited early and like him he experienced the conflict of Protestantism and Catholicism from his upbringing:

'. . . My father & mother lived and died papists: and only I, by God's merciful providence, was educated in the true protestant religion, from which I never swerved towards either extreme, not when it was most dangerous to profess it & most advantageous to quit it. I reflect not upon any who have held another course, but will charitably hope that though their changes happened to be always to the prosperous side, yet they were made by the force of present conviction. My brothers and sisters . . . were very fruitful & very obstinate (they will call it constant) in their way . . . But . . . I am taught by nature, & also

---

[16] e.g. his letter to Hyde from Caen dated May 29, 1651, printed in Carte *Original Letters* ii, 5. See also Hyde's letter to Ormonde dated March 14, 1645 printed in Carte *Ormond* vi, 268–9: 'I have not the vanity to believe myselfe in any degree known or remembered by your lordship, though I have had sometimes the honour to wayte on your lordship in London, but I have a great ambition to bee received by you, as one who holds your Lp in singular admiration.'

[17] *Nicholas Papers* i, 276.

[18] Carte *Ormond* iv, 418. The figure given is £868,000.

[19] *ibid* i, 18.

by instruction, that difference of opinion concerning matters of religion dissolves not the obligations of nature; and . . . I own, not only that I have done but that I will do, my relations of that or any other persuasion all the good I can . . .'[20]

This profession, made as an old man, is like everything else about him, true from youth to age. 'I think his whole life was a straight line, if ever a man in the world's were so.' The judgment is the more telling in that it comes from a highly intelligent and critical member of the next generation, Sir Robert Southwell.[21] One of Strafford's last requests before his execution was that his Garter might be conferred on Ormonde (characteristically he refused it on the double ground of his own youth and of the value such an honour put in the King's gift at so difficult a time). Yet in May 1642, when Hyde was preparing to leave London and join the King at York, the Commons were voting Ormonde a jewel worth £500 and sending a messenger to the House of Lords to invite their support in pressing the King to make him a Knight of the Garter. Few members of that most honourable and noble order can have had their claims advanced from such opposite points of the political compass.[22] Fewer still can have so well deserved it.

The two men met at last in Paris at Christmas 1651. As usual Hyde had had a hellish journey, culminating in a prostrating attack of gout. Although the summons to Paris reached him early in November he did not set out till the middle of the next month, arriving in Paris on Christmas Day. He had delayed his departure in the hope of co-ordinating his arrangements and dividing his expenses of travel with Nicholas, who had also been bidden to Paris, together wth two younger members of the exiled court who were returning from The Hague. Since one of them was Lady Anne Douglas it is possible that she might have been to The Hague to see her mother, the Countess of Morton, off to Scotland. The date on which she left Henrietta Maria's court is not known but she was certainly in Scotland by the end of 1652.[23] By mid-December it was clear that Nicholas was not well enough to face the journey, so Hyde travelled with the other two.

Nicholas for all his staunchness of character was apt to be tetchy, even querulous. He was forever accusing Hyde of keeping things from him, of pretending to value him more than he really did, of having more funds than he had, even of living more comfortably. At this time Hyde had his suspicions that Nicholas's illness was what we should call psychosomatic. He knew that he was depressed by the Queen's hostility. Indeed after he had arrived in Paris Nicholas wrote to tell him that when his money ran out he was going to go back to England 'and

[20] *ibid* iv, 572–3.   [21] *ibid* i, x.
[22] *ibid* i, 280; v, 310.   [23] *Cal. Clar SP* ii, 171.

bid them do with me as they list. If the King cannot protect an honest man in his honest ways from his mother's unjust displeasure, what honest, faithful men will serve him?'[24] It is very rare that Hyde, himself by all accounts a choleric and irritable man, replies in any but soothing terms, except for his occasional exasperation at Nicholas's mania for enciphering matter involving no requirement of secrecy. Neither Hyde nor Ormonde doubted for a moment that he was the wisest and most experienced counsellor available to them as well as having the best intelligence, obtained from a high level and at a high price, from the usurping government in London.

The triple alliance of Hyde, Ormonde and Nicholas was to outlast their service to the King and to reappear in everything that Clarendon wrote about the history of his time. At the moment of its forging in Paris Hyde wrote to Nicholas on January 13, 1652, 'In my life I never knew a worthier person than my Lord of Ormond, nor more impossible to be swayed or guided by any but public and noble rules, & to the best ends; & with this he loves and esteems you heartily.'[25] When he wrote he was still feeling wretched: '. . . since my coming to Paris . . . I have not been well one hour.' As soon as he had recovered he pressed Nicholas to abandon his scheme of retiring to England and to come and take the Secretary's place, else 'the King will be forced to make some unworthy choice'. The plea is reinforced by the use of Ormonde's name.

What in fact happened was that for the whole of the next two and a half years that the Court remained in France Nicholas, residing in Holland, retained the office of Secretary while Hyde did the work. At first the reason was undoubtedly Nicholas's poor health and increasing age. A winter journey through country that was either being fought over or else in the forlorn and dangerous condition that constant warfare induces was not lightly to be undertaken. Nonetheless, in spite of occasional half-hearted expressions of a readiness to make the journey, no serious move was made to do so when the days lengthened. Perhaps he came to see, and Hyde tacitly to assent, that he was both better off and more useful where he was. He had, what Hyde so sorely missed, the present support of a devoted wife and family. He was not distracted by the intrigues of jealous courtiers. At The Hague he was in one of the best listening posts in Europe and at the point of departure for clandestine activities in Scotland. He was, moreover, increasingly doubtful that France was the right place for the court to be.

Hyde had always been of that opinion and soon became even more passionately convinced of it. At first he was so delighted with the improvement in the King's application to his duties, and with the

---

[24] *Nicholas Papers* i, 285.   [25] *Clar. SP* iii, 42.

unqualified support he seemed ready to give to the policies that he had championed, that he was happy to lose himself in the work to be done. 'It is now but newly day break & yet within less than this hour I shall be troubled with so many people that I must give over writing, & the King requires us to be with him in Council by eight of the clock . . . I am obliged to keep good hours, for if I do not go to bed by ten, how shall I rise by five?' he wrote to Nicholas barely a month after he had settled in.[26] But only a few weeks later the old frustrations of serving a Stuart sovereign had knocked the gilt off the gingerbread: 'Oh Mr Secretary, this last act of the King's in making Mr Crofts a gentleman of the bed-chamber, so contrary to what he assured me, makes me mad & weary of my life, as not knowing hereafter how to be confident of anything. Upon my word I desire nothing so much as honestly to get into a corner to enjoy my wife and children, and to say my prayers & study, for I shall never be able to indure this kind of life.'[27] Crofts was the Jermyn type of Royalist émigré who thought the maintenance of their own luxurious style of life a sufficient, indeed self-evident, raison d'être. He had a comfortable country house near Paris to which the King could retire when he needed to recruit his health and spirits. To honour such contemptible self-indulgence when men were every day risking their lives and losing their lands and fortunes was not only cynical and frivolous: it was foolish.

The first two months of Sir Edward Hyde's experience as Charles II's first minister encapsulate the fifteen years that were to follow. No one could have had a shrewder, saner, easier-tempered, more approachable master than the King: no one could have enjoyed a more confidential relationship, cemented, it would have seemed, by years of daily intimacy. Yet it was from start to finish impossible for Clarendon to have any confidence in it at all. It was not that Charles II was disloyal to, or even secretly distrusted, his great servant. On the contrary, when attempts were made to displace or discredit him, he shewed him decisive support. It was rather that he appeared to want both conviction and principle. His character perplexes, enrages, excites and amuses because it is never in focus. Both those who admire and those who deplore him seem agreed that he set a high value on the wise and the good and saw through rogues and fools, though he might not care to reveal, still less to act on, these insights.[28] Hyde was the first but by no means the last of the able and perspicacious men who served him to be baffled by these discontinuities. Suddenly, for no discernible reason, the chain of policy breaks. It is of all deficiencies the most disconcerting. Laziness, malice, dishonesty all have their own logic and

[26] *ibid* 45 February 3, 1652.   [27] *ibid* 59 April 13, 1652.
[28] For a fuller exposition of all this see my *The Image of the King*, 151–3.

can, to an extent, be allowed for. Even stupidity, by definition unpredictable, yet shows its own warning light.

'As not knowing hereafter how to be confident of anything.' At the very outset of this long partnership Hyde had grasped its chief and abiding hazard. Yet at the very end, even after it had been dissolved and he had been, as he thought, unfairly disgraced and, as few could doubt, treated with the basest ingratitude, he still appears to have retained the same fundamental conviction of the King's goodwill that he began with. '. . . the truth is, it is our parts to use our utmost endeavour to prevent the King's doing anything that is amiss, but when it is done to make the best of it . . . for the King is an excellent man, & if he hath good men about him he will answer all the expectation the world can have of him,' he wrote to Nicholas in May 1652.[29] Just over a year later he told the same correspondent: '. . . the King loves both you & me, & thinks us very honest & useful servants, yet he will sometimes use another of whom he hath not so good an opinion as well or better than either of us.'[30]

Belief in the King's goodwill was necessary to Hyde's sanity. As he came to recognise towards the end of his life, he shared Archbishop Laud's unfortunate aptitude for putting people's backs up. 'It will always be too visible in my face to all standers by (which is a great infirmity) what company I keep out of choice and friendship & what out of obligation & necessity . . . you know my fault . . . I am too open, too plain.'[31] To this want of courtliness (a shortcoming not evident in the letters he wrote to people he did not like) only a part of the hostility he felt round him can be attributed. Jealousy, resentment, outright opposition to everything he stood for were widespread in a circle which as he himself observed had nothing to do. The Queen had always seen him as her most formidable opponent. His recent usefulness over the Duke of York had so far recommended him as to permit her to offer quarters for his wife and family in the Louvre in exchange for toeing her line in the King's Council. The inevitable refusal confirmed her enmity, now strangely reinforced by Hyde's old friend Sir John Berkeley, lately in her bad books as chief among the evil counsellors of the Duke of York. Berkeley was certainly nettled by Hyde's part in that affair. But what had infuriated him, had indeed made him an implacable and lifelong enemy, was Hyde's meddling in his unsuccessful courtship of the Countess of Morton. Vain and quarrelsome as Berkeley was, a much milder man would have been exasperated by the vast letter that Hyde felt moved to write to him from Antwerp on July 28, 1651.[32] Prosy generality succeeds to prosy generality. A page and a

---

[29] *Clar. SP* iii, 65.   [30] *ibid* 170.
[31] *ibid* 45, 94.   [32] Clar. MS 42 f.119.

half, say a thousand words, are taken up on the duties of friends to give advice and on the caution to be exercised in matrimony. 'A man is not a friend because he means and wishes very well, no more than a man is married because he is in love.' The argumentation, prolix and contrived, is substantially the same as in the *Essay on Friendship* written in Montpellier in 1670. As if that were not enough another page and a half are devoted to the disadvantages of acting precipitately. Berkeley had already showed the whites of his eyes at Hyde's criticism of the opportunist policy that had led the King to accept the label of Scotch Presbyterianism. 'According to your singular & accustomed justice, you mingle heaven and earth together in your complaints against me, and the rest of your servants, & are all this while so overweening, as you imagine we should esteem those invectives favours,' he had written in March 1650,[33] robustly rejecting the holier-than-thou pretensions of men who claim that they are governed solely by principle. In a later letter he criticises temperately but trenchantly Hyde's fundamental proposition that the King's case, since it rests on the law of the land, cannot admit of concession or bargaining. He warns his friend against the high moral line. 'There is a raging disease amongst us of sainting each others proselytes & condemning those mutually that differ in opinion with us . . . But I know you are so free from this infirmity . . . as well knowing that it is as impossible for you to cease loving me, as it is for me not to continue to love & honour you, though our senses in particular things disagree, as they do at this present.'[34] It was a shot across his bows that Hyde chose to disregard.

Other minor courtiers arched their backs and hissed. Lord Thomas Wentworth wrote him an abusive letter, accusing him of lowering him in the King's esteem. Lord Gerard wished to challenge him to a duel. Senior and more powerful figures went about the business with a little more finesse. The Earl of Norwich with the suavity of a courtier who had charmed James I, Charles I and Henrietta Maria wrote to Nicholas: 'Sir Edward Hyde . . . is certenly a most unfortunat man . . . for you will never find that any party, be it Presbiter, Independent or Cavalier, will be contented to come under his government.'[35] Nonetheless he and Hyde appear to have liked each other. Hyde told Nicholas that he loved him 'with all my heart, though he be faulty to me without the least cause, & is so unsteady & unsecret and unthrifty'.[36] Such was certainly not the case with Sir Edward Herbert, the Attorney-General soon to be made Lord Keeper, and Sir Robert Long, Nicholas's junior colleague as Secretary of State. Both men

[33] *Clar. SP* ii, 530.   [34] *ibid* 540.
[35] *Nicholas Papers* ii, 320. June 1, 1655.   [36] *Clar. SP* iii, 92, August 30, 1652.

seem to have hated Hyde as bitterly as they opposed his policies. Both stood high in the favour of Henrietta Maria.

Herbert had been known to Hyde since those far-off days when they had both acted with Bulstrode Whitelocke as joint impresarios for the Inns of Court Masque that was to wipe away the stain of Prynne's *Histriomastix*. He had come up against him again when the Court was at Oxford in 1643 and had found him then the man whose conversation was most like sense without being it as was humanly possible.[37] Subsequent experience confirmed this impression. 'Of all the men in the world I cannot understand Mr Attorney, nor will any compliance with him serve his turn, for he hath no opinion, but lives by perpetual contradiction & opposition of all other men's opinions.'[38]

Long was a well-connected Exchequer official of more than dubious reputation. There had been accusations not only of corruption but of private and possibly treacherous correspondence with the enemy. It was the open revival of one of these charges that led to his being forbidden the Council Board. On the maxim that attack is the best form of defence he ascribed this to the malice of Hyde, whom he was unwise enough to accuse of being in Cromwell's pay, indeed to assert that he had actually called in on Cromwell on his way back from Madrid in 1651.[39] These absurd, and easily disproved, accusations were eagerly seized on and publicised by another old enemy from Hyde's days in the south-west, Sir Richard Grenville. Long, perhaps out of the prudent cowardice of the born liar, had diffused these rumours rather than risk open accusation in the spring of 1652. Grenville, who was not in Paris, only heard of them a year later, but instantly brought formal charges against Hyde in a letter to the King. Another six months elapsed before before the matter was heard before the Council, during which time Herbert and Jermyn attempted, unsuccessfully, to have Hyde suspended until his reputation was cleared. In dismissing the accusations in January 1654 the King forbade both Long and Grenville the Court. Undeterred, Long then combined with Lord Gerard to report private conversations of a year earlier in which Hyde had spoken with his usual force and freedom of the King's indolence and love of pleasure. This again was formally brought before the Council. Hyde, with the uprightness that best became him, admitted that he might very likely have used the words alleged against him. The King crushed the charge by saying that the expressions were no more, indeed rather less, than Hyde habitually used to him in reproving his conduct to his face and that he had never taken them as offensive or disloyal.

So handsome and candid an avowal of trust might seem to be

[37] *Life* VI, 27.   [38] *Clar. SP* iii, 125, December 14, 1652.
[39] Lister, i, 379–80, iii, 63.

conclusive. But was anything, noble or base, wise or weak, ever conclusive about Charles II? Even Hyde for all his heroically charitable, steadfastly asserted belief in the fundamental goodness of his master's nature did not think so. 'In a word the King is thought to be too favourable to me, and truly he is more angry at the combination than I wish, but on my conscience he knows more of it than I do.' Hyde's words at the end of a letter to Nicholas reporting this affair contain the same sense made explicit over Crofts' appointment: 'As not knowing hereafter how to be confident of anything.' Not having Frances's courage and loyalty to sustain him made the two and a half years in Paris seem ever longer and more trying.

It was also the time of his bitterest poverty. Throughout the exile he exclaims, often in half-amused astonishment, at the emptiness of his pockets and at the impossibility of any relief. But in Paris even the little that there was, in the shape of a contemptuously small pension from the French Court to the King, was channelled through Henrietta Maria who was quite unscrupulous in cutting off this trickle if she thought it would give her bargaining power. Even the meals her son ate at her table were charged against his allowance. For militant Church of England men like Hyde who stood in the way of her policies the husks that the swine did eat were the appropriate diet. He was in fact entirely dependent on remittances from friends and relations in England and, most important of all, on what his credit could raise locally. Besides, indeed above, his own necessities there were the expenses incurred in discharging his duties: 'I have not had a Crown these two months,' he wrote to Nicholas on November 22, 1652, 'but borrow, that is Edgeman [his faithful secretary] borrows (for so God help me I have no credit) every week two crowns to fetch my letters from the post (they come to no less) & to buy paper and ink, and my wife is in the meantime in as sad a condition as can be imagined.'[40] Nicholas in reply complained of his own want of means to carry out his responsibilities. 'I have as much reason as any man living to join with you in that thrift,' answered his friend, 'yet I cannot avoid the constant expense of 7 or 8 livres the week for postage of letters, which I borrow scandalously out of my friends' pockets . . . those which concerned my own private affairs would be received for 10 sous a week, so that all the rest are for the King, from whom I have not received one penny since I came hither . . . & yet it is to no purpose to complain, though I . . . am cold for want of clothes and fire, & owe for all the meat I have eaten these three months and to a poor woman who is not longer able to trust [i.e. give him credit], and my poor family at Antwerp (which breaks my heart), is in as sad a state as I am, and the King as either of us, being in

40 *Clar. SP* iii, 120.

these very personal distresses, yet I am not able to avoid and you must not be angry if I put you sometimes to the charge of a single letter, which it is not possible for me to decline . . .'[41]

Six months later at midsummer 1653 things were no better: 'five or six of us eat together one meal a day for a pistole a week, but all of us owe for God knows how many weeks to the poor woman that feeds us. I believe my Lord of Ormond hath not had five livres in his purse this month & hath fewer clothes of all sorts than you have, and yet I take you to be no gallant.'[42] Hyde and Ormonde were living at this time in the Palais Royal, occasionally moving to St Germain, just to the west of Paris, when the French court required their quarters. This is one of the very few allusions Hyde makes, and that only indirectly, to the humiliation of perpetual shabbiness in the smartest place in the world. He was still his father's son and thought honest poverty no shame. 'Keep up your spirits, and take heed of sinking under that burden you never kneeled to take up. Our innocence begets our cheerfulness; and that again will be a means to secure the other. Whoever grows too weary and impatient of the condition he is in will too impatiently project to get out of it; and that, by degrees, will shake, or baffle, or delude his innocence. We have no reason to blush for the poverty which is not brought upon us by our own faults.'[43] The words he had written to Nicholas six years earlier at the beginning of his exile were his maxim still.

[41] *ibid* 124.   [42] *ibid* 174.
[43] *ibid* ii, 310 quot. Lister i, 377.

XIII

Policy and Practice

W<small>HAT</small>, in these two and a half unhappy years in Paris, was Hyde trying
to do? How, hampered by poverty, opposed by the Queen, sniped at
by the men of pleasure who surrounded the King, did he set about it?
The policies and priorities that he worked out there remained, barring
the few swerves always and everywhere incident to the conduct of
affairs, constant until he and his master returned to the acclamations of
their countrymen in 1660.

The enemy, until death removed him in September 1658, was
Cromwell. Although he did not assume the position of Head of State
until 1654 he had established himself in supreme power by executing
the King and crushing the Levellers in 1649. The subjugation of
Ireland and Scotland had reinforced his impregnability and had
destroyed any hope of maintaining a Royalist redoubt behind which an
army might be embodied. If Cromwell was to be got rid of, there were
only three ways to do it: a general rising, a coup d'état or assassination.
They were not, of course, mutually exclusive.

Almost every Royalist scheme other than Clarendon's would have
made these secondary to, or dependent on, an invasion by foreign
troops. It was the spectacular failure of the first of these projects, the
Scottish, that had brought Hyde from the sidelines to the centre of the
field. But there were still a host of schemes for enlisting the help of the
Pope, Cardinal Mazarin, the Duke of Lorraine, the Dutch, the
Spaniards — all at a price naturally. Since the price necessarily in-
fringed either the territorial sovereignty or the religious laws that
formed part of the civil constitution of the country, Hyde would have
none of it. The core of the Royalist position, in his steadily repeated
view, was that these things were not negotiable. If, for instance, the
laws against the Roman Catholics were to be relaxed that could only be
done by the King in Parliament, not by either acting on their own. If
the proposition was, as the Queen certainly advocated, that Roman

Catholicism should become the official religion of the Royal House then the Royalist party would melt in the night. Foreign assistance in money, ships, arms, was eminently desirable. He himself had gone to Madrid to try to obtain it. His old colleague Colepeper had been strikingly successful on a similar mission to Moscow. Even the sybaritic Crofts had brought back from Poland a small surplus over his own travelling expenses. No time was lost in sending a special embassy to the Imperial Diet with the same objective, though perhaps the envoy chosen, the expensive and epicurean Lord Wilmot, now raised to the earldom of Rochester, owed this agreeable appointment to the King's friendship rather than to Hyde's judgment.

All this was well enough. No hare-brained, half-baked military adventures. No short cuts that only ended in cutting off the ground on which the Royalist cause stood. But was it not easy for critics to damn such principles as a façade for futility and inertia? Hyde's profound insight into the process of history as an organic movement that rejected political implants left his strategy entirely exposed to such an accusation. Waiting on events, allowing a situation to develop, may be the path of wisdom but can hardly be an easy policy to sell. The character and habits of the King made it harder still. Cromwell's reported remark to Lord Broghill who had proposed a solution to all constitutional problems by marrying Charles to one of the Protector's daughters — 'He is so damnably debauched he would undo us all' — is a sample of the reputation he was beginning to earn. Action, even unsuccessful action, would do much to retrieve this. Hyde himself recognised as much. 'It is too true & cannot be denied that the King is exceedingly fallen in reputation, which cannot be recovered but by some bold attempt, besides I must tell you he is so much given to pleasure that if he stay here he will be undone; add to this the usage of the French towards him is not to be endured.'[1] This was written on June 27, 1653. But what 'bold attempt' was feasible? In February of that year during the war between the English Commonwealth and the Dutch Charles had volunteered his services as a naval commander[2] but the offer had not been taken up. At the same time preparations were being made in Rotterdam for landing General Middleton in Scotland to head a rising in the Highlands. At best only a guerrilla campaign was envisaged but it might offer the King an opportunity of sharing the hardships and dangers of his supporters. 'This I will assure you,' wrote Hyde to Middleton on March 28, 1653, 'that rather than ly still heare and dreame out his tyme, nay if he finde he can no other way to give the Rebells worke, our master will keepe you company in the Highlands of Scotland.'[3] In fact it hardly started before it ended in complete disaster. Both Middleton

---

[1] *Clar. SP* iii, 173.   [2] *ibid* 141.   [3] Clar. MS 45, f.193.

and his equally indestructible courier, Peter Mews, a former don and future bishop, were lucky to escape with their lives.

For either a general rising or a coup d'état, according to Hyde's understanding of historical forces, time and the movement of opinion in England were required. God would work his purpose out if his servants submitted their wills to his. This did not of course excuse inaction. It was the clear duty of the government in exile to maintain the most extensive and immediate contact with those people and those bodies of opinion through whom this great work might be achieved. That was the most important single task of Hyde's years as Charles II's minister. But, before turning to this major pre-occupation, what of the minor question of assassination? Was such a method open to a gentleman and a Christian? Could it conceivably be reconciled with an organic view of history developing itself as an expression of the will of God?

On the evidence of his own letters Hyde would have answered 'yes'. Twice he countenanced, even actively supported, attempts to assassinate Cromwell.[4] Similarly in private correspondence he condoned the murders of the Commonwealth ambassadors, Dorislaus at The Hague and Ascham at Madrid, by Royalist exiles. Publicly he was bound to deplore them, especially the second in which a member of his own diplomatic mission had taken part. Any competent lawyer — and Hyde was more than that — could construct an argument on the basis that a régime which had defied the law and religion by killing the Lord's Anointed had put itself outside all law. Like the pirate on the high seas it was *hostis humani generis*, fair game for anyone to knock on the head. But Hyde was not only a lawyer. He was also a philosopher, a historian and a devout Christian who had made a critical examination of the political and moral controversies of Europe. As a controversialist he must have known — none better — the scholastic tag *'dolus latet in generalibus'*, the catch is concealed in inferring the general from the particular. As a historian no less than as a man of affairs he must have known how dubious were the moral credentials of almost any government if too minutely inspected and how destructive the principle of conducting international affairs on the basis of moral approbation. Yet the author of the *History of the Rebellion*, so justly admired for its magnanimity and its humanity, could write to Secretary Nicholas, 'But it is a worse and a baser thing that any man should appear in any part beyond sea, under character of an Agent from the Rebels & not have his throat cut.'[5]

---

[4] Lister, i, 425. It is even possible that Hyde was party to a plan to poison Oliver. His agent in Rome wrote to him on February 12, 1656, 'The powder for Sir Gilbert Talbot is given to Mr Allestree', *Cal. Clar. SP* iii, 252. Both Talbot and Allestree were daring secret agents.

[5] *Clar. SP* iii 144, February 20, 1653.

What are we to make of this? What would Falkland have thought of such an opinion? The bravoes who would break in and murder a man while he was at supper in an inn would have been out of place at Great Tew. Can one even imagine Hyde himself taking part in such a scene? The truth is that he was, and partly knew himself to be, a man of passion. Ready as he was to appeal to reason, sincere as he was in his hatred of war and violence, the warmth of his temper often led him into unfairness and inconsistency. 'God send me to deal with men of passion who will be angry when they are contradicted & provoked . . . An obstinate dulness is a temper there is no contending with.'[6] This opening sentence of a letter (to the King!) tells the reader a great deal about the man who wrote it and administers a salutary backhander to his biographer.

He was also not always as fastidious in the practice of political morality as in his professions of it. Trafficking in honours is not to be spoken of in the same breath as assassination or terrorism but the following story for all its triviality involves an interesting reversal of moral roles. Two years after the Court had left Paris, in October 1656, Hyde wrote to the King from Antwerp about a very rich Royalist living in the town who had fought in both Civil Wars and finally at Worcester, Charles II's only experience of battle. Although he went under the name of Sir William Harte he had not, as he confided to his friend and fellow Royalist Sir Richard Page, ever been knighted. In fact he did not even know who his father was. If the King could be prevailed on to rectify the position by dubbing him he was ready to offer '£100 & some other conveniencyes'. Sir Marmaduke Langdale, the ex-commander of the Northern Horse and head of an ancient recusant family, had recommended this plea to Hyde, who, it may be inferred, thought that £100 would be nice to have. By return of post Ormonde wrote, on the King's behalf, a stern refusal. '. . . the King will at no hand heare of knighting the gentleman you mention . . . saying that he being capable of shuch an imposture . . . is in nothing else to be credited & would make some unhansome use of it if it should be conferred upon him & so his ma^{tie} should be accessory to his cheates . . .' Hyde wrote back applauding the King's decision. (How much was it his, how much Ormonde's?) He had by this time sought out the man who 'denyes anything of imposture, professing that he is a Baronett & desyred the other as of right . . . the truth is I knowe not what to thinke of the man . . . he is a very odd composition & like nothinge I have seene: he seems not of partes to cozen anybody & his expenses are greate & discharged with ready money . . .'[7] How it was possible to be a Baronet if one did not know who one's father was is only one of the

---

[6] *ibid* 302.   [7] Clar. MS 52 ff.296, 301, 312.

mysteries of this strange episode. But it is diverting to see Hyde reproved by Charles II for impropriety.

A further instance involving double standards of moral judgment (of which there are many in the *History*) may be cited from the summer of 1657. A crew of Royalist émigrés reinforced by half-a-dozen ruffians from Bruges set out across the North Sea in an open boat, found their way into the mouth of the Thames and landed on the Isle of Thanet in the middle of the night. They then broke into the house of a rich city merchant, dragged him out of bed and kidnapped him. The old gentleman — he was seventy — was according to Hyde none the worse for his experiences and was tranquilly awaiting the payment of his ransom at Bruges. They would have taken his son too but for the entreaties of a wife who was expecting his child in a few days. Hyde praised their courtesy and approved the ransom of £1,000 — a huge sum in the mid-seventeenth century — payable in Bruges. They had already seized all the cash in the house amounting to some £500. Ormonde, to whom he reported these exploits, seems to have evinced less enthusiasm than his friend expected. 'Why have you no mind that we have any more such expeditions . . . are there any objections against it?' Hyde's inquiry seems curiously naive. It was not long before he was himself anxious to get out of the business as best he could. The 'old curmudgeon', in spite of threats of hanging, issued most indiscreetly in the King's name, refused to be bluffed.[8] The denunciatory thunderbolts that would have been hurled at such conduct on the part of a Cromwellian force can be easily imagined.

We may shake our heads and sigh over the inconsistency (to take the kindest view) of so high-minded a man. But before we flatter ourselves that we are holier than he we should remember that in his own family he had suffered outrages enough. His cousin Harry Hyde had been beheaded in 1651 for nothing more than having asserted his right to represent Charles II at Constantinople. The ambassador appointed by the Parliament had had him put aboard an English ship and sent back to London where he was found guilty of High Treason.[9] Clarendon had tried to dissuade him and thought the mission 'ridiculous'. But his cousin 'had a strange prejudice to Common Lawyers & trusted me with little of his disieres'.[10] Even uglier evidence that Hyde had not misjudged the capacity for cruelty and wickedness inherent in Cromwell's government comes from the end of the year 1656. His sister had gone down to stay in the country with his first wife's family. 'Suddenly upon a Sunday morning there came three armed men, two of them

[8] *Clar. SP* iii 354–5, and Clar. MS 56 f.39.
[9] R. W. Ramsey. *Studies in Cromwell's Family Circle* (1930), 181–194.
[10] Clar. MS 41 f.177.

messengers sent from the Councell of State . . .' They used violence on
her and took her off, in a state of shock, to Marlborough and then to
London. She was unable to eat and already, on the journey, showing
symptoms of nervous distress. Kept at first under arrest in the house of
one of her guards she was intensively interrogated. In a final coup, she
was woken up in the middle of the night and dragged off to prison.
The application of terror was too much for her. She lost her reason and
died a week later, not recognising her familiar priest who was allowed
to visit her when it was clear that she was dying.[11]

Personal experience, personal anxieties, can hardly be irrelevant to a
man's ideas. What Hyde tried to do, and more especially the means he
considered, may be better understood by taking such matters into
account. Assassination and reprisal have been first discussed not
because they were first in importance but because they appear so out of
character as to demand immediate examination. The principal aim of
Hyde's policy, the resuming of the ancient track so disastrously abandoned in 1641 without recourse either to foreign intervention or to
another civil war, is so evidently coherent with the evidence of what he
said and did and wrote as to require no such explanation. There
remained the question of means.

The first essential was not to dissipate or dishearten by clever, short-
term expedients the natural force of conservatism that such a policy
expressed. This aspect of Hyde's policy, which brought him into conflict at one time or another with almost all his fellow-exiles, has already
been sufficiently treated. It was essentially negative. The positive side
was to maintain in England itself a belief in the real, not remote, prospect of such a resumption and to make the presence of such a body of
opinion palpable. The conservative temper is often hard to distinguish
from a sluggish acceptance of things as they are. Yet Hyde's policy
depended on galvanising the one and shaming the other. At the
moment of decision, whose timing no one could foresee, an instant
appearance of armed strength would be needed. A secret structure of
military cadres must therefore be maintained and, if possible,
supplied with saddles, pistols and such easily concealed cavalry equip-
ment. Obviously it would be impossible to prepare a force capable of
taking on Cromwell's army. The assumption must be that that force
would have been in some way neutralised, either by divisions amongst
its own officers and men or by winning over a substantial part of it to
the Royal cause. All this required the maintaining of a considerable
underground organisation, with couriers, agents, networks, and the
rest of it. Such an organisation could also be employed to gather

---

[11] *ibid* 53 f.73, 56 f.132. Letter from Jane Silvester. The date September 29 must, I think, refer
to 1656.

intelligence and money as well as to initiate political diplomacy by testing the sympathies and loyalties of men prominent in government or the army. Many of those who would broadly have agreed with Hyde in 1640 were, after taking the opposite side in the war, beginning to think that they might agree with him again. And in the decade that had passed a lot of old faces had gone and new ones had appeared. Young men now in their early twenties had been boys of ten or eleven when the war broke out.

This consideration leads to the second, and more difficult, question raised by Hyde's policy. Granted that the Restoration was to be an all-English affair, with even the Scots and the Irish kept out if possible, would not the Royalist-Church of England bloc have to attract some other great body of politico-religious opinion — in the loose, unsatisfactory terminology of the day, either the Presbyterians or the Independents? Secretary Nicholas, Hyde's closest confidant, thought that they would and plumped for the Presbyterians. Hyde, on the whole, thought it much better to leave it to God and to the passage of time to unbecloud their eyes. But if such an alliance was necessary, a hypothetical admission, he would prefer the Independents, largely because such a union would be of its nature self-dissolving. The Independents were independent because they did not agree with anyone else. A rooted, coherent body such as Nicholas and he belonged to was bound by the simple force of historical gravity to weigh heavier in the scales than such ideological thistledown. The Presbyterians were another matter. The English variety might not be such a bigoted and intractable lot as the Scots but their leaders, especially their clerical leaders, were bound to insist on conditions that would undercut the foundations on which he had, from the start, based his position — no alterations to church and law except by King and Parliament.

The proper aim in his view was to divide the opposition, rather than to make alliances with any of its component parts. Individuals, yes: parties, no. Thus at different times Hyde or his agents entered into close co-operation with the Leveller, John Wildman, and the old Ironside and extreme independent, Colonel Sexby. Such arrangements were limited and pragmatic. No attempt was made at forming an ideological coalition. The common object was to get rid of Cromwell, both parties tacitly reserving their right to do down the other once that happy consummation had been achieved. Rather charmingly Sexby wanted to know whether Charles II at a personal meeting would require overt marks of deference that would offend his own egalitarian principles and was instantly reassured on the point. Good manners are possible even among plotters.

Contact was established with these and other disillusioned or disaffected supporters of what was later to be called the Good Old Cause

— the phrase dates from the last stand of the English Republic in 1659 — by the Royalist underground. The composition and activities of this body, if shape it could be called that shape had none, occupied the greater part of Hyde's working day and waking thoughts until the very eve of the Restoration. It was not of his making. Indeed many of the senior figures in it, Old Cavaliers who had ridden with Rupert, were hostile to him both personally and politically. There was however a kind of Young Turk movement within it, headed by the daring John Mordaunt, that came in the last years of the exile to dominate the rest, and certainly to enjoy Hyde's support, almost to the extent of monopoly.

To write the history of Royalist conspiracy in England is fortunately unnecessary since it has already been admirably done in a work of that name[12] by Professor David Underdown. In one point where his final verdict differs from Clarendon's it may however be worth considering an alternative interpretation.

According to Professor Underdown the clergy, with a few notable exceptions, played little part in conspiratorial or other secret activity such as fundraising.[13] Clarendon did not think so. This might be ascribed to prejudice. The Church of England has had no more robust champion. But that is not the same as an uncritical estimate of its clergy: '. . . clergymen who understand the least and take the worst measure of human affairs of all mankind that can write and read.'[14] Such a judgment seems an even bolder retort from pew to pulpit in the twentieth century than in the seventeenth. The tribute that Clarendon pays to the conduct of the clergy during the Interregnum is thus all the more telling. It is to be found towards the end of one of the last books that he wrote (the dedication to Charles II is dated May 10, 1673), *A Brief View and Survey of the Dangerous and Pernicious Errors to CHURCH and STATE in Mr Hobbes's Book entitled LEVIATHAN*. 'They discharged the expense of many expresses, which were frequently sent to the King, & from him which amounted to a great charge . . . & often transmitted such sums of money to his Majesty himself as were very reasonable supplies to him in great distresses . . . I . . . hold myself obliged to Justice & truth to give this testimony, since all the particulars are well known to me, having at that time the honor to be in some trust with his Majesty, & thereby the full knowledge of what then passed.'[15] Clarendon is provoked to this declaration by Hobbes's ignoble opportunism. 'It was below the education of Mr Hobbes, & a very ungenerous & vile thing, to publish his *Leviathan*

[12] *Royalist Conspiracy in England 1649-1660* (Yale, 1960).
[13] *op. cit.* 182-4 & *passim*.   [14] *Life* I, 69.
[15] *op. cit.* (2nd ed. Oxon 1676), 308.

163

with so much malice and acrimony against the Church of England when it was scarce struggling in its own ruines . . . the true Clergy sometimes lost their lives upon the scaffold, sometimes in Gibbets for the greater disgrace . . . & others died in Prisons . . .'[16]

The warmth of Clarendon's feeling has led him to exaggerate the frequency of public executions. But it is not so easy to check the numbers of those who died as a result of imprisonment or other mistreatment. What is much more interesting than attempts to reconstruct a Royalist martyrology is Clarendon's emphatic assertion of the part played by the clergy in transmitting secret messages. It is well known that Cromwell had in John Thurloe one of the ablest counterintelligence controllers in our history. The collection of papers that guaranteed his immunity at the Restoration revealed on their publication in 1742 how effective he had been both in intercepting and decoding secret messages and in penetrating Royalist networks. Hyde had early recognised the insecurity of communication that bedevilled all Cavalier conspiracy. As one of his most trusted agents, Captain Titus, wrote to him in October 1656: 'Our futility brings uppon us the same effects which Dishonesty would doe, which is to ruin our friends & deprive ourselves of Trust. This is the best spye & intelligencer Cromwell hath.'[17]

It would, surely, be natural in so dangerous a traffic to rely most heavily on those of a man's most intimate acquaintance who had shewn both steadfastness and ingenuity in resisting the new régime. If well chosen, such agents would cover their tracks and leave little by which Thurloe, or the harmless enquirers of later centuries, could run them to earth. An obvious candidate for Hyde to choose as agent in England was Gilbert Sheldon, Warden of All Souls and future Archbishop of Canterbury. Hyde had known him well at Great Tew and had made trial of his dexterity and resolution in securing plate and money from the Oxford colleges in the very early days of the war when there were no royal forces anywhere near. He had observed, from abroad, Sheldon's skilful and daring obstruction of the Parliamentary Commissioners sent to purge the University of Royalists in 1647. During the time that he was ambassador in Madrid he was in secret correspondence with him and deeply anxious for his safety: 'The other letter with the W is for the honest Warden, which I pray thee send to him by the first conveyance. I do looke every post to heare that he is at Antwerpe, for it is not possible he can sleep quyetly in that cursed ayre, or be longe out of a gaol if he stay ther.'[18] The same anxiety is repeated a month later and again a month after that.[19] 'Can it be possible that in the midst of these new

---

[16] *ibid* 305–6.
[18] *HMC Bath MSS* ii, 88. February 20, 1650.
[17] Clar. MS 52 f.353.
[19] *ibid* 89, 90.

threates and others the Warden can finde it safe to stay in that cursed country?' Yet just before Hyde left Madrid in the spring of 1651 there is a marked change of tone. 'Thou wilt remember me when thou writest to the honest Warden, & tell him I am very gladd that that ayre continues still so wholesome that he dares venture his constitution in it.'[20] It is hard to imagine why Frances Hyde should have been in regular correspondence with Sheldon unless they were both links in a secure chain of secret intelligence.

An even stronger hint of what Sheldon may have been doing in the years after he was ejected from All Souls is given by his choice of retreat. This was in one house or another in that part of the Trent Valley where Leicestershire, Derbyshire and Nottinghamshire meet. Here his elder brother Ralph had his estate. And here too, at Staunton Harold, just over the Leicestershire border, Sir Robert Shirley established a redoubt of Anglicanism that still breathes defiance: the church, built under the Republic in the old Laudian style, is surrounded by a curtain wall. Shirley, as the Clarendon State Papers abundantly demonstrate, was as fearless and effective in providing funds and intelligence in the Royalist underground and for the court in exile as anyone before Mordaunt came on the scene in 1656. He was in fact Mordaunt's cousin and may well have introduced him to that world.[21] After his arrest in the backwash of the plot for a Royalist rising in 1655 he was imprisoned in the Tower till his death from smallpox in November 1656. During this period he produced a comprehensive plan for the remodelling of the loose, incompetent and often conflicting Royalist secret networks into one organisation to be controlled by the bishops and clergy.[22] The ardour of his attachment to the episcopal order is gently satirised in a contemporary Royalist ballad of a distinctly anti-Clarendonian character:

> Wee Prisoners all pray that brave Shirley may
>   bee gently assest in your books
> Cause under the line hee has payd a good fine
>   To the poore Common wealth of ye Rooks.[23]

His proposals bear the strong impress of Sheldon's ideas. For it is not only the Royalist underground but the Church itself, as its active embodiment, that is to be remodelled. Here, in a document produced by a layman under the Protectorate, is a succinct statement of what Sheldon would try to do when he became Archbishop after the

---

[20] *ibid* 95.   [21] *Cal. Clar. SP* iii, 49.
[22] *ibid* 47–50. Underdown *op. cit.* 181–6 for a criticism of them.
[23] Clar. MS 50 f.290.

Restoration. Cause and effect are not hard to discern. Sheldon spent three or four years at the house of Shirley's mother-in-law at Bridgeford, Nottinghamshire, itself only a few miles from Staunton Harold.[24] That Sheldon was a frequent visitor and often acted as chaplain there is clear from another source: '[In Sir Robert Shirley's] family the service of the Church of England was regularly kept up all through the rebellion by Sheldon and Dolben.'[25] Shirley also made Sheldon one of the three trustees of an annuity for disseminating Anglican propaganda.[26]

Sheldon's partner in maintaining the Anglican liturgy at Staunton Harold, John Dolben, was secretly ordained priest by Henry King, the poet-Bishop of Chichester, in 1656. A year later he married Sheldon's niece, the daughter of the squire of Stanton, Derbyshire. That he did not confine his activities to the Trent valley is clear from Anthony Wood's laudatory mention of him as one of the group of three ejected members of the University of Oxford who defied the authorities by celebrating the Anglican rites in a house near his own opposite Merton. One of the others named by Wood, Richard Allestree, was a Royalist agent and courier who, like Dolben, bore the scars of the Civil Wars in which they had fought as laymen. Dolben's intelligence, daring and happy knack of getting on with people made him an obvious choice for clandestine activity.

It is the argument in this extended gloss on the two contradictory statements of Clarendon and Professor Underdown that the absence of any record of conspiratorial activity is, in all ages, the mark of the successful conspirator. One thinks of Dr Schacht's reply to the question why he did not, if he was opposed to Hitler, join in the plot of July 1944, that it was unwise to act with conspirators who kept lists. What explanation other than recognition of outstanding and hazardous service can be found for the rapid and conspicuous preferment with which these independent-minded, not particularly well-connected clergymen were rewarded at the Restoration? Sheldon as Warden of All Souls and a notably inflexible loyalist, ex-chaplain to Charles I, friend to Lord Chancellor Clarendon, was obviously a candidate for the episcopate. Indeed he was on every list of the half-dozen or so put forward for consecration during the Interregnum when it seemed that the dwindling handful of old men might end the Church of England's claims to episcopal continuity by dying off. In fact he went straight to the see of London and within three years to the Archbishopric of Canterbury. Dolben, who had never even held a benefice and had only been ordained for four years, immediately became his archdeacon and

---

[24] Thoroton *Antiquities of Nottinghamshire* (1677) 2nd ed. 1790 vol i, 296.
[25] *Theologian & Ecclesiastic* vi, 80.   [26] *Cal. Clar. SP* iii 385.

in 1662 Dean of Westminster. By the end of the reign he was Archbishop of York. Allestree, whom we know to have been a secret agent,
like Dolben a promising young Oxford don when the war broke out,
was given the most sought-after of all pieces of ecclesiastical patronage
(one of the very few tenable by a layman), the Provostship of Eton. All
these appointments could certainly be defended on merit. But in the
England of Charles II it is usual to look for subsidiary qualifications.

Sir Robert Shirley was of all Hyde's secret correspondents the one
who most closely resembled him in combining a practical approach to
immediate problems with a deeper interest in theology and church
order. What other agent would bring the judicious Hooker and the importance of maintaining intercommunion with the Eastern Churches
into a despatch about the reorganisation of the King's party in
England? Yet it was Shirley who was in touch with Wildman the
Leveller and who recognised the need for a proper structure and
finance to maintain it if Royalist activity were ever to come to anything.
It was his young cousin, John Mordaunt, who in the crucial period immediately preceding the Restoration was to establish himself as the
most effective agent in the field.

Whatever Hyde's preferences in the matter may have been he had
neither the power nor the qualifications to design and control a single,
all-embracing secret organisation. The only sustained attempt at setting up an over-riding authority was the formation of the Sealed Knot
(the subject of one of Professor Underdown's chapters) late in 1653.
The distinction and interest of its membership, the melodramatic
choice of its name, have perhaps distracted attention from its non-
performance. Like almost everything to do with the Royalists from first
to last it was, through the pride and touchiness of its members, less
than the sum of its parts. Two of its six members, Lord Belasyse and Sir
Richard Willys, had been involved in what came near to a brawl in the
King's presence over the replacement of the one by the other as
Governor of Newark in 1645 and had subsequently to be restrained
from fighting a duel. It seems that this quarrel was still unabated. Both
Willys and another member, Colonel John Russell, were friends and
old comrades-in-arms of Prince Rupert, whose hostility to Hyde was
notorious. Yet the strict condition of the Knot's communications with
the exiled Court was that no one except the King, Ormonde and Hyde
were to be made privy to their activities. They certainly represented the
true blue Royalism that would have no truck with Presbyterians. In the
Continuation of the *Life*, written in Montpellier in 1670, Clarendon's
prose throbs with enthusiasm as he thinks of them. But were they not
in fact a trifle too true blue? Belasyse was a Roman Catholic aristocrat
whose Royalism was that of a natural Cavalier, not that of a constitutional lawyer of strong Anglican convictions. There were two with

167

whom Clarendon had some affinity: Sir William Compton, a paragon of all the military and public virtues as well as a man who could charm the sharply critical Samuel Pepys; and Edward Villiers, brother of the beloved Lord Grandison who had fallen at the taking of Bristol. Both his mother and his sister Lady Morton were, as we have seen, the objects of Hyde's deepest attachment.

The history of the Knot, and of its penetration by Thurloe through Sir Richard Willys, has been told once and for all by Professor Underdown. Though it certainly impinged on Hyde's conduct of affairs and on his understanding of what was going on in England it was by no means his only source of information or his only instrument of action. There is no evidence that it contributed to the formation of policy, unless it added by the weight of its caution — or as Mordaunt would have argued its inertia — to Hyde's reasons for waiting on events.

The two Royalist risings that went against this principle and for whose ignominious failure Hyde was rightly or wrongly held to blame were those of Penruddock in Wiltshire in 1655 and Sir George Booth in Cheshire in 1659. In both cases they were instances of partial ignition of what had originally been envisaged ('planned' seems too kind a verb) as a general conflagration. In both cases cold feet, incompetence, lack of central direction and, above all, effective communication left these luckless outliers to take on a battleship with a pea-shooter. Hyde was caught, as any politician in real life is caught, between irreconcilable necessities. He had to keep up the morale of the Royalists at home and prevent them lapsing, as they so easily could, into a self-protective acceptance of a régime that on the whole was not too irksome. On the other hand he did not believe that an armed insurrection would achieve anything unless it were preceded by some evident change of political heart. Like the atomic weapons of the twentieth century the military strength of Royalism would only be useful if it was never used. A certain consciousness of the inconsistency in his position is perhaps revealed in the harsh and unfair judgments he passes on the leaders of these hopeless ventures. Penruddock is censured for his humanity in saving the lives of the Judge and Sheriffs appointed by the Protectorate who were hauled out of their beds at Salisbury in March 1655. Clarendon even implies that the rising might have succeeded if more bloody-mindedness had been shewn at the start '. . . as if works of this nature could be done by halves . . .'[27]

The general view of Royalists both at home and abroad was more favourable to Penruddock. Peter Mews at The Hague reported the feeling that 'for the miscarriage of the business' Hyde was to blame: '. . . if not the sole, yet the cheife manager of this designe, the whole weight

---

[27] *Hist.* XIV, 132.

lyes upon him.'[28] Later in the year he found the same current of opinion at Rotterdam: '. . . it was said that the King needed not a lawyer to dispute the right or justice of his title, swords being more needful than words . . .'[29] At home the news, so infuriating to Cromwell, that his expedition against Hispaniola, commanded by Penn and Venables, had only managed to capture Jamaica was compared in a Royalist ballad to the military planning of the exiled court, now removed from Paris to Cologne:

> Jaymaica relations soe tickle ye nations
> And Venables looks soe Sullen
> That every one cryes the designe was as wise
> as those that are fram'd at Cullen.[30]

The conduct of military operations lay outside Clarendon's experience and talents, as he was the first to admit. Both as chief minister in exile and after the Restoration he did his best to avoid a policy that required them. When he was overtaken by events and the shooting started he refrained from meddling. That he should shoulder the blame for blunders and failures is the common lot of politicians.

---

[28] *Nicholas Papers* ii, 267.   [29] *ibid* iii, 19.   [30] Clar. MS 50 f.290.

XIV

Rising Men

CLARENDON'S ideas were formed by the reading and conversation of a generation that was mature if not already ageing in the days of Charles I's personal rule. Pym and Selden, Falkland and Chillingworth, even the shades of Donne and Ben Jonson, whom he had known in youth, peopled his mind. His political experience, naturally enough, lay largely with younger men.

The politicians with whom he co-operated or contended in the early years of the Restored Monarchy — Shaftesbury and Buckingham, Arlington and Danby, William Coventry and his brother Henry — seem to come fresh on the scene, almost to inaugurate a new era. Yet almost all of them were known to him in the years of exile and adversity; known not just as individuals but in the context of activity and ambition and connexion. In one way or another most of them had come up against him. Naturally he loomed larger in their world than they did in his. But his keen awareness of people, his immediate and often intemperate reaction to them that make him such a lively historian, contributed to his difficulties as a politician. A blander, less sharply defined personality would have made easier those accommodations without which the traffic of politics comes to a halt.

With Shaftesbury, then as Colonel Ashley Cooper the young Royalist local commander in Dorset, Hyde had already come into contact in the dispute with Prince Maurice over the Governorship of Weymouth.* Hyde had taken Cooper's side, probably out of his violent prejudice against Maurice. Cooper's subsequent adherence to the Protectorate had removed him from the concerns of Charles II's chief minister. Buckingham had pursued a much more devious path that had in its endless windings and turnings brought him all too often to Hyde's attention. The fatal Villiers connexion, how it returned to

* See above p. 5.

dog him. For not only the Hydes, but the Aylesburys, Frances's family, were clients of that house. Her father had risen high in the service of the first Duke. Her brother Will had been acting as continental agent for his son the second Duke, negotiating the sale of part of the Buckingham picture collection shortly before he decamped to England in the unhappy circumstances already described.* Buckingham himself made several attempts to strike a bargain for his immense estates, first with the Commonwealth and finally with Cromwell, but the Protector, with his famous judgment of men, consistently refused to trust him. In the meantime Buckingham made a name for himself as the declared enemy of Hyde, Nicholas and Ormonde. When their fortunes went down, his went up. He accompanied the King to Scotland in 1650 and was with him at the final débâcle at Worcester. Consequently when Hyde was recalled to the direction of policy at Christmas 1651 he could rely on the steady and unscrupulous enmity of one whom Ormonde, the personification of courtesy and good temper, tersely characterised as 'that vile man'.

Hyde's relations with the future Earl of Arlington, then plain Sir Henry Bennet, were to follow a more complicated pattern. In the *Life*, written when Clarendon was again and finally in exile, Arlington gets rough treatment. Yet of all that royal entourage who went on to high office at the Restoration he was one of the very few who shared Clarendon's cultivation of mind. 'He never plays, but reades much, having both the Latine, French and Spanish tongues in perfection: has traveled much, & is absolutely the best bred & Courtly person his Majestie has about him.'[1] Thus John Evelyn in 1677, a quarter of a century after they had first met in Paris as exiles. Like Clarendon, he was of modest social origins and had, like him, gone up to Oxford a younger son intended for a parson. They had other things in common. Both were disliked, Bennet indeed loathed, by James, Duke of York to whom he had the misfortune to be secretary. Both enjoyed the friendship of the brilliant, mercurial George Digby, Earl of Bristol. Both were in the bad books of Henrietta Maria. They were thus often on the same side and Bennet was an easy man to get on with. After he had been relieved of his duties in the Duke of York's household and sent to Hyde's old post as ambassador in Madrid the letters they exchanged were notably free and open. Indeed in her admirable biography of Arlington Violet Barbour long ago made the case that Bennet was a natural ally whom Clarendon in his years as Lord Chancellor antagonised by snubbing and frustrating.

Of course as he grew older Clarendon became goutier, tetchier, more often tired and cross than genial and amusing. But there were

* See above p. 142.   [1] *Diary* (ed. de Beer) iv, 118.

some conspicuous characteristics that must always have jarred. Bennet was relentlessly smart: a social climber, a lover of luxury, a worshipper of display. In this his affinity was very much with the King, not with the Chancellor. And he was evidently not serious about his religion.

This lies at the root of another wanton dissipation of perhaps even more valuable support. Readers of Pepys's Diary will remember, for its rarity as much for its steady repetition, the unqualified praise bestowed on Sir William Coventry: 'the best Minister of State the King hath', 'the activest man in the world', 'by my troth I do see more reall worth in him then in most men that I do know'. By the time Clarendon came to describe his character in the *Continuation* he had a long score to settle. Coventry had often opposed his measures with success in the House of Commons; he had done so less successfully but more offensively at the Privy Council board; and finally he had joined with Arlington in achieving his dismissal. Objectivity was hardly to be expected. Yet even there he allows some of the qualities that enraptured Pepys. 'His parts are very good, if he had not thought them better than any other man's; and he had diligence and industry, which men of good parts are too often without . . . and he was without those vices which were too much in request, and which make men most unfit for business and the trust that cannot be separated from it.' Drinking and whoring were presumably what Clarendon had in mind. In Parliament he admits that he had 'very much reputation of an able man. He spake pertinently, and was always very acceptable and well heard.'

Against this, 'he was a sullen, ill-natured, proud man, whose ambition had no limits, nor could be contained within any'. His high opinion of himself and his contempt for experience and seniority are bitterly and repetitiously recounted. On the personal level 'he did not dissemble in his private conversation (though his outward carriage was very fair) that he had no kindness for him [i.e. Clarendon], which in gratitude he ought to have had; nor had he anything to complain of from him, but that he wished well and did all he could to defend & support a very worthy person, who had deserved very well from the King, against whom he manifested a great & causeless animosity, and desired to oppress for his own profit, of which he had an immoderate appetite.'[2]

Clarendon's warmth of temper is the only clear and true element in this passage. If he had any claims on Coventry's gratitude the evidence has not survived. The 'very worthy person' whose past loyalties rather than present usefulness are, significantly, selected for commendation is probably Carteret, Clarendon's host in Jersey. The only other possibility is the futile Sir John Mennes whose incompetence at the Navy

2. *op. cit.* 401–3.

Board is so vividly depicted by Pepys. Mennes had been Clarendon's comrade in exile, good company over a song and a glass as Pepys confirms: indeed Mennes has left for posterity an agreeable ballad about a Christmas entertainment given by Clarendon to the King and exiled court at Xanten in 1654.[3] Coventry and Pepys were entirely right to do their best to have him put out to grass. As for the accusation that Coventry was avaricious and corrupt, a recent scholarly investigation confirms his uprightness so much admired by Pepys and his anxiety to eliminate the system of *douceurs* that was generally accepted in the naval administration of his time.[4]

It is easy now to see why Clarendon at the end of his career had his knife into Coventry. But why should he have taken against him in the first place? His brother Henry was always a great favourite of his, and his father, who had been Lord Keeper, is one of the few ministers of Charles I's pre-Civil War government to earn Clarendon's whole-hearted approval in the *History*. A good deal later in the *Continuation* Clarendon looses off another broadside at William Coventry. Among the thunder of that cannonade there is one telling condemnation: 'He had no principles in religion or state.' It seems an absurd assertion to make of one of the few Restoration politicians whose incorruptibility was thought to verge on the priggish. But it is true to Clarendon's earliest perception — or would prejudice be an apter word? 'The truth is, he hath good parts, but he is void of all Religion,' so wrote Hyde to Nicholas in June 1652 when Coventry was in Paris.[5] He also noted the friendship between him and Sir Henry Bennet and that both of them were in the circle of Will Crofts and Wilmot.

Of course at that stage he did not have to bother about a couple of clever young men who did not have that reverence for their seniors that Mr Hyde had had when he was a clever young man. Men of far inferior ability like Crofts and Wilmot were of much greater concern because of their unfortunate influence on the young King. Wilmot would certainly have presented a threat to Hyde's position if he had survived to the Restoration. His extraordinary ascendancy as a royal favourite, dating from the shared adventures of the six weeks that followed the battle of Worcester, was demonstrated by his elevation to the Earldom of Rochester (substituted at the last moment for that of Danby) in December 1652. This drove a coach and horses through Hyde's avowed policy of creating no new titles and filling no vacant offices until the Crown enjoyed its own again. Yet this humiliation was not personally

---

[3] Clar. MS 49 f.245.
[4] *Camb. Hist. Journal* xii (1956) 107–25 V. Vale, 'Clarendon, Coventry and the Sale of Naval Offices'.
[5] *Clar. SP* iii, 77.

resented. In his letters to Nicholas he consistently declines the Secretary's invitations to manoeuvre against him or even to run him down.[6] That Wilmot would not have recognised a principle in religion or state if it had been served up to him in its own gravy he knew perfectly well. The character he drew of him a decade after his death[7] leaves the reader with no illusions. But quite clearly he found him an easy man to get on with (anyone with a bottle and two glasses found that) and, within limits, to do business with. His laziness made him a bad correspondent on the various diplomatic missions in which he was employed but that is almost the only complaint about him in Hyde's letters. They were never, in Hyde's understanding of the word never could have been, friends. Wilmot's second wife, then living in Paris, was a St John and thus a cousin of Hyde's through his mother. Hyde was evidently fond of their eldest son: 'I cannot think of anything to add but my continued complaint that you do not write to your son, who every week is piously inquisitive after you when your letters come, & somewhat out of countenance when he finds many paquets come without any for him. He is an excellent youth and you cannot be too fond of him.'[8] A few months later he was lamenting his untimely death 'in as wicked an Age as ever was he was an Innocent and Virtuous a young man as ever I knew'.[9] Hardly the reputation that his poet-brother was to earn.

Clarendon enjoyed the friendship of the young and took trouble to please and encourage them. His relations with his own children have already been cited. Nothing in the Clarendon State Papers is more charming than the courtesy and ease of his correspondence with Nicholas's son John, 'My good tutour'. So far from the busy statesman talking down to his young friend he commissions him to buy books for him in Holland and to obtain a complete catalogue of the works of scholars such as Salmasius and Vossius, both printed and in manuscript ready for the press. 'I am so farr from murmuring at your want of diligence that if I would quarrel with you it should be for your excess of civillity and putting yourself to unreasonable paynes to comply with my desyres . . . you are a greate husbande and very skillfull in the marchandise of books & truly if I gett those safe into my hand (as I hope I shall shortly do) I will not take treble the money for them: whatever directions you send for payment shall be punctually & at a minute observed . . .'[10] That is the way in which the eminent should address young men in their late twenties. The financial priorities revealed in this letter are interesting. Spot cash will be found for the purchase of books; but in the preceding winter Hyde had written to John's father,

[6] e.g. *ibid* 128, 129. [7] *Hist.* VIII, 169. [8] Clar. MS 46 f.155v.
[9] *ibid* f.289. [10] *ibid* f.365.

'I am so cold, that I am scarce able to hold my pen, and have not three Sous in the world to buy a faggot . . .'[11]

It was over the treatment of the young that Clarendon's friendship with Bristol, proof, it had seemed, against every folly and excess, first began to show signs of wear and tear. To obtain some promised preferment he had made his son turn Roman Catholic. '"Oh, Mr Secretary, I do confesse to you this last parte makes me ashamed of my old friend."'[12] Far worse was to follow. A daughter who had been brought up in England was sent for and, much against her will, installed in an English nunnery in Ghent. Her father promised that there would be no question of her becoming a Roman Catholic, still less a nun. The abbess introduced her to 'a young half-witted man of a good family and a competent fortune' who promptly made overtures of marriage. Without stopping to consider his character or to investigate his circumstances Bristol at once pressed his daughter into the necessary change of religion 'and then frankly gave her up to a perpetual misery, which she entered into from the day of her marriage: which, considering all the circumstances, would have brought much grief of mind to another parent . . . nor did he more consider the loss of a child, in an adventure which probably might bring some convenience to him (for himself was still first, if not sole in all those considerations) . . .'[13] That he should himself become a Roman Catholic in the winter of 1659, when the defeat of Sir George Booth's rising had apparently extinguished all hopes of a Restoration, came as no surprise to Charles II or to Ormonde, though Hyde was somewhat stunned. After all that, Bristol's attempt to stage a come-back by moving for Clarendon's impeachment of High Treason in July 1663 can hardly have had power to shock.

Bristol, alone of Hyde's friends, was ideally suited to the life of exile. His restlessness found a repose that political stability denied him. An adventurer, he responded to the challenges without having to stay for the consequences. His courage, his intelligence, his command of languages, his good looks, his noble birth dazzled the Frenchmen and the Spaniards from whom he coaxed, apparently without effort, one glittering appointment after another. By turning Papist in 1659 he counted on rising to high position in the service of the King of Spain, a country where he was as much at home as in his own. When in 1669 Clarendon came to write the character sketch of him just quoted he could still, in spite of everything, not entirely repress the amusement and affection of so long a friendship. Bristol was one of the few of his intimate correspondents who could twit him with his faults of censoriousness and quick temper and who could dare to laugh at him.

[11] *Clar. SP* iii 126.   [12] *Cal. Clar. SP* ii, 237.   [13] *Clar. SP* iii supp. lxix.

In November 1656 when the exiled court was, as usual, desperate
for money Hyde was trying to hurry on the payment of the allowance
made by the Spanish King to his English ally. The final hurdle was the
signing of an order by the Governor of the Netherlands with whom
Bristol had at once established the best of relations. Hyde pestered
him to get the order signed at once. Bristol, exasperated, explained
that he had had a gentleman waiting outside the Governor's door all
day, but without success 'because his highness played all the afternoon
at tennis. I believe you will thinke it a faulte that I demanded not the
letter from the Secretary of the Chamber & that I carryed it not to him
my selfe to signe with his racquet.' Warming to his work he derides his
friend's bureaucratic request for copies of such of the governor's letters
as refer to the affairs of the English court: '. . . such a thing as I beleeve
nobodye ever dreamt of but yourself that ever had to doe with Princes.
Lett me take the liberty to tell you that if you will have business well
dispatcht at a Secretaria soe ill served as this you must get some little
blade of the office whoe upon gratification may make it his businesse
upon the place to see such things as appear of nothing & yett perhaps
are of great consequence punctually & timely dispatcht . . . I hope this
lesson will make you wise for the rest of your life . . . In the meane
while God give you a better temper . . .'[14]

Such good-humoured plain speaking was impossible to Secretary
Nicholas who was for ever taking offence at what he considered his
old friend's want of frankness. Was Nicholas imagining slights where
none existed? Hyde evidently thought so, from his constant expostu-
lations, after Ormonde or some other third party had shewn him a
pained letter from the Secretary. Indeed as the reams of paper
covered with Hyde's most rapid, ill-formed hand unfold themselves,
all dashed off without art or hesitation, thinking aloud, recalling the
day's frustrations, flitting from family and friends to bores and
bugbears, it seems strange that their recipient should complain of not
being told enough. Other men receiving a much less ample measure
protested on opposite grounds. Yet Nicholas, a staunch supporter
from first to last, would not have repeated complaints that might
easily be turned against Hyde unless he thought he had good
grounds. No doubt he was over-sensitive. No doubt his consciousness
that Hyde was doing his job for him during the Paris years intensified
this. Still there was a sly, secretive side to this open, passionately com-
municative person. He could hardly have survived if there hadn't
been. Without a real pleasure in bluff and deception he could not
have achieved what he did for Charles I's cause in the propaganda war
of 1641–2. He put the same arts to use, and perhaps enjoyed the

14 Clar. MS 53 f.38.

The Hanneman portrait, probably painted c. 1654, here vividly conveys Clarendon's unhappiness and frustration in that dark time as well as the mental and moral energy with which he fought against them. Another version is reproduced on the jacket.

Frances, Lady Clarendon. If the identification, which rests on the inscription, is correct this must have been painted about the time of her marriage.

Sheldon. Painted by Samuel Cooper in 1667. Dated by the artist who also gives the sitter's age as 69.

Morley. Drawing after Lely. Both friends from Great Tew days, both appointed Executors and Overseers in the will of 1666 (see Appendix I), Morley was much the closer to Clarendon both personally and in his religious opinions.

Falkland (attributed to Van Dyck). 'That unparallel'd lord'. The founder and the inspiration of Great Tew.

George Digby, later second Earl of Bristol, by Justus van Egmont. His character clearly fascinated Clarendon, perhaps because it was in so many respects the antithesis of his own.

William Villiers, Lord Grandison. Studio of Van Dyck, from the Clarendon collection. A cousin of Clarendon's first wife, he fell early in the Civil War, leaving a daughter who, as Charles II's principal mistress, was to prove a formidable enemy.

John Earles.
A friend from
Great Tew
days 'who
never had nor
ever could
have an
enemy, but
such a one
who was an
enemy to all
learning and
virtue'.

174

Lady Morton, sister to Lord Grandison, and during the early years of exile the recipient of Clarendon's most intimate confidences. Copy of a Van Dyck by Van Leemput.

Three close colleagues: Cottington, from a portrait Clarendon had copied for his collection; William Shaw, the devoted secretary and amanuensis of his last exile; and Sir Alan Broderick, his cousin who saw him through the trials of 1667.

The Paris that Clarendon knew in the late 1640s and early 1650s
from two drawings in the Sutherland collection.

An allegorical rendering of Charles II's policy, deplored by Clarendon, of attempting to regain his throne by the help of the Scots. The young king is being armed against the hydra of rebellion while in the background his father's execution is depicted outside a Venetian version of the Banqueting House.

The infant Prince of Orange, later as William III to share the throne with Clarendon's grand-daughter, caracoles in front of a Low Country townscape so familiar to the Chancellor in the late 1650s.

The Loggan portrait
engraved from the life
(1666).

Anne Hyde by
Hanneman
c. 1655–6. The
erroneous
inscription was
added in the next
century.

MADAME DE CANTE CROIX

Ormonde, the portrait after Lely from Clarendon's collection.

James, Duke of York, attributed to Charles Wautier, painted at the time of his liaison with Anne Hyde in the late 1650s. The Duke was then serving in the Spanish army.

Samuel Butler by Soest. Clarendon's request for the licensing of the first, second and
third parts of *Hudibras* is preserved in the State Papers.

Charles II and his Queen, Catherine of Braganza. The portrait of the King was
painted by an unidentified artist shortly before the Restoration; that of the Queen,
by Lely, some years later. Both were originally in the Clarendon Collection.

KING. CHARLE
THE 2.^{D.} QVEE

The Lely portrait in Lord Chancellor's robes.

same thrill of being unsuspected even by his closest colleagues, during the exile.

The most successful instance of this was a pamphlet, printed in England in 1656, though bearing the publication date of October 31, 1655, entitled 'A letter from a true and lawful member of Parliament, and one faithfully engaged with it from the begininge of the warr to the end, to one of the Lords of his Highnesse Councell'. Hyde (for the manuscript in his own hand survives in his papers) assumed the character of what he might so easily have been, a moderate conservative Parliament man, determined to curb the illegalities and excesses of Charles I's government. From his standpoint he attacks the arbitrary penalties inflicted on the Royalists by the Protector's government, not because they were inflicted on Royalists but because they were arbitrary and therefore just as illegal as anything done by Star Chamber. He pooh-poohs talk of combination between the Royalists and the Levellers against Cromwell (which in fact was, as we have seen, being actively pursued) and shakes his head over the degree of toleration shown to Roman Catholics by the Protectorate: '. . . the swarming of those Jesuits which are now croaking amongst us . . . as if no laws were in force for their punishment.'[15]

The most convincing disguises are those that shadow the truth. How much of the young Mr Hyde who sat in the two Parliaments of 1640, how much of the future historian, is in this passage, never in his lifetime owned by the author: 'When I was returned to serve my country in Parliament, I brought with me all that affection to the Liberty & Benefit of my Country as the condition of it required, & all that Reverence and duty to the King that was agreeable to the Oaths . . . I had no more desire to alter the fundamental Government of Church & State than you have to restore it. I will not deny to you that after a short time of sitting there, the continual Feaver of the House made my pulse beat higher too, and the prejudice I had to some persons in power, & authority, from whom, as I thought, I had received some hard measure, lessened my esteem & opinion of the Court . . . made me think my self in the number of those who were to govern all the World, & insensibly I found myself a greater man, than I had before imagined I was. I chose the conversation of those who were believed most intent & solicitous to free the subject from the vexations & pressures he had been made liable to . . .'[16] The style is lighter, nimbler, than that of the *History*. It is cleaner, more compact than the untidy, vivid sentences, straggling into an infinity of parentheses, of his letters. Is it perhaps closer to the speeches that seem to have pleased the Long Parliament or to the informal expository manner that so delighted

[15] *ibid* 51 f.58.   [16] *ibid* f.5.

Pepys at a meeting of the Tangier Committee in October 1666? There is, once the authorship is disclosed, a recognisable touch of the master's best controversial manner:

'What is become of those two swelling names, which for so long time filled our mouths, & under the shelter of one of which all men took sanctuary, the *Presbyterians* & the *Independents*? Is there one man of either party, who without renouncing the principles of his party, is in credit or trust with you?'[17]

It is however the authorship, not the style or the content of this accomplished essay in psychological warfare, that makes it remarkable. As the editor of the *Calendar of the Clarendon State Papers* pointed out, Hyde not only deliberately misleads his close friend Ormonde: '. . . there is a letter come out to one of the Protector's Council which makes Cromwell mad, who swears that it is by Hollis & that he will destroy him for it; Hollis is generally believed to be the author.'[18] He even continues, when any need for secrecy was long past, to throw dust in the eyes of posterity. At the end of the fourteenth book of the *History* he mentions that the King 'caused such an answer to be made . . . as if . . . by one who had been always of the Parliament side and who was well pleased to see the cavaliers reduced to that extremity . . .' In a first draft of this passage, written as part of the *Life* in May 1670, he owns both his authorship and the idea of deception. The King had simply commanded him 'to write some discourse' on Cromwell's penal impositions.[19] He struck it out when re-editing the text for inclusion in the *History*. Why, if the story were worth mentioning at all, should he omit the element of chief interest? Perhaps it showed, on reflexion, too much of the young Mr Hyde, too little of the Earl of Clarendon.

Whatever occasional reservations he may have made in telling Ormonde and Nicholas what he was doing and thinking, they were in effect by far the closest of his many associates. To them he would open his mind, as he would to no one else, on such dangerous and delicate subjects as the King's character and reputation. They were indeed the elder statesman of Royalism. Of the others, death, in battle, on the scaffold, and latterly from old age or hard service, had claimed nearly all. The surviving grandees, Hertford, Southampton, Newcastle, had gone into hibernation either at home or on the continent. Apart from Bristol whose trail still flared across the sky there was only Colepeper. And he had to a large extent isolated himself, first by supporting Henrietta Maria against Hyde and Nicholas and then by undertaking an embassy to Moscow soon after Hyde had gone to Madrid. Its success — Tsar Alexis had been prompt and generous — had not raised his standing as might have been expected, perhaps because the Queen

[17] *ibid* f.57.   [18] *Cal. Clar. SP* iii 171.   [19] *Hist.* XIV, 151.

and the insatiable Jermyn had been its main beneficiaries. Colepeper remained in touch with the Court rather than a member of it. Perhaps Charles II looked a little askance at a Counsellor who was so much approved by his mother. In effect he played no part in the politics of the exiled court, though his extraordinary sense of potentialities and the acuteness of his judgment appear in a striking letter he wrote to Hyde on Cromwell's death in September 1658. No one else judged the course of events or outlined the tactics to be adopted both in general and in particular with such penetration. His sudden death immediately after the Restoration removed a man who had been a rival at the Court of Charles I, not a contender for the favour of Charles II.

One survivor from Charles I's time who was to outlast and outlive Clarendon was Sir Edward Walker — not, it must be admitted, a major figure but important enough and tiresome enough to take up a good deal of his time. 'Indeede your favourite Sir Edward Walker is a troublesome correspondent & not to be indured', he told Nicholas in July 1653. He had been kicking up a great fuss because, as Garter King of Arms, he had not been employed to convey that honour to the Court of Sweden. A crushing retort from Hyde made no impression. A year later the correspondence was still in full swing. 'Why should you wonder that a Herald, who is naturally made up of embroidery, should adorn all his own services & make them as important as he can? I would you saw some letters he hath heretofore writ to me in discontent, by which a stranger would guess he had merited as much as any General could do, and was not enough rewarded.'[20] In the meantime he had been allowed to present the insignia of the Order to the Elector of Brandenburg who had entertained him nobly. He grumbled about that too, apparently arguing that he had not been granted the travelling expenses to which his office entitled him. He had greeted the arrival of the young Duke of Gloucester from England early in 1653 by preparing a paper 'touching the bearing of differences in the armes of the younger sonnes of the Kings of England', not perhaps the most urgent preoccupation of that hard-pressed court. In spite of this absurd behaviour he was appointed one of the Clerks of the Council at the Restoration and put in charge of the arrangements for Charles II's coronation. He was still in office when Clarendon was dismissed. His *Historical Discourses*, in which the importance of heraldry is stressed, were published after his death 'which he had done whilest living but to avoid the affectation of Praise'.[21] His modesty was rewarded. They proved no serious rival to the *History of the Rebellion* which had appeared three years earlier.

[20] *Clar. SP* iii, 236.   [21] *op. cit.* ed. Hugh Clopton (1705). Postscript to the dedication.

XV

From Paris to Cologne and Bruges

So much is established, so much evidence has been critically examined, concerning Clarendon's years of power as Lord Chancellor that it is on the cob-webbed obscurity of the two long, gestatory periods of exile that light may more profitably be directed. In the first he was generally under pressure; the daily correspondence of a government that had next to nothing in the way of secretariat or resources, the maintenance of an elaborate secret intelligence system, the plots and intrigues of disgruntled allies and hidden enemies, the personal anxieties of a man often separated by his duties from a wife who needed his comfort as he needed hers and from children to whom he was devoted. In this first exile, at any rate from the beginning of 1652 to his homecoming in May 1660, he was always busy and always short of time and money. In the second, between his dismissal in 1667 and his death in 1674, he had adequate means and all the time in the world. The fact that he was equally active in both periods demonstrates his inexhaustible intellectual energy. In the first he was always surrounded by people, reacting to them, attempting to influence them, talking to them, writing to them. In the second he was on his own. A widower, he was, very occasionally, visited by English travellers. Correspondence with England was strictly forbidden him, except for members of his family who had to submit their letters to the censorship of the Secretary of State. If he wrote letters himself, no more than a handful have survived.

The first exile however is the best documented passage of his life. If he spent the second writing books he spent the first writing letters. It is there that he draws, unselfconsciously, the self-portrait that, with more art and some retouching, he has given us in the *Life*. The material for the portrait is almost endless. Much of it, as is the case in so many full and fruitful lives, is tediously repetitive. The tedium, however, consists in the fact of repetition, not in the ideas or the style of that which is repeated. What makes it worth wading through is that this is the final phase of a statesman's formation, of his training for the exercise of power. After 1660 he had seven years as a minister wielding quite exceptional authority, followed by seven years expounding for posterity the lessons of his life in works of history, autobiography, controversy and moral reflection, none of which were published in his lifetime. In the first seven years he was doing, in the second teaching. Preparation was over.

Something has been said about Hyde's principles, about ends and means, about the friends with whom he worked most closely and about some of the men whom, both in exile and after the Restoration, he accepted as colleagues with a more or less marked lack of enthusiasm. This has sometimes necessitated sacrificing chronology to coherence. It has always meant narrowing the view of a multifarious life to a single point or a single person. Perhaps the distortion so imposed may be lessened by supplying a framework of time and place.

By the spring of 1652 Sir Edward Hyde had settled, not altogether cheerfully, into the routine of life in Paris as the effective head of the English government in exile. English, be it noted: both then and later he did all he could to distance himself from the affairs of Ireland, which he was happy to leave to Ormonde, and of Scotland which was in any case a separate kingdom. He had the unswerving support of Ormonde, the staunch friendship and invaluable information of the Dutch ambassador in Paris, Boreel, and the general if unreliable backing of the King. On the other hand he was wretchedly poor, often ill and depressed by yet another parting *sine die* from his wife and family. He did not like Paris, of which he had seen quite enough on his journey to and from Madrid. The Queen, assisted by the French government, lost no opportunity of humiliating him and, much worse, his master. Had he had money to buy books and pictures and to live in the style proper to his position, had he been treated with the courtesies and civilities that the French court knew so well how to extend, no doubt it would have been another story. He was not indifferent to climate or to the beauty of buildings and the grounds in which they were set. But all his old resentments and suspicions of the French were confirmed and intensified. It was not just Paris. France was no place for a self-respecting Englishman whose first loyalty was to the Church and the laws of his country and thus to the King as their visible embodiment.

Apart from one unexplained journey with Ormonde to meet Lord Digby at Poissy in March Hyde spent the first six months of 1652 in Paris. On July 26 the English court moved to St Germain and stayed there till September 21.[1] During this absence from Paris a Venetian historian arrived who was anxious to consult so important a source for a

---

[1] *Clar. SP* iii, 53, 85, 100.

book he was writing about the English Civil War. Hyde declined his request for a number of reasons. First of all the difference of language 'would beget a thousand errors in both of us . . . Then the reading his papers, which I hope are in Latyne, must take me up much time, & how patiently he will attend my leasure I know not, men of those faculties being oftentimes supercilious enough.' And then there was the delicate question of relations with Venice which had recently booted out the drunken and disreputable court hanger-on sent by Charles II to represent him. The provocation was ample but the manner necessarily reflected on the King. The Most Serene Republic was on the point of recognising the Commonwealth. Hyde would nonetheless answer in writing any questions that were sent to him 'for such Men must not be disobliged, much less provoked'.[2]

The winter of 1652–3 was spent in Paris, mostly at the Palais Royal. In the spring Prince Rupert arrived, raising hopes of captured treasure from his long cruise, begun before the trial of Charles I. In spite of appetising reports of chests of chocolate and indigo, bars of steel and elephants' teeth being landed at Paimboeuf and Le Croisic, of tempting offers made by merchants for the prize vessels, of high prices promised by the Superintendent of the Magazine for the guns of the King's ship *Swallow*, nothing was left over once Rupert had paid off the crew and cleared his accounts. Doubtless there was peculation and incompetence. Certainly Rupert could be relied on for high-handedness and want of tact. The business, profitably hampered by the French port authorities, dragged on for nearly a year. When Hyde and his master at last realised that they were going to get nothing, not even the price of the *Swallow*'s ordnance, their rage knew no bounds. Hyde had never liked Rupert but had been brought to recognise his effectiveness as a commander and a disciplinarian, even to support his appointment as admiral, when the Revolted Fleet, unpaid and ill-led, began to disintegrate in 1648. From now on both as statesman and historian he felt himself thankfully released from any obligation to be fair.

By the summer of 1653 Hyde had come to take his own indispensability as a fact, and a not altogether welcome one. 'Surely if the Marquis of Ormond and Sir Edward Hyde were dead, the King would never commit any business which he cares for to the conduct of the Lord Keeper [Herbert] whom he perfectly abhors; but I must tell you Sir Marm. Langdale, Wansford [Christopher Wandesford, son of Strafford's right-hand man] and Lord Keeper have not been without such a plot.'[3] Lord Keeper Herbert was very thick with Prince Rupert and on excellent terms with the Queen and Jermyn. Langdale, the

---

[2] Clar. MS 49 f.237.   [3] *Clar. SP* iii, 181.

recusant who had commanded the Northern Horse, was a natural enemy to everything Hyde stood for. The old divide between the Swordmen, who wanted no nonsense about Parliament and the Common Law, and the Royalists, who based the King's right firmly on these two foundations, was always ready to open.

Hyde's spirits were further lowered by a long, unexplained illness of the King's which exposed him to the perils of blood-letting and such dangerous expedients as enabled seventeenth-century doctors to kill those they could not cure. Fortunately his constitution survived these ministrations but a change of air was prescribed and on October 3 the King and Hyde moved to Condé's château at Chantilly. The original plan had been to stay for five or six days.[4] In fact they remained for six weeks. The King would get some hunting (not Sir Edward Hyde's preferred recreation). But the heavy rain kept them indoors the first week and then they determined to stay as long as the weather stayed fair, which it did till near the end of November. The King had by this time come to share Hyde's passionate desire to be quit of Paris. The coldness of the French court confirmed the intelligence from every quarter that Cromwell and Mazarin were working for an alliance. To speed them on their way the French had promised full payment of the King's pension, now many months in arrear, if they would leave France within ten days of its receipt. Rochester was commissioned to find out if they would be welcome at Cologne and to buy 'a good sett of Coach Horses, of seven, in those parts, & to bring them with you for he is told they are the best of the world'.[5]

The King's recovery and the prospect of escape raised their spirits. But nothing in the world of politics and diplomacy moves quickly for people without power. As the winter dragged by Hyde became so depressed as to talk of retiring. 'The condition I am in breaks my mind and wastes my spirits so much that I cannot hold out long,' he wrote to Nicholas on February 6.[6] A fortnight later he was for some days 'so indisposed all over that I am neither able to write nor read, & not without very great pain to dictate'.[7] The illness would not go away. On March 20 he reverts with enthusiasm to his plan for retiring with Nicholas: 'when I can get into that blessed retreat we now speak of, I will not desire to hear any news, or to hold any other correspondence than what is necessary to draw supplies of money to us, but to study and learn to die, which I would gladly do if I had finished those papers which I have a great mind to leave to the world for the honour of our poor Master, of whose memory I find few tender enough.'[8] He suggests Cleves in the Emperor's dominions but if Nicholas would rather live under the

---

[4] *Cal. Clar. SP* ii, 259, *Clar. SP* iii, 193, 199.   [5] Clar. MS 46 f.303.
[6] *Clar. SP* iii, 216.   [7] *ibid* 220.   [8] *ibid* 226.

Spanish government 'let us go to Gueldres, which they say is the sweetest and cheapest place in the Seventeen Provinces, and where nobody would take notice of us'. Perhaps the desire to resume work on the *History* was the first sign of returning health. By March 27, having been bled four times and purged so often that he is actually lean, he can walk again and expresses a cautious hope that the worst is past.[9] By early June he has quite recovered his élan. Prince Rupert has left for Germany. Sir Edward Herbert, after a series of interviews in which the King shewed admirable firmness even when pressed by the Queen and Jermyn, has surrendered the Great Seal. The departure from Paris is now certain.[10]

Early in July they set out, the King for Spa in the United Provinces where he was to meet his sister, the Princess of Orange, and Hyde for a month's leave with his wife and family at the house in Breda to which they had moved from Antwerp in the autumn of 1653. It was the Princess's kindness to which they were beholden for living rent-free. She was to add to it a few months later by appointing 'the girle', Anne Hyde, the apple of her father's eye, one of her maids of honour.

During this period of recess when the King was refreshing his spirits by balls and suppers, and his minister was recuperating his in a contented domesticity, a silence descends. Apart from drawing up a scheme of expenditure that would enable the King to live within the pension paid by the French, an academic exercise since the delights of Spa had already plunged him deep in debt, Hyde issued no state papers and, apparently, wrote no letters. The financial regulations for the Royal Household are of interest because they show who was, so to speak, borne on the books and in what order of precedence. Apart from Ormonde, Hyde's only real friend is the King's sometime tutor, John Earles.[11] By the beginning of September the wheels of correspondence start to creak slowly round. By the end of the month King and minister are in business again at Aachen (the Government of the United Provinces, hostile to the House of Orange, would not let the Princess entertain her brother in their dominions). In October, to Hyde's pleasure, they had established themselves at Cologne. He enthused at the time over 'the strange delightfulness of this Citty and Countrey . . . (which sure is admirable)'[12] and recalled at Montpellier the broad elm walks that crowned its ramparts, superior to those at Antwerp.[13] The contrast with Paris was certainly marked. The city authorities were honoured to receive them, the neighbouring Duke of Neuburg generous and hospitable, though his Duchess, plain and lumpish by Clarendon's account, 'confirmed the King in his aversion

---

[9] *ibid* 228.
[10] *ibid* 245-6.
[11] Clar. MS 49 ff.4-5.
[12] *ibid* f.87v.
[13] *Hist.* XIV, 111.

from ever marrying a German lady'. Part of this satisfaction in their new surroundings must be attributed to the fact that Anne Hyde's removal to the Princess's court enabled her mother and her brothers to close the house at Breda and join the head of the family. The ending of separation gave him his second wind.

Paris, however, had not done with them. Hardly had they settled into Cologne before news came of Henrietta Maria's attempt first to seduce and then to bully the young Duke of Gloucester into becoming a Roman Catholic. This was one of the only two occasions on which Hyde records seeing his master make no effort to disguise his fury.[14] No other single act could have rendered the restoration of the house of Stuart a political impossibility. Only Henrietta Maria's determined and contemptuous ignorance of things English could have led her to contemplate the absurdities of a papal war of reconversion by which she attempted to justify her defiance of the strictest injunctions left by her husband and her son. Hyde saw at once the sly hand of Mazarin turning her folly to the ruin of England and the advantage of France. As outraged as Charles, he managed a potentially disastrous situation with tact and wisdom. The choice of Ormonde as special envoy to Paris was brilliant. The Queen and the French held all the cards. They could open and shut frontiers and prisons, turn on and cut off the current of money and credit on which their adversaries absolutely depended. The person of the Duke was in their hands. His tutor, Lovell, who had been his companion from childhood, was sent packing in spite of his own and his pupil's protests. The Duke's indeed were stronger than Lovell's. He shewed throughout the affair a courage, a self-reliance and a steadfastness remarkable for a boy of fifteen. That was Hyde's one stroke of luck.

The letters containing the alarming news were held up in the French post-office. The first that Hyde heard of the affair was in a long and feebly self-exculpatory letter from Lovell, who was apparently ready to accept defeat on terms that would enable him to go on a tour of Italy. '. . . theyr sentence was that removed I must be, but with all fayrenes and a provision be made for me . . . Because I am like to have leysure enough my purpose is to seeke ease to my minde by putting my body to some more paine, in travaileing farther into the world.'[15]

Hyde's reply though swift and sharp was temperate. He and the King 'wondered exceedingly (not without some trouble)' why he had delayed an instant in warning them what was afoot. 'But that which troubles me most is that you seem to have given over the game, and to

[14] *Clar. SP* iii, 258 to the Princess of Orange.
  Clar. MS 49 f.151 to Colepeper. Both November 20, 1654.
[15] *ibid* f.92 Lovell to Hyde, October 19, 1654, see also Lovell to Morley *ibid* ff.90–1.

be even upon the point to travel, and ready to depart from your charge, as soon as it shall be wished by those who have reason to be pleased with your absence . . . I doubt not but God will preserve the Duke from his misfortune, and give him grace and courage to resist this temptation [He had been promised a large, immediate and secure income from Church preferments]; if he should not, can you think a journey into Italy seasonable for you, and that your reputation will not suffer exceedingly by it?'[16] Compared with the tone taken by the King to his brother — 'If you herken to her [the Queen] or to anyone else in that matter, you must never thinke to see Englande or me againe' — this is the cooing of a dove. Until Ormonde could arrive — and the young Duke had already been under pressure of every kind for a month before Hyde had heard a word — Lovell was the only thread by which a connexion could be maintained.

Ormonde made good time. On November 27, a week after his arrival in Paris, he reported fully on every aspect of the matter, which by his inflexibility of purpose and courteous outspokenness he had brought under control. The French government were deeply involved — which, as he pointed out to the Queen, could hardly be irrelevant to their strenuous cultivation of a Cromwellian alliance. He had found the young Duke of Gloucester staunch, loyal and highly intelligent. He had wisely involved the Duke of York, always liable to rash and independent action, in his negotiations with the Queen. He had even made use of Lord Jermyn, whom both the King and Hyde suspected of complicity in the Queen's machinations, in finding a secure lodging for the Duke where he could not be threatened or cajoled. By early December the Queen, still refusing to see her son or to give him her blessing unless he turned Roman Catholic, admitted defeat by leaving Paris. On December 18 Ormonde and his young charge were on their way to Brussels. Disaster had been avoided and that without an open and public breach in the Royal Family.

It is perhaps officious to remind the reader of the formidable trivialities which Ormonde and Hyde were left to face whether in success or failure. Raising the money to pay for the Duke's journey cost Ormonde almost as much time and effort as the diplomatic victory that had made it possible. When they at last reached the frontier of the Spanish Netherlands on New Year's Eve they were kept waiting all night at the customs because there had been a delay in forwarding their pass. The Duke caught a chill which turned into a fever. The fortnight's delay that ensued, and the consequent medical expenses, exhausted the money needed for their onward journey[17] — and so on and so on.

---

16 *Clar. SP* iii, 256–7, misdated November 10 for November 20.
17 *Cal. Clar. SP* iii, 1, 5. Ormonde at Antwerp to Hyde.

None the less the year 1655 began well for Hyde. He was reunited with his wife and children. Cologne not only suited him much better than Paris but offered the King far less in the way of distraction and of undesirable company. And the Gloucester affair had strengthened his hand with a much-needed success.

The breathing-space was a short one. By February the movement of resistance to Cromwell that had been stimulated by his establishment of the Protectorate in December 1653, was intensified by his arbitrary dissolution of his first Parliament in January 1655 into rumblings of revolt. The want of organization, of any clear chain of command in the Royalist underground, has already been stressed. A fiasco of greater or lesser proportions must have appeared the most probable outcome. But what was the court in exile to do? The King could not sit still and take no notice. On the other hand a rousing call to arms that simply exposed his bravest supporters to the vengeance of an efficient military dictatorship was not a mistake he could afford. A strategy that limited the damage was the best. The King must be ready to appear at once as leader of a victorious party if by the chance of events Cromwell were to be overthrown. Otherwise he must keep his head down.

Accordingly about the middle of February the King slipped away from Cologne incognito, accompanied only by Ormonde, who with Hyde and Nicholas was the only member of the court privy to the plan. This was that Charles should hold himself in instant readiness on the Dutch coast, waiting for news of the projected risings in the south-west, in East Anglia and in the north. Hyde, accompanied by his wife, moved soon afterwards to Breda where he would be within easy reach both of the King in his concealment and of Nicholas at The Hague. A number of exiled Royalists of some standing had already crossed to England to open channels of communication or to assume command if the revolt came to anything. Several were caught but Sir Joseph Wagstaff got through to the south-west as did Rochester to the north. Wagstaff took part in the only tiny operation to result from this vast, unwieldy scheme, the Wiltshire revolt of Penruddock and Grove. The East Anglians and the men of Kent cried off and the Northerners were able to disperse in time. Cromwell's government had had ample warning, from the indiscretion of booby squires and from Thurloe's excellent domestic and foreign intelligence system. Nearly all the potential leaders were behind bars before there was any hint of trouble. Hyde, it seems, had never had high hopes. By the kindness of the Duke of Neuburg he had travelled to Holland in great comfort on a boat that provided two excellent meals a day and allowed him to sleep every night in his own sheets. When he had established himself he intended '. . . falling to my book and . . . not to stir till some very good or very bad news calls me away . . .'[18] Perhaps he was less philosophical than he made himself out. The dismal news from England, particularly from that best-loved, best-known corner of it where for a few hours the King's right had been asserted, could not leave him unmoved.

Spring, late in coming, found him low and irritable. 'It is yett so much worse than winter that it poures every day and the winde is so sharp that it hath given me the tooth ache which hath tortured me these 4 or 5 dayes beyonde my patience: indeede I do not knowe that any kinde of weather hath had such an influence upon my body & minde ever since I was borne,' he wrote on April 21.[19] He quarrelled bitterly with Nicholas's friend and protégé, Peter Mews, the daring agent and courier who was to become President of St John's College, Oxford and Bishop of Winchester. In 1655 Mews had the front-line soldier's impatience with obstruction from the politicians and the staff, and shewed it when Hyde refused to disclose the King's whereabouts. 'His raylinge at me . . . proceedes from a sawcy, pragmaticall roote,' wrote the resentful Chancellor.[20] Depression, failure, poverty were taking their toll of his resilience. He stayed on in Holland to arrange for his cousin James Hyde, a practising doctor, to go over to England to try to raise some money for the support of his family, an expedient of which the English government were immediately informed by their spies. He was still there in May, still complaining of worse health than he could remember.

He and the King were back in Cologne a few weeks later. Despondency at the easy triumph of Cromwell was soon forgotten in the new possibilities opened by the now certain Anglo-French alliance. This meant that a Royalist alliance with Spain was highly probable; but that, though desirable in itself, was not without its embarrassments. Any alliance with Spain must mean a rupture with Portugal, regarded in Madrid simply as a rebellious province of the Spanish realm, not as a sovereign state. It would be bitter ingratitude to spit in the face of the one European country that had actually taken risks and suffered penalties for upholding the dubious rights of Rupert's squadron against the naval might of the Commonwealth. And what might the most Catholic King require in the way of undertakings to protect his English and Irish co-religionists if, by his military and financial support, the King should enjoy his own again ? These questions were further complicated by the backing that the Spaniards had already given to Sexby, the Leveller, in his plots against Cromwell. Hyde had, in theory, no objection to a strictly limited co-operation with him. But here again the situation was bedevilled by a mischievous, meddling,

[18] *Clar. SP* iii, 267–8.   [19] Clar. MS 50 f.31.   [20] *Cal. Clar. SP* iii, 31.

and wholly fearless family of Anglo-Irish Roman Catholics called Talbot. Two of them were monks, which if anything seems to have made it easier for them to racket about Europe, intriguing, interfering, making promises and assuming powers for which they had no shadow of authority. Vainly Hyde struggled to have them comprehensively disowned by the King and confined to the cells of their mother houses by their ecclesiastical superiors. For years together his correspondence bulges with fury at the elfin irresponsibilities of this terrible pair. A third brother, a soldier, came nearest of all to assassinating Cromwell, subsequently escaping from the Tower of London with the family genius for eluding restraint in any form. Sexby they regarded as their personal property, and indeed there were natural affinities. But the exasperation of attempting to conduct negotiations with the most dilatory court in Europe while the Talbots were forever cutting in or going over his head or behind his back at least made Hyde's adrenalin flow.

Early in March 1656 the King left Cologne, accompanied by Ormonde, to press the Spanish authorities in the Netherlands to the settling of an alliance. The Royalists had something to offer. The Irish Regiments in the French service could be brought over (after due notice given to their French employers) and Royalism itself, supported with Spanish arms and money, could be of considerable value in distracting the energies of the Cromwellian government. There were a number of details to be settled before the exiled court could move its base from Cologne to the Netherlands. Was the King to be formally recognised by the Spanish Governor or was he to live incognito? Was the French pension, cut off by Mazarin's alliance with Cromwell, to be replaced by a Spanish one? Were the regiments recruited from the Irish brigade to have their officers commissioned by the King of England though paid by the Spaniards? Was the King to be accommodated in the capital, Brussels, or in Bruges or Ghent? Would the large debts incurred by the court at Cologne be settled, as Hyde repeatedly insisted, before its removal? He got his way on this point, as he did in the choice of provincial Bruges as a more modest and suitable seat for a pensionary court than metropolitan Brussels. In April, only half-recovered from yet another incapacitating fit of gout, he left Cologne with his wife who was now approaching another confinement. Breda had been chosen for her lying-in. It was from here that Charles II, exultant at the conclusion of what must have seemed an eternity of negotiation, summoned the Chancellor 'to make as much haste as your gouty feet will give you leave' to Bruges on May 7.[21]

Bruges was to be his permanent base until the eve of his master's

[21] *ibid* 299.

restoration. He was often on the move in the Netherlands, spending quite long periods at Brussels, Ghent and Antwerp, as well as odd nights at smaller towns such as Alost that lay on the main routes. Probably he knew this rich and highly developed part of Europe better than he did France, Spain or Germany. If he seems to have been indifferent to its charms it must be remembered that he had been an exile for nearly ten years, and the prospect of return seemed to have moved no closer. 'You cannot think in earnest that I am in love with Bruges,' he wrote to Nicholas in May 1657, 'or would not choose rather to lyve in any place I was ever in in my lyfe . . . having no opinion of the ayre, of the water, or the people; I had rather remoove into England than to any other place . . .'[22] The best years of his life were passing; frustration, poverty, anxiety about the King's weaknesses of character, the little room left him for good talk and congenial company, made cheerfulness harder. On the other hand the Spaniards, exasperating as might be their interminable procrastination in everything, above all in paying out money, were not, like the French, determined to insult and to humiliate. Eight years later when as the returned King's chief minister he was instructing the English Ambassador to Madrid he recommended to his particular kindness 'Mon. Oginate [Oñate] . . . a person of very great Parts and as much a Gentleman as I know any. When the King first came to Bruges this Gentleman was the principal person in Authority there . . . the truth is, his Civility to the King and the Respect to him (which upon my Conscience proceeded only from his Duty to his Master for he is as good a Spaniard as lives) made that place supportable & pleasant to him & to us all.'[23]

Hyde's chief executive responsibility during these years was towards those Royalists in England who were active in conspiracy, intelligence or transmission of funds. Although his judgment of people he did not know was generally shrewd, markedly more so than that of his colleague and friend Sir Edward Nicholas, he was apt to be influenced by the prejudices of friendship and of family connexion. It is difficult to believe that the garrulous and not unentertaining Alan Broderick would have been given so much rope and taken so seriously if he had not been Hyde's cousin. Professor Underdown has described the increasing acrimony between him and John Mordaunt, for long the white hope of the livelier Royalists who sought a brisker pace than the ceremonial slow march of the Sealed Knot. Hyde's position as the chief to whom both men reported became impossible when they accused each other of outright treachery. Both were extremely vain and difficult men: but Mordaunt, when it came to energy and daring, outclassed his rival. On the whole Hyde handled secret activity with a sure touch. His

[22] Clar. MS 54 f.264.   [23] *Original Letters . . . of Sir Richard Fanshaw* (1724) i, 74.

sense of security was rarely at fault. He did not blab. He did not, like Nicholas, suffer from a passion for enciphering low-grade intelligence. 'In truth that which is in its nature to be secrett, lyes in a little roome, & is ever lost by makinge the bulke to big,' he told Nicholas in November 1653, an axiom that might profitably be remembered in our age of classified information. The Secretary seems not to have taken the point. 'Do not take it ill if I grumble at your immoderate usinge your cipher which is growne so familiar to you that I suppose writinge it is no trouble to you but vexes those who are to decipher it.' Hyde complained six months later.[24] He did, it is true, overestimate the safety of the easily broken numerical ciphers employed in his correspondence but in that age of mathematical innocence who was to know what clever Cambridge dons could get up to? Both Pepys's tutor at Magdalene, Samuel Morland, and his later friend at the Royal Society, John Wallis, would have earned their keep at Bletchley Park.

Best of all, the breadth of Hyde's acquaintance gave him a background knowledge that few surpassed. When Manning, the spy planted by Thurloe who was ultimately shot by his fellow Royalists in a wood near Cologne, arrived at the exiled court Hyde suspected him at once because various statements he made about common acquaintances struck him as out of character. He noticed people.

It may seem off-hand to dispose of so important a field of Hyde's activity over so long a period in so summary a fashion. But such an admirably thorough and lucid account is available in Professor Underdown's work that the story needs no re-telling. Rather perhaps it may be more profitable to enquire into Hyde's own life of the mind. That he was itching to get back to his history is evident. Did he ever tinker with what he had written, or make notes for its revision and extension? When he talks of 'falling to my book' does he simply mean that he is going to read? Probably, but not certainly. Even when he was Lord Chancellor of England at the height of a war, passing sleepless nights over the mounting Bills of Mortality occasioned by the Great Plague, he found, or made, time to write. 'I find myself insensibly ingaged in my olde exercise of writinge, which I have discontinued since my coming into England, & it is not easy to me as it hath beene.'[25] From his reading and his enquiries about books it can be seen how much he was occupied in equipping himself to write history. Among his regular correspondents his agent in Rome, an English Benedictine, John Wilford (*alias* in the letters Richard Clement) was often asked questions about the Papal archives. With John Cosin, the deprived Dean of Peterborough and ex-Master of Peterhouse, now and for the whole of

---

[24] Clar. MS 47 f.93, 48 f.202.
[25] Bod.L MS Add. C 303 f.104. Clarendon to Sheldon, August 24, 1665.

the exile chaplain to the Royalists in Paris, he runs the whole gamut of Church history from the Fathers to the controversies of their own day. While they had been in Paris together Cosin had, at Hyde's request, written a Latin defence of Anglicanism, against which the Queen was tirelessly employing the intellectual and material resources of her native country. He continued to scour the Paris bookshops (even in those lean years he had formed a considerable library) for Hyde's requests. One passage from a letter Hyde wrote to him from Breda in May 1656 is of interest not only because it shows the critical faculty he brought to bear on his extensive reading but also because it foreshadows Edward Gibbon in its opinion of Julian the Apostate.

'Concerning Julian, I confesse I have a good mind to have a better opinion of him than the Fathers have. I know no reason why (since his virtues are not inferior) I may not thinke as well of him at least as Trajan & the best of the Heathen Emperors. And I hope it is no want of reverence to the memory of St Gregory or St Cirill to believe neither of them did know the Emperor so well (though it is true one of them saw him once or at least was where he might have seene him) as Ammianus Marcellinus did, nor could as well know the manner of his death, which is as punctually set down as that of any man's can be who is hurt in battell, yet the weapon which stuck in his flesh was the same his ennemyes used & the manner of his death & his wordes . . . was with the calmnesse & resolution gallant men in that tyme died, who believed they were in the right.

'And it may be if those good Fathers had informed themselves dispassionately they would have found his Apostacy (which was that worthily makes him odious to them) to be no other than that he succeeded Christian Emperors without having ever been a Christian himself . . .'[26]

There was no time, however busy he might be, at which Clarendon's mind was not reflecting, comparing, relating and, ultimately, questioning — activities essentially characteristic of the historian. It did not matter whether the subject that engaged him was ten centuries away or ten minutes. He was firmly convinced that the conduct of affairs and the writing of history were interdependent; his maxim, already quoted, is categorical: 'There was never yet a good History written but by Men conversant in Business.'[27] For his own understanding of the historical process the converse was no less true. It was only by such an insight that, if one accepted that history expressed the divine purpose, it was possible to escape the crude criterion of success, by which Cromwell, for example, interpreted the course of

[26] Clar. MS 51 f.267.   [27] *Tracts* 180.

events. There was room in this philosophy for the concept of the fruit-ful error. Hyde made this point explicit in a letter to Nicholas in October 1657:

'I think there is nothing more necessary to make us wiser than recollecting what we have done amiss, but let us have another rule to judge of what hath been done amiss, than merely by the success, other-wise men who must give counsel will be much discouraged; you give some instances in which I may be a reasonable considerer, having had no share in the counsel, and yet am far from censuring those who had. For his Majesty's journey into Scotland, you were against it, and if I had been with you I should as much have dissuaded it, yet I think neither you nor I do now wish that he had not gone, and if he had not, he would have been thought to have overslipped an opportunity to have recovered his three kingdoms. You were for the King's journey hither [he was writing from Brussels] and I against it, yet I know no reason that you should repent your advice since you thought it the most prob-able to produce good effects; and I am sure I have reason to be glad he came, if he had not, would not all the world have said, if he had fol-lowed his own business all would have been well? When we have faith-fully advised what to our understanding is best, let us not be out of love with it because it hath not success.'[28]

Occasionally it was possible to turn historical research to practical advantage. His reading shewed him that in 1576 Queen Elizabeth had lent £40,000 to the States of Flanders 'for repayment of which with interest the several corporations of Antwerp, Ghent, Bruges & Ypres became bound'. James I and Charles I had both at different times at-tempted, unsuccessfully, to recover this. Charles II now offered to wipe the slate clean 'if the Corporations, beginning with Antwerp, will now lend him such a sum as may well consist with their present condi-tion'.[29] The claim was not met: but since it was not pressed it may have been tacitly dropped in exchange for the exiguous supplies that did at length arrive from the Spanish government.

In spite of the ever-increasing severity and frequency of the gout Hyde travelled a great deal more at this period than he had done dur-ing the years in Jersey or Madrid or Paris. Partly this was because Breda seems to have been the appropriately-named choice for his wife's virtu-ally annual confinements and he had to get her there, visit her, and bring her back; partly it was because the war with France, in which the Royalist government was now a co-belligerent, involved the shifting of the centre of power to wherever the army command might be. But largely it was because Charles II enjoyed the sensation of independence induced by being on the move and had better means and pretexts for

[28] *Clar. SP* iii, 372. [29] *Cal. Clar. SP* iii, 178.

doing so than when his mother had held the financial trumps. Not that there was much, or even enough, money. But there was some. The allowance of wine and beer for a household of some eighty-seven persons dated April 26, 1657 is some way from the breadline.[30] And Hyde's own travelling expenses, though not luxurious, are not bleak. Mostly he travelled by waggon, which was slow and tiring. In August 1657 he was summoned to Brussels and took Frances, once again expectant, part of her way:

'Though we left Bruges by 8 I assure you we gott not to Gand till neere 5 & the next morning we were in our wagons by 7 & parted at the door; I heare my wife was bitymes at Antwerp but it was past 6 before I came hither [Brussels], so you will believe I spent little of that night on businesse with the Kinge, for the truth is the waggon makes me very weary and an ill dinner very angry . . .'[31]

Shortness of temper was certainly growing. Even old friends like Ormonde and Bristol are offensively reproved for not writing: 'The King . . . begins to believe his business would have been done as carefully if you had both stayed here . . . If you know anything of good to relieve us you are not well natured to keepe it from us. Your man Oneale may have leasure to write though you have not . . . I am only well enough to write this, otherwise (though out of torment) in no good ease & such a distemper as makes me looke for more torment.'[32] 'Your man Oneale' is a sufficiently insulting description of a courtier and soldier whose subtlety, intelligence and courage Hyde unwillingly admired.[33] But the letter supplies its own explanation. Hyde was living a thoroughly unhealthy life, unalleviated, as was that of so many of his contemporaries, by the long hours in the saddle imposed by the need to get about. Even when he left Madrid in 1651 he had been doubtful whether he could still ride post. No subsequent journey seems to have been made on horseback except for a two-day ride from Xanten to Brussels in December 1656 that left him 'sufficiently tyred & galled'.[34] He ate and drank heartily while leading an entirely sedentary life; his girth was the frequent object of pleasantries by his old friend Bristol; no wonder he was liverish and gouty.

30 *ibid* iii, 278–9.
32 *ibid* 54 f.201 May 10, 1657.
34 Clar. MS 53 f.98.

31 Clar. MS 55 f.310.
33 For his character see *Hist.* VIII, 268.

XVI

Fresh Allies and False Hopes

T𝐇𝐄 𝐒𝐏𝐀𝐍𝐈𝐒𝐇 Alliance altered the balance of power within the exiled court of Charles II — if 'power' be not too ironic a word. Frustration, impotence, would have seemed more accurate descriptions to the people involved. But the very fact that there were now English, Irish and Scots troops serving the English King in alliance with Spain against the French, in their turn powerfully supported by Cromwell's Redcoats and a well-found squadron of the English fleet, meant that, as in the Civil War, the swordmen went up in importance and the political counsellors went down. Those who combined both functions, as did Ormonde and Bristol, moved to the centre of the Royalist stage. Since Ormonde and Hyde were in perfect sympathy this made little difference in his case. Indeed the selflessness of Ormonde's service, as his friend makes clear in his *History* as well as in his contemporary correspondence, shone as bright as that of Hopton or Capel or Falkland. With Bristol it was another thing altogether. To his considerable military experience and his brilliant courage Bristol added his mastery of languages, his lifelong familiarity with Spanish manners, his dazzling charm and his restless experimentalism. He was on the closest terms with the Spanish military and political magnates, Don John, the Marquis of Caracena, Don Alonso de Cardenas, who were by no means on close terms with each other. When it came to getting the Spaniards to pay up, Bristol, as we have seen, was the man to whom Hyde, however grumpily, had to go cap in hand. This was not the right order of precedence for a Chancellor of the Exchequer, still less for a Lord Chancellor of England to which office he had been appointed in July 1657.

Charles II had pressed the Lord Chancellorship on Hyde nearly four years earlier when Herbert, in alliance with Prince Rupert and the Queen, had tried to oust him and had been asked to surrender the Seal as a result. Hyde had refused then, partly on the principle of no rewards or promotions until the King enjoyed his own again, partly on the subsidiary grounds that if the Seal were held in abeyance no grants of royal favour could pass it. Perhaps by the middle of 1657 he felt that the additional authority conferred by the highest office under the Crown was necessary to him in a world where Bristol had got the bit between his teeth at Spanish headquarters and where the conflicting leaders of the Cavalier party in England needed checking and controlling. Perhaps, too, his own relations with the King required a gracious acknowledgment of so signal an honour. That both Ormonde and Hyde were deeply concerned at the King's negligence of his own reputation, his image, is evident from an exchange of letters dating from January 1658.

'I must now freely confess to you,' wrote Ormonde, 'that what you have written of the King's unseasonable impatience at his stay at Bruges, is a greater damp to my hopes of his recovery than the strength of his enemies, or the weakness and backwardness of those that profess him friendship: Industry,[1] courage and many accidents may overcome those enemies and unite and fix those friends; but I fear his immoderate delight in empty, effeminate and vulgar conversations, is become an irresistible part of his nature, and will never suffer him to animate his own designs and others actions with that spirit which is requisite for his quality and much more to his fortune.'

It was not so much that they objected to his womanising — even Hyde, sterner about sex than the aristocratic Ormonde, accepted that 'Kings are of the same mould and composition as other men & must have the same time to be made perfect'[2] — or to his gambling with money he did not possess. It was the lamentable people like Lord Taaffe who, sharing these amusements, were setting his tone. Lucy Walter and her variously attributed offspring were bad enough. In 1656 she had appeared with them in London. Arrested and sent to the Tower, she had given the Protectorate propagandists a field-day by carelessly allowing them to find Charles II's warrant for her pension among her effects. On her deportation Charles had caused a scandal by trying to obtain custody of his son by force. Hardly had that died down before she appeared in Brusssels in August 1657 where she had an English exile stabbed in the street.[3] Luckily he escaped with his life. Duelling, whoring, gambling, the favourite pursuits of the King's particular friends, threatened the reputation that belongs to a national image even in poverty and in exile. Dignity, even austerity, as General de Gaulle showed from 1940 to 1944, is essential to its exploitation.

---

[1] *Sic* in Ormonde's holograph in Clar. MS 57 f.56. *Clar. SP* iii 387, perhaps following Carte's transcription, has 'modesty'.
[2] *Clar. SP* iii, 71.   [3] *Cal. Clar. SP* iii 352.

Next to the dangers of loose living, perhaps partly consequent, are those that arise from engaging in dubious financial transactions. With the connivance of the Spanish authorities and encouraged by Bristol the King had agreed to use his influence with Don John to obtain the post of Financial Commissioner for Cardenas's secretary, Mottet. For a consideration, of course. Hyde's horror, and outspoken condemnation are amply documented in his correspondence. The story foreshadows the strains of his relations with the King after the Restoration.

In spite of the Protean deviousness of the monarch and of the censorious uprightness of the minister, those relations were surprisingly close. That Hyde, from first to last, felt real affection for the King, a protective, quasi-paternal affection that could be bruised but not quenched, seems evident from his private as well as his public writings. When Bishop Burnet, who did not himself witness this relationship but moved among and talked with those who had, wrote that the Earl of Clarendon doted on the King,[4] the rough stroke of his language hits off, as it so often does, a truth that more delicate workmanship might obscure. The King's feelings were not, on the evidence, deep or constant: but the tone of his letters suggests an easy, good-humoured frankness. After all, they had gone through a lot together and were still every day facing the same common exasperations: the tireless intrigues of the Queen Mother to involve the Royalist cause with that of Roman Catholicism, the stream of recommendations sent by her to Jermyn for people who were known to be double-agents or, worse, the procrastination of the Spaniards that made it impossible to co-ordinate plans for supporting a Royalist rising in England and the everlasting hammering on the permanently-closed shutter of the Spanish government cashier. 'This scurvy usage puts me beyond my patience, & if I were with Don Juan I should follow your councell & swere two or three round oathes,' wrote the King to Hyde on June 18, 1657, adding two days later, 'I have lost all patience, & give all men that have or shall have to do with mony to the divill.'[5]

The King was then at Brussels, anxious to join the army in the field and show himself to his troops. On July 15 he addressed a letter to Hyde 'For my Lord Chancelour', evidence that the appointment had been made although Hyde was not sworn in and did not receive the Seal until January 13, 1658, a few weeks after Herbert's death in Paris.[6] On July 30 Hyde wrote in terms of warmest sympathy to his master:

'Though I have been longe prepared to beare untowarde usage enough from these people, yett the informacion you were pleased to

---

[4] *Supplement to Burnet* ed. H. C. Foxcroft.   [5] Clar. MS 55 ff.43, 50.
[6] Lister i, 440.

give me in yours of the 27th makes the carriage so much worse than I expected, that I know not what to say: I thinke you see playnely that they have not only noe minde that you should come to the Army, but that they resolve to keepe you from it, and if you shall break through the difficultyes they lay in your way, it is playne enough they will receave you with such countenances, as you cannot but grow quickly weary of their company: I beseech you therefore to consider whither it be not better to change your minde yourselfe, & lett them know that you have done so, & really thinke no more of seinge them till they make themselves more worthy to be seene, but retyre hither with as much resentment & sullenness as you can . . .'[7] Hyde had had a long experience of playing from weakness and knew that it was no good to knuckle under.

The Spanish alliance offered the near prospect of military support on a major scale. Discussions of 'the great business' — the invasion of England — took place in October 1657 and moved into top gear two years later, in September 1659, when Hyde and Colepeper conferred with Caracena and Cardenas about where the landing should take place. Colepeper favoured Romney Marsh, the Earl of Bristol (whose views were presented by proxy) the Suffolk coast near Orford or Southwold. The Spaniards were apparently in earnest and shocked Hyde by insisting that the Duke of Gloucester should neither be present nor informed of the meeting.[8] Perhaps they thought him too young to be trusted with military secrets. From the depths of disarray Spanish professionalism in war and diplomacy was apt to surface with disconcerting suddenness. It may easily be believed that Hyde was less enraptured by such a prospect than the bulk of his fellow exiles. Had he not from the days of defeat in the Civil War insisted that England must work out her own salvation? In his retirement and reflection he read over Macchiavelli, an author of whom he is generally critical, but in his commonplace book he transcribed with approval his conclusion 'that a Prince should rather take any other course than seeke to bringe auxiliary forces and souldyers into his Country'.[9] Perhaps his experience as ambassador at Madrid had convinced him that nothing would, in fact, ever be done. In any case, unlike Macchiavelli the historian and philosopher of history or, come to that, Edward Hyde the historian and philosopher of history, he was, in this context, a man of affairs acting within the limits so imposed. It would be absurd to wave away Spanish military support even if one did not really believe in its actuality. As in the doctrine of the Fleet in Being its potentiality was a military and political fact in its own right. As such it was taken into account in the drafting of a Proclamation in the autumn of 1657 that

---

[7] Clar. MS 55 f.223.   [8] Clar. MS 56 f.164, 64 ff.89–5.   [9] *ibid* 126 f.60.

outlines the Declaration of Breda that was to follow two and half years later. In both a general clemency and oblivion is withheld only from the Regicides. In the Proclamation of 1657 Hyde has inserted into this clause in his own hand 'or who pleaded as Councell learned in the Law against his life'.[10] The *trahison des clercs* was, in his eyes, the worst betrayal of all.

Hyde's ideas surely shaped the phrasing that would, it was hoped, reconcile Englishmen to the presence of Spanish troops: '. . . taking armes against soe powerfull a Tyrant . . . it hath pleased God allsoe at the same time to give unto us by the friendship & generous Piety of our Deare Brother the King of Spayne the power to strengthen their meritorious harts & hands with ours and our Dearest Brother the Duke of York's presence at the head of a considerable army.'

The conjunction of the two brothers was itself an achievement. James as a result of the Spanish alliance had had to throw up a successful and lucrative career in the French army, much to the annoyance of his mother. His insistence on bringing with him the touchy and quarrelsome Sir John Berkeley led at once to trouble. The King forbade Berkeley the court. James retaliated by dismissing Henry Bennet, never a favourite with him and the especial abomination of Henrietta Maria, whom Charles had appointed as his brother's secretary and chief adviser when he quitted Paris in 1654. James's tantrums seem always to have imposed a need for travel both as symptom and as cure. The breach was healed by a journey of reconciliation culminating in a visit to their sister, the Princess of Orange. The civilities shown to visiting royalty proved dangerous. 'At Damm the garrison gave them a volley', from which the King, observing the standard of small arms drill, wisely took evasive action. Two of his courtiers, slower off the mark, were wounded, fortunately not seriously. At Sluys one of the colour party was shot in the head, another in the neck and a third slightly wounded. 'Methinkes any ill manners may be dispensed with rather than such salutacions,' wrote Hyde to Ormonde when he had got safe back to Breda.[11] The dissension had been settled by promoting Jack Berkeley to the peerage as Lord Berkeley of Stratton and by sending Bennet to Madrid as ambassador.

Bennet, originally Bristol's protégé, had hitherto enjoyed Hyde's good opinion though never his friendship. His engaging worldliness struck an answering note with the young King but not with the older minister. Nonetheless anyone who was so consistently and so unfairly abused by the Queen and the Duke of York was bound to find himself defended by Hyde. And he was intelligent and well-read. His dispatches from Madrid however were received with a coolness that the

10 *ibid* 56 ff.366–7.   11 *ibid* 53 f.302.

King once or twice remarked on. Were they perhaps too enthusiastic, too presumptuous in suggesting lines of policy? To the King himself they were deferential to the point of flunkeydom: the fullest titles, the soapiest phrases are employed whenever the ambassador turns towards his master. And now that Spain was a full ally the Madrid embassy was a much more important position than when Sir Edward Hyde had gone there to write his *Reflections on the Psalms* and to distance himself from the execution of policies that he had opposed with all the force of his deepest convictions.

The Spanish alliance did not in fact deliver the goods. The French, whom Cromwell upbraided for their dilatoriness as much as Hyde and Ormonde cursed the Spaniards for theirs, at last succeeded in taking Mardike and Dunkirk, largely thanks to their English allies to whom the fortresses, in accordance with the treaty, were handed over. Mardike fell in October 1657. James, Duke of York, who was serving in the Dunkirk garrison met the Cromwellian commander, apparently at his initiative, among the sand dunes of the coast a month later. He was accorded his royal style of address, a fact at once reported with amazement at Whitehall. The General was instantly recalled. His successor and the Duke met at the Dunes in the battle of that name the following May in the fiercest of the fighting. The Spaniards were routed and Dunkirk became an English possession. Cromwell's military ascendancy was complete. A landing in England was out of the question.

The Lord Chancellor can hardly have regretted this. Perhaps he saw more significance in the Duke of York's earlier meeting in the Dunes than in his defeat there. He had the sense of his own age in the same way that we have the sense of ours. Party labels and the schematizing of historians flatten the three-dimensional quality of perception. Recording the passage of the Grand Remonstrance by a handful of votes and Cromwell's remark to Falkland on that occasion, he had written, 'So near was the poor kingdom to its deliverance.' Hyde never lost the awareness that things might easily go the other way, that men change their minds, behave better or worse, respond now to this pressure, now to that. Feelers were out in many quarters in England. Apart from the Levellers, sworn enemies to Cromwell, there were great figures like Fairfax who had conspicuously withdrawn from the scene, great supporters of Cromwell such as Lambert who had been alienated, important commanders such as Mountagu in the Navy and Monck in Scotland of whom various Royalist relations had high hopes. These people might well rally to the King. Two years later nearly all of them had.

Hyde's chief colleagues during this last phase of the exile were once again the men he had worked with in Charles I's government in Oxford fifteen years earlier — Nicholas, Bristol and Colepeper, who had long returned from his diplomatic expeditions to settle, apparently, at the court of the Princess of Orange. From time to time he came to meet Hyde, once at least escorting Anne to see her father. His circumstances seem to have been, for some unexplained reason, easier than those of the others. He advances money to buy coach-horses for the King: he lends Ormonde £50. He seems to know what is going on but to play little, if any, part. This suited both Hyde and Nicholas, who had both found him more bother than he was worth. 'I had rather be Secretary Nicholas on foot than Colepeper in a coach,' wrote Hyde to his friend. Nicholas was still the steady, professional royal servant to be relied on utterly. But the statesman whose judgment Hyde most valued, whose support in managing the King and the rest of the royal family he found indispensable, was Ormonde.

Early in 1658 Ormonde had volunteered for a secret mission to London, to evaluate the conflicting networks and if possible to reconcile them, above all to form a judgment of the real possibilities of a rising and of the prudence of committing the person of the King to it. In spite of his great height, his disguise was not penetrated. He met the people he had come to meet, changing his lodging every night, sleeping in his clothes, always making sure of a back way out. He cost no lives and brought back a conspectus of the situation that could have been obtained in no other way. Yet it was not his brilliant success that delighted Hyde so much as his safe return. 'Yours without a date was so very wellcome to me for the assurance it gave me of your safety that I impute that parte that lookt like melancholique in it rather to your warynesse that you would not rayse our expectance than that indeede you were yourself in any dejection of minde . . .'[12]

There are deceptive similarities between the twentieth and seventeenth century usages of war. In Ormonde's secret visit and its dangers we recognise a pattern made familiar in the clandestine operations of 1939–45. Yet only a few months earlier Ormonde's eldest son the Earl of Ossory had been granted a pass by Cromwell to cross the Channel to recover his health. Ossory had had to find a large security and to promise not to act against the régime:[13] and this after several months' imprisonment in the Tower on suspicion of active Royalism. Two years later, in October 1659, Hyde supervised the arrangements for Ossory's marriage to Emilia Beverwaert, a daughter and co-heiress of a very rich though illegitimate scion of the Orange family. Ormonde was absent, attending the King at Fuentarabia. Hyde's letter[14] to him, vast, careful and affectionate, is unusually interesting evidence of the close personal friendship that existed between them. The substance of it is the kind of advice that accountants and tax lawyers now dispense at a high price.

---

[12] *ibid* 57 f.123.   [13] *Cal. Clar. SP* iii, 354.   [14] Clar. MS 63 f.240.

The sums involved in the marriage settlement between two families of such enormous inheritance required such attention. And Hyde, before becoming Lord Chancellor, had had in the far-off days of the 1630s a flourishing practice in such matters. What more natural than that he should, with enthusiasm, place his skill at the service of his friend? Like the Hydes and the Nicholases the Ormondes were a large and affectionate family. But their social and economic standing, their status in the hierarchy of their age, imposed differences on their mutual relationship. The letters between Hyde and Ormonde are entirely frank and easy — it would be difficult to think of Ormonde's good manners and good nature rendering any relation otherwise — but they are not unbuttoned. Clarendon's nature was various enough to respond to different qualities. The impulsive outpourings that are prefaced by 'Oh Mr Secretary' are no more and no less revealing than the formal ordering of his thoughts invited by Ormonde's polite patrician charm.

Royalist hopes, downcast by the loss of Dunkirk in May, leapt up at the death of Cromwell in September 1658. Hyde's reaction was guarded rather than ecstatic. He counted on events moving for the King, but wanted to wait on them: 'we shall have advantages offered, if we do not hurt ourselves upon projects:'[15] Compared to the astonishing prescience and brilliant analysis shown in Colepeper's letter of September 20[16] his judgment was sound but lacking in flair. Colepeper not only picked the winner, Monck, but predicted how he would run and provided some highly professional riding instructions. As a feat of political ante-post betting it has never been surpassed. Clarendon on the other hand discounted Monck's potentialities till very late in the day.

Partly this may have been because he stood too close to the main Royalist sources of intelligence in London while Colepeper was at a distance. The men Hyde listened to most, Mordaunt and Broderick, though scornful and jealous of each other, were both champions of the same idea, namely to do a deal with Cromwell's sons while the Protectorate lasted and after that, or as an alternative, to strike a bargain with one of the Army leaders, Fleetwood if a Cromwellian were favoured, Lambert if a more pronounced emphasis on Parliament were likelier to succeed. Hyde's own preference was for another Cromwellian, Edward Mountagu, the Commander in Chief of the Fleet at the time of Cromwell's death. It was a shrewd choice. Mountagu, like Monck, was a master of bluff. He could hide his real intentions from his closest associates. His cousin and confidential secretary Samuel Pepys has candidly recorded his own failure, for all his sharpness of observation, to perceive what game his master was playing.

---

[15] *Clar. SP* iii, 409.   [16] *ibid* 412–14.

The course of events between the death of Cromwell and the Restoration has recently been examined by Dr Ronald Hutton[17] who has brought to it a fresh eye as well as an abundance of fresh material. The activities of Clarendon's chief agents and informants are lucidly disentangled in Professor Underdown's work already cited. But what was uppermost in the mind of the tiring, irritable, gout-wracked man of vision whose policies had preserved the Royal cause from the disastrous adventurism to which so many of its votaries had wished to commit it?

The core of his position had consistently been that Royalism rested on the Law and on the Church of England. His personal interest in theology and Church history was lifelong. Had not Great Tew offered the delights of a perpetual *convivium theologicum*? The last works of his retirement were to show an undiminished zest for such controversy. Even now, after a dozen years of poverty and exile and incessant political correspondence, he turned with enthusiasm to the letters of travellers such as Isaac Basire who were doing all they could to keep open the contacts between the Eastern Orthodox and the Church of England that Laud had fostered. Closer at hand he continued to extend his patronage, meagre but in the circumstances magnificent, to the exiled Dean of Wells, Robert Creighton, who had for some years been engaged in transcribing and translating into Latin a Greek history of the Council of Florence. In October 1658 the work was nearing completion but the learned editor's funds were exhausted '. . . for every sheet of that paper I payed eleven stivers and could get nothing abated though I bought a half Rheme together'. The books Hyde had promised to send by water had not arrived 'but I am a man very unhappie in books though no man loves them better'. Both they, and a small supply of money, were urgently needed. 'I confesse (my Lord) it is very unseasonable to trouble your Lordship with these perfunctory triffles of myne, in this Knott and coniuncture of great affayres . . . I know your Lordship hath much to do at this tyme & the world is bigg swoln with an extraordinarie hope of the success of your great counsells, and much is looked for from your Lordship who sitts at the helm, whose noble parts, wisdome & loyaltie, are perspicuous & manifest as the sun at noonday to those who want not understanding.'[18] Six months later the Dean wrote to his patron in renewed agitation. Stephen Fox had failed to send the funds that Hyde had ordered to enable him to move from Utrecht and settle at The Hague so that he could confer with the great Vossius. Vossius was both a fellow scholar and a rival editor. The prestige of the King, to whom the book would

---

[17] *The Restoration: a political and religious history of England and Wales 1658–1667* (1985).
[18] Clar. MS 59 f.2

be dedicated, of Hyde as its sponsor and of Creighton himself were all at risk, 'yett I have gott so prettie a start of him & his printer that should they be importunat they should never overtake me till doomsday'.[19]

Hyde's interest was not simply ecumenical. It was both scholarly and controversial. The big battalions of Papist historiography were to be smitten hip and thigh. 'Your Lordship desires to know what this book contaynes that the Roman Catholics may take ill . . . ther is not any one paragraph in all the twelve sections wher businesses are transacted that doth not manifestly bewray a knack of Legerdemayne . . .'[20] The Greek account, according to Creighton, was 'a thing so cleane if not contrarie yet diverse' from the Roman one and retailed many instances of improper pressure.

By September 1659 the book was nearly ready for press. Hyde criticised the fulsomeness of the epistle dedicatory to the King. '. . . no Gentleman is sooner out of countenance by being over commended . . . You have not nor you cannot say too much of the candour of his mind; of the justice & gentleness of his nature.'[21] It was published at The Hague in 1660. Ten years later its author, now a very old man, was promoted to the Bishopric of Bath and Wells.

Maintaining a fighting front against papal pretensions was a pleasure. Duty, urgent duty, called for measures to preserve the episcopal succession of the Church of England. Only a handful of the pre-Civil War bishops survived: all were old, some like Duppa physically frail, others like Matthew Wren worn down by nearly two decades of imprisonment. Sir Robert Shirley had drawn attention to the problem before his own premature death in the Tower.* It was the subject of much correspondence between Hyde and his most active and courageous agent among the clergy, Dr Barwick. The Lord Chancellor was not a High Churchman of the school of Archbishop Laud or Mr Gladstone.† As a historian his view of the apostolic succession would more probably have coincided with that of Macaulay. The Great Tew Circle, except for Sheldon, were latitudinarian by temper and by conviction. The churchmen he particularly liked and admired, Morley, Earles and Sheldon himself, were not consecrated bishops till after the Restoration. The only bishop of his own communion with whom he could easily get in touch was Bramhall, Bishop of Derry. He was not, in Hyde's view, much of an advertisement for his order. He had come near to public disgrace by the part he had played in the conspiracy against Hyde which Sir Richard Grenville had mounted in 1653.

---

* See above p. 165.
† Who, as a schoolboy, made a digest of the first five books of the *History* (BL Add. MS 44802 C). Two outraged marks of exclamation against one of the nineteen propositions, *viz.* that Parliament should approve the creation of Peers, are the only indications of opinion.
[19] *ibid* 60 ff.359–60.   [20] *ibid*.   [21] *Clar. SP* iii, 567–8.

Called on by Ormonde to produce the evidence on which he had repeated stories of Hyde's receiving a pension from the rebels, he cringed and equivocated, hinting that such enquiries might violate the secrecy of the confessional.[22] His alacrity in attempting to secure a commission on the sale of prize goods at Flushing, where he happened to be living, did not become the dignity of a bishop.[23] His reliance on the reported prophecies of a three-month-old child born with a double tongue as grounds for belief in the King's restoration[24] could hardly have recommended his critical intelligence.

To Hyde the importance of episcopacy was not sacerdotal but territorial and disciplinary. The mechanisms of the Church of England for the appointment of bishops exemplified their function. The *congé d'élire* from the King, as Supreme Governor, the ratification of his choice by the cathedral chapter, could only take place when Church and King enjoyed their own again. Consecrating bishops *in vacuo* might smack of the Roman Catholic appointment of dignitaries to sees *in partibus infidelium*, dioceses, that is, which only existed on paper. In the navy of his day there was no such thing as the *rank* of captain, only the *post* of Captain of such-and-such a ship. In the Church of England a bishop, a dean, a rector, were similarly circumscribed to a local habitation.

From such premises Hyde was a staunch upholder of the priestly office. Time and again he complains that the King has been too long without the services of a chaplain. In his own practice we have seen the care that he took both when he was living in Antwerp as a private householder and as Ambassador in Madrid. In entrusting the religious education of his favourite child to his old friend George Morley he bore witness to the same principles.

Thus once again in the rapid scene-shifting that followed the fall of the Protectorate Hyde found himself the target of criticism from those who advocated now an undertaking with the Presbyterians, now with the Fifth Monarchy men who, in immediate expectation of the Second Coming, were hesitant to take the oaths against government by a Single Person, lest they might exclude the Ancient of Days. To suggestions from Bennet at Madrid that the time might have come to enlist the support of the Pope he remained as obdurate as ever.

That policy had begun to look attractive in the autumn of 1659 after the ignominious collapse of the Royalist rising, headed by Sir George Booth, which Mountagu had come within an ace of supporting by his sudden withdrawal of the Fleet from its station at the entrance to the Baltic. His steadiness of nerve when he arrived off the Suffolk coast to find not so much as a dog barking justified Clarendon's confidence.

---

[22] Clar. MS 46 f.318, 47 f.11.   [23] *Cal. Clar. SP* ii.   [24] Carte *Original Letters* ii, 206–8.

How confident had Clarendon himself been in the success of the rising? As far as can be judged from his contemporary papers, very much so. Naturally his letters to agents in the field would convey such a message, whether he felt it or not. But there seems every reason to think that his optimism was genuine. Otherwise he would scarcely have given his blessing to the King's secret journey to the French channel coast in mid-August with the object of embarking for England at a moment's notice. Optimism indeed was perfectly rational. The English government was unstable. The army, the great sanction of Cromwell's dictatorship, was divided. Some prominent officers and leading Cromwellians, even the ex-Protector Richard himself, had privately indicated their readiness to welcome the King. Everywhere rich and powerful landed families who had fought for Parliament in the Civil Wars were coming into line, fearful of the threat to the social order presented by the Quakers and other sectaries. Hyde's own particular contacts, Mordaunt above all, were co-ordinating all these forces. The rising was expected to embrace all southern and central England from Dover across to the Severn. Sir George Booth's efforts in Cheshire were to be the crowning glory. In the event he found himself playing a solo when he had prepared for a concerto.

What had gone wrong was what always went wrong. The feebleness, bombast, quarrelsomeness and indiscretion of the Royalists had enabled the authorities to forestall them. And the Sealed Knot had once again excelled themselves in discouraging and disorganising the party they were supposed to lead. At the last moment Mordaunt performed prodigies in putting the whole creaking machine into reverse and saving the lives that would otherwise have been thrown away. The uselessness of the Knot did at last raise some suspicions that were soon to be all too thoroughly confirmed. As early as August 11 Hyde wrote to Broderick, one of the young activists: 'the King cannot comprehend why Sir Richard Willis should be so shy and wary as he hath always been, and never yet contrived one design, and opposed all; if therefore he be neither come over hither upon the King's letter, or in the field with our other friends, you must never communicate any particular resolutions or the names of persons with him . . .'[25] Soon afterwards Samuel Morland, now high in Thurloe's intelligence secretariat, provided damning evidence, including letters in Willys's own hand, of his treachery. This Morland himself had now decided to imitate on a more spectacular scale, sending over copies of secret documents and ciphers as well as extremely accurate details about which Royalists were playing a double game. In return he was given the Garter.

Was it an early instance of the monarch's engagingly cynical sense of

[25] *Clar. SP* iii, 542.

humour that prompted him to reward this thorough-going betrayal with the bestowal of one of the highest orders of Christian chivalry? What *can* Sir Edward Walker have thought or said, if indeed he was ever told? Perhaps it was the expected explosion of this self-inflating bullfrog that induced Clarendon in a moment of mischievous malice to agree to so manifest an impropriety. For the Garter was actually sent — by secret courier — together with the promise of 'somewhat that shall make you wear it with more delight'.[26] Morland entrusted this precious, but perhaps compromising, token to his father-in-law in Normandy for safe keeping. *Sed quis custodiet ipsos custodes?* Morland's father-in-law '. . . did out of joy communicate ye same to his brother M. de L'Ambrun, Mr D'Ornal Hautcour his cosin & divers other persons of great quality in France, & some copies of ye letters were taken, as one of my wives brothers . . . has confessed'.[27] This premature disclosure gave the King and Hyde an escape from so discreditable a commitment. When Morland presented himself at Breda on the eve of the Restoration, 'my Lord Chancellor advised me by the mouth of Mr Henry Howard to deliver back ye aforesaid letter to ye King, which accordingly I have since don'.[28] Sir Edward Walker could breathe again. Morland was compensated with a baronetcy and a pension of £500 but continued to harbour a sense of injury at not being made Under Secretary of State, which, he claimed, the King and the Chancellor had promised him.

But in the summer of 1659 his intelligence of Royalist doubledealing only deepened the gloom and disappointment felt by the émigrés. The King, accompanied by Ormonde, Bristol and O'Neale, set out at once for Fuentarabia where Spain and France were conducting negotiations for a peace treaty. Bennet at Madrid had long been urging his master to put in an appearance in the hope of enlisting the joint support of the two great Catholic powers in restoring him to his throne.

It was a move to which Hyde was strongly opposed. The weakness of his master's position was so naked that a posture of supplication must at all costs be avoided. Disheartened, distrustful of two out of the three companions the King had taken with him, he lacked the physical resilience of his younger years. On September 25 he wrote to his scholarly protégé Creighton that since the end of August he had been 'indisposed in my health and having not till within these few days recovered . . . vigour of body and mind'. The interval of health was short for on October 18 he wrote to Ormonde that he had been confined for twelve days '. . . but they say 'tis nothing but a cold & all will

[26] Clar. MS 62 f.188, 61 f.355.   [27] *Nicholas Papers* IV, 258–61.
[28] *ibid.*

be well.'[29] The bedridden frustration of his years as chief minister of the restored monarchy was casting its shadow before.

The difference between the temperament of master and servant was never more evident than in these weeks that followed what looked like the final Royalist fiasco. Weariness and depression wore down the older man. But the King, to whom the disappointment must have been bitter, set off southward in, apparently, the best of spirits, open to every pleasure that the journey might put in his way. He was, it seems, in no hurry to arrive. In fact the peace conference had broken up by the time he did so. He therefore decided, on the strength of Bennet's constant urging of a personal meeting with Don Luis de Haro, the chief Spanish minister, to pursue his journey to Madrid. From Saragossa he wrote to Hyde on October 15 a letter of such tranquil enjoyment that, whether it be compared with the Lord Chancellor's own state of mind or with his complaints of travelling the same route ten years earlier, could hardly mark a stronger contrast:

'. . . having mett many pleasant accidents & not one ill one to any of our company, hardly so much as the fall of a horse, but I am very much deceaved in the travelling in Spayne, for by all reports I did expect ill cheere & worse lying, & hetherto we have found the beds & especially the meate very good, the only thing I find troublesome is the dust & particularly in this towne, there having fallen no rayne on this side the Perinaeans these 4 months. God keepe you & send you to eate as good motton as we have every meale.'[30]

The diplomatic circumstances of this expedition were not so happy. The King had been misinformed. Don Luis had not yet returned to Madrid and flew into a passion of rage and suspicion at finding a visiting monarch (unannounced) between himself and his capital. Charles was abruptly recalled to the frontier where the minister was calmed and the King cheered by the unfamiliar pleasure of a payment in cash. Ormonde was granted a friendly but non-committal audience by Mazarin. The little party set out on the return journey in November. They spent a night at Chartres but do not appear to have noticed the glass. They went to Paris so that the King might mend the family fences with his mother. On Boxing Day he was back in Brussels. More than a year had passed since the death of Cromwell. The great powers whose rivalry might have provided him with a re-entry had made peace and turned their backs on him. It did not seem likely that the New Year would be a prosperous one for Royalism. Yet the short-term analysis of Colepeper and the long-term projection of Hyde were, as we know and they did not, on the point of historical ratification.

---

[29] *Clar. SP* iii, 567–8, 583–4.   [30] Clar. MS 63 ff.135–6.

XVII

On the Eve of Restoration

ON JANUARY 1, 1660 Monck began his famous march from Coldstream that has given its name to his regiment. The force he commanded — well-found, regularly paid, purged of politically active officers — was the most formidable single body of troops in the country. Its entry into London on February 3 left Pepys deeply impressed. Even he, close as he was to his cousin Mountagu and ideally placed to hear all the political gossip of London and Westminster, was in the dark as to Monck's intentions, which Colepeper had correctly divined in 1658.

Hyde was even slower than Pepys. The news of Monck's declaration for a free Parliament which had set London alight with bonfires on the night of February 11 (February 21 by the New Style calendar employed on the continent) reached Brussels four or five days later. Three weeks after that Hyde was still sceptical of Monck's crypto-Royalism, though eager to exploit the favourable possibilities of the situation that he had created.[1] Yet his steady conviction of the course to be steered took him by dead reckoning through the fogbank of failure and depression. Things and people were what they were: the art of the statesman was to make the best of them. On November 21, in the trough of Royalist collapse, he had written '. . . when the corruption, or the defects are so universal, except we could make a new people, we cannot be sure to be without the old usage; therefore we must not only not seem to know what hath been miserably done by some persons, but do all we can that they may themselves think as well of themselves as is possible, and recover again their courage towards themselves before they can make use of it towards others.'[2] Faith in the divine providence did not contradict but rather underpinned his sceptical realism. 'I, who have no other method of judging, but by

---

[1] *Clar. SP* iii, 701. Letters dated March 17 to Mordaunt and to Hatton.
[2] *ibid* 609.

what I know men say, and what I know men do', he had written to Ormonde at about the same time.[3] He would certainly have endorsed Pepys's advice to be most slow to believe that which we should most wish to be true. 'It was never harder for me to make a judgment of the state there than now,' he wrote to Bennet in Madrid on January 10, trying to keep him informed of what was happening in England. The letters he received from London, he said, simply reflected the 'constitution' of the men who had written them.[4]

Tactics in any case were not in themselves interesting to him. Principles and perspectives were. Supposing a Restoration to be imminent and granted that it must be established on the old foundation, what elements in the political and ecclesiastical constitution invited encouragement or needed checking? Neither Church nor State was in the condition to resume where young Mr Hyde and his friends had been forced to leave off in 1641.

To take politics first it seemed that the tide most likely to carry the King home after so many wanderings was the fear among the upper classes that the old framework of society was in danger. They had been alarmed by blood-curdling texts from the Old Testament bandied about by sectaries who might take them altogether too literally. If that were so, might there not be a danger of an oligarchy, somewhat on the Venetian model, that would reduce the balancing power of the King? This was urged by Mordaunt in a letter of February 6, 1660. 'There is so insolent a spirit amongst some of the nobility that I really feare 'twill turne to an Aristocracy, Monck enclining that way too.' A few days later Hyde wrote to Broderick suggesting the immediate issue of a pamphlet exposing the political and economic vices of the European republics it was fashionable to admire. Venice and Genoa could be taken as examples of political tyranny, the United Provinces and the Hanse of high taxation and the maintenance of standing armies.[5] The ferment of political ideas distilled by Harrington, Henry Neville* and the other members of the Rota Club, which fascinated Pepys and Aubrey, was not at all to the taste of the Lord Chancellor. Freedom of discussion among the learned at Great Tew was one thing. Dissemination of subversive notions in a capital which was changing its government every six weeks was another. If Clarendon would have agreed with Disraeli in denouncing a Venetian oligarchy he would have drawn back in horror from Tory Democracy. 'Dirty people of no name.' There is no getting away from that detestable phrase,

---

* Clarendon's protection of this interesting figure after the Restoration elicited a charming letter describing Rome and Roman society in 1666. In it he affirms both his personal gratitude to the minister and his loyalty to the restored monarchy. Clar. MS 84 ff.78–9.

[3] *ibid* 610.   [4] *ibid* 641.

[5] Clar. MS 69 ff.191–2, 190.

employed in one of the latest of his writings, the critique of *Leviathan*.[6]

The immediate practical problems a restored Royalist government would have to face were two: the Army and the ownership of land. How the force that had made and unmade governments could be controlled and if possible dispersed into its constituent atoms by the latest of its own creations was a puzzle that could only be solved by the actual process of Restoration. If Monck as effective military dictator were to be the agent, then presumably he could manage the means of his power and it would then simply be a matter of securing his co-operation in dismantling the juggernaut. There was no point in theorizing. The matter would have to be dealt with on an *ad hoc*, day-to-day basis. But the land question was susceptible of rational analysis. Plainly if legal title were to be restored, if the Crown and the Church were to repossess what had been taken from them, if Royalist landowners were not to be penalised by the King they had served as they had been by the usurper, there would be a great number of rich and powerful people turned out of estates that they had acquired in the last twenty years. A more combustible tinder for disaffection could hardly be imagined, especially as many of the intruders would be exactly the sort of people, like Monck himself, whom it was essential to conciliate. Wisely it was recognised that money spent on compensating or reimbursing the loser would be a prudent investment. It did not matter much which proprietor, the old or the new, was left in possession as long as a body was not created with a grievance against the restored régime. The formula of remitting such questions to a future Parliament, which would be able to raise the necessary finance, was unexceptionable. It was later adopted in the more delicate matter of punishing those guilty of rebellion, treason, even under the comprehensive language of the Declaration of Breda, of regicide itself.

By the time that Declaration was issued, on April 14, 1660, the Restoration was certain. Ten days earlier Monck, canny to the last, had received his cousin Sir John Grenville, one of that great Royalist family with whom Hyde's relations had ranged from admiration (Sir Bevil) to loathing (Sir Richard). Verbally, but not on paper, Monck had professed transports of loyalty, stipulated his own conditions (which left politics and religion pretty well alone) and recommended the King to move out of Spanish territory with all convenient speed. All this presented no problem. His terms were accepted *in toto*. The King, Ormonde, Hyde and Nicholas left early one morning for Breda, having successfully disguised their intentions from the Spanish authorities, drafted the brief Declaration that was to bind the wounds

[6] *op. cit.* 319.

and soothe the fears of twenty years of war and revolution, and sent
Grenville back almost by return of post. Mountagu, who had by great
good fortune been reappointed General at Sea, had already given
secret pledges of loyalty. Lawson, who commanded the powerful
squadron in the Thames, was reckoned a sympathiser of the Anabap-
tists and therefore likely to oppose a Restoration. But to everyone's surprise, including Mountagu's, he led his men into the royal service with
the same wholeheartedness that he led them into action against the
Dutch. The new Parliament, or Convention, elected in April, was as
overwhelmingly Royalist as the City of London. As the King wittily
observed it seemed that he had only himself to blame for having been
away from home so long.

Where a tide runs so strongly and so suddenly it is, as Clarendon's
first and best biographer pointed out, impossible to demonstrate individual responsibility for or control of the course of events. But Hyde's
correspondence substantiates Lister's apt metaphor of the 'pilot, borne
along with his vessel by an impetuous current, dexterously avoiding in
his onward course, the dangerous rocks on either side. That he arrives
at the desired haven, seems the sole work of the resistless current; and
the spectators on the shore are not aware of the care and skill by which
that port is reached in safety.'[7]

He had more than ever to check the constant pressure to do deals
with particular parties. Remission of disputed points to a future Parliament was his steady principle. And the active proclamation of a
reconciling, not a vengeful, spirit was its complement. The general
principles were simple. Their application to a host of individual cases
each standing in a different degree of political obliquity and each com-
manding stronger or weaker support in quarters that had to be conciliated, without, in so doing, distorting an emergent balance and
stability, was a delicate and an exhausting business. By the middle of
April Hyde, a glutton for work and a correspondent of indefatigable
zest, told Lady Mordaunt that he was so short of sleep that he could
hardly hold his head up and scarcely knew what he was writing.[8]
Nonetheless he did not abate his learned correspondence; and when,
at last, the gold began to flow into the long-parched channels of the
émigré court his first request to Cosin in Paris was to obtain all the
books printed at the Louvre, particularly the Byzantine historians.
And, at last, the luxurious connoisseurship that was to issue in his collection of portraits, in the adornment of the house and park at Cornbury and finally in the building of the great house in Piccadilly, could
shake itself free from two decades of constriction. The books were not
to come in their everyday clothes. They were to be sumptuously bound

[7] *op. cit.* i, 482–3.   [8] *Cal. Clar. SP* iv, 637.

and gilded. In fact Cosin was to engage the services of a binder and a 'doreur' . . . 'for no Book is well bound here [Breda] but by ye imployment of two or three severall trades.' To lure over a good binder Hyde was ready to offer travelling expenses to include a wife and three children, a free house, and a guarantee of work at the same prices as in Paris, paid in advance. The 'doreur' would be offered the same terms except that there would be no family allowance.[9]

Though he scarcely ever mentions his own family in his correspondence, financial relief was timely indeed. Frances gave birth somewhere towards the end of March to their last son, James. For once she was with her husband in Brussels and had to be left behind when he accompanied the King to Breda. From a letter of Sir Charles Cotterell's to her eldest son Henry it is clear that she had been safely delivered by March 30.[10]

Clarendon — for so at this period we increasingly think of him although he was not in fact raised to that earldom until the coronation on April 20, 1661 — has been generally credited for the tranquillity, the smoothness, of the Restoration and for the fact that it was accomplished without foreign interference. Criticism, often virulent, has come from two quarters. The first, voiced by contemporaries, came from the Old High Cavalier, future High Tory, party. In 1660, so this version goes, the King could have written his own contract. The demoralisation and division of all opposing political forces was so complete that all he had to do was square the crafty but fundamentally stupid Monck (which, indeed, he lost no time in doing) and then he could have established a monarchy far stronger than that of his father or his grandfather. The Convention would have settled on him what revenues he liked. It was only that friend of Pym and Selden, Hyde, up to his old tricks, who agreed a settlement that he knew to be inadequate so that the King and his successors should never be independent of Parliament.

The second attack, later in its mounting but supported by a far wider spread of opinion, is summed up in the historical expression 'the Clarendon Code'. This is short-hand for the intolerant, exclusive policy in the Church Settlement enforced by the Parliament that met in 1661. This legislation was passed during Clarendon's Lord Chancellorship. The burden of the charge against him is that although he did not write this, or anything like it, into the terms of 1660 it was only because he was biding his time. He hated Presbyterianism. He thought Independency absurd but potentially dangerous. He was implacably opposed to Roman Catholicism and was ready to stop up any loophole of toleration through which the Old Serpent might slither.

[9] Clar. MS 71 ff.221 & 328. [10] *Cal. Clar. SP* iv, 610.

Much of the ground on which this last contention is based is incontestably true. But recent scholarship[11] has, to say the least, cast considerable doubt on the necessity of any such inference. In both cases the matter is made no easier by Clarendon's own subsequent account, as historian or autobiographer, of what he thought and said and did at the time. Throughout his second exile, the period during which he wrote of these subjects, he was always hoping that Charles II might relent and allow him to return. This, not an Olympian objectivity, was at the forefront of his mind. He would not have thought much of a historical critic who did not recognise so natural a preoccupation.

In attempting to explain or even to establish the actions and motives of so intelligent and so complicated a man at so critical a juncture the safest tests of evidence seem to be contemporaneity and coherence. Is this what he said or did at the time? What relation does it bear to the political principles to which he had stood with such tenacity? Judged by these criteria there is no positive evidence that Clarendon whittled down proffered revenues so that Parliament's traditional power of the purse might be preserved as a check on an overmighty King. There is, too, a general agreement among historians that the yield of the revenues settled on the Crown fell far short of the estimate, at least for the first half of the reign. And in spite of Clarendon's long tenure of the Exchequer there is no reason to believe that he had any expert knowledge of public finance. Or, to judge from his management of his own affairs in the years of prosperity that were opening before him, of finance in general. If Clarendon did secretly design to clip his master's wings it is difficult to believe that his success was achieved by skill rather than chance.

This does not mean that his old adversaries of the High and Dry Cavalier party may not have been right in imputing such motives to him. Judged by his own steady insistence on the interdependence of King and Parliament on each other in a kind of constitutional symbiosis it would seem very much in character. But was such fine tuning of the public finances a method that sorted with his genius? It hardly seems probable. In any case a much more obvious and familiar expedient for attaining his object lay to hand in the policy, already referred to, of involving Parliament inextricably in the settlement of that most fundamental question, the ownership of land whose title had changed hands through the action of the usurping government.

But what of the Church question? Was Clarendon, as he has so often been represented, the wicked uncle responsible for the stealthy reintroduction of an intolerant establishment after all the fair promises of a liberty to tender consciences, promises that the King, not generally

[11] Notably that of Professor G. R. Abernathy.

admired for his integrity, was to do his best to keep? It is sometimes argued that Charles II's inclination towards religious tolerance was simply a function of his own crypto-Catholicism: that he was ready to allow a freedom of worship to Dissenters, not out of a general Christian charity or an enlightened magnanimity, but because it was the only means open to him of relaxing the laws against the Papists: and that Clarendon, perceiving the black-gowned figure in the shadows, set out to thwart him. This view has been elaborated to provide an explanation of the displacement of Clarendon in the King's favour. Charles, bent on toleration, resented the obstructiveness of his minister and turned to Bennet and others of a younger, looser generation.

Such truth as there is in this is disclosed by the rationalisation of hindsight. To represent Clarendon as the champion of a vindictive, persecuting Church is the reverse of the truth. As Sir Keith Feiling long ago demonstrated in a fine paragraph of his *History of the Tory Party*: 'The one thing most certain about Clarendon is that he was not author of "The Clarendon code".'[12] Evidence subsequently adduced by Professor G. R. Abernathy[13] shows him secretly using his formidable powers as a draftsman and a propagandist against the policy with which he was publicly associated, an echo, if faint, of his political ventriloquism of 1641 and 1642. The necessities of politics, the private convictions of a profoundly religious mind, the dialectical adroitness of a professional advocate, the perspectives of a historian and the *trompe l'oeil* of an autobiographer complicate the evidence of his words and his actions. As the most recent historian of the *Re-establishment of the Church of England* has well written. 'It must be confessed that Clarendon has made it very difficult for us to read his mind.'[14]

It is the argument of this book that it is in his choice of friends that he is best understood. In the early months of 1660, who stood closest to him? Ormonde in politics (which in the seventeenth century included the political regulation of the public expression of religion in doctrine, discipline and worship). In religion *tout court* surely it was those two survivors of Great Tew who had also shared his exile, intimate friends of a lifetime, George Morley, who had been his own private chaplain and the catechist of his favourite child, and John Earles, who had been tutor and chaplain to the young King. Of Ormonde's largeness of mind and distaste for bigotry it is hardly necessary to speak. Of his political awareness of the need for reconciliation, tact, plain good manners, there is evidence at every stage of his long career. And what of the two Churchmen? In that age of vociferous partisanship they were more concerned to listen than to pronounce. Earles, like

12 *op. cit.* 104.   13 *Trans. American Phil. Soc.* 55 part 2 (1965).
14 I. M. Green *op. cit.* (1978) 204.

Clarendon, had in his youth sacrificed to the Muses, but his publications include no controversial theology. Morley published nothing until he was in his eighties — an extraordinary example of humility and self-restraint in so eminent a divine. Both men were to be singled out by the touchy and combative Presbyterian leader, Richard Baxter, as charitable, fair and constructive in the official conferences between the two sides that followed the Restoration. If a man is known by the company he keeps there cannot be much doubt of Clarendon's principles. This is not of course to deny that he disliked Presbyterianism and thought that it had a lot to answer for in the troubles of his country. There is nothing necessarily hypocritical in his saying so, in his wishing it as little success as possible, in his encouraging those responsible, after the Restoration, for the settlement of Ireland and Scotland (two countries altogether foreign to him) not to give it an inch.[15] England, for which he was responsible, which he knew and loved, demanded the putting into practice the spirit of Great Tew.

Morley was sent over in April, when the Restoration was already a virtual certainty, to hold preliminary discussions with both Churchmen and Presbyterians. His letters to Clarendon[16] are evidently written on the assumption that the militant Churchmen must be reined in and the conciliatory Presbyterians encouraged. He wished to promise their leaders substantial preferments, Deaneries, Canonries at Westminster or St Paul's, the Provostship of Eton, the Mastership of the Savoy. The only obstacle he foresaw was that of episcopal ordination which might be demanded by the statutes. For this he proposed two possible remedies: one, to take no notice of the fact, and the second, which he favoured, to arrange 'a hypothetical re-ordination by Bishops'.[17] Even the second would have been coldly received by Charles I and Archbishop Laud: the first would have made them turn in their graves. Already it was clear that bishoprics would be offered them if they could overcome their scruples. Within the next eighteen months Clarendon was repeatedly to press the Presbyterian leaders to accept three of the vacant sees, unsuccessfully except in the case of Reynolds who became Bishop of Norwich.

There were of course survivors of the Laudian school, some of whom such as Matthew Wren or Bruno Ryves were ready to deal out the harsh treatment they had themselves received, while others such as John Barwick, who had risked and suffered much for the King, were less exigent. Juxon, the senior surviving Bishop, who went to Canterbury, had always been courteous and gentle to opponents in spite of

---

[15] *ibid.* Dr Green, in his full, fair survey of the subject argues that there is.
[16] printed in *Clar. SP* iii, 722 ff. and Abernathy *op. cit.* 64.
[17] *Clar. SP* iii, 738.

his intimacy with both Charles I and Laud. Duppa, who had been Charles II's tutor before the war, was too old and infirm to do more than assist in the consecration of new bishops and to press the claims of Hyde's old friend Sheldon to the active leadership that Juxon could not give. Even at Great Tew Sheldon's friends had said that he was born to be Archbishop of Canterbury. He did not in the least mind standing up to people more powerful than himself. He had done so with Archbishop Laud, and again with the Parliamentary Commissioners appointed to purge the University of Oxford. He was to do so again with Charles II in reproof of his open adulteries. Clarendon's warm friendship with him was certainly nourished by admiration for his fearlessness and his integrity. 'The honest Warden' — how much that adjective expressed in the years of defeat and demoralisation. Sheldon's weight and force carried him to the front. In every scheme for rejuvenating a perilously senescent episcopate his name had been prominent. Did Clarendon perhaps feel a touch of misgiving at the very quality he had so much valued? Within two years of the Restoration he had reason to. But there is no evidence that he did. The letters he wrote him at the time of the Plague show all the old affection.

With the stern, unbending High Churchmen who had shared his exile Clarendon's relations were not close. With Cosin, who had scandalised Puritan Cambridge by introducing incense into the chapel at Peterhouse, he was on correct but by no means intimate terms. Clarendon rightly valued the knowledgeable eye of so notable a bibliophile in scouring the Paris bookshops. His learning could be pressed into service against the Papists. The long years of holding the thin red line of Anglicanism against the overwhelming forces of Henrietta Maria could not go unrewarded. Cosin's appointment soon after the Restoration to the great see of Durham was the culmination of a career characterised by tenacity, ability and ambition. The rigorism with which he administered it was, similarly, his own.

The other prominent Laudian of the diaspora, Bishop Bramhall, was, as we have seen, Clarendon's bitter enemy. His promotion to the Archbishopric of Armagh may well have been supported in a negative sense by the Lord Chancellor in order to keep him from that of York. Bramhall's predecessor, Archbishop Ussher, had, according to George Morley, reached essential agreement with Richard Baxter 'in half an hour' when they had discussed ecclesiastical polity. Clarendon would not have been as accommodating as that. But it is clear that he pressed the Presbyterian leaders to accept bishoprics before filling a single vacancy with the most deserving candidate from the ranks of divines who had suffered for their loyalty.[18] It is perhaps significant that

[18] I. M. Green *op. cit.* 84.

Sheldon's first message to Hyde, conveyed by Morley in April 1660, was to warn him of the dangers of too liberal a spirit in the distribution of places.[19]

In the same letter Morley condoles with Hyde on the loss of 'one of your children . . . though that was a thing I could not but apprehend before I came away'. A few days earlier Sir Charles Cotterell had expressed apprehension about the health of an otherwise unmentioned son Charles.[20] The entrances and exits of his children are rarely remarked by their father. Was Charles perhaps 'your young soone Mince' who blotted a letter written by his mother in October 1658?[21] The raising of the Standard in 1642 and the Restoration in 1660, the formal opening and closing of the great struggle in which Clarendon was both actor and historian, were both marked by the tombstone of a son. He mentions the first, in passing, in his autobiography simply to illustrate how little time great events leave for private grief. He had referred to it once, twelve years after the event, in a letter to Sir Charles Cotterell commiserating with him on a similar loss.[22] So attached a husband and father could not, even in the extraordinary exhilaration of 1660, but have felt a wound. How much even this most copious, most unreserved, of correspondents leaves unsaid.

[19] *Clar. SP* iii, 736.
[21] Clar. MS 129 f.34. See Appendix II.

[20] *Cal. Clar. SP* iv, 610.
[22] Clar. MS 47 f.357.

XVIII

Triumph

THAT Hyde might carry all before him on a tidal wave of political success was widely feared, not least in the Royalist party. His enemies there were legion: the Queen and her adherents at the Louvre, who had cultivated good relations with the Presbyterians as a counterweight to Hyde's policy; the old Cavaliers who had charged with Rupert or Langdale; the young courtiers who clustered round the young King, some of them very recent recruits to Royalism; the country squires who looked to the restored monarchy to secure them against social disturbances and distrusted, instinctively, a metropolitan intellectual who had spent the last fifteen years out of the country. Even before the Restoration took place determined efforts were made to get rid of him. 'Sir Edward Hyde hath doubtless great enemies' reported a correspondent on April 13, 'and 'tis believed confidently that if the Parliament make conditions with the King (which is supposed) there will be great heaving to remove him from his Council. I have lately been credibly informed that a great person (one whom he hath formerly obliged) will put to his whole strength to give him a lift.'[1] On May 4 Mordaunt wrote to Hyde warning him of Manchester's activity in spreading 'a very ill opinion of you' and citing Monck and his wife as examples of his audience.[2] The campaign was evidently serious enough to provoke counter-activity. On May 7 Broderick reported: 'My Lord Southampton saith it were not only injustice, but impiety to displace your Lordship, or prevent your entrance with his Majesty, who, next under God, that gave him his title by birth, have rendered his education equal to that title . . . who have furnished his princely heart with all that can become a Throne. *And those only who desire his Majesty should rule irregularly, that themselves might gain advantage by new confusions, would take from him so useful, so excellent a*

---

[1] *Clar. SP* iii 728.   [2] *ibid* 739.

Minister. These things I am commanded to repeat, and they all wish they may be repeated to his Majesty by the sight of this letter.'[3]

Here is the manifesto of the Clarendonian party. Twice in the *Continuation* of his autobiography Clarendon describes Southampton as his 'bosom friend', a term he also applies to Ormonde. They were the two whom the King, in the autumn of 1660, chose to break to the Lord Chancellor the devastating news that his daughter, Anne, the eldest, cleverest and best loved of his children, was pregnant by the Duke of York and had been secretly married to him. The shock of grief and shame all but unhinged him. The King's sympathetic understanding of his great servant was never shown to better advantage than in the choice of messengers. This event, and its consequences, colouring as they did the rest of his life, will shortly be considered at greater length. It forces its way in here because the choice of Southampton, and not an old family friend like Sir Edward Nicholas or Anne's own confessor, George Morley, shows the bond between the two men to have been of a depth and strength that nothing in Hyde's correspondence or general account of his life would have led one to expect.

The friendship between the two men arose, as in the case of Ormonde, entirely from working together in public affairs. Southampton, the son of Shakespeare's patron, was two years older than Hyde. Entering Eton (attended by a page) at the tender age of six he had gone on at twelve or thirteen to St John's College, Cambridge. He succeeded to the earldom at seventeen and then spent ten years abroad, mostly in France where he married the striking young Huguenot beauty whose portrait now hangs in the Fitzwilliam Museum. Returning in the middle 1630s to his estates, he was made the victim of one of the fiscal rackets (in this case the Forest Law) by which Charles I sought to obtain a revenue that did not require the sanction of a Parliamentary vote. Small wonder that in the Short Parliament of 1640 he had been one of the minority in the House of Lords who had supported the Commons resolution that redress of grievances should precede supply. At this point his views might have seemed to agree with those of Pym and Bedford, Essex (Clarendon stresses his close sympathy with Essex) and, indeed, of Clarendon himself. It was over Strafford that fissures began to open. Clarendon's own position, though he nowhere makes it plain, seems to have shifted between his original allegiance to Pym and an uneasy neutrality. Southampton, like Sir Philip Warwick, faced the odium of being placarded as Straffordians, much as they disliked the man and disapproved of his policies. From that moment Southampton moved on to the ground of constitutional Royalism that Hyde was to develop so brilliantly.

[3] *ibid* 744. Author's italics.

The two men may have met in the high political excitement of 1640 and 1641. They were certainly together in the rain-sodden gloom of Nottingham in August 1642 when the Standard was raised (and almost instantly blown down). From then on they must have seen a great deal of each other. Southampton had been made a lord of the bedchamber in June 1641 and a Privy Counsellor six months later. All the time that Hyde was at Oxford with the King they worked in the closest partnership, and never more closely than in the two peace negotiations, at Oxford in 1643 and at Uxbridge in 1645. Writing at Moulins in 1672 he does not disguise how much the more sincere, the more ardent, in this pursuit the servant was than the master. 'He had all the fidelity that God requires, and all the affection to the person of the King that his duty suggested to him was due, without any reverence for or compliance with his weakness; which made him many times uneasy to the King, especially in all consultations towards peace, in which he was always desirous that his majesty should yield more than he was inclined to do.'[4]

It was after the failure of the Uxbridge negotiations that their paths divided, in a purely physical sense. Hyde was sent off as one of the Council appointed to attend the Prince of Wales with consequences already described. Southampton, too, was one of those originally chosen for this service by Charles I but begged off on the grounds of a recent second marriage (it was in fact some three years old) and a family too young either to be left on their own or to face the dangers and disorder of the South-West.[5] Had he accompanied Hyde through the years of defeat and exile, it seems probable that he rather than Ormonde would have become the Chancellor's most intimate political partner. England, not Ireland, was their common background and paramount concern. They had come to know each other well and to champion together policies distasteful to the swordsmen who had been in the ascendant in the years at Oxford. Southampton indeed, after Hyde had gone, dared to speak in Council in terms that led to his accepting a challenge from Rupert. The duel — to be fought on foot with pistols as Southampton was small and not very strong — was only prevented by their colleagues at the last moment. Southampton's tastes, too, were much closer to Hyde's. He was bookish, physically lazy, and did not take enough exercise. What with the gout, and the even more agonizing stone, he was, after 1660, like his old friend more often prostrated with illness than active in court and council.[6] How unlike Ormonde, who even in his old age began the day with two hours on horseback, got privately and regularly drunk, and at sixty was still fit enough to tip the kidnapper to whom he had been tied out of the saddle and to survive the fall without ill effects.[7]

[4] *Cont.* 1074.   [5] *Hist.* VIII 280.   [6] *Cont.* 1076–9.   [7] Carte *Ormond.*

Above all Southampton was by Clarendon's account his own mirror image in religion. 'He was a man of great and exemplary virtue and piety, and very regular in his devotions; yet was not generally believed by the bishops to have an affection keen enough for the government of the church, because he was willing and desirous, that somewhat more might have been done to gratify the presbyterians than they [the bishops] thought just. But the truth is, he had a perfect detestation of all presbyterian principles, nor had ever had any conversation with their persons, having during all those wicked times strictly observed the devotions prescribed by the Church of England; in the performance whereof he had always an orthodox chaplain . . .'[8] He might have been writing his own epitaph. The passage certainly contains all that he would most wish to read there on the subject that from his young manhood had been his chief preoccupation. Cardinal to his Christianity were serious, practical morality: the private life of prayer: order, a decorous order, in public worhsip but not such as to invest bishops and priests with any general or undefined powers: a rational, neutral, tolerance of Presybterianism combined with a vigorous personal rejection of its forms and tenets. Again there is the sympathy of self-portraiture in the concluding sentences on Southampton's religion: 'But that which had the strongest influence upon him, and which made him less apprehensive of the venom of any other sect, was the extreme jealousy he had of the power and malignity of the Roman catholics . . . and he did believe, that the King and the duke of York had a better opinion of their fidelity, and less jealousy of their affections, than they deserved; and so thought these could not be too great an union of all other interests to control the exorbitance of that.'

These passionate convictions (the epithet is Clarendon's own) are closer by far in nature and intensity to his own than the spacious, cool air of good breeding in which Ormonde approached such questions. Ormonde's sincerity is supported by an uprightness of life and an absence of deviousness or malice that Clarendon no doubt recognised as the fruits of the spirit. Besides, his charm of manner, by all accounts, made him irresistible. But Southampton's temperament, interests, activities were far more congenial. It is hard to resist the conclusion that if Southampton had not stayed behind and played out the drama through all the closing scenes that Clarendon missed — the surrender of Oxford, the negotiations with the Army, the trial and execution, the vigil in St James's Palace, the burial at Windsor — he, not Ormonde, whom Clarendon only got to know in 1652, would have been the friend and confidant of the exile.

What Hyde owed to Ormonde was the development of a quality

---

[8] *Cont.* 1080.

already present though often overshadowed, that of uncynical but undeceived realism. He made him more of a man of the world, particularly in his dealings with difficult or unsatisfactory people. 'When the corruption, or the Defects are so universal, except we could make a new people, we cannot be sure to be without the old usage.' 'I have no better opinion of the honesty of the age than you seem to have, and do not look that conscience and repentance shall dispose men to lose all they have got.'[9] The man who so expressed himself had come a long way from the moral fist-shaking of the letters written as ambassador in Madrid. Ten years of disappointment and frustration have to be taken into account: but so in the case of Clarendon does the company he kept.

The contrasting influence of these two bosom friends may be glimpsed in the most delicate of all the issues that threatened Clarendon's relations with his master, that of Lady Castelmaine. Southampton like Clarendon showed his disapproval of her establishment as the King's *maîtress en titre* by a steady refusal to acknowledge not only her power and her influence but even the fact of her existence. No grant from her royal lover would receive the sanction of the one as Lord Treasurer or the other as Lord Chancellor. Of course there were ways of enriching her and even of granting her noble status without going through these channels. It is perhaps significant that her husband, Roger Palmer, was created an Irish, not an English, earl. Ormonde's attitude was less assertive of what Shaw's Mr Doolittle dismissed as middle-class morality. He did not object, as his own life had shown, to great men keeping mistresses. But he did join Clarendon in deploring the King's 'immoderate delight in empty, effeminate and vulgar conversation'[10] and, after Charles's marriage to Catherine of Braganza, in opposing his insistence on forcing his wife to accept his mistress as a lady of her bedchamber. The difference is developed in Newman's critique of Burke's famous phrase: '. . . Vice itself lost half its evil by losing all its grossness.'[11] Ormonde stood for the aristocratic, man-of-the-world virtue of decency: Southampton and Clarendon for principle. In the court of Charles II people who stood for either were easily confused.

These three men occupied in May 1660 the chief executive, advisory and judicial positions in government. By adding the aged Secretary Nicholas, who was a Clarendonian of the earliest vintage, the number could be stretched to four. But Nicholas was simply too old and too exhausted to take more than a nominal part in affairs. Indeed it was Clarendon himself who, to the resentment of his old friend, supervised

[9] *Clar. SP* iii 609, 702.   [10] *Clar. SP* iii 387, Ormonde to Hyde January 27, 1658.
[11] *Idea of a University* n.i. (1925), 201.

the terms of his redundancy in October 1662. Old age and ill health were mowing, not thinning, the ranks. Hertford and Colepeper died within a few months of the Restoration.

Of the two men who had the most obvious claims on the King's gratitude for restoring him and occupied the most solid base of military and naval power, Monck and Mountagu, it was the second and less powerful though more politically minded with whom Clarendon enjoyed the better relations. Like Ormonde, Mountagu had easy manners, a calm temper and a wife whose charm and kindness are attested by every scrap of evidence that survives, notably the *Diary* of the sharply critical Pepys. Created Earl of Sandwich at the Restoration, Mountagu was from that moment until the fall of the minister in 1667 reckoned a Clarendonian. It was not that he shared Hyde's religion — according to Pepys he was a sceptic — or the views of history, law and society derived therefrom. He was not an intellectual, but, again like Ormonde, was a member of the ruling class whose instinct was to support government. Before he became a Clarendonian he had been a Cromwellian. The transition was not a difficult one to make. Mordaunt had tried to nerve Richard Cromwell to take the initiative in restoring the monarchy. Henry Cromwell, the abler brother, thanked Clarendon in the handsomest terms for the treatment accorded him: '. . . your lordship (being above making an Interest by trampling upon the fallen or by being bitter against things that come to pass by God's secret providence) have most nobly & Christianly patronized me in it even to successe.'[12] Cromwell's brother-in-law, John Wilkins, the brilliant Warden of Wadham during the Interregnum, had ecclesiastical preferment heaped upon him: his protégé and successor at Wadham, Walter Blandford, became Clarendon's chaplain and succeeded Morley as confessor to Anne, Duchess of York.[13] To a surprising degree Clarendon and Cromwell valued the same qualities in their colleagues and subordinates.*

Monck was of an altogether different colour. A professional soldier of much the same social rank as Hyde or Mountagu, he had not shared their advantages of wealth, upbringing or education. Worse still he had married a wife whose snobbery, rapacity and general ill-breeding had roughened a nature already close and crafty. No wonder Hyde had been a late convert to his beneficent intentions. His relationship to the Grenvilles, a family with whom Clarendon was not on good terms, did

---

* One of the last and most touching of Clarendon's letters, written 'in a hand at best illegible and now shaking through much weaknesse', was to Lockhart, once Cromwell's Governor of Dunkirk and Ambassador to France. After Clarendon's fall he was re-employed by Charles II at the Paris embassy. Printed in Lister iii, 484–5.

12 BL Add. MS 4159 f.74, April 9, 1662.

13 George Morley *Several Treatises* . . . (1683) xiiii.

not help. But clearly, if the new régime were to survive and gather strength, he had to get on with him. Very likely Monck, when out of reach of his wife's jealous malevolence, thought so too. In fact, after a guarded beginning, they seem to have recognised in each other the quality that Pepys grudgingly admitted in Monck, that he was 'stout and honest to his country'. At the time of the Plague when Clarendon had to follow the court to Salisbury and Oxford he wrote to Sheldon, then Archbishop of Canterbury:

'I sweare to you I have the same sense and apprehension of hearte that your grace hath with reference to the Generall who cannot avoyde exposing himself to many daungres & good God in what case now were all if we should loose him? and yett I do envy you both that you have the frequent opportunity to visitt and comforte one another and I do often and heartily wish that I were admitted to the same happinesse.'[14]

The passage shows what a sense of duty, given time, can do. It is impossible to imagine Clarendon and Monck, as private citizens, enduring each other's company for half an hour. But after twenty years of making himself agreeable to Henrietta Maria's favourites and Charles II's companions Clarendon could maintain an easy working relationship even with people he detested as heartily as he did Lauderdale and Robartes, both of whom had, in the past, done their best to destroy him. He was himself uncommonly good company. The Ciceronian solemnities of his prose style sometimes lead one to forget this. Both Evelyn and Pepys who saw more of the society of their own time than most men are emphatic on the point. Bishop Burnet who did not know him clearly thought that he allowed his wit and his perception of the ludicrous altogether too free play.

It is a criticism that has also been levelled at Charles II. For all their differences of temperament, character and taste there were, particularly at the beginning of the reign, points of congruence. Both men had a sense of humour: both favoured religious toleration: both were anxious to let bygones be bygones. In the last two they were against the most powerful tides of political opinion, as manifested in the Cavalier Parliament that met in 1661. The anxiety of the King and Minister to broaden the base of the régime and to bury hatchets exposed Clarendon to a mounting fury of Royalist resentment, exemplified in the bitter jest that the Act of Indemnity and Oblivion achieved Indemnity for the King's enemies and Oblivion for his friends. The only counterweight to the minister's unpopularity was the favour of his master.

In May 1660 this looked deeper and firmer than ever. The King had backed the minister when there was nothing to show for his policy. Now the minister's judgment and the King's trust had been

14 Bod.L Sheldon Papers. MS Add. C.303 f.104.

triumphantly vindicated by events. Yet the cheering and the drinking of healths had hardly subsided before their differences began to appear.

The first and far the most dangerous was the marriage between the Duke of York and Anne Hyde. As soon as it was made public one of Pepys's friends observed that it would 'prove fatal to my Lord Chancellor',[15] an opinion finally endorsed by Clarendon himself and generally shared by contemporary observers. Mazarin, who thought that Clarendon had engineered it, could not understand how so wise a statesman could have done anything so foolish. Naturally his enemies asserted his responsibility; and, by extension, his contriving the King's subsequent marriage to a barren Portuguese princess so that his own grandchildren should inherit the throne. The first public assertion of the charge was made by Clarendon's old friend, now turned his embittered detractor, the Earl of Bristol, in the tenth article of the impeachment he moved against him in the House of Lords in the summer of 1663. It was then too early to be sure that Queen Catherine would not produce an heir. The marriage was barely a year old: there were rumours of a pregnancy in 1664 and, after a serious illness, a miscarriage in 1666. It is inconceivable that Clarendon or anyone else could have possessed the gynaecological expertise necessary to such a prognosis. Bristol instead alleged legal chicanery: that Clarendon 'had broak of ye match with Spayne & others; . . . and had contrived ye K's marriage by a Romish preist, contrary to ye lawe of ye land, that thereby ye succession might be hereafter questionable.'[16]

The charge, whether made by contemporaries or by those who later had reason to blacken his name, rests on malice not evidence. No one who reads his own account in the *Life* can doubt its truth. The anguish of deep feelings deeply outraged is unmistakable. There can be no doubt of his devotion to his elder daughter or of his antipathy, long evident, to his son-in-law. What father in his right mind would wish to commit the happiness of a favourite child to so distasteful a figure? The public admission that she had been the Duke's mistress for many months before her hole-and-corner midnight wedding, itself necessitated by her advanced pregnancy, cut his pride to the heart. Such a thing would never have happened had she been living with her father and mother. It was the loose idleness of Court life that had undone her, the court of the King's indiscreet and wilful sister Mary of Orange, no doubt made yet more giddy by the presence of his aunt Elizabeth of Bohemia, the Winter Queen. Anne Hyde had seen her parents only at rare intervals since she had become a Maid of Honour in 1654, mostly when her mother came to Breda to lie in. In the year of the Restoration

---

[15] *Diary* i, 284.   [16] Lister iii 247.

this fixture had been transferred to Antwerp so that she seems to have seen nothing of her family for some two years before she rejoined them in London in the summer of 1660. The date and place of her betrothal to the Duke is controverted by its principals. In their sworn attestations both agree on the date of August 9, 1659, though the bridegroom opts for 'Hounslardike in Holland', the bride for 'Breda in Brabant'.[17] By February 1661 when these transactions were officially minuted by a Privy Council 'purposely called for declaring the certainty of the marriage' the Duke and Duchess were agreed on Breda as the place but had shifted the date to November 24.[18]

It hardly seems probable that the Duke endeared himself to his father-in-law by his behaviour after the wedding solemnised by his own chaplain in Worcester House, where the Chancellor was then living, after everybody else had gone to bed about midnight on September 3 in the presence of Ormonde's son, Ossory, and Anne's personal maid. The Duke began to get cold feet: could not the whole business be called off, the contract cancelled, the marriage annulled? All too obviously it had been consummated. A posse of his boon companions swore to having had carnal knowledge of the Duchess. Of course it was entirely untrue, as was soon established and confirmed by the complete retraction of his friends. The bishops made it plain that they would not, indeed could not, bend the rules of matrimony. The marriage was an accomplished fact. A scandal of its nature sufficiently notorious had thus been gratuitously defiled. Through the years of poverty and exile the Chancellor had kept his reputation and that of his family unspotted. Now on the morrow of his triumph the royal cesspit had been emptied over him and his.

The clearing of his name was neither easy nor cheap. The King, grasping the fact that there was no going back on what had been done, threw his full weight behind his minister, did what he could to comfort him, and forced the rest of his family to acknowledge his brother's wife. Henrietta Maria's fury at finding herself connected to her most inveterate, most successful, political enemy, who was not even a member of the aristocracy, can be imagined. Even her youngest son, the Duke of Gloucester, by all accounts the best natured of the family, opined that his sister-in-law smelled of her father's green bag. It was the King who insisted that the Chancellor should at once take a peerage to secure the privilege of that order. From June 1 he had sat on the Woolsack as plain Sir Edward Hyde: on November 6 he took his seat as Baron Hyde of Hindon, a village in the Wiltshire heartland of the family.

There were difficulties and dangers enough that autumn: the

[17] Clar. MS 74 f.128.   [18] *ibid* f.138.

disbanding of the army, the rumours and rumbles of revolt, the cautious advance through the minefield of the land question, the prevention of vendettas under the pretext of punishing political offences, the question marks that still hung over the two great issues that had precipitated the Civil War, the Church and the Militia. To take a hold on expenditure was urgent. Disbanding the Army meant finding money for mountainous arrears of pay. The same was true of the Navy, which could not safely be reduced to the old peacetime skeleton force of the first Stuarts and even of Queen Elizabeth. The acquisition of Dunkirk looked splendid on the map, but disastrous on the national balance sheet. Pre-industrial economies could not support these vast expenditures. And it was not to be expected that a young King entering on his inheritance after years of scrimping would set an example of financial prudence. For Clarendon everything depended on the King. He could not afford to lose any of the capital built up by years of personal service and successful advice. Suddenly, at a stroke, his daughter's unimaginable act in making him father-in-law to the heir to the throne wiped it out. He was in debt to the King, not the King to him.

He had not long to wait before this was brought home to him. In the early summer of 1662, when he and Ormonde remonstrated with the King over his bullying his young, convent-bred Queen into accepting Lady Castlemaine as a lady of her bedchamber, Charles wrote to Clarendon, indicating that the letter should also be shown to Ormonde.

'. . . whosoever I find use any endeavour to hinder this resolution of myne (excepte it be only to myselfe), I will be his enemy to the last moment of my life. You know how true a friende I have been to you. If you will oblige me eternally, make this businesse as easy as you can, of what opinion soever you are of; for I am resolved to go through with this matter, lett what will come on it; which againe I solemnly sweare before Almighty God. Therefore, if you desire to have the continuance of my friendship, meddle no more with this businesse, except it be to beare down all false & scandalous reports, and to facilitate what I am sure my honour is so much concerned in: and whosoever I finde to be my Lady Castlemaine's enimy in this matter, I do promise, upon my word, to be his enimy as long as I live . . .'[19]

The invocation of the Deity adds a nice touch to this profession of personal honour when the purpose of the letter is considered. Its snarling, threatening tone hardly needed such reinforcement. 'You know how true a friende I have been to you.' The bill for Anne Hyde's misconduct was being presented for payment.

[19] Lister iii 202–3.

Next to the shame and grief that his own child had so betrayed what he stood for was the revulsion at the child of his old friend Grandison flaunting her whoredom, tainting the sacred mystery of kingship at last delivered from the hands of the heathen. The rich denunciatory language of the Old Testament prophets was all too familiar to the ears of seventeenth-century Englishmen. Barbara Villiers gave it form and substance. And that it should be her, of all people. The only child of a man who had given his life for the King: the niece of the woman, Lady Morton, whom he had long and dearly loved: the granddaughter of that Barbara Villiers, still alive, who had supported him with her affection and her prayers in the terrible bereavement of his first marriage. It was one of his longest, most intimate connexions. The two families had been neighbours at Westminster before the Civil War. Barbara had been baptised at St Margaret's in the same year as his son Laurence. Had it not been for the war they might have grown up together, perhaps married. Was she not, one might guess, the inspiration of that famous, furious, indictment of the society that had grown up in the years of disorder drawn by Clarendon in his last exile?

'. . . the time itself, and the young people thereof of either sex having been educated in all the liberty of vice, without reprehension or restraint . . . Children asked not blessing of their parents; nor did they concern themselves in the education of their children; but were well content that they should take any course to maintain themselves, that they might be free from that expense. The young women conversed without any circumspection or modesty, and frequently met at taverns & common eatinghouses . . . The daughters of noble & illustrious families bestowed themselves upon the divines of the time, or other low & unequal matches. Parents had no manner of authority over their children, nor children any obedience or submission to their parents . . .

'In a word, the nation was corrupted from that integrity, good nature, and generosity, that had been peculiar to it and for which it had been signal and celebrated throughout the world . . . the very mention of good nature was laughed at and looked upon as the mark and character of a fool; . . . In the place of generosity, a vile and sordid love of money was entertained as the truest wisdom, and any thing lawful that would contribute towards being rich. There was a total decay, or rather a final expiration of all friendship; and to dissuade a man from any thing he affected, or to reprove him for any thing he had done amiss, or to advise him to do any thing he had no mind to do, was thought an impertinence unworthy a wise man, and received with reproach and contempt.'[20]

[20] *Cont.* 36–8.

'The Lady', as Clarendon calls her, disdainfully admitting her to a place but not to a name in his book, certainly satisfied the last part of this description. 'A gay wife, great expenses, slender fortune': thus was her husband's condition described to him a few weeks before the Restoration.[21] Lady Castlemaine's love of money, and her vindictiveness, seem to have been the strongest, most consistent elements in her character. That Clarendon felt bound to hate as a harpy a person whom he would have wished to love as a daughter made the relation all the bitterer. Most contemporary authorities agree with him in seeing her as one of the most venomous, most unrelenting, of those who turned the King against him.

But the most effective agent of this process was Clarendon himself. He had never lacked, never was to lack, a high opinion of his own quality. The Christian virtue of humility, which his prayers, his *Reflections on the Psalms* and other writings show to have been real enough, did not extend to social relations or public affairs. People, not only his rivals and his critics, thought him pompous, overbearing, too full of himself. He was, after all, a very mighty subject who laid himself open to the charge of being overmighty. Both Lord Chancellor and Chancellor of the Exchequer until he resigned the post in May 1661 in favour of the Treasurer's nephew Sir Anthony Ashley Cooper (newly ennobled as Lord Ashley), his was the voice that carried the note of authority, whether he was speaking in the House of Lords, at the Council Board or in the inner committee of Government loosely charged with the conduct of Foreign Affairs. In the Coronation Honours he was created Earl (having declined the offer of a Dukedom as likely to incite envy). A few months earlier he had succeeded Hertford as Chancellor of the University of Oxford, perhaps the honour he valued most. Although he was not avaricious, had indeed, like Walter Scott, a grand carelessness about money when he believed himself reasonably secure, lands and riches were heaped upon him, directly by the King and collaterally by Ormonde and his colleague Orrery, from the Irish revenues. Offered the loan of Worcester House by its owner, the Marquis, 'without requiring from yr. Lo. one penny rent (yet that only knowne between yr. Lo and me)'[22] he first concentrated his attention on extending and improving Cornbury, the house and estate near Oxford which he was granted in 1660.[23] Hugh May was employed as architect and landscape gardener. Here he would be surrounded not only by the books and papers he had begun to amass in the penury of

---

[21] *Cal. Clar. SP* iv, 655.

[22] Lister iii 108. Clarendon states in his autobiography that he paid a rent of £500 a year. In fact the figure seems to have been £400. *Cal. Clar. SP* v, 305.

[23] V. Watney. *Cornbury and Wychwood Forest* (1910) *passim*.

exile but by the great collection of portraits he was intent on forming. This would preserve the likenesses of all his closest friends and associates, indeed of all those eminent on the Royalist side however much he might have disapproved of them; even some who had been in arms against the King but had subsequently redeemed their errors were to be admitted. Edmund Waller, the poet, was granted a place though Clarendon as Chancellor blocked his appointment to the Provostship of Eton and dealt faithfully with his cowardice and his treachery in the *History*. Would figures such as Blake ultimately have gained admission? Cromwell and Ireton, Lambert and Vane could hardly be allowed into the Chancellor's house. But great historical personages, Cardinal Wolsey, Archbishop Warham, Thomas Cromwell, the Cecils, were to be included.

A royal grant of land on the north side of Piccadilly extending from Coventry Street to Hyde Park Corner presented the Chancellor with an opportunity for building a London house. The largeness of mind that has been so much admired in the *History* was given free rein in the conception of Clarendon House, designed by Sir Roger Pratt and built between 1664 and 1667. Its magnificence was seized on by his enemies to inflame public opinion against his mightiness and to infuse it with the idea that only corruption on a huge scale could have enabled a man who had inherited so little so spend so much. 'Dunkirk House' it was nicknamed, implying that the sale of Dunkirk to the French, which the Chancellor had negotiated in 1661, had provided a good part of the money. There was in fact no substance in this rumour: and Clarendon was merely carrying out a decision of government in which, as a purely military and strategic question, he had accepted the opinion of his expert colleagues. Sir Robert Southwell, most impartial of witnesses, has left the clearest testimony on the matter, in answer to an enquiry, nearly forty years later, from Clarendon's son Henry, the second Earl:

'I came not to Whitehall till towards the end of 1664 when the Business of Dunkirk was over, soe that what I learnt concerning that affair was by accident when I was at Madrid about October 1667 and when the Earl of Sandwich was Ambassador Extraordinary there.

'The Discourse was then warme, how France was expending vast Sums at Dunkirke & how dangerous these preparations might prove to England. But His Excellency seemed to despise them as Fancyes, saying that the Coast there was so tempestuous & the grounds so changeable & rouling upon every storme, as never to leave a certain steerage to that Port. And it was (said he) upon full consideration hereof, & the Charge of that Garrison, that I was the first Man that ever moved the King to part with It, although my Lord Clarendon, who is now thrown out, has undergone the Blame.

'This [is] what past in open discourse at his Excellency's Table . . .'[24]
Not only did Clarendon refuse the enormous bribe offered by the
French: he informed the King of it, who laughed at the idea of not taking it. If for no other reason — and there certainly were others — he
was too proud to be corrupt. He accepted the customary perquisites
and payments of his numerous offices. Bureaucracy in the seventeenth
century was a turnpike, not a free highway maintained at the public
expense. Those who used it expected to pay a series of tolls at each administrative checkpoint. Clarendon took much less in the way of
honours and rewards than he was offered. He refused a dukedom: he
refused the Garter: he refused a grant of rich fenland worth in the
money of his time £20,000 a year. His former close friend Bulstrode
Whitelocke is almost alone in accusing him of extortion, grumbling at
having to pay £250 for his pardon to pass the Great Seal and such-
like.[25] Doubtless Clarendon felt that for twenty years Whitelocke had
had his share of good things and that a re-adjustment would be in
order. He always despised people who put wealth and comfort first;
and this, rightly or wrongly, was his interpretation of Whitelocke's
political conduct. Whitelocke, after all, had taken service with a
régime that had proscribed his old friend Hyde, expropriated his
possessions, persecuted his family, without, so far as is known, raising a
finger in his help or defence.

Disappointments, jealousies, resentments were bound to spring up
and to spread, however and by whomsoever the Restoration had been
effected. What more natural, indeed inevitable, than that they should
focus on the political architect who concentrated in himself its principles and its authority? The unwieldy figure, laden with honours,
carpeted and curtained with the gold-encrusted robes of the Lord
Chancellor of England, would of itself have provided a sitting target.
That he should have married his daughter into the Royal Family, and
not just the outer branches but have grafted his stock into the immediate line of succession, raised him to an eminence as vertiginous as
that achieved by any other favourite in that century of favourites,
Buckingham, Richelieu, Olivares, Mazarin.

So, at least, his triumph looked from the outside. His own private
correspondence, especially that with Ormonde after his old friend left
England in the summer of 1662 to take up his Lord Lieutenancy in
Dublin, shows how precarious he felt his own position to be, how
unfixed the King's purposes, how dark and uncertain the prospect.
Nonetheless cheerfulness kept breaking in. 'Amonge all my faultes,

---

[24] Letter transcribed in Speaker Onslow's notes on Clarendon's *Life* (1759) II, 329 now in University of London Library.
[25] Ruth Spalding, *op. cit.* 239ff.

you know sullennesse is none. I throw that however alwayes off, in an houres conflicte.'[26] It is this note, of cheerfulness, almost of conviviality, that he struck so characteristically in his address to the Convention Parliament of 1660:

'. . . The King is a suitor to you: makes it his suit very heartily that you will join with him in restoring the whole Nation to its primitive Temper and Integrity, to its old good Manners, its old good Humour and its old good Nature; Good Nature! A Virtue so peculiar to you, so appropriated by God Almighty to this Nation, that it can be translated into no other language: hardly practised by any other People . . . If the old Reproaches of Cavalier and Roundhead and Malignant be committed to the Grave, let us not find more significant and better words to signify worse things: Let not Piety and Godliness grow into Terms of Reproach . . . and let not Piety and Godliness be measured by a Morosity in Manners, an Affectation of Gesture, a new Mode and Tone of speaking . . . Very merry Men have been very godly Men; and if a good Conscience be a continual Feast there is no Reason but Men may be very merry at it . . . Be but pleased yourselves and persuade others to be so; contrive all the Ways imaginable to your own Happiness and you will make him the best pleased and the most happy Prince in the world.'[27]

---

[26] Lister iii 226.
[27] *CJ* Sept 13, 1660, 172–4. I have altered 'appropriated to' to 'appropriated by'.

XIX

The Administration of Clarendon

OF THE great historians who have written on Clarendon's ministry (Clarendon himself excepted) Macaulay is the one who best satisfies the qualification insisted on in Clarendon's Essay on the Active and the Contemplative Life. It is however the prejudices of Holland House rather than the insights gained in the administration of India that characterise the stock representation of a decent old thing out of touch with his age offered to the reader of the *History of England*. One point however that Macaulay makes has such important and obvious truth in it that its exaggeration prompts reflexion: 'Toward the young orators, who were rising to distinction and authority in the Lower House, his deportment was ungracious: and he succeeded in making them, with scarcely an exception, his deadly enemies. Indeed one of his most serious faults was an inordinate contempt for youth: and this contempt was the more unjustifiable, because his own experience in English politics was by no means proportioned to his age. For so great a part of his life had been passed abroad that he knew less of the world in which he found himself on his return than many who might have been his sons.'[1]

The circumstantial content of this accusation is irrefutable. Clarendon had been abroad for far too long: he was out of sympathy with the Cavalier Parliament elected in 1661 and exacerbated this by tactless and overbearing behaviour: the members of the House of Commons who were soon determined on his destruction were almost all younger than he. But did he despise them because they were young? Had he, in Macaulay's phrase just quoted, 'an inordinate contempt for youth'? When he died in 1674, an exile, broken and forgotten, one of his young friends wrote to inform another of the private arrangements for his burial in Westminster Abbey. The recipient of the letter, Sir John

[1] *op. cit.* ch. 2.

234

Nicholas, Edward's eldest son, had also been the recipient of some of Hyde's most charming letters in the 1650s. The writer, Henry Coventry, was the elder brother of William, one of Hyde's most redoubtable critics. How many statesmen would have taken the trouble, as Hyde did, to write to an Ambassador, Rochester, telling him how his son watched every post for a line from his father? How many fathers have lived so happily and affectionately with their own children and have been so warmly and so movingly remembered? He liked the young.

It may be argued that these examples are confined to family life. But a no less telling refutation, set in a wholly professional context, may be found in a letter written to Ormonde on November 10, 1666 about promotions to the Irish bench: 'Wee have a greate many very extraordinary younge men growinge up in the professyon of the Law, who in a few yeares will be fitt for any places, and then I hope wee shall be able to supply your Benches upon any vacancy . . .'[2]

William Coventry and Sir Henry Bennet, from 1663 Lord Arlington, are certainly examples of rising politicians whom Clarendon gratuitously antagonized, snubbing them, thwarting them, and finally in his retrospective survey undervaluing them. But in both cases it was not their youth that aroused his hostility, though he used his own seniority as a weapon against them. Bennet indeed he had originally befriended and supported when the Duke of York was set on his destruction. Sheer unreasonableness, sudden antipathy, is not unknown among politicians, particularly among those of warm temper. He was in any case not without his reasons. Bennet had identified himself with the frivolous set of courtiers on whom the Lord Chancellor fixed a basilisk stare of disapproval. And Coventry he had long suspected of having no religion.

It might perhaps be more profitable to look at Clarendon's relations with the young members of the Cavalier Parliament from their end, not his. To ambitious young men like Edward Seymour or Sir Thomas Osborne, later Earl of Danby and Duke of Leeds, the men in office were the men who stood in their way. The old bull would have to be dealt with before the young could have his own way with the herd. And Sir Thomas Osborne doubtless bore a lively grudge against the man who had been the prime mover in abolishing the Court of which his father had been Vice-President, the Council of the North. Unlike the Convention Parliament of 1660, the Cavalier Parliament of 1661 did not regard the abolition of the Prerogative Courts by Pym and young Mr Hyde twenty years earlier as good riddance. They were quite ready to rip up the old wounds, to get their own back on their enemies,

[2] Carte MS 47 f.128.

to re-open the issue of crime and punishment in the late troubles. Clarendon and his master were alive to the extreme dangers of any such proceeding. In any case the Declaration of Breda could not be disavowed without public shame. On the whole they managed to hold the line. The most serious breaches of its spirit were in the field of religion. The liberty promised to tender consciences had offered hopes not only of a reasonable toleration of Dissent but of widening the basis of the national Church so that it would comprehend the moderate men of all opinions. The Act for settling Ministers that had passed the Convention Parliament was in the judgment of the most recent historian of the Restoration settlement 'a triumph for moderation in an immoderate age'.[3] Its aim was to cause the minimum of dislocation. Episcopal ordination was not insisted on as a qualification for incumbency. Clergy whose loyalty and orthodoxy were in doubt were to be vetted by a committee of three royal chaplains, Sheldon, Earles and Morley, Clarendon's closest ecclesiastical friends and all three Great Tew men.[4]

This was not what the Cavaliers had in mind, as they very soon made plain. The Bishops were restored to their seats in the House of Lords. The Solemn League and Covenant was on their vote burnt by the Common Hangman in Palace Yard. The political base of Presbyterianism was attacked by the Corporation Act of 1661. The Presbyterian clergy who would not accept the necessity for episcopal ordination and the formularies of an Anglicanism distinctly higher than that of Great Tew were ejected on St Bartholomew's Day 1662. Presbyterianism as a major political and religious force was in effect destroyed. This, not a religious revival, was the object of the exercise. Clarendon, as has been said, did not like Presbyterianism. Unlike some who now appeared as higher Churchmen than he, he had declined to attend the Huguenot chapel at Charenton when he was at Charles II's court in Paris.[5] But he

---

[3] I. M. Green *op. cit.* 49.

[4] *ibid* 53. Professor R. S. Bosher characterises them as 'three leading Laudians': reasons for disputing this categorisation may be found above, p. 215.

[5] The history of Clarendon's attendance at Huguenot temples during both his first and second exiles is thoroughly set out by his eldest son in a letter to Hickes, the Non-juror, dated October 22, 1707 (Bodleian Library MS Eng. hist. b.2 f.77). Henry recalls the efforts made 'to get King Charles to goe to the Temple at Charenton in the time of his exille, and how much my Lord Clarendon opposed it; as in truth he did, and always valued himself for having soe done'.

During his second exile at Montpellier '. . . he never was at any of them above once or twice at most, wch he thought enough . . .' Henry indignantly rebuts the accusation brought by a French controversialist that his father ever allowed arguments of political expediency to prevail over his religious convictions. '. . . the basest scandal the Author could blast my Lord Clarendon with . . . 'Tis eminently known the Statesman and the Protestant were never different personages in my Lord Clarendon . . . he always laying it down for a Fundamentall that the interest of the King and of the Church of England must be the same.' Only weeks before his death at Rouen he had written to his son 'shewing the reasons why he would not frequent the Assemblys at Quevilly'.

took his religion too seriously to want to use it as a weapon in the scramble for power and office. Believing that the Divine providence was at work in history he was anxious to leave as much as possible to its operation and not to stir up resentment by the officious scrutiny of religious opinions which he did not share. Like Queen Elizabeth he did not want to make windows into men's souls. In all this he was closer to the King than to his old friend Sheldon. The evidence for his sentiments permeates this book. The evidence that his contemporaries recognised or suspected as much is to be seen in the fact that when he fell it was the Presbyterians alone who tried to support him.

Yet, having said that, difficulties at once appear. Clarendon did in fact express objections, legal objections not theological, to a minister not episcopally ordained having the right to receive tithe, on which clerical stipends were founded.[6] It is easy to find material for the contention that he was glad to see the Church of England in its full canonicals, its liturgy re-established, its cathedrals rescued, its revenues restored, its institutions and its political powers revived, triumphant over its enemies. He disliked dissent. He hated and feared fanaticism. And not without reason. Pepys was not the only citizen of London to whom Venner's rebellion in January 1661 gave a nasty shock. Plotting was the obsession of political activists in late seventeenth-century England. If Charles II's government seemed to over-react this may have been caused by the amateurishness of its intelligence system compared with the extreme efficiency of Cromwell's. Clarendon's resolute opposition to any modernisation of the machinery of government may in its turn have contributed to this. No one really knew how secure the restored monarchy was. Sir John Plumb in his examination of the *Growth of Stability in English Politics* has suggested that even in the court itself confidence was none too robust.

Clarendon's acceptance of toleration was a victory for his mind over his prejudices. He liked nothing better than lambasting Presbyterians and Independents in his letters. It was also a victory for magnanimity over past grudges. It is much easier to be tolerant towards people in the distant past who have done one no wrong than towards contemporaries who have set themselves to destroy what one loves. Clarendon's toleration was no overflowing of a diffused charity towards the human race. Still less was it the by-product of indifferentism.

Its nature is best shewn by the proviso, designed to accommodate the moderate Presbyterians, that he attempted, unsuccessfully, to introduce into the Act of Uniformity. This would have accepted the scruples of ministers who could not bring themselves to wear a surplice or, when baptizing, to make the sign of the cross. Pepys reports in his

---

[6] Lister iii 100, I. M. Green 211.

entry for March 21, 1662 the 'great differences' this proposal provoked: 'And though it be carried in the House of Lords, yet it is believed it will hardly pass in the Commons.' Events confirmed his forecast. The Venetian Resident, writing on the same day in almost identical terms, concluded that the Chancellor, though no Presbyterian, thought that party worth conciliating '. . . to have it on his side in case of need'.[7] What may well be the authoritative statement of his position is to be found in an anonymous pamphlet on which the Oxford antiquary of his time Anthony à Wood has written, 'Penned as tis said by Ed. E. of Clarendon.'[8] The style and content support the attribution.

Second Thoughts; or the Case of a Limited Toleration stated according to the present Exigence of Affairs in Church and State. The careful circumscribing of the plea is exactly consonant with the grudging recognition that there *is* a case. And the epigraph *Nihil Violentum Durat* — 'Nothing violent lasts' — is eminently Clarendonian. The arguments deployed are largely pragmatical and historical with a distinct infusion of Hobbesism. The starting point is the weakness of the country in the face of so many potential enemies. Division is an unaffordable luxury. Realism comes next: the country is as it is, not as we would wish it to be. This is followed by the time-honoured formula: 'What is the alternative?' 'Let the Opposers of a Toleration shew us a safe and ready way to rid the Nation of all Non-Conformists, though I confess I am no Friend to Force and Violence, especially in Matters of Conscience . . . But if this be impossible to do, and if the Method by them prescrib'd . . . serves only to exasperate, not to carry off the peccant humour, I must conclude that the good of the Nation is either not rightly understood, of not justly pursu'd by them.' Next, the argument from Futility: 'Compulsion may bring many Hypocrites, but no real Converts . . .' and then, as we might expect, from History: The Court of High Commission persecuted Sectaries and Nonconformists with a zeal that united them in resentment. 'And to what Power and Strength they grew by this union was too fatally known by the Famous Mischiefs they did.' Finally there is the clinching analysis: 'Mankind in general is constantly true to nothing but their Interest; how much that over rules Conscience in all Religions is but too visible in the World . . . And therefore the great Art and secret of Government is to make it the Peoples Interest to be True and Faithful to their Governors.' Clarendon had not read Hobbes and Macchiavelli for nothing. He reinforces this argument by pointing out the prevalence of Nonconformity among 'the Sea-fareing Men, and the Trading Part of the Nation'. 'Nature hath so placed this Island that whenever we are Masters at Sea we are Umpires of this part of the world; so that we must always Rise or

---

[7] Quot. *Diary* iii 49 note 1.   [8] Bod.L Wood 614(15).

Fall in Plenty and Power, as we encrease or decay in Traffic and Navigation.'

Does all this sound too calculating and mercenary for the philosopher of Royalism? Clarendon had been a successful barrister, had known how money was made, before he had embarked on a political career. His travels had given him exceptional opportunities of observing the economic life of northern Europe. However anxious his critics are to write him off as a romantic rhapsodist of the England he had known as a child, however much ground he has given them by the intemperance of his language about the England of Cromwell and Charles II, his own insistence on his qualifications as a historian, must not be forgotten. He was indeed a man of affairs 'conversant in Business'. In the speech on the adjournment of the Convention already quoted, he commended two practical measures as of the highest priority: the setting up of a Council of Trade and a Council of Plantations.[9] In the principles of his foreign policy, alliance with Portugal, cultivation of good relations with France, avoidance of war with the Dutch which so many people were clamouring for, he showed the same clear apprehension of the national interest in developing trade and navigation.

But although in this carefully limited and pragmatical criticism of religious coercion he claims the support of the New Testament: 'Both the Precepts and Example of our Great Master and his Disciples are directly Opposite to it', he explicitly rejects giving the Nonconformists any share 'in Offices and eminent places of Trust'. Toleration is what he is advocating, not equality. That question answers itself. 'Let the *Presbyterians* meet in their Halls, the *Fanaticks* in their Barns, the *Papists* in their Garrets, shall the Church of England Assembled in her Cathedrals fear the Competition of Rivals every way so inferiour to her, in force of Arguments and Reason, in exterior Decency and Gravity, and in the Credit of Publick Authority?'

In fact the forces against comprehension within the Church and toleration outside it were too intractable. The Cavalier Parliament was bad enough. But the Presbyterian leadership also was stiff and prickly. If Richard Baxter had taken the opportunities offered there would have been at least three voices to speak for his school of thought on the restored bench of bishops instead of only one. And the suspicion that the King's championship of toleration merely masked a secret leaning to Roman Catholicism was widespread in well-informed circles. Ludicrously the conversion of Lady Castlemaine, hardly a serious theological thinker, to the Roman obedience allied her with Clarendon on the issue: 'the Lady is the great champion of the Presbyterians . . . next

---

[9] *CJ* 1660, 172–4.

one of your frinds [i.e. Clarendon] the fiercest solicitor these ministers have.'[10] So wrote Ormonde's London correspondent, Daniel O'Neale, no doubt grinning to himself.

It is easier to disentangle Clarendon's notions on the question from his later writings (when he had nothing to do but clear his own mind) than from what he said and did when he was the central figure in government. He had to take account of so many forces with which he must act, not least his own deep conviction that a minister of the Crown was a servant, however much he might deplore his master's perversities and however much he might seek to dissuade him from them. He was like an old family retainer who allowed himself what some would consider gross insubordination in speech while feeling himself bound in the end to do what he was told.

The King and his minister certainly did what they could to protect the Nonconformists from the fierce intolerance of the Cavalier Parliament. So much is common ground. But historians are divided as to the Chancellor's real convictions and the true zeal displayed.[11] Whatever the truth may be it is also certain that he and the King saw the matter differently, however they might concert their actions. From this it is deduced by those historians who doubt the Chancellor's sincerity that the issue of religious toleration was decisive in turning the King away from his old mentor to younger and more pliant advisers. Others argue that it was not ideology but gout. From December 4, 1662 to March 13, 1663 he was confined to his bed. A disastrous if heroic attempt to preside at the opening of the Law Term in Westminster Hall in January brought a severe relapse. It was the first time he had stirred outside his house for ten weeks.[12] This was the crucial period at which the King attempted to circumvent the persecuting legislation of his Parliament by a Declaration of Indulgence emanating from his regal quality as the fountain of justice and mercy. In the unsuccessful campaign to secure Parliamentary assent to this watering down of their measures Bennet was the Counsellor on whom the King relied. He had succeeded Nicholas as Secretary on October 15, 1662. Was this a move against the Chancellor? In the fits of self-pity which frequently engulfed him he suggested that it was, remarking years later in his autobiography. 'It cost the King in present money and land or lease, very little less than twenty thousand pounds, to bring in a servant whom very few cared for, in the place of an old servant whom everybody loved.'[13] Yet Clarendon had pressed his old friend to accept retirement and thought

10 Carte MS 32 f.3.
11 Of recent authorities Dr D. T. Witcombe and Dr I. M. Green doubt him while Professor G. R. Abernathy argues the other way. Dr Ronald Hutton in general warns his readers against relying on his veracity.
12 Carte MS 47 f.22 January 24, 1663.   13 *Cont.* 438.

the conditions generous.[14] Bennet, no doubt, would not have been his choice as successor but it was hardly reasonable to expect the King to submit the nomination to him.

We may be faced by conflicting evidence about Clarendon's opinions but there is no ambiguity about his health. The gout never left him for long. His absences from the Council became more regular than his attendance. The attacks form a major preoccupation of his correspondence.

'Few men know how to choose well for themselves. You know how sollicitous I have been this longe tyme to deverte my gowte from the Springe, a jolly and vigorous season, to the winter, believing that November and December beinge good for nothinge but to ly in bedd and sitt by the fyre would be best to have the gowte in. And I have had my wish, for as I had the last fitt this tyme twelvemonth, so it seized me agayne the same tyme, about a week before the end of the Tearme and in 2 days cast me on my bedd; since which tyme I have not been able to stirr from it. But alasse ther is great difference betweene havinge any sicknesse or payne in a frost and in the Springe. Those terrible frosts have broken mee on the wheele and after 25 dayes torment, without beinge able to sett either foote to grounde, I have cause by every nights torment to conclude that the worst is not yett past, excepte this Thaw, which hath held six or seven houres and is like to hold, continue . . .'[15]

Thus the Chancellor to his closest friend, Ormonde, now and for the rest of the Clarendon ministry away in Dublin as Lord Lieutenant. This as much as his ill-health reduced the supply of spiritual oxygen. Nicholas had gone. Southampton was constantly incapacitated by the gout or the stone. As early as October 1662, a bare three months after Ormonde's departure, Clarendon was writing to him, in cipher, of the King's shortcomings:

'That which breakes my hearte is that the same affections continew still, the same lazynesse and unconcernednesse in businesse, and a proportionable abatement of reputation; and this makes a greater impression upon my mind and spirits than heretofore, by my not having that faithful bosome I had to discharge my selfe into, nor that friend, nor any other who is ready to beare that parte in speaking plainly and honestly in proper seasons.'[16] Six months later he was in deeper depression: '. . . the truth is, since your departure I have had so unpleasant a life as that, for my own ease and content, I rather wish myself at Breda, and have hardly been able to restraine myself from making that suite.'[17] From time to time he perks up. Sullenness, as he truly said, was not one of his faults. The King has seemed readier to

[14] Lister iii 228-9.
[16] Lister iii 227-8.
[15] Carte MS 47 f.18 December 13, 1662.
[17] *ibid* 244.

listen to him. But the marvellous resilience of the long, apparently hopeless, years of exile has left him. Hardening arteries, the gout, the penalties of taking no exercise and little care for diet, must surely have contributed. But, for a man who needed so deeply to communicate, the psychological deprivation must have taken an even greater toll. He was not in good form. And, not being in good form, he had to a degree lost his touch.

His mishandling of Arlington (as Sir Henry Bennet now advanced to an earldom had become) went beyond loss of touch. In obstinate, self-destructive fury it exhibited the character of a rogue elephant. Clarendon blocked him over the Post Office, a reasonable perquisite for a Secretary of State in view of its value in gathering intelligence. Far more foolishly, as Dr Hutton points out,[18] he blocked him over the Paris embassy which would have taken him out of the country again. Ormonde, that civilized smoother of ruffled feathers, seems to have tried to urge a reconciliation. Had he, perhaps, been prompted to use his good offices by the King?

'The Kinge hath done his parte towards the reconciliance you men-cioned' wrote the Chancellor on June 19, 1663, 'and I hope it will be such as it ought to be and prove usefull to his service . . . but you know there is a mutuall confidence necessary that must come by degrees. I use all freedom and opennesse, and when any thinge is shewne mee of dispatch, as frequently it is, I do excepte and admire as I see cause . . . for without all doubte all derections and orders of importance should be carefully worded and with great cleerenesse; busynesse is a new language that men are not suddaynly acquainted with . . .'[19]

The passage echoes a phrase of six months earlier: 'I told him [Bennet], by that time he had writ as many declarations as I had done, hee would find they are a very ticklish commodity.'[20] Ten years earlier such a master-to-pupil tone might have been acceptable. In 1663 it was not. Arlington's fastidiousness, conspicuous in his taste for literature and the arts, did not extend, as Clarendon's did, to the company he kept. Buckingham, Castlemaine, Bab May, the King's boon companions, were natural allies against the old man. Yet Arlington, and even more William Coventry, were serious poli-ticians, not adventurers. It was Clarendon's fault, not theirs, that they found themselves working against him with people empty of principle, derisive of vision.

Clarendon's want of tact united the political world in a desire to be done with him. His personal dealings with the King are neatly epitomised in the notes that passed between them at the Council table.[21] A later sample from the spring of 1663 shows him, in a letter

[18] *op. cit.* 193.   [19] Carte MS 47 f.56.   [20] Lister iii 233.   [21] Ed. W. D. Macray (1896).

of his own to Ormonde about assignments on the Irish revenue, helping to construct the alliance of resentment that was to destroy him. Clarendon had urged the danger of holding up money desperately needed by the Irish administration and had secured a favourable decision. 'Bennet hath all the credit and enough lessened mine, promised me it should be immediately sent away, but the King on Sunday entered upon a deliberate and formed discourse with me how inconvenient such assignations would be in this time of necessity when all money ought to be applyed to his own occasions. I told him that he assigned nothing that was his owne and that he was only trusted to dispose the money according to the intention of the Act of Parliament. He said he would debate it with me . . .'[22] It is easy to believe that one who put the King so brusquely to rights made the remark with which his enemies in the Commons taxed him in moving their impeachment: that 400 gentlemen were only fit to give money and did not know how an invasion was to be resisted.

Hated by the young Turks in the Commons who saw him (correctly) as the chief obstacle to a Cavalier vendetta, resented by the King as overbearing, by the Presbyterians and Dissenters (incorrectly) as the author of a harsh penal code, by Sheldon and the stern unbending Churchmen as unsound, detested by Castlemaine *et al.* as the enemy of the permissive society they were inaugurating with such *éclat*, the Chancellor needed all the arts of pleasing, at which, in the past, he had shown himself so adept. Instead he crashed head-on into hazard after hazard, changing course erratically, unwillingly, and always too late. Even his unrivalled historical sense of the times he was living through betrayed him. In the spring of 1663, in an attempt to outflank the House of Commons' flat rejection of a Declaration of Indulgence, a Bill was introduced into the Lords to give the King statutory power to dispense with the Act of Uniformity. Clarendon, long absent from the Woolsack in the agonies of gout, addressed the chamber in opposition to a measure which his parliamentary judgment must have told him did not stand a chance, much as his master might have wished it to succeed. The proposal differed from the free grace of a Declaration of Indulgence in that the toleration would be granted by letters patent to specified individuals who would of course expect, and be expected, to pay for the privilege. The Crown would thus obtain both an extension of powers free from Parliamentary control and a source of revenue independent of the House of Commons. In a phrase, apt indeed, far, far too apt, that haunted him when he came to write his autobiography, 'he said "it was ship-money in religion, that nobody could know the end of, or where it would rest; that if it were passed Dr Goffe* or any

---

* See above, p. 123, for the object of this allusion.   [22] Carte MS 47 f.39 March 1663.

other apostate from the church of England might be made a bishop or archbishop here, all oaths and statutes and subscriptions being dispensed with"".[23] 'Ship-money in Religion'! How that description must have rung in the King's ears: what echoes from the (unpreserved) speeches of the young Mr Hyde must have stirred in the memory of his auditory. Two birds brought down with one stone: King Charles I and King Charles II.

That Clarendon, early in his administration, came to occupy what Bagehot called a dignified rather than an efficient position is common ground among historians. David Ogg dated the decline of his power from the summer of 1661, Dr Hutton dates it from the end of 1662.[24] Which of them Clarendon would have agreed with would have been a matter of mood. His letters to Ormonde by June 1663 show him settled into an acceptance, however hurt and resentful, of the fact. 'I cannot tell what to say to you of myselfe, beinge better able from what you write to me to conclude how the world goes heare than from any observation of my owne: . . . I have stoode still & looked on only, so that I am sure ther is no thought of alteration in me, yett the countenances are not the same they have beene . . .'[25] '. . . the truth is, I am so broken with it that were it not for the hope of once more seeinge you, & consultinge togither, and trying like good men what wee can, I would passyonately contryve the gettinge into some corner, and to be forgotten.'[26]

Passivity, a sort of political hibernation against a spring whose coming seems ever more unlikely, is the note most continuously sounded, at any rate when it is a question of his taking an initiative either public or private. But his exhortations to Ormonde are a very different matter. Careless himself about putting his finances in order, he is constantly chivvying his old friend: 'I would be gladd to heare a good testimony of your having entered upon any good husbandry upon your owne estate, which is that which must be relyed upon when all is done. I pray gett my Lady Duchesse to give George Lane [Ormonde's secretary] derections to send me some informacion of that affayre, how you provyde to pay your debts, what progresse you are making towards it and how your fortune is now managed. I

[23] *Cont.* 590. Clarendon here places the incident in 1665. I have followed Lister (ii, 211–2) and David Ogg (2nd ed. i, 204) in preferring 1663. Dr Hutton (p. 197 and p. 347 notes 60 and 61) lucidly sets out the difficulties of accepting Clarendon's version of events and summarises the views of other scholars. Whatever the exact circumstances I cannot believe that Clarendon would have invented in such sharp and painful detail a scene so unflattering to himself and so harmful to any possible interest of his.

[24] Ogg i, 205, Hutton 191.

[25] Carte MS 47 f52 June 6.

[26] *ibid* f.55 June 13.

suppose my Lord Ossory manages his aparte . . .'[27] A year later he returns to the charge, questioning Ormonde closely on his 'managery' of his estate. 'I cannot be quyett till you give me some satisfaction in these particulars . . . which upon my conscience you are apter to forgett than any other bodyes.'[28]

In government he takes the same forward line. Ormonde must not ride on too easy a rein. 'For Gods sake defend yourself from importunityes and learne to deny: you have sent 2 or 3 promises unreasonable enough to Mr Sollicitor, quyght contrary to all rules: be not so confident of our wisdome that we will always stopp what you lett passe.'[29] Ten months later after the detection of a plot to surprise Dublin Castle: 'I do beseech and conjure you to make all possible hast in the prosecution and execution of those who are notoriously guilty.'[30] How well the two men knew each other and how profound was Ormonde's understanding of his own nature. 'The steady pursuing your owne rules will at last produce a full conformity from all persons . . .' wrote Clarendon, 'and I do not thinke you will meete with any obstinate obstruction, provyded you take the hardheartednesse upon yourselfe, which you must do, how untowardly soever you do it.'[31] 'I cannot,' wrote Ormonde, after the discovery of the plot, 'much boast of being master of the temper necessary for the government of as ill a sort of people as, I think, inhabit any part of the earth. But I know I am also destitute of that power which should make them good or keep them from doing hurt.'[32] There is an acceptance of the limitations imposed by the realities of life and an honest admission of his own that is wholly characteristic.

What did Ormonde and Clarendon, feeling themselves more or less impotent spectators, think they could, or should, do? A lifetime spent in hanging on when there are few signs of relief doubtless makes tenacity a reflex action. Patience, cousin, and shuffle the cards. Besides, if they could do nothing much themselves except in a negative way, they could protect and encourage the younger men whose abilities and principles recommended them. A great deal of their correspondence is taken up with this. Clarendon tells Ormonde how well he thinks of the young Lord Cavendish and of Mr Temple, the future Sir William,[33] though it was in fact Arlington who launched him on his diplomatic career. Henry Coventry for whom Clarendon obtained the Swedish embassy was another of their joint protégés, having served Ormonde in the Irish administration before resuming the diplomatic career that he had begun during the exile.

[27] *ibid* f.3v September 1, 1662. [28] *ibid* f.72 November 7, 1663.
[29] *ibid* f.1 July 19, 1662. [30] *ibid* f.52 June 6, 1663.
[31] *ibid* f.28. [32] *ibid* f.143. [33] *ibid* ff.56, 67–8.

Both men felt a strong obligation to reward past loyalty, intensified when this was entwined with the ties of kinship. Clarendon recommended to Ormonde his cousin and erstwhile secret agent Alan Broderick while admitting his unsuitability for any judicial office. In his letters, he found, 'there is always more of passyon with reference to thinges and persons than is agreeable to a person who is to judge all interests and praetenses . . .'[34] Mere family connexion was of itself sufficient. Sir Hugh Middleton, 'a Baronett of the 3rd descent & a proper, well-built gent — an officer lately at Dunkerke, a Captain of Foot', is recommended on the ground that 'he hath marryed a Cozen German of myne by whom he hath a good fortune . . . £2 or £3000 which together with his commande I should hope would be the foundacion of a competent fortune'.[35]

Most powerful of all was the motive of old friendship. Perhaps the most telling instance of this is a letter written in a hand still crabbed and halting with gout dated January 30, 1664:

'This is the first letter I have undertaken to write since this day nine weeks that I wrote to your Grace and though I have this day begunn another letter to you I have no hope to finish it, beinge indeede very weake: but I should be very ill natured, if I did not summon all my strength togither, to recommende this particular affayre to you, which concerns an old friende and companyon of myne, at my first comminge to Oxforde, and whom I have long enquyred after of all my friendes who knew Irelande and believed to be longe since deade.

'Dr Burly, who havinge lyved many yeares in Irelande was by my Lord Staforde [Strafford] made Deane of Emley and prebendary of St Patrick's in Dublin — the valew of both doth not exceede fifty pounds per an. These small praeferments (of which he was abundantly worthy) he injoyed many yeares before the warr: but was afterwards dryven out of that country and when I thought him deade longe since I finde him in a poore vicaridge not far from Cornebury. He is a very learned, worthy man but so infirme in health, and broken by age (though he be not above 4 or 5 yeares elder than my selfe) that he dares not thinke of returning into Ireland but disyres me to be a suitor to your G^{ce} on his behalf that he may retayne the small profitt of those his places after havinge beene so longe without them, and I do most earnestly desyre & conjure you to take him so farr into your protection, I meane only so longe (for I do not think it fitt men should lyve heare and have praeferments there) till I can provyde better for him heare which I am sure I will endeavour from this moment (for till within these few days I knew not he was livinge)

[34] *ibid* f.50.   [35] *ibid* f.24v.

and hope ere longe to offer him. I pray your effectuall order in this that the good old man, may know from his friend, that he is in your protection.

'I did not thinke I could have writt this much, so that you may expecte more this night or very shortly.'[36]

Ormonde wrote to the Archbishops of Dublin and Cashel and the thing was done.[37] Perhaps the good old man was too broken in health for Clarendon to obtain any English preferment for him; at any rate when he died in 1671 he was still Rector of Ducklington.[38] But the letter tells one a great deal about the Chancellor's sense of duty and of priorities. His disapproval of clerical absenteeism is characteristic. So is his putting the necessities of an old friend, however insignificant on the political scale, before the discussion of larger issues. One may admire, one may deplore. Clarendon's most attractive virtues were inextricably bound up with his most tiresome limitations. Like so many men of strong loyalties and high intelligence he was equivocal in his recognition of the truth that change is the law of life. The speech in which he had commended the setting up of Committees for Trade and for the Plantations was a notable example of his intellectual grasp of the country's essential interests and their future development. Yet his heart was not in it. He did little or nothing to follow up this admirable beginning. In administration in general he was the enemy of modernisation and reform. As Sir Keith Feiling long ago pointed out Charles II was entirely right in championing, and Clarendon wholly wrong in obstructing, the establishment of Commissions and Committees to take over the work of the great medieval officers of state, such as the Treasurer. Young Mr Hyde would not, one may guess, have taken this line. But Lord Clarendon was worn out, overworked, ill and politically lonely. Each condition aggravated the other as Clarendon himself seems to have recognised. 'I cannot say all you desire to heare of my health . . . and it may be my uneasynesse of minde may contribute somewhat to my indisposition of body . . . but I am not able to turne myself from my apprehensions on the behalfe of the publique . . .' he wrote to Ormonde in April 1663.[39]

Quotation from so intimate a correspondence may provide the best evidence of a man's thoughts and feelings but it does not necessarily, or even probably, convey the impression he made on his contemporaries. We know how Pepys and Evelyn looked on him as the embodiment of cheerful, self-confident good company. In 1665 his second surviving

---

[36] *ibid* f.79.　　　　　　　　　[37] *Cal. Clar. SP* v, 400, 403.

[38] Burley's will and inventory (Oxon CRO W.I. 6/4/23) show his estate to have been a very modest one. More than two centuries later Clarendon's *History* was to find its definitive editor in another Rector of Ducklington, the Rev. W. Dunn Macray.

[39] Carte MS 47 f.46v.

son, Laurence, was about to marry Lord Burlington's daughter. Burlington, who was not a member of Clarendon's circle, wrote him a letter in which, after praising his abilities and services, he came to the real point: '. . . if I may be so sawcy as to use so plaine a worde I love you for being master of (what very few great persons in this age possesse) tenderness & good nature.'[40]

[40] Clar. MS 83 f.156.

XX

Life as Lord Chancellor

Seven fat years followed by seven lean ones might seem an apt description of the fortune that awaited Clarendon when in 1660 he returned in triumph with his master. Materially it is largely true. Politically, psychologically, dare one say spiritually, the years of power were years of impoverishment. Frustration, disillusion, depression, above all loneliness are the notes that swell or diminish but never die away. In the last exile, when his circumstances defined themselves almost in these terms, they are heroically absent.

At the Restoration Clarendon was rewarded as he deserved. Charles II may not have had a warm or a generous heart, but he had none of his father's stinginess. Lands, sinecures, grants of money, were heaped on the Lord Chancellor, whose office was in any case a lucrative one. Clarendon made no attempt to compute his receipts* (or even calculate his approximate financial latitude and longitude) until he was called on to rebut charges of corruption. That they were large enough to render such an exercise unnecessary was the clear assumption on which he formed his style of life. Never, even in the hardest times, mean or parsimonious, he had now no reason to be. 'If riches increase, set not your heart upon them.' His practice exemplified the injunction of the Psalmist.

His vocation as a historian, disclosed to him in the dark hour of Royalist defeat, had already inspired him to begin collecting papers, books and pictures. As long ago as 1651, on the eve of his return from Madrid, it will be remembered that in the directions he gave his wife for finding suitable accommodation a study where he could house and use these collections came high on the list. That he was an epicure in the matter of bindings is clear from his letter to Cosin already quoted.

---

* A partial transcript of the will made by Clarendon in January 1666 will be found in Appendix I. His particular bequests provide valuable evidence of his wealth.

That he read widely and thought life unsurrounded by books a naked and brutish thing is evident from every period of his life. In pictures his taste seems to have been almost exclusively for historical portraiture, and that again principally in the times he had known and meant to write about. Some portraits he had commissioned while still in exile;[1] it is even possible that he then acquired a few Dutch and Flemish sub-ject pictures that were to form part of the collection. But this was nothing to the magnificent gallery he had assembled by the time of his fall, on the housing of which he spared no expense.

The first home designed for it — and for its founder — was Corn-bury Park, near Oxford. This handsome royal hunting-lodge had already been done up in the 1630s. Clarendon commissioned Hugh May to add a new wing (with a long room on the ground floor for the picture collection), a stable block and a chapel (designed in partner-ship with John Evelyn in 1664 but not built till 1677). Hugh May had been a Royalist exile like his brother Baptist ('Bab'), one of Clarendon's most vindictive enemies among Lady Castlemaine's circle. He had been deeply influenced by the buildings he had seen in Holland, where the early exuberance of Renaissance ornament had been, by this time, chastened and refined. Clarendon took a close interest in his activities, particularly in the landscaping. On February 3, 1663 he wrote from London to his son Henry who had been joined at Cornbury by his younger brother Laurence. May was there too, waiting for a load of young trees that Clarendon had ordered through his agent at Purton. The delivery was short: 'However I pray lett all the holes be digged that the Gardyner may plant the trees as they come: for I sup-pose there will be a fortnight's time to sett in after you returne . . . if you think fitt, lett Hugh May sett out foure rounde or square places in which the Gardyner may be appointed to sett all manner of seedes . . . of Ashe, Walnutte, Haslenutts, Acornes and the like, which in 3 or 4 yeares will be a fyne thicket, and in a little more tyme will be copses. I am sure you do not forgett to sett all the lyme trees which were kept togither in the garden when I was ther: Hugh May I hope will carefully looke over my memoranda and discourse upon them . . .' He expresses the hope that they will return as wise as Hugh May and that in each suc-ceeding month they 'will send down somewhat to beautify Corne-bury'.[2] Every line breathes fond proprietorship: and almost every line supports the view his son expressed to another correspondent: 'Hugh May rules all here.' His ascendancy was accepted with good humour. Preserved among the Clarendon papers in the Bodleian is an order of

[1] *Burlington Magazine* XC, 98, XCII 73–80. Robin Gibson *Catalogue [of Portraits in the Collec-tion of the Earl of Clarendon]* (1977), pp. viii–ix, 128–9.
[2] Clar. MS 79 f.64.

Hugh May as 'Judge of the Architects' that Edward, Earl of Clarendon shall pay the Duchess of York £20 in settlement of a wager between them.[3]

Cornbury had been granted to Henry Danvers, lately created Earl of Danby, just before the Civil War. He had already occupied the house as Ranger of the Royal Park for a quarter of a century and it was he who had commissioned Nicholas Stone to build the new front in 1631, together with the gatehouse for the Botanical Garden at Oxford which still looks across the bottom of the High to Magdalen. His younger brother, Sir John Danvers, an even greater and more extravagant connoisseur of architecture and landscape gardening, inherited the estate in spite of all that Danby had done to prevent it. For while Danby had been an ardent Royalist, Sir John had not only sided with the Parliament but had been a prominent Regicide. Luckily for him he had died before the Restoration but his attainder meant that his estates were forfeit. The descendants of Danby's sister, his original legatee, had a claim that was settled for £20,000, a gift from the King to Clarendon, but some other adjacent lands of Sir John's were added to the original estate and Clarendon bought yet others. It was to be a property worthy of the viscountcy that Clarendon took as his second title, by which his son Henry was thereafter known.[4]

Purton, to which his thoughts had so often turned in exile, remained his property. He corresponded with his agent about estate business: but it was now only a tributary to a greater river. Cornbury was his seat. Its proximity to Oxford, where he had succeeded the aged Marquis of Hertford (raised by Charles II to the Dukedom of Somerset) as Chancellor in October 1660, was a notable convenience. It enabled him to entertain the King when he visited the University or — as in 1665 — held a Parliament there because of the Plague. It also gave him better hopes of entertaining his old friends, survivors from Great Tew, such as Earles and Morley and Sheldon, whose Oxford connexions were still strong. His letters are full of projections for these delightful houseparties, too seldom achieved. Sheldon was always too busy, Earles too often ill.

In September 1663 both the King and the Duke of York were expected for the partridge shooting. Most inconveniently the King had suddenly expressed a desire to visit the University. As Sheldon pointed out it was impossible at such short notice and at a time of year when the University was practically empty to make a fitting preparation for his entertainment. 'I heartily wish my self one of your number,' he wrote

---

[3] *ibid* 129 f.80 n.d.

[4] On Cornbury Park see V. Watney *Cornbury Park & Wychwood Forest* (1910) and article by C. Hussey in *Country Life* cviii, 922.

to Clarendon, 'but I find so much to do at Lambeth . . . that I can only solace myselfe with thinking of the happiness of my friends who are abroad, and in the meane time remaine a prisoner here.'[5] He hoped to communicate further by Earles, then Dean of Westminster, who had just been nominated to the see of Salisbury. Earles reluctantly had to cry off. He was very unwell and anxious 'to goe downe [to Salisbury] as soone as I am qualified for it, and if I cannot long sitt in that Church I shall be glad to lye there in the company of my friends under ground which are as many I believe, as there are above it'.[6] He was older than Clarendon and felt himself wearing out. 'Perhaps to me *quod deffertur aufertur* [what is postponed is given over], for though your Lordship I trust may live many summers yett, I that am now in my 65th yeare and under all these infirmityes look upon every month as a yeare and every yeare as an age, and therefore cannot so well stay for my friends',[7] he wrote from Salisbury the following May. His self-mocking humour still flickers over the embers of his life. 'Indeed your Lordship gives me that health you wish me in being so much concerned in it and though when I look upon my very inconsiderable selfe, I finde no reason why you should be so, yett when your Lordship says it I finde more reason to beleeve it & am very much comforted in that thought.'[8] The two friends were to meet again the following year when the Plague drove the court first to Salisbury (where Clarendon lingered) and then to Oxford for the Parliament, which Earles as a bishop felt bound to attend. He died soon after his arrival and was buried in the chapel of his old College, Merton.

Morley, the third of the Great Tew bishops, seems to have been less hobbled by overwork or failing health. Twelve years older than Clarendon he was to outlive him by ten, retaining in his eighties great vigour of mind and body. As Bishop of Winchester he was Visitor of five Oxford colleges and took his duties seriously. In September 1663 he wrote to his friend, applauding his conferring with the Heads of House towards a reform of the University. A man of personal frugality he cited Clarendon's cousin Frank Hyde as a pattern of prudent living amid the conspicuous consumption of seventeenth-century Oxford '. . . as well clad and as much like a Gent (for he allwayes had a Beaver Hatt and silk stockings) as any Fellow of a House'. And all this was contrived on £20 a year. Morley, a generous host, concluded the letter with the encouraging assurance that he was obtaining his friend 'a hogshead of the best wine in towne' and sending it in bottles to Worcester House.[9]

Worcester House was Clarendon's London base until the last few

5 Clar. MS 80 f.171.   6 *ibid* f.199.   7 *ibid* 80 f.214.
8 *ibid* 81 f.265.   9 *ibid* 80, f.198.

months of his ministry. If the lease had been renewable there seems no reason to suppose that he would have built himself the house which he, in common with all the world, came to see as a cause of his undoing. Besides Cornbury, which was to be the family seat and the repository of his collections, he had also bought in 1660 a substantial house at Twickenham, particularly convenient when the King was at Hampton Court or Windsor, and easily accessible from London. In the will he drew up at Cornbury on January 20, 1666 he left it to his second son Laurence and does not make any suggestion as to its being sold.[10]

Clarendon House, 'my house in the fields' as he describes it in the 1666 will,[11] was not, as some have thought, an arrogant architectural manifesto, long meditated in the impotence of exile. In fact the idea of it does not seem to have occurred to him until the spring of 1664. On Easter Eve he wrote, half defensively, at the end of a long letter (not that any are short) to Ormonde:

'I will now tell you an odd tale of myselfe, which you will hardly believe. Do you think it possible, that I, an old fellow, a beggar, am aboute to builde a house in St James's Fields, and yett this is true God helpe me. The Lord and the Lady will not suffer me to keepe this house beyounde the Tearme I have, which is Michaelmasse come twelve-month; wher to rent another house I know not, and being condemned to spend at least halfe my dayes besydes nights within doores, meethinkes it should not be unreasonable to make myselfe as much ease and pleasure ther as is possible and by this kinde of argumentacion I am launching out into that sea not havinge wherewithall to finish half I goe aboute.'[12]

Half defensive, half defiant, the Chancellor may have been, but there were to be no half measures about the project. Sir Roger Pratt, the architect of great country houses now alas mostly demolished or mutilated, was engaged to design what was, after all, 'my house in the fields', not a city mansion. He appears to have been in charge of the interior decoration: at any rate he certified the bills of the master-craftsmen, carvers, plasterers, painters and the rest, including a bill of £311. 10s. 6d from Robert Streeter, the King's serjeant-painter, which suggests a wall or ceiling painting of some extent.[13] Hugh May seems also to have been consulted since he certified one of the carver's bills.[14]

Perhaps Clarendon's experiences with May made him more watchful, both as to financial control and as to the tendency of *virtuosi* to disdain the convenience of their clients. During his prolonged absence

---

[10] *ibid* 84, f.38. For Clarendon's purchase of York House, Twickenham see *V.C.H. Middlesex* iii, 148–9
[11] See Appendix I.   [12] Carte MS 47 f.94v.   [13] Clar. MS 85 f.425.
[14] M. Whinney and O. Millar. *English Art 1625–1714* (Oxford, 1957), 139 n.6.

from London occasioned by the Plague, the Oxford Parliament and his subsequent prostration at Cornbury he addressed a series of letter to Sir Alan Broderick in London that betray his anxiety on both counts. They show, too, a certain awe of 'Mr Pratt', fresh from the building of Kingston Lacy, as well as a real pride and delight in the project. What evidently worried him most was that this gentleman-aesthete might take no notice of such mundane considerations as the weather. 'I longe to heare that the roofe and coveringe is on, that we neede not feare rayne, which wee are to expecte in some aboundance; if we were secure in that pointe, I should be without any impatience'[15] he wrote on December 10. A week later the receipt of a letter from another friend who has visited the site 'almost perswayded me to make a journey thither, to see the Roofe raysed upon the grounde before it be carryed up to the topp. I wish it were at highest for the apprehension of the mischieve the rayne will do gives me some trouble, and methinkes no tyme should be loste in coveringe the Pavilyone with leade now the Plattformes are on, that at least so much of the house may be safe.' On New Year's Eve the downpour at Oxford drove him to urge yet again '. . . coveringe of the whole, and then I shall be out of payne, for whatever my good friends say I shall finish it within by those degrees that are fitt, without putting myself to inconvenience of any kinde'. On January 2 'Good Allan' is told that 'Nothinge will satisfy mee till you send me worde that you walke dry in every part of the house, and then as much patience as you can desyre . . .' On the 7th he hears, at last to his relief that the roof is on. But are the bricklayers at work in this open weather? How many bricks are there? And how much timber? Cannot the ground be levelled and 'they cause the cross walls to runne . . . the gardyner might finde himselfe some worke, who I believe hath his wages for nothinge . . .'

Both the Clarendons, though pleased to have secured Pratt's services, were evidently anxious that he should not get the bit between his teeth:

'I am gladd Mr Pratt is so cheerfull. My wife longes to see the [? draft] of the Chappell, and then shee will bee gladd that worke should be hastened. I hope Mr Pratt will not [put] the whole worke into any one hande, but contracte by the roome with one, that we may be able to sett others on worke to, and first finish those roomes of which we are to have first use. I would be gladd my owne joyner should finish my Library, which I hope he may do, and if ther be neede he may gett 2 or 3 to helpe him, and if Mr Pratt advizes him I doubte not he will do the worke well. I pray send me worde how much he hath done towarde it.'

---

[15] This, and all the quotations in these two paragraphs, are from the Brodrick MSS in the Guildford Muniment Room, 1248/10 ff.82, 84, 86, 88, 113.

This request was repeated a week later on December 17. Had Pratt approved the joiner's work and had he given him directions for wain-scotting, window shutters and doors? 'I would have him derected to make a good doore for my study, and I suppose Mr Pratt will have the out doores of the house at least of Oke.' Clarendon is disturbed to hear that 'Mr Pratt is giving some derections towards the paving of the Sellars which I told you longe since must not be done, for ther is not yett one stone there which must be used to that purpose or within doores, all which are there beinge to ly abroade of which I pray advertize Mr Pratt carefully'.

In addition to the marble that Ormonde was sending from Kilkenny* Clarendon had ordered an unspecified amount from Purbeck and authorised the purchase of 'those Marble Stones in Scotlande Yarde if they be not excessive deere'. Pratt is commended for insisting that the chimneys be set up before the roof is covered with lead, a grudging admission that haste to keep out the weather may have partly defeated its own object: 'therefore I wholy referr that to Mr Pratt.' But in his letter of January 23 suspicion still lingers that the patron's special requirements may not be properly respected: 'I will have as much roome for bookes in my study as I can, but it may be I may change the forme of those between the windowes, and if ther be not some greate inconvenience in it, I desyre my owne joyner may do it, which I am sure he can do, if Mr Pratt will derecte him; but if he will not take the paynes to derecte, I know not what to say.' He cannot here deploy the assistance of Frances as in the exterior setting of the house: '. . . methinkes though Mr Pratt will not yett consent to the planting Elmes before the house, in which at last my wife will have the better of him, he should be content that this yeare be not lost, but that such as he will admitt to be sett behinde the stable may be planted before the season is past and methinkes the rayle, one single rayle, should be sett the whole length before the house.'

That Clarendon, for all the boldness and *brio* with which he 'launched out into that sea', never felt easy about tying up so much money in the house is obvious from the will he made less than two years later. It was not so much that he felt that he was showing himself too magnificent for a subject: it was his expertise in advising clients on their financial dispositions that told him that his own were top-heavy. The house, he admits, 'hath cost me much more money that in common discrecion a man of so meane a fortune should lay out in buildinge, yett I had some reason for it . . .' He explicitly releases his son from any obligation to keep the house in the family. '. . . I do intirely referr it to his discrecion to sell it, if he findes it convenient . . .', whereas selling Cornbury would made him turn in his grave. At both houses 'my deere wife shall have and injoy during her naturall life, what appartiments and lodgings she shall chuse to make use of . . . which she shall injoy as her owne . . .' If Henry sells Clarendon House 'he is to provyde such a house in London for his mother during her naturall life as she shall be well pleased with: as I make not the least doubte that he will always be desyrous to please her in all thinges, and that she will be as kinde to him and the rest of her children as she hath alwayes bene.'[16]

Here, in the core of this self-revealing document, we touch the mainspring of the Chancellor's life. The friends of his early manhood and maturity were sundered by death or distance or decline. The companionship, and intimacy of family life has supplied their place '. . . as it was one of the principle ends I proposed to my selfe in all my buildings, that I might injoy the company of my wife and children, upon whom I have always looked as the greatest blessings god Almighty hath bestowed upon me, so when I am deade I heartily wish that they will lyve togither as much as ther severall occasyons will permitt, and I doubt not but that they will always be a singular comforte to each other'. This embraced his surviving daughter-in-law, Laurence's wife 'who in her selfe deserves as much from me, as can be imagined, and whom I looke upon with the hearty kindnesse of a father, and as a singular honour voutsafed by god Almighty to my family'.[17]

His favourite child Anne had by marrying into the Royal Family transcended this domestic circle. In his will he leaves her a gold cup, 'conceavinge it not decent in many respects to present her with a greater legacy'. Towards her husband he professes that he 'hath always and in all tymes *out of the conscience of my duty* borne the highest devocion to his person . . .' The italicised phrase surely contains the higher quotient of truth. So intelligent and cultivated a man must have been grateful for the barrier of rank that kept him from the close society of so stupid a son-in-law. Evidently he saw a great deal of his York grandchildren and is one of the earliest witnesses to that sweetness of temper that distinguished Queen Anne. Writing from Oxford in October 1665 to the retired but still querulous Secretary Nicholas he sends him the good wishes of his family '. . . and I must tell you I have gotten a girle into it since I saw you that is the best natured and best humor'd childe in the worlde . . .'[18] Queen Anne had been born that February.

Of his younger children Edward, the second of that name,* had died of smallpox just over a year before the will was made.[19] Perhaps

* See Appendix II for Clarendon's children.
[16] Clar. MS 84 f.40.   [17] *ibid*.   [18] Clar. MS 83 f.253.   [19] Bod.L MS Add. C.308 f.17v.

the sudden death of this young Christ Church don three months short of his twentieth birthday had made the father think of setting his affairs in order. The second daughter, Frances, born in the middle 1650s, was handsomely treated: an outright legacy of £5,000 plus all her father's gold plate not otherwise assigned, to a minimum value of £5,000 which sum the executors were to make good if the plate did not reach it. She was strictly charged not to marry without her mother's consent, or, if her mother were dead, her eldest brother's. In fact she did not marry until 1675 when both her parents were dead, but her bridegroom, a connexion of John Evelyn's and gentleman usher to James, Duke of York, would certainly have passed muster.

The youngest son, James, born just before the Restoration, was to receive an annuity of £200 for life 'and is as much as I am able to leave to him, except god shall give me a longer life'. It seems that he turned out unsatisfactory. His brother Laurence, a kindly figure, mentions his aversion to study. His naval career of rather less than a month, before he was drowned in 1682 whilst accompanying his brother-in-law the Duke of York to Scotland, seems to have started too late to be taken seriously. Had his father noticed premonitory signs at the tender age of five? It hardly seems likely: but the disparity in provision is strange.

Apart from his family there are no legatees specified by name, except for the ceremonial bequests of gold cups to the King, the Duke of York, and the two Queens, Henrietta Maria and Catherine of Braganza. The servants are liberally provided for, but none, not even the private secretaries with whom throughout his life he got on so well, is personally mentioned. The old friends, Sheldon, Morley, Southampton and Sir Jeffrey Palmer, who are appointed as executors and overseers, are to be rewarded as such, but of Ormonde and Nicholas, or of younger friends such as Henry Coventry, there is no word. Even more astonishing nothing is said of the great picture collection he had been so active in forming.

This is in marked contrast to the careful arrangements for his books and papers:

'. . . to my sunn Cornbury all my library of bookes and papers which are in my house at Worcester house which I desyre he will keepe togither (for which I have builte a particular roome in Clarendon house) and suffer to descende to the heyre of the family, descended from me, and because the good will or curiosity of many of my friends who have to good an opinion of me, may possibly desyre that some of my papers may be published, which I have not for many yeeres perused, and which were writt in my retirement, and when I was without those conveniences of bookes and other helpes, which in such exercises are necessary, I do entirely leave the publishing or not publishing all or any of them of what sorte soever to the discrecion and will of my sunn

Cornbury, wishing him that he first take the advice of my very worthy friends, the Lord Archbishop of Canterbury, the Lord Bishop of Winchester, Lord Chief Justice Bridgeman, Sir Jeffry Palmer, His Majesty's Attorney generall and Sir Heneage Finch, His Majesty's sollicitour generall, or as many of them as he can prevayle with to peruse and correct the same, which beinge done lett him publish or not publish what he thinkes fitt.'

The preservation of the historical materials he was still assembling was never absent from his mind — witness the architectural provision made for them. Did he envisage employing them himself? Government and the gout left little time for literary activity. On the evidence of the will just quoted he had not so much as looked at what he had written nearly twenty years earlier. Yet perhaps the turning of his mind to the ultimate destination of his papers released a spring that was soon to press him, in loneliness and misfortune, to his true vocation. The first, and only, sign I have found during his time in office follows a few months after the making of the will. At the end of August 1665 he was in Salisbury, having followed the Court first to Hampton and then on to avoid the Plague. In a most interesting series of letters to Sheldon, who had stayed behind at Lambeth, occurs this passage: '. . . I havinge at the present more upon my hands than I can dispatch within my tyme, for I must tell you I finde myself insensibly engaged in my olde exercise of writinge, which I have discontiued since my coming into England, and it is not easy to me as it hath beene.'[20]

What was he writing? The manuscript of the *History*, which anyway he would hardly have carried round England with him, shows no sign of tinkering that would fit this context. Nor does that other unfinished work to which he was soon to return, his *Reflections on the Psalms*. Some of the pieces in *A Collection of Tracts*, posthumously published in 1727, bear no date or place of composition but none seems an obvious, or even likely, choice for a politician agitated about a war he had not wanted and a growing natural disaster which he could not see how to control. We do not know: but we do know that he was again addressing himself, after the floods of memoranda, of interminable drafts of diplomatic instructions, of legal and political pronouncements, of long self-unburdenings to Ormonde, to the task of formal literary composition.

The letters to Sheldon open a more extended, balanced view of the Chancellor's life than the far larger and longer series addressed to Ormonde. Those letters were written to a colleague in high office, usually against the clock, squeezed in between the arrival of the Irish mails, which was generally at night, and the departure of the govern-

[20] *ibid* MS c 303 f.104.

ment bag. The writer was often tired, oppressed by a sense of isolation and impotence, and bound by the self-disciplinary code of a lifetime not to neglect any matter of business before allowing his mind to play on the larger issues of the day. The insatiable litigiousness of the Irish, the endless disputes over the land settlement, the plain lawlessness of a nobility disinclined to honour any obligation they found irksome, the constant simmering and not infrequent outbreak of rebellion, the permanent and desperate need for money, occupy page after page of browning ink, written from edge to edge without a margin, indeed often with a word divided, the writing crowding up to the ceiling of the page or scurrying along its wainscotting. Every now and then there is a breathing-space. Clarendon's mind turns to the negotiations he was conducting on behalf of Ormonde and his wife — who is always remembered wth affection — for the purchase of Moor Park. In the end, on March 21, 1664 he concludes for £10,500 — '£500 lesse than I ever hoped to have done . . . and remembering how much the beauty of this place depends upon the guardens and well keepinge the walkes, and how little care people who sell such seates use to take in those particulars from the tyme they are resolved to parte with them, you shall do well to send such derections to us for the entertayninge the gardyners and other necessary people to keepe all fayre'.[21] Sometimes too the dry, mellow wit that entranced Pepys is allowed to play on great affairs. This letter, written by the head of the government in the middle of the Four Days Battle,* the guns clearly audible in London and the English fleet known to be divided and in terrible danger, has the classic touch:

'. . . you may be sure I will use all the importunity I can for present mony but I do confesse to you I know not yett wher or how to finde it: you knowe how many other thinges we have to thinke of, and that wee are not very good at thinkinge. The truth is, wee are at this houre in some trouble of spirritt in expectacion of newes from the fleete, which by the noyse wee have hearde yesterday and all this night, wee conceave to be in sight with the Duch . . .'

He goes on to explain that Rupert 'with 20 good shippes' had been detached to intercept the French squadron under Beaufort which had been reported leaving the Mediterranean and is now thought to be in the latitude of La Rochelle. They may be trying to join the Dutch; or, 'if he hath some landmen on Boord, and some horse, as are reported wee are more apprehensive of some designe upon Irelande . . . and therefore it will be a greate blessinge of god if you have prepared for his recepcion by crushing this insurrection . . .' As he writes, letters arrive

---

* See pp. 268 and 270.
[21] Carte MS 47 f.89.

from the joint commanders-in-chief. Monck's, written at noon the previous day, reports the Dutch fleet in sight: Rupert's, written at four in the afternoon from St Helens, reports the receipt of the King's orders on which 'he was making all hast with a good winde to return to the fleete'.

Three centuries later the reader can feel the tension; but the writer can still find time for his friends: '. . . I have promised the good old Secretary Nicholas to putt your Grace in minde of some contingency dew to him upon a former assignment, I thinke by your procurement, I am sure you will do all you can for him . . . It is now almost 8 of the clocke, and no more newes come, but the noyse of the Gunns still hearde, I dare no longer keepe my packett up . . .'[22]

By contrast the letters to Sheldon are written, not from the centre of affairs, but from Salisbury, Cornbury and Oxford, the England, almost, of the Great Tew past they had in common. They immediately precede the meeting of Parliament in Oxford, occasioned by the Plague, and much of the correspondence, or Clarendon's side of it, is taken up with arrangements for it. As ex-Warden, and now Visitor, of All Souls, Sheldon was entitled to some say in the disposition of the accommodation in that College. Clarendon, who was also Chancellor of the University, never tires of assuring him that 'All Souls is assigned wholly to your Grace's disposall, that when you have made choice of your owne accommodation, you may likewise choose your neighbours and provyde for those whose company you like best: Secretary Morrice hath a sunn a Fellow there, seems to be a very prety man. He hath very modestly desyred me to recommend his Father to your Grace that with your permission he may injoy the chamber in the other syde, very distant from your lodgings and which he said he could well accomodate for his father.'[23] It is difficult to imagine a twentieth-century Fellow of an Oxford College taking so deferential a line. Perhaps the absence of the Warden, who had evidently not yet taken up his residence after his election only a month earlier, left these two masterful men in possession of the field. 'I have been putt to a little chydinge of the sub-warden,' writes Clarendon loftily, 'I believe there is some peevishness in that house.'[24]

As might be expected the episcopate is a prominent topic. Clarendon is anxious that the bishops from the more distant sees should not be put to the trouble of coming to Oxford for the Parliament. Even Bristol qualifies for this excuse. 'If you have a 3ᵈ parte of the Bpps. with you it will be very well.' And the King 'has dispensed with us all for our roabes with very good reason for I know not how wee could gett them hither'. Naturally there is a good deal about filling vacancies on

---

[22] *ibid* ff.113–4.   [23] Bod.L MS Add. C.303 f.110.   [24] *ibid* ff.116, 120.

the bench. Dr Blandford, the Warden of Wadham, Clarendon's own chaplain and his daughter Anne's spiritual director, was, it seems, unwilling to accept the see of Oxford. 'I will when I come to Oxford use all my interest . . . to perswade him,' writes the Chancellor from Salisbury, '. . . I will not give it over, and if the Bpp of London stickes to us . . . wee shall overrule him.' It was not only that Blandford was evidently a man of uncommon quality who had entered the university as a servitor and had been one of the distinguished circle that gathered round Wilkins, the Cromwellian Warden. It was also that Morley, their old friend, was pressing the claims of William Fuller, Bishop of Limerick, one of the few bishops whom Pepys approved: '. . . one of the comeliest and most becoming Prelates in all respects that ever I saw in my life.'[25] 'Though in good earnest I love Christ Church well,' wrote Clarendon, 'I do not thinke it an equal reason for making a Bp. because he is a Christ Church man, which may expose that noble foundacion to more envy than it can beare.' He goes on to deplore the unwisdom of translating Irish bishops before they have had time to set their own house in order. For Morley, in his loyalty to his college, was running yet another old Christ Church man, the Bishop of Ferns, as a candidate for Bangor. Here he got his way. The Bishop was nominated to Bangor in 1665 but incontinently died before he could be instituted. Clarendon and Sheldon prevailed with the Warden to accept Oxford; but only two years later Fuller obtained the far richer see of Lincoln.[26]

Clarendon's concern, as so often, seizes on practicalities. 'And now I am upon that Argument of improving Bpp[rics] I must informe you of a proiecte for the puttinge of this poor Bp of Oxford (when there shall be one) into such a state as may inable him well to beare the dignity and infinitely do good to this Diocese. It is a particular we have sometimes spoken of, but know not how to make it practicable, by annexing the sinecure of Witney which I cannot imagyne the Bpp of Winchester will be unwilling to consent to. Dr Bridooke* who is now ther,offers very freely to resigne it to that good end, and to expect such a recompense and in such tyme as the King and you shall thinke fitt. It is I believe worth more than the Bpp[ric] (beinge neere £400 p.a.) and hath a house fayre enough for a Bp to live in and then is seated in that parte of the country where the authority, example and hospitality of the Bp is most wanted. I pray thinke of it as a worke worthy of your Grace's tyme.'

The proper remuneration of bishops was not the only practical

---

* Ralph Brideoake, like Blandford a scholar of humble origins whose qualities of mind and character impressed both Royalist and Parliamentary patrons.

[25] *Diary* ed. Latham and Matthews vii 209–210.

[26] All unattributed quotations in this and the succeeding paragraphs are from Bod.L MS Add. C.303 ff.104–26.

matter to which he addressed himself in these letters. The question of how the Archbishop was to make the journey from Lambeth to Oxford at a time when the Plague, already widespread, was seeping over the Thames valley was much discussed. As early as September 5, while he was still in Salisbury, he had worked out a plan:

'If you are not able to make your journey in one day and give notice to Sir Richard Powell, whose house at Sharbrooke [Shottesbrooke] 3 or 4 myles from Reddinge, and not a myle out of the way, I dare say you will be very welcome, and it will make your journey very easy to you. Methinkes it should be very convenient to you [to send whatever] you can suppose you shall want (and may thinke you will want)* at Oxford in your own Barge which your owne watermen can easily carry thither and if you are sure they are sounde ther is no daunger in it, and they may go away the day before you . . .'

A week later he writes from Cornbury:

'There is another place I am sure is not out of your way which is Raddinge, and there you may lodge very well at Will Armourer's, who will take care that your horses be in a secure place, but I do not heare that there is any sicknesse there.'

On reflection this became his preferred solution:

'Cornbury Munday night this 18 September

'. . . I am sorry to heare that the sicknesse is at Windsor & Eton which I did not know before your letter, but was that very minute givinge leave to Mr Dugdale to visitt his wife at Windsor but I revoked that leave as soon as I received yours.

'. . . the greatest daunger is that somebody who is not sounde may crowde into the company of those who must flocke hither at the first sittinge of Parliament. When you have thought about it you cannot pitch upon so good a place as Will Armorer's at Reddinge for your lodginge. I would by no meanes you should venture to lodge in any Inn, how free soever the towne is thought to be.'

Again on September 26 he returns to the charge. Will Armorer who is now in Oxford will be back in Reading in two or three days and will arrange for Sheldon's servants to be quartered in 'wholesome places'. But the Archbishop, as his friends knew, had a will of his own. On September 28, in the last of these letters, he concedes defeat:

'. . . I thinke you resolve well for your journey, from aboute Maydenhead you may well make your journey hither but you shall do well to avoyde Henly.'

Minutiae are the refuge of minds burdened with great affairs. The war was enough in all conscience. But the Plague . . . the thought of its possible effects, the sense of powerlessness, nagged mercilessly. 'I do

---

* A distinction invisible to any but the head of the legal profession.

thanke your Grace with all my hearte for keepinge me wakinge all this night with the dismall newes of the continuance of the Bill [of Mortality] to the same number of the last weeke with only an abatement of 3 of the plague but I do not thanke my Lord Arlington for suffering me to labour under that affliction till this morninge when he tells me that by my Lord Mayor's letter it appeared the decrease is not lesse than 1833 which is a blessed refreshment . . .' Sheldon's figures were nearer the truth, as Clarendon soon found out. It was the coming of the cold weather that was to turn the tide. Nonetheless, two hundred and fifty years before the aetiology of the disease was established, he fought with what weapons he had. From his letter to Sheldon of August 24 it seems that both of them had penetrated beyond the generally accepted notion of a miasma. '. . . I am very glad of your observacion that it is knowne by what meanes the sicknesse comes into any house, which makes it manifest that the ayre is not infested . . .' he took the strictest precautions he could about sanitary cordons, maintained apparently during the court's stay in Oxford by '. . . the King's guardes, those of the university being too weake for that service'. And legislation might be framed in the light of what he had learned: 'I wish you would bring with you, upon your owne observacion and those advertisements you meete with, some good materialls for an Acte of Parliament to meete with those mischieves, which fall out in the tyme of a great contagion.' It might have been his father writing.

Clarendon's confidence that the session would pass off without difficulty proved justified. 'I hope notwithstanding the contagion that we shall have a full appearance and a liberall supply,' he had written to Henry Coventry, then ambassador at Stockholm, on September 4.[27] In fact the turn-out was low: but in three weeks the business was done and an enormous sum voted. For once it was neither the King's boon companions nor the embittered Cavaliers in the Commons that spoilt his pleasure in dividing his days between the University he loved and the country house in which he took such pride. It was health — the country's and his own. To anxiety over the Plague was added a fierce and prolonged visitation of the gout so agonizing as to make him fear for his reason. By December 11 he had recovered enough to write to Ormonde to tell him of the seizure 'on the sudden in one night' so severe 'that I had no spirrits to supporte me'. Parliament had just assembled but he was for a time wholly unable to collect his thoughts. Although his London house should by this time have been weatherproof he does not expect to be back there before the beginning of February.[28] He managed to return to his house at Twickenham during the last week in January but the journey to London brought on 'a larger

[27] Longleat. Coventry Papers LXIV.   [28] Carte MS 47 ff.100–1.

and a sharper torment than ever before'. It was not till March 18 that he
was even capable of handling his papers.[29]

By then the cold months had brought down the incidence of the
Plague. The long spell away from London that it had entailed — a
month or more at Salisbury, nearly five months at Oxford and Cornbury — was to prove his last sight of the places he loved best in
England. Of the early connexions with Salisbury, of his pride in Cornbury, enough has been said. But no distinction was more valued, no
duty more punctiliously discharged, than his Chancellorship of the
University of Oxford.

It was not always free from acrimony. As Professor Hardacre points
out in an excellent article,[30] his imposing his connexion by marriage
Heneage Finch as second burgess for the University in the Parliamentary election of 1661 was widely resented. That his son Laurence
should be returned as senior burgess was accepted readily enough. His
letters to the strongly Presbyterian Principal of his own old house,
Magdalen Hall, were openly offensive but it was the Principal's refusal
to conform under the Act of 1662 that led to his ejection and subsequent replacement by the Chancellor's cousin, James Hyde, who had
taken his doctorate in the famous medical school of Padua and was to
succeed to the Chair of Medicine at Oxford in 1665. James's elder
brother, Alexander, was actually consecrated Bishop of Salisbury in
New College Chapel during the Chancellor's stay in Oxford, in succession to John Earles, but did not live long enough to make any mark.[31]

These honours for his kinsmen were not seized on by his detractors.
By the standards of his day the Chancellor was free from nepotism.
Murmurings arose in the University about the number and quality of
the names submitted for honorary degrees: but as Professor Hardacre
points out the dons themselves were the prime movers in devaluing
that currency. As conservator and protector Clarendon was an outstanding Chancellor. He rescued the authoritative copy of the Laudian
statutes, lost in 1648, from the papers of his friend Sheldon; and it was
his initiative that induced the Archbishop to endow the theatre that
bears his name. Most interestingly and characteristically, he refused to
allow the formidable Dr Fell as Vice-Chancellor to bend the rules
governing the election of proctors: 'The logic of the late ill times having introduced so many inconveniences and mischiefs by distinguish-
ing between the equity or intention and the letter of the law, I am not
willing to open that door to any decisions in the University . . .'[32] As a

[29] *ibid* ff.104–5.
[30] P. H. Hardacre 'Clarendon & the University of Oxford 1660–1667' *British Journal of Educational Studies* ix (1960–1) 117–31.
[31] Wood. *Athenae Oxonienses* ed. Bliss iv, 832.
[32] Clar. MS 77 ff. 304–5 quot. Hardacre.

disciplinarian he was both firm and enlightened, ridding the University of a senile Master of Pembroke by declaring the office void in October 1664, and recommending that John Locke should be allowed to proceed to the degree of Doctor of Medicine without first taking the baccalaureate in Physic. This last recommendation was not accepted.

Clarendon has been censured for his academic conservatism. He did nothing to promote the new philosophy that animated the Royal Society. His only attempt at modifying the course of study was to recommend an exercise in rhetoric for B.A.s before taking their M.A. But it might be argued that he proved himself a friend to those like Blandford and Christopher Wren who belonged to the circle of the new philosophy, that he showed a commendable scepticism towards the lecture as a useful means of instruction and that he was anxious to endow the teaching of such necessary social accomplishments as riding and dancing. The crabbed cast of mind too often associated with the ancient universities was his aversion. He wanted scholars to be able to hold their own with soldiers, lawyers, courtiers, men of fashion.

If he had been accused of stiffness, not to say harshness, towards Dissenters and especially Quakers, the Chancellor of the University of Oxford could not then conceivably have taken any but a strict line. A century later Dr Johnson, no bigot in religion, applauded the expulsion of six dissenting students from St Edmund Hall: 'I believe they might be good beings, but they were not fit to be in the University of Oxford. A cow is a very good animal in the field, but we turn her out of a garden.' Too many spiteful and outrageous acts were too fresh in too many minds for the large-minded tolerance that everyone is ready to concede to those who have done them no injury.

In one instance Clarendon has been specifically accused of vindictiveness. Describing the activities of the Earl of Bristol in the winter of 1660, Dr Ronald Hutton writes: 'Clarendon, whom he had displaced from power nearly twenty years before, reacted with an almost childish spite, using his own new authority as Chancellor of Oxford University to dismiss Bristol from its Stewardship.'[33] The authority cited for this statement disproves it. It was not until the end of April 1663, when Clarendon's authority was anything but new, that he wrote to Dr Blandford, then Vice-Chancellor and soon, as we have seen, to become Bishop of Oxford:

'. . . I have forborne replying . . . till I could resolve what was to be done in that affaire. It is notorious enough that my Lord of Bristoll hath brought an incapacity upon himselfe [by virtue of his conversion to Roman Catholicism] of continuing in the Office of Steward to the University but his Patent being for his life, and himselfe being a Person

[33] Hutton *op. cit.* 168.

of so great Parts and Endowments I was not willing that hee should by any Act of the University find himself deprived of the relacion he had to them and therefore I resolved to speake very freely to him and told him what I should doe if I were in his place whereupon he hath very frankly and with greate Expression of affecion and Reverence to the University resigned his office into my hande. And I have upon conference with my Lords the Bishops of London and Winchester [Sheldon and Morley] made choice of a very noble Person to succeed him, the Earl of Bridgwater. It is true he was never a member of your University which is to be imputed to his misfortune not his fault, being kept from it by the wickedness of the times, and since that would not suffer him to be of Oxforde, he would not suffer himselfe to be of Cambridge . . .'[34]

The accusation of childish spite might surely be better levelled at Bristol himself, who three months later attempted to impeach his old friend of High Treason on grounds so absurd that even those who had been itching to get rid of Clarendon hastened to dissociate themselves from the move. As Dr Hutton makes clear[35] the effect was to check the erosion of the Chancellor's position, even to restore his relations with the King to something approaching their old wary correctness. Execution had been stayed.

[34] BL Add. MS 14269 f.33.   [35] *op. cit.* 202–3.

XXI

A Fatal Year

THE YEAR 1666 had long been regarded with foreboding. Its numerical combination of 1000 — a naturally awe-inspiring figure — with 666, the number of the Beast in the thirteenth chapter of the Book of Revelation, seemed sinister. Clarendon himself, not a superstitious man, alludes to it in passing: 'I wish with all my hearte the yeare 66 were expired, which would much contribute to mens recovery of ther witts.'[1] The public disasters of the year, beginning with the Battle of the Four Days in June and ending with the Great Fire of London in September, strengthened an ugly national hysteria, to which he may here have been alluding. Certainly in the wake of the Fire he was quite specific: 'I must tell you, since I was borne, I never knew so greate a sharpnesse and animosity against the Roman Catholiques, as appeares at this present, I meane amongst persons of quality and condicion . . .' and again seven weeks later '. . . ther beinge the greatest jealosye throughout the whole kindgome of the Papists that ever I knew in any tyme and wher it will end god knows.'[2]

His last eighteen months of office were to be as daunting and as exhausting as anything he had experienced in a quarter of a century's service to the Crown. It was not, as we have seen, until the middle of March that he was even up to dealing with his papers. By the middle of April he had 'not yett recovered any strength, beinge not able to walke without beinge ledd'. By May 5 he was 'so recovered that I goe every day to Westminster Hall . . . but am in truth so weake that till yesterday I was not able to climbe the stayres to Whitehall, and am not the better for the adventure'.[3] Yet for all his infirmities and for all his

---

[1] Carte MS 47 f.113 Clarendon to Ormonde. June 2, 1666. There is a certain play with astrological projections in his famous speech to the Convention Parliament; and his horoscope, cast after the Restoration, is in BL Add. MS 6419 f.38.

[2] Carte MS 47 f.127 September 22 and f.128v November 10, 1666.

[3] *ibid* f.108 and f.110.

repeated descriptions of them his resilience was still astonishing. Within a month of the letter just quoted he was to display, in the crisis of the Four Days Battle, a calmness and strength that show no sign of failing power or weakening nerve.[4] He was pressing on, amongst hazards of a misbegotten, ill-conducted war, with the building of a house on which both Pepys and Evelyn lavished praise. Pepys and his colleague, Sir John Mennes, Clarendon's fellow exile of the 1650s, rode their horses over the site in February 1665 and exclaimed at the magnificence of the conception. A year later though it was by no means finished Pepys 'went with trouble up to the top of it and there is there the noblest prospect that ever I saw in my life, Greenwich being nothing to it. And in everything is a beautiful house — and most strongly built in every respect — and as if, as it hath, it had the Chancellor for its maister.'[5] As the months went by and the staircases were finished he took his friends and relations to admire it, culminating in July in a visit with his wife when they walked upon the leads.[6] Sir Roger Pratt's directions and the bills of masons, joiners, plasterers, carvers, plumbers, locksmiths, painters, bricklayers, stone-cutters and builders' merchants, occupying twenty-five pages of R. T. Gunther's *The Architecture of Sir Roger Pratt* (1928), support Pepys's opinion. But as with Hugh May at Cornbury the Chancellor was an interested patron, not an idle spectator. 'I thanke you for the new hopes you give me for my Chimneys', he wrote to Ormonde (at the height of his anxieties over the Four Days Battle) 'if the stone comes to Bristoll I have taken care for the transmitting of it hither.' This was, almost certainly, Kilkenny marble from the Duke's estates. Pratt had directed that 'the Chimnypeeces in ye great roomes are soe to be fitted upp y^t they may agree with ye mantlepeeces of marble to be sett up there hereafter'.[7]

The large conception of Clarendon House infused itself into the portrait collection. 'I have been three times at Mr Lilly's to sit for my picture by my Lord Chancellor's command,' wrote Heneage Finch, later first Earl of Nottingham, in August 1666.[8] It seems probable that this was not an isolated instance. 'Many of the post-Restoration portraits in the collection,' writes Mr Gibson, 'suggest a dating in the mid-1660s rather than directly after the Restoration', and quotes a passage in Evelyn's diary for 1668 as evidence that it had not been completed by the time of Clarendon's final exile. Indeed as late as March 1667 Evelyn sent Clarendon a list of forty-two persons to be added to it.[9] The

---

4 See above, p.259.   5 *Diary* vii, 42.   6 *ibid* 220.
7 Carte MS 47 f.113 June 2, 1666. R. T. Gunther. op. cit. 156. I am grateful to Mr Howard Colvin for this suggestion.
8 Quot. Robin Gibson *Catalogue* . . . (1977), x. This paragraph derives almost entirely from this authority.
9 Evelyn *Diary* (ed. de Beer) iii, 520n.

presentation of originals by Van Dyck, Lely and others became an obvious means of recommendation to the Chancellor. Mean accusations that he extorted masterpieces from penniless Royalists ruined by their loyalty were refuted a century ago by Lady Theresa Lewis,[10] widow of his first biographer. The example of Finch just quoted shows Clarendon directly commissioning Lely, whom both he and his daughter patronised extensively. Lely and members of his studio were in many cases employed to copy existing pictures rather than to paint *ad vivum*. As Mr Gibson points out: 'The accusation that Clarendon had plundered unfortunate Royalists for goods, pictures and money is best answered by the visual evidence of the pictures themselves. Most of the pre-Civil War portraits are copies, of which the originals are still in the family collections for which they were painted.'

The Clarendon Gallery was at once the counterpart of the *History* and an expression of his two master passions, friendship and love of learning. The great historical figures are there, not only of his own period and not only of his own side. But so are, or were, his friends and his family: even some who were once his friends but were so no longer, such as Edmund Waller, included no doubt for his eminence as a poet. The great pictures of great people, Strafford, Clarendon himself, Charles I, Charles II, are framed with the magnificence with which he bound his books. A large part of the collection still remains happily in the possession of the present Earl, though in the course of three centuries divisions of inheritance and subsequent sale have removed some of its splendours. Some portraits, that of Finch for instance, have disappeared altogether. No complete list of the collection survives. Unlike the great collections formed in Clarendon's youth by Arundel, Buckingham and Charles I it was not inspired by connoisseurship but by iconography, the desire of a historically-minded patron to preserve the likenesses of the men and women who had played a large part either on the wide stage of public affairs or in the intimate theatre of his own life.

To dwell on its contents, to speculate on its omissions, to guess at the identities of unknown sitters, are temptations that must here be resisted. The works of Lady Theresa Lewis and Mr Robin Gibson, already cited, show how important the subject is to any understanding of Clarendon. Among the illustrations to this book is his full-length portrait in his Lord Chancellor's robes, seated with his seal-bag. The original Lely from his own collection, recently identified by Sir Oliver Millar, it seems more alive, less glossy, less oily, than the engraving of it that forms the frontispiece to the *History*. The face is sharper, better-coloured, healthier, with something of the solidity of George Monck.

[10] In her *Lives of the friends and contemporaries of Lord Chancellor Clarendon* (3 vols 1852).

Although Clarendon had hoped that his new house would be ready to receive him it was to Worcester House that he returned. He was there during the whole of that electric summer, as beautiful and as perilous as that of 1940, disaster and triumph blazing across the sky. It was from Worcester House that he wrote the letter at the height of the Four Days Battle.* The country was still picking itself up from the punishment of the Plague. The psychological, social and economic damage had to be reckoned with. The destruction of a divided fleet by a superior enemy was only narrowly avoided in one of the bloodiest sea battles ever fought in home waters. The ships had limped into their harbours, ragged and torn, some without so much as a mast standing. Yet within a fortnight Clarendon was writing to Ormonde: 'Our fleete will be ready within 20 dayes, in better condition than ever, which will be much sooner then the Dutch can be.'[11] In spite of his courage and his confidence, he was feeling his age. In the last week in July he 'underwent as terrible a payne by a defluxion upon my shoulder, and afterwards upon my whole backe as I ever felte. It is farr from beinge gonne yett [August 4]. You have few of these Alarumms of age which must now every day grow upon me and putt me in minde that it is tyme to retyre from the noyse and throng of businesse and leave it to men of more vigour and dexterity, and who consider less what others thinke, when anything is amisse . . .'[12]

This recognition that he was no longer physically up to the direction of affairs is the more convincing because the letter was written when the war had suddenly started to go much better. Ormonde had subdued the rising at Carrickfergus and Rupert and Monck had won an outright victory over the Dutch in the St James's Day Fight. Once again as in the first battle of the war the failure to press a close pursuit had allowed the enemy to scramble to safety across the shallows that protected their anchorages. But there was no doubt in the Chancellor's mind of the magnitude of the success. 'Lett me now congratulate with you, for your good success against the Rebells, then in the budd, and havinge putt that kingdome into so good a posture for the recepcion of an enimy, and for our greater successe in so signall a victory which in respecte of the slaughter and the irreparable damage the enemy sustayned by it is very prodigious. I make no doubte you will cultivate the former by a very rigorous examinacion and prosequcion of those who had the least hande in that foolish designe, and if they whose names are to the declaracion that was founde in the foole's pockett were reall subscribers ther ought not a man, be he of the Clergy or the Layty, be

---

* See above, p. 259.
11 Lister iii 436 June 16 (misdated 18). Carte MS 47 f.116.
12 *ibid* f.120 Clarendon to Ormonde.

suffered to lyve. Nothinge can praeserve or secure Irlande but such severity.

'I hope wee shall make good use of the blessinge god hath given the kinge heare, his ma^ty beinge so little exalted with it that he hath rather increased than lessn'd his desyre of peace . . .'[13]

A week later he again emphasises the Dutch losses, especially in men: '. . . so that if they had all other thinges ready they will hardly be able to man ther shipps and every day or night the maryners who are on boarde throw themselves into the water and escape . . .'[14] By the following week he has heard the news of 'Holmes's Bonfire', a brilliant fireship operation that destroyed upwards of a hundred richly laden Dutch Indiamen as they lay at anchor in Vlie Roads.[15] Ormonde is exhorted to take a more positive view:

'I am sorry to see your so fainte expressions of the posture you are in to despise any invasion. I assure you we see letters . . . so full of courage and disdayne of the French that a man would thinke you want only ships to the conquest of Britany itselfe. I confesse I do not thinke M de Beaufort himself will have the courage to visit you this yeare, yett you cannot be to cercumspecte . . .

'The late prodigious outrage we have committed in Holland, upon ther shipps and ther towns* . . . of which they had not the least apprehension and which without the most dismal consternacion that ever fell on men they would have resisted and repelled in the instante, hath putt them all out of ther witts. God Almighty works still wounders for us.'

So optimistic is Clarendon that even domestic politics seem, for once, set fair:

'I know not upon what grounde you have so terrible apprehensions of transactions in Parliament heare, save that I know you correspond with those who have no minde to crosse anythinge that makes a noyse. I am very farr from that consideracion and that apprehension and am morally sure that if the Kinge uses his endeavours and be resolute himselfe, which he ought to be, and which I presume your reasons will make him: it will never passe the House of Commons it selfe and less the house of Peeres . . . I thinke I have tyred you: I am sure I have my shoulder.'[16]

The measure to which Clarendon refers must from the context of their correspondence be the Bill to prohibit the export of Irish cattle into England, a trade which was the one hope, in Ormonde's view, for

---

* The troops accompanying Holmes's expedition had burnt the pacifist Mennonite town of Westerschelling.

[13] *ibid*.   [14] *ibid* f.122v. August 11.

[15] For this see my *Man of War: Sir Robert Holmes and the Restoration Navy* (1969) pp. 148–61.

[16] Carte MS 47 f.125v August 18, 1666.

the recovery of the shattered Irish economy. The English landed interest, so overwhelmingly represented at Westminster, was determined not to open the home market. Clarendon remained absurdly overconfident until the last moment. On September 22 when the Bill was actually before the House, he wrote: 'The Parliament seems very passionate for the dispatch of it, and I know not how it comes to passe, many have no minde to oppose it, who do not thinke it reasonable: But the King seems to me to be resolute against it, and if he continue so, and declare it warmly, I am still of opinion that it will not passe both houses, but I must tell you few are of my minde . . .'[17] William Coventry, writing on the same day, gave Ormonde a far shrewder assessment: '. . . this day was read in the house of Commons a bill against Irish Cattle (which your letter in the close seemed to foresee). I was not in the house when it came in, it was ordered to be read a 2[d] time on Wensday next and noe doubte it will have a speedy passage in the house of Commons, and I believe noe hard one in the Lords house alsoe, and if it should be resisted by the King it would be the greatest dissatisfaction to the Parliament that can be imagined. I am sorry to tell your Grace such ill newes, but undoubtedly this is truth as to men's inclinations heere.'[18] Coventry, whom Clarendon detested, and Arlington, whom he resented, are the two correspondents sourly alluded to in his letter of August 18. As this instance suggests, Ormonde seems to have found their information more reliable than that of his old friend.

Ireland, perhaps understandably, provokes Clarendon's fiercest reactions. He had never been there, probably had never thought about the country until the disastrous rebellion of 1641 upset the delicate balance that he and his friends were trying to construct in the early months of the Long Parliament. In so far as it had entered his political calculations his dislike of Strafford would perhaps have inclined him to sympathise with those who resented his arbitrary and forceful administration. The massacres and atrocities of 1641 broke on England's consciousness like a tidal wave, overwhelming justice, reason and historical analysis. It was yet another gift to the propagandists of antipapal hysteria. Clarendon recovered enough to deplore in his *History* the inhumanity shewn to Irish Catholic prisoners in the Civil War and to arraign Cromwell for his foul acts at Drogheda and Wexford in his *Short View of the State and Condition of Ireland*.[19] But that work,

---

[17] *ibid* f.126v.   [18] *ibid* f.464.

[19] First published in London and Dublin (separate editions) in 1719–20. Almost certainly written in Cologne between 1654 and 1656 '. . . with the Assistance of the Duke of Ormond, and by the help of Memoirs furnish'd by the said Duke . . .' See the scholarly note by William King, Archbishop of Dublin, on the verso of the half-title of the Dublin edition '. . . much more correct than that of London'.

The date 1659 printed on the page-head (p. 13) of the Oxford edition of 1849 cannot be that of its composition.

written in defence of Ormonde's conduct as Lord Lieutenant from 1642 to 1650, betrays a bland self-righteousness about England's civilising mission in Ireland that provokes the reader's scepticism. '. . . the improvement of land, the erection of buildings, and whatever else might be profitable and pleasant to a people, which were advantages and ornaments that the policy and industry of that nation was utterly unacquainted with, till they were acquired by the skill and labour of the English, planted, and living charitably, friendly, and hospitably amongst them . . .'[20] Quite so.

Although Clarendon explicitly disclaims any general imputation against the Irish nation or the Roman Catholic part of it,[21] the consideration of what Ormonde had had to contend with obviously strengthened his prejudices and informed his reactions. The constant refrain of Clarendon's letters as Lord Chancellor to Ormonde as Lord Lieutenant is to exhort him to act out of character and be stern, if not savage. Fear and firmness must be his maxims. Considering that Ormonde knew the problem and personalities involved from first-hand experience unrivalled in extent and that his relations both with the King and with their colleagues in government were so manifestly happier than Clarendon's, this vehemence and assurance is the best evidence of what his enemies could plausibly represent as an overbearing arrogance. It must never be forgotten that Clarendon's early training had been in the law. Certainty, clarity, open-and-shutness were what he hankered after. That these commodities are not always on offer in politics he had learned as a man of affairs. But like the rest of us he did not always remember his lessons. Prejudice and reflex must be allowed for in the most open-minded of men.

Nowhere is this truer than in the fortification of long-held opinions:

> To observations which ourselves we make
> We grow more partial for th' observer's sake.

As ambassador in Madrid Clarendon had, or thought he had, discovered that the Spanish wine growers in the Canaries were exploiting the exclusively English market for their produce. On his return in 1660 he found that the price of Canary had risen from £20 a pipe in 1640 to £36. In a narrative whose tedium and complexity strains the loyalty of the most devoted reader he tells us how he ultimately solved the problem by inducing the merchants to ask for a charter of incorporation, so that the Spaniards would be offered a single price which they would have to take or leave. The interruption of the trade by the Dutch War and the large stocks held in the warehouses by some

---

[20] *op. cit.* p. 15.   [21] *ibid* p. 19.

merchants who had purchased at high prices led however to grievances and hard cases, and thus to accusations that the Chancellor had been bribed. These were revived at his fall and the Canary patent was instantly revoked.[22] So proud was he of the expedient — 'nor is ther any other way under heaven to subdew the people of those Islands to the rules of traffique and commerce' — that he repeatedly pressed Ormonde to adopt it in Ireland.[23]

This mood of optimism flushed with complacency was destroyed by the Great Fire. A bare fortnight after Clarendon had written to Ormonde exulting in the economic damage inflicted on the Dutch by the burning of a hundred merchantmen the city of London was engulfed in flames. Vast wealth roared up in the holocaust. The Dutch, the greatest sea power in Europe, in alliance with the French, by now the rising land power, faced an England already weakened by the Plague and apprehensive of disaffection in Ireland and Scotland. The government of Charles II was far from secure. To the man who had achieved the Restoration and still stood at the head of affairs, the political shock must have been profound.

It was not only, perhaps not even primarily, political. Pepys, a generation younger and rarely touched by the tragic sense of life, has recorded the moral and psychological shock caused by the obliteration of the world in which he had been born and bred. Bombing, motorways and developers have steeled twentieth-century Englishmen to these disorientations. To Clarendon, rooted in, nourished by, continuity in whose violation he consistently saw the visitation of God's displeasure, such a cataclysm must have put his courage and his faith to a severe trial.

Of its direct impact on him the only evidence is a letter[24] written to Ormonde from Berkshire House, where he and Frances had taken refuge with the Burlingtons, his son Laurence's in-laws. It is dated September 22 (the Fire broke out about two in the morning of Sunday the 2nd and was not brought under control until the night of Wednesday the 5th).

'. . . it is not in your power notwithstanding all descripcion made to you from heare to imagyne the generall distraction all men have been [in] these last 3 weekes: my parte, though I have not undergone any insupportable losse (yett I have lost more than I meane to bragg of) my trouble and disorder hath beene enough, for whilst I was at Whitehall (indeede upon so reasonable a conclusyon that many houres would not passe before Worcester House should be reduced to ashes) the terrible

[22] *Cont.* 610–30.
[23] Carte MS 47 f.112 June 2, 1666 and f.124 August 18, 1666.
[24] *ibid* f.126. The transcription printed in Lister iii 440–1 is not accurate.

apprehensyon my wife was in, caused all my goodes to be throwne into lighters for Twitnam, and into Cartes for my new house and other places, so that I cannot yett bring anythinge in order, or so much as find all necessary papers. To Worcester House I can returne no more, for besydes that my Tearme is expyred at Michaelmasse, it would be unspeakable and a chargeable trouble to returne thither, so that I make all the hast to putt my family into my new house and hope myselfe to be ther before Allhollandtyde [November 1st], and in the meane tyme my wife and I are sheltered by Lady Burlington in 3 or 4 roomes in Berkshyre House, wher I must acquiesce till it be counsellable to remoove to my owne, when I have roomes enough ready to receave all my family . . .'

As usual this took much longer than he had expected. The servants moved in about Christmas but it was Easter before he and Frances slept their first night there.[25] The Burlingtons were admirable hosts: 'We live with great satisfaction in each other; and truly the addition he hath made to my poore family, hath brought me infinite content.'[26] But as early as November 24 he was dreading the gout. 'The season of the yeare makes me looke every day for the visitacion of my old companyon: and I wish heartily (though it be like to cost me deere enough) it were the greatest calamity I am to looke for. Oh, god send us peace or you and I shall see ill dayes agayne.'[27] The Dutch reception of Charles II's overtures had been equivocal. Even when negotiations did begin, the regular emergence of new obstacles raised the Chancellor's doubts as to their intentions. Of the communications (known to very few) between Louis XIV and Charles II that were to culminate three years later in the Treaty of Dover he had no inklng. His foreboding that foreign affairs would trouble him more than the gout proved justified, though the attack, when it came, was a severe one, confining him to his room from the beginning of January to early March. By the 25th, though still weak, he could walk unsupported.[28]

Up to this point, however dark and dangerous the outlook at home and abroad, he had had, to all appearances, the general though never reliable support of the King. At least the King had moved decisively against his most inveterate enemy, the Duke of Buckingham, dismissing him from all his offices and issuing a warrant for his committal to the Tower on February 25. But at the end of March, just as the Chancellor was shakily getting on his legs again, a blow fell which he and his eldest son, revolving in retrospect the course of events that

[25] Clar. MS 85 f.165 Clarendon to Nicholas March 25, 1667.
[26] Lister iii 450 Clarendon to Ormonde March 8, 1667. 'Barkelye' is a misreading for 'Barkshyre'. Carte MS 47 f.134.
[27] Carte MS 47 f.130 Clarendon to Ormonde.
[28] *ibid* f.132v February 2, 1667: Clar. MS 85 f.165.

swept him from power, came to see as fatal. This was the elopement of Frances Stuart, 'la belle Stuart', the famous court beauty most ardently desired by the King, with his cousin the Duke of Richmond. There seems little doubt that the King's passion and the lady's obdurate refusal to become his mistress had led him to consider the possibility of making her his Queen. When Catharine of Braganza had nearly died in the spring of 1664, Frances Stuart's chances of succeeding her were highly rated. When the Queen recovered, the only means of bringing about this union with its fresh chance of legitimate offspring was by divorce. The King privately consulted Archbishop Sheldon as to the circumstances in which the Church would allow this. More publicly, and perhaps in anticipation of ecclesiastical obstruction, he provoked widespread speculation by attending the hearings of Lord Roos's attempt to obtain a divorce by Act of Parliament. All this Clarendon knew and deplored, leaving his master in no doubt of his opinions on this and other aspects of his marital delinquency. The King must have been used to this, even if his tolerance and good humour were wearing thin. But in this particular context so cynical and suspicious a man could hardly have failed to notice, and was in any case often reminded by his courtiers, that Clarendon's grandchildren could only be prevented from succeeding to the throne by the King's having legitimate children of his own. These it was now clear Catharine could not give him. Finally, and it would seem to Charles's mind conclusively, Frances Stuart had consulted Clarendon when her newly widowed cousin, the Duke of Richmond, had secretly offered her marriage and Clarendon had told her that such an offer was not lightly to be put aside.* The secrecy, the fait accompli, all pointed to the minister having taken the chance of thwarting his master's designs and securing the succession to the throne for his own descendants.

So at least Charles, in a rare burst of uncontrolled fury, gave the astonished Cornbury to understand when the Chancellor's son ran into him on the steps of Frances Stuart's lodgings. Cornbury later recounted the scene to Bishop Burnet who accepted it as a sufficient explanation of Clarendon's fall. Most modern authorities find a wider range of causes. Indeed they crowd so thick and fast that it seems invidious to grant the primacy to any.

Underlying everything was Clarendon's own personality: his wit, his force, his overbearingness. Age and arthritis had not softened his asperities. The suppleness and readiness to please of the young Mr Hyde had long disappeared under the weight of responsibilities and the consciousness of power. His relations with his most efficient

---

* Clarendon categorically denied any such involvement in a later letter to the King. See below, p. 292.

colleagues Arlington and William Coventry were bad. His parliamentary judgment and management had failed over the Irish Cattle Bill. His obstinacy over the Canary Patent had further exacerbated opposition. His unwisdom in employing an army of workmen to build a private house of palatial magnificence at the very moment when sailors were starving for want of pay and there was nothing in the exchequer to fit out a fleet inflamed his unpopularity. The war was still unfinished, still unpaid for. He might not have been in favour of it: in fact we know that he was not. But he had been at the head of affairs since 1660 and the war, no less than the Clarendon Code, lay at his door. Perhaps most corrosive of all the acids that were eating away at the foundations of his ministry was the resentment of Cavaliers who had not been rewarded with office or wealth. Any administration runs this risk. The longer it lasts, the more numerous its supporters in the House of Commons, the greater the danger. There is never enough to go round.

How violent and how dangerous a storm was rising against the Chancellor in the House of Commons was foreshadowed by the impeachment of Mordaunt, the brilliant and daring Royalist agent of the years immediately preceding the Restoration. If anyone personified the Clarendonian policies that had brought the King back it was he. An attack on him, mounted in the full panoply of impeachment, was a political initiative, not a judicial inquiry. At the Restoration Mordaunt, already raised to a viscountcy, had been appointed Constable of Windsor Castle. Never the most equable of men he was soon involved in a fierce quarrel with a minor official whose post entitled him to lodgings in the Lower Ward. As it happened the man had established himself and his family in the Garter House, itself the perquisite of that Order, which the King was anxious to revive. He ordered the Constable to obtain vacant possession which Mordaunt, with more alacrity than good manners, proceeded to effect. A file of soldiers marched up, the furniture was thrown out, the young son of the house was frightened (it was alleged) out of his wits and died shortly afterwards. Mordaunt was further accused of seducing or attempting to seduce the man's daughter and of throwing him into prison in the Castle when he attempted to stand as Parliamentary candidate for the borough. How much truth there was in all this we shall never know. Given Mordaunt's record and temper there was probably some, a conclusion supported by his readiness to accept a royal pardon. The immediate and important effect of the impeachment which was sent up to the Lords in January 1667 was to embroil both houses in a furious jurisdictional squabble, which held up financial supply (and everything else), thus further exposing the weakness of the administration's Parliamentary management.[29] But

[29] There are good accounts in both D. T. Witcombe and Ronald Hutton *op. cit.*

for the Chancellor the presage was darker still. This was the first attempt of the reign to impeach a peer (barring Bristol's fiasco), the first, in fact, since Strafford. Mordaunt was known to be a friend. The rumble of approaching thunder was in the air.

How alive was Clarendon to his danger? Seen from his vantage point was it indeed so great as it looks down the perspective of subsequent events? Granted his belief that he was, when all was said and done, indispensable to the King, and that the bonds of loyalty and affection between them were, in effect, indissoluble; granted, too, that the war, that mine that might blow them all to glory, was about to be defused, was the prospect so very frightening? These assumptions were, in a very short time, to be falsified: but it does not follow that they were false, still less that they were unreasonable, in the early spring of 1667. The revolt of the Scottish Covenanters had been crushed at Rullion Green at the end of November. The trouble in Ireland had been largely dealt with. 'You shall do well to finish your little thieving rebellion as soon as may be,' he wrote to Ormonde on March 8.[30] No doubt the young puppies round the King were sneering, the jumped-up politicians like William Coventry and Henry Bennet intriguing, the discontented Cavaliers in the Commons growling. But there was nothing new about that. 'It seems the present favourites . . . have cast my Lord Chancellor upon his back, past ever getting up again.' When did Pepys, one of the best-informed witnesses we have, write that? In May 1663, nearly four years earlier.

The rain of blows that fell on him in the spring and summer disabled him from controlling or repelling the multitude of forces that were making for his overthrow. There was the Frances Stuart affair. And then, within weeks of each other, a series of deaths: first that of Southampton, the Treasurer, for long an agonised victim of gout and the stone and thus a negative rather than the positive ally he had once been. Against Clarendon's vigorous opposition he was replaced not by another great nobleman but by a Commission, an indecent administrative and constitutional innovation of the late ill times, whose members included William Coventry and Lord Ashley, names to be mentioned with a shudder. Southampton died on May 16. Later the same month Clarendon's grandson, the Duke of Kendal, was buried in Westminster Abbey, followed in June by his elder brother the Duke of Cambridge.

Clarendon's grief at the death of an old and long-ailing colleague was sharper than at the loss of his two young grandsons, though he thought their death the greater public calamity. The terms in which he wrote to Ormonde on June 1 bring out the contrast: '. . . besydes the publique calamity in the Duke's children, in which I thinke every good

---

[30] Lister iii 450.

Englishman concerned, and even the government itselfe, I have lost a frende, a fast and unshaken frende, and whether my *only* frende or not, you only know and how fast you can stand against all temptacions and assaultes of which I must tell you I do not make the least doubte in spight of all men's vanity . . .'[31]

His distress is evident from his admitting to having left unanswered five of Ormonde's letters written over a period of nearly three weeks. But in the very next paragraph he has happily lost himself in labyrinthine hints that Ormonde has not been well advised in resisting the claims of the Duke of York's Admiralty agents to some of his lands: ' . . . you may very reasonably conclude that I would in friendship advertise you what I thinke upon that pointe, if I believe you in the wronge, and yett I must say agayne to you, what I have to say upon that subjecte is fitter for discourse than writinge . . . Of this if you will promise to forgive me, if after all this preamble it prooves to be impertinent, I will in my next write to you at large, and you will then best determine it yourselfe; for the present I tell you truly I am not yett enough composed myselfe against all my uneasinesses . . . and do bring my selfe very unwillingly to this very taske of writinge now.'

For all Clarendon's warmth of heart and warmth of temper, there is a curious touch of coquetry in this intimate letter to an intimate friend. Ormonde himself thought so. ' . . . I must complaine of the ceremony you use in desiring my leave to deale freely with me in that inconsiderable question between the Duke's servants heere and mee . . .'[32] Perhaps when deeply moved the Chancellor naturally reverted to the literary idiom of his youth, the age of Donne and of Ben Jonson, which by the Restoration had come to seem artificial. His kinsman and close political supporter, Sir Alan Broderick, who had been granted leave from his duties as a member of the Commission for the settlement of Ireland to attend on Clarendon, confirmed to Ormonde the reality of his distress: ' . . . Sure I am the death of my Lord Treasurer and of ye Dukes . . . have extreamly discomposed my Lord.'[33]

Broderick's letter of June 8 brought the first news of what was to prove a disaster of unimagined proportions. On the previous day the Dutch fleet had sailed into the approaches of the Thames and anchored in the King's Channel. On the 10th they were in the river. Late in the afternoon Van Ghent's squadron captured the fort of Sheerness at the entrance to the Medway, opening the way to the most spectacular feat of arms ever achieved by an enemy fleet in British home waters, culminating on the 12th in the capture and towing away of the *Royal Charles*.[34] If the brilliance and the daring were beyond praise,

---

[31] Carte MS 35 f.461.   [32] *ibid* 48 f.461 June 11, 1667.   [33] *ibid* 35 f.465.
[34] For the best account of all this see P. G. Rogers *The Dutch in the Medway* (1970).

the feebleness and incompetence of the English were beneath contempt. No excuse could possibly be acceptable for allowing an enemy, whose preparations had been amply reported by reliable sources, to penetrate in force to the heart of England's principal naval base without encountering any serious opposition. Public opinion was by turns incredulous, panic-stricken and finally outraged. The restored monarchy, its ministers, its servants, the very fabric of society were shaken as if an earthquake had followed the Plague and the Fire. Scapegoats would have to be found. Readers of Pepys's *Diary* will remember how that outstandingly able and effective public servant shook in his shoes. Clarendon, the unpopular head of a devastatingly discredited ministry, was in a far more exposed position.

Broderick's letters to Ormonde describe the situation from the vantage point of the Chancellor's most intimate circle. On June 15, the morrow of the disaster with the Dutch still poised, perhaps, for further triumphs, he wrote '. . . so stupendious a negligence in all sorts of officers no story mentions nor can anything lesse than a Miracle praeserve us. My Lord Generall [Monck] wished not to outlive the first view hee had of their miscarriages at Chatham and would have bin well content to dye on the place . . .' A week later he gives a memorable picture of Clarendon:

'In the course of my life I never saw my Lord so intire. I watch almost like a spy on my excellent Patron to observe every variation and though I had from my infancy reason to believe Him a right good man, and from my elder observation a right good Statesman, nor I, nay (if I may presume) your Grace or any about Him ever saw so miraculous an immoveableness. Sometymes it suggests a good Omen, otherwhile I think of Cato, or that excellent representation of Horace in the broaken Sphaere, *Impavidum faerient . . .*'[35]

The allusion to one of the greatest poems in ancient literature would have gratified his master. *Iustum et tenacem propositi virum* . . . The opening line, describing the honest man who will not swerve from his purpose, might have been the motto of his years, his grand years, when he stood for principle in the ruins of a cause. *Impavidum ferient ruinae*. No need of a hypothetical future tense. The ruins of a collapsing world *had* struck him and had found him unafraid.

Such strengths carry their own weaknesses. His resistance to putting the Treasury in commission and his 'extraordinary preference for my Lord Bridgwater [as Southampton's successor] gave greate advantage to ye other pretenders' — even in the eyes of so friendly a witness as

---

[35] Carte MS 35 f.478 and f.488. The quotation is from Odes III, 3. The false quantity would have been unthinkable to a man of Broderick's social and political antecedents in the eighteenth or the nineteenth century.

Broderick.[36] In the wake of the Medway disaster it was inevitable that there should be an urgent demand for the recall of Parliament. Indeed so stout a champion of established institutions as the Chancellor might have been expected to forestall it. In fact he opposed it on two grounds: one, a legal technicality that irritated everybody including, by his own account, the King,[37] that a Parliament once prorogued could not be recalled before the date specified in the prorogation. The correct procedure would be to dissolve and issue writs for a new election, the last thing that anyone wanted to be bothered with at a moment when a Dutch landing was a distinct if unlikely possibility. The other, stronger and more practical though politically more dangerous, was that the necessity, being immediate, required an executive not a parliamentary remedy. What exactly Clarendon said at the Council Meeting on June 25 cannot now be established. Pepys, writing on that very day, reports that the Chancellor 'told the King that Queen Elizabeth did do all her business in 88 without calling a Parliament, and so might he do for anything he saw'. That surely has the ring of authenticity. Clarendon himself writing in exile five years later explains his recommendations and admits that in defending them he might have used imprudent and unguarded language:

'It is very probable that in the earnestness of this debate, and the frequent interruptions which were given, he might use that expression (which was afterwards objected against him), "of raising contribution as had been in the late civil war." Whatever it was he said it was evident at the time that some men were well pleased with it, as somewhat they meant to make use of hereafter, in which his innocence made him little concerned.'[38]

Did he also say, as was alleged, that '400 country gentlemen were only fit to give money, and did not know how an invasion was to be resisted'?[39] It certainly sounds in character. His outspokenness was a function of his clear conscience. As he himself recognised:

'The Truth is; the chancellor was guilty of that himself which he had used to accuse the archbishop Laud of, that he was too proud of a good conscience. He knew his own innocence, and had no kind of apprehension of being publicly charged with any crime.'[40] In the event he was overruled and Parliament was recalled for July 25.

In spite of this rebuff, in spite of the rumours flying round political London and of the popular demonstrations against him, the cutting down of his trees at Clarendon House, and the daubing of *graffiti* on its walls, the Chancellor maintained his serenity. Broderick contrasted it with the general mood:

'Sure I am since my earliest observation I have not found so generall

---

[36] *ibid* f.465.   [37] *Cont.* 1103.   [38] *ibid* 1105.   [39] Lister ii 402.   [40] *Cont.* 1117.

discontent and irresolution in ye minds of Men; my Lord, as I formerly told your Grace, is in truth ye firmest and least disturbed of any I either converse with, or hear of, which certaynly is not only the effect of his Innocence, but observing ye universall consternation, hee was ashamed to be afrayd of hee knew not what. The Warr (as your Grace is witness) hee never advised. The peace (at Oxon) hee endeavoured. Hee had no share in ye derection of ye warr, much less in detayning our 1st and 2nd rate fregatts in port to ther destruction . . .'. Nonetheless Broderick seems to have seen which way the wind was blowing, for he urged Ormonde to come over so that he might '. . . give a Turne to many things I dare not mention of deeper concerne . . .'⁴¹

All that Broderick says about the war and its conduct is perfectly true. The military experts and the Commanders-in-Chief must bear the responsibility for not seeing that defensive measures they had ordered had in fact been carried out, for their inexcusable neglect of first-class and highly alarming intelligence, for their explicit reassurance of the King, on the very eve of the Dutch coup, that all was safe and well. Yet it is the business of politicians to be sceptical of expert advice. Clarendon, though he had had, as we have seen, some only too justifiable qualms, had allowed himself to accept that the treaty was in the bag. Or almost. 'It is to greate a presumpcion to conclude anythinge upon the supposition of a peace before it be very notorious,' he had written to Ormonde on May 11, 'but I confesse I doe believe you are free from those apprehensions you might reasonably have from the warr and therefore I doe heartily wish you would make as many reflexions as you can upon what advantage poore Irelande may gett from a good peace, and I do wish you would contryve as much exportacion as you can of the Natives, for plantacion or any other way, and draw as many English and Duch over in ther places as you can, and your greate men of lande shall be very good husbands in givinge good encouragement to both, though with some present expense.'⁴²

The absolute necessity of the peace had dominated his view of policy for many months. When at last it came it seemed to him to outweigh even the recent disaster in the Medway and the threat to his own position. On July 13 he wrote to Ormonde in a shakier hand, to thank him for his condolence on the death of Southampton.

'I am not yett recovered to so good humour, besides that the excessive hott weather makes me unfitt for any thinge, to take any delight in writinge, but the extraordinary kindnesse of yours of the 2 of July, and the greate civillity of my Lord Ossory upon the delivery of it, oblieges me tell you that though I am not at all surpryzed, nor can be, with your freindshipp, yett I am not without delight in the manner you expresse

⁴¹ Carte MS 35 f.522 July 2, 1667.   ⁴² *ibid* f.413. This document is not calendared.

it. You say you do not well know what wee are doing or what we purpose to do. I am sorry you do not. I hoped that they who do had
made you of the councell. I am sure I know neither.

'You know how many miracles and how seasonably God Almighty
hath wrought for us: trust me, none hath fallen out in a more lucky
houre than this of the peace, which I looke upon as concluded, since
the King hath consented to all things all other parties under ther
hands requyred as necessary to the peace, though some men will still
doubte it in order to doinge somewhat else, which will do us no
good.

'I guesse by some of your expressions, for which no question much of
your intelligence hath given you too much grounde, that you thinke
me in some straights with reference to my selfe, which no doubte some
of your frendes desyre to see me in, and it is no wonder you should
apprehende that when many have come out of London [i.e. the City]
to see if my house hath not beene pulled downe, and all the affronts we
have lately undergone in the Ryver hath beene brought upon the
Nacion by the Chancelour: yett after all this I am the same man you left
mee: and consequently as much only of the least apprehensions for my
selfe. I have done nothing I ought to be ashamed of, or my frends for
me: besydes that I am marvellously praepared to leave all I have to do
to wiser men.

'I will not deny to you that there are some naturall results from the
pryde of a very good conscience which are a little troublesome, and it is
not in my power to thinke, with all my humillity and submissyon,
which is very reall I hope, that I am aboundantly well used, but all
these [? scars] will quickly vanish and I have no cause to thinke that the
King is without some kindnesse, and opinion of my honesty and good
meaninge. I hope god Almighty will conducte him through all the
difficultyes he is to go through, which when the peace is concluded, he
is still to contende with, and now only capable of beinge contended
with, by this blessinge of peace, and which the continuance of the warr
would have rendered insuperable, and yett (which is most wounderful
to me) some of your frends who have not been bredd to the trade
would have beene well pleased if the warr continued. If I saw we did
anythinge to deserve those greate mercyes God Almighty every day
pours out upon us, I should recover some courage and hope to see you
agayne.'[43]

Long as this extract is, reluctant as its writer professed himself to put
pen to paper, the letter flows on — 'Since my hande is in' — to Irish
affairs in general and in particular, to Ormonde's dispute with the Lord
High Admiral's underlings, to his want of adequate judicial advice.

[43] *ibid* f.535.

Clarendon's sense of the divinely ordained inequality of man is strikingly illustrated in an allusion to the death of his grandsons:

'I wish all men who have the same obligacions had the same sense of the judgment and displeasure of god upon the Nacion in the loss of the Duke's children as you have, but I assure you I observe no such temper, and it is easily passed over, as if they were in the ordinary Bill of Mortality.'

A week later came the first sign of the worst that was to be borne. 'My Lady Clarendon this day begins to drink ye waters at Tunbridge, ye Doctors hoping her speedy recovery. My Lord is in good health, save yt he eat too much cocumber yesterday', wrote Broderick on July 20. On August 3 he told Ormonde: 'I am newly returned from waiting on my poor Lady Clarendon who continues very ill at Tunbridge.' On the 6th she was brought back to Clarendon House 'very weake but wee hope in no danger.' On the 9th at seven in the evening she died, having lain speechless for forty-eight hours: 'my Lord can neither write or direct me what to say to your Grace.'[44]

The rule that misfortunes never come single is perhaps more merciful than it first appears. During Lady Clarendon's last illness the recalled Parliament had met but, thanks to the timely arrival of the articles of peace, had been summarily prorogued to its original October date. If the mood in which it met had been a dangerous one, tempers had not been improved by an expensive and uncomfortable journey through heat that even the Chancellor in the airy splendours of Clarendon House had found oppressive.

> The portly *Burgess*, through the Weather hot
> Does for his Corporation sweat and trot.
> And all with Sun and Choler come adust;

The King might buy time by dismissing them but the price was clearly going to be formidable. Stunned by grief at 'so sudden, unexpected and irreparable a loss, that he had not courage to support',[45] the Chancellor perceived no alteration in his master's attitude towards him. A few days after Frances's death the King paid him a personal visit of condolence. Ten days later the Duke of York came to him in great agitation to tell him that the King, fearing his impeachment by the re-assembled Parliament in October, wanted him to give up the seals of office.

To say he was thunderstruck would be to understate his incomprehension. But, to borrow his own noble words, his enemies had found out a new kind of consolation to him, which his friends could never have thought of, to enable him to bear that more insupportable misfortune.

---

[44] *ibid* ff.559, 595, 607, 624.   [45] *Cont.* 1133.

XXII

End Game

CLARENDON'S dismissal, as Dr Clayton Roberts first pointed out in a brilliant article,[1] should be clearly distinguished from the attempt to impeach him which resulted in his flight and subsequent exile. The course of events, not least his own robust reaction, made the two episodes look as if they were both part of a single convulsion. But the second was by no means the necessary, still less the intended, effect of the first.

That Clarendon must go seemed obvious to many intelligent and informed contemporaries such as Pepys and Sir William Coventry, and has appeared equally obvious to historians as sympathetic to him as Sir Keith Feiling. His fall was a simple demonstration of the law of gravity. In political, personal, even physical terms the ground on which he stood was being washed away. Isolated, old, bereaved, gouty, he could not have been kept standing much longer. The shock of the Medway disaster would have brought down a far stronger bastion. This is to state matters in pragmatic terms. Viewed morally and philosophically, which is how Clarendon looked at history, the perspective is altogether different. Questions of right and wrong, of good men and bad men, of purpose, not the mere totting up of figures in the balance sheet of events, are the questions to be considered. This assumes, of course, that there *is* a purpose in the existence of the universe and in the experience of humanity. Clarendon, in common with most men of his time and of preceding ages, made that assumption. He is only remarkable in the vigour and consistency with which he applied it to the understanding of the world he knew.

Sententious this may sound: but it perhaps goes some way to explain why both he and some of those who had worked with him found his dismissal dumbfounding. What seems, in that situation, to have been

[1] *Cambridge Historical Journal* XIII, 1–18 (1957).

inevitable seemed to him inexplicable. And here, surely, something must be allowed for the peril in which every supporter of the restored monarchy felt the régime to be. There was a big sea running and somewhere ahead the crash of breakers. Clarendon who saw himself, and had often heard himself described, as the helmsman could not believe that the captain would choose that moment of all moments at which to order his relief at the wheel. He was not alone in his perplexity. Ormonde, who corresponded regularly with a wide range of courtiers, ministers and Cavalier M.P.s some of whom Clarendon regarded as his enemies, was equally at a loss.[2] The same incredulity is evident also in the letters written to Ormonde by Arthur Annesley, Earl of Anglesey, a colleague of both men in government, who had recently exchanged his Irish Vice-Treasurership for the Treasurership of the Navy. Level-headed and hard-working, Anglesey personified the conciliatory Presbyterianism that looked to Clarendon as the guarantor of the Declaration of Breda against Cavalier revenge and reaction.

Lady Clarendon had died on August 9 and had been buried in Westminster Abbey on the evening of the 17th.[3] At some unspecified date during that week the King had paid the Chancellor a personal visit. Letters of condolence flooded in of which Henry Coventry's, written from the treaty negotiations at Breda, perhaps best expresses the feelings of his closest friends. The news of her grave illness had made him 'very unfitt for the buisienesse wee have yett left and more for the iollitys and exaltations that are expected from us. If God Almighty hath beene pleased to bereave you of her, I do from the bottom of my hearte condole with you, and have only this to say that blessings so greate as shee are proportioned only for such as have virtue and constancy enough wisely and patiently to submitt to God's will in the losse of them, and such an one I estime yr. Lpp. though I acknowledge this a tryall sufficiently rude.' On hearing her death confirmed by the next post he wrote: 'It were greate presumption in me my L^d to presume to offer you any arguments for your better bearinge so greate an Affliction. They are from your owne great treasury of wisdome and religion those materialls for comfort are to be supplied.'[4]

Within a week of the funeral the Duke of York, whose unwavering support of his father-in-law in his time of trial perhaps blotted out earlier impressions, came to Clarendon House to tell the Chancellor that the King wished him to surrender the seals forthwith. The reason given was to prevent his impeachment when Parliament reassembled. Clarendon scouted the idea. He knew himself to be innocent. He was

[2] Carte MS 48 f.471 Ormonde to Clarendon September 6, 1667.
[3] *ibid* 35 f.644 Broderick to Ormonde. Chester *op. cit.* 167.
[4] Clar. MS 159 ff. 62, 64. August 16 and 19, 1667.

not afraid of the House of Commons. But he thought that if the King showed signs of being so it would rapidly become unmanageable. Both those who wanted to retain Clarendon and those who wanted to get rid of him began to lobby and to agitate. Ossory told his father Ormonde that '. . . the Dutches has bin with teares to mediate for her father . . .' Her brother Cornbury had attacked Arlington as the author of the trouble but Ossory had refused to accept this, while offering his own service to the Chancellor. He strongly advised his father to stay in Ireland and not to burn his fingers. He would in any case certainly be accused of extravagance in making so expensive a journey.[5] The King hesitated. On August 25 he sent Monck, twin pillar of the Restoration, to reason with Clarendon and, if possible, bring back the seals. Again the Chancellor demurred, requesting and obtaining a personal audience of the King next day, Monday, August 26. Anglesey, writing to Ormonde on the 27th, gives the evidence of a usually shrewd and certainly well-placed observer:

'My last [of August 24] gave your Grace an intimation of things a doeing here which made me wish your presence. The next day after [the 25th] the businesse concerning my Lord Chancellor's looseing the great seale became no longer a secret but was so publickly knowen that many out of zeale to justice and the King's service interposed with his Majesty on his behalfe that at least he might be left to a faire tryall, and not boaren downe by the cry of the people, and yesterday the Chancellor was in ye morning at his chamber at Whitehall whither his majesty came and they had long discourse together, ye Duke of York also present. In conclusion his Majesty said he would consider further, and the businesse seems to cool more this day, but what the issue will be I shall not take upon me to foretell . . .'[6]

He was to witness it three days later:

'I was yesternight [August 30] with his majesty when Secretary Morrice who was sent with a warrant to ye lord chancellor for ye greate seale brought it to Whitehall and his majesty shutt it up in his cabinet . . .'[7]

Clarendon's own account in the *Life*, written some six years after the event, on the whole agrees. But he also tells us what passed at the audience on the 26th. 'The King seemed very much troubled and irresolute; then repeated "the great power of the parliament . . . and that his own condition was such that he could not dispute with them, but was upon the matter at their mercy."'[8] This provoked a lecture from the Chancellor on the dangers of letting Parliament get above itself.

---

[5] Carte MS 220 f.274v ? August 28, 1667.   [6] *ibid* 217 f.404.   [7] *ibid* f.405.
[8] *Cont.* 1141. A shorter account, written within only two years of the event, is to be found towards the end of his *Vindication. Tracts* p. 85. See below, p.320.

'And thereupon he made him a short relation of the method that was used in the time of Richard the Second . . . And in the warmth of this relation he found a seasonable opportunity to mention the lady with some reflections and cautions, which he might more advisedly have declined.'[9] Throughout the two-hour audience Clarendon emphasised 'that he had no suit to make to him, nor the least thought to dispute with him, or to divest him from the resolution he had taken, but only . . . most humbly to beseech him to let him know what fault he had committed . . .'[10] To throw off an old servant in circumstances that must otherwise suggest either a yielding to court intrigue or a failure of nerve in the face of Parliament would, he argued, inflict serious, perhaps irreparable, damage on the monarchy.

The King might be excused for failing to see what this meant if it did not mean maintaining the Chancellor in office. It is hardly surprising that at last he rose and left without a word after the disquisition on his relations with Lady Castlemaine, 'not well pleased with all that had been said; and the duke of York [hardly himself a pattern of tact] found he was offended with the last part of it. The garden, that used to be private, had now many in it to observe the countenance of the King when he came out of the room: and when the chancellor returned, the lady, the lord Arlington, and Mr May [Bab, the brother of Hugh] looked together with great gaiety and triumph, which all people observed.'[11]

It is a famous scene. Pepys, even at second-hand, conjures up its most vivid image: Lady Castlemaine in déshabille running out into her Aviary and standing 'joying herself at the old man's going away'. Another memoirist, intimate with the court and particularly with the Duke of York, gives Clarendon an appropriate last word: 'O madam, is it you? Pray remember that if you live, you will grow old.'[12]

* * * *

No one who knew Clarendon doubted that he would survive the hammer blows that in a mere three weeks had destroyed both his domestic happiness and his public career. On September 13 Ormonde wrote from Kilkenny about his dismissal:

'You have doubtlesse long before this can come to your hands fixt on a much better method than I can prescribe. The substance of the misfortune befallen you is not without many presidents familiar to you in History, and some your owne experience can furnish. Circumstances

9 *ibid* 1142. 10 *ibid* 1137. 11 *ibid* 1143.
12 *Memoirs of Nathaniel, Lord Crewe* (Camden Society, 1893).

may agravate or aleviate but the succors from within are what makes all crosses more or lesse supportable.'[13]

On the 14th Broderick wrote from Clarendon House:

'Yesterday afternoon my Lord Holles and Mr Coventry arrived at Whitehall [from Breda] and in the evening made a visitt to my Lord Chancellor, much concerned in the alteration . . . My Lord hath taken phisick these 2 dayes according to his course in Autumn but is in good health and very cheerfull . . .'[14]

Not every friend showed such open loyalty. But Clarendon even derived a certain amusement from observing these backings and fillings. Towards the end of September he took advantage of the return to Ireland of Ormonde's land agent, Captain Edward Cooke, to send a letter that would not be opened and read by his enemies:[15]

Clarendon House
24 September 1667

Though I have great reason to take heed what I write and what I say and therefore have given over sending all letters by the post yet I satisfy myself that this bearer will carefully deliver into your hands this scribble; and yours of the 6th [about Lady Clarendon's death] is so full of kindness that I must not leave it unacknowledged.

The truth is, I know not what to say the world is so much altered since I writ last. The great affliction I lay under in the unexpected loss of my wife, which I did not apprehend full two days, had I thought pretty well prepared me to quit this world; yet I cannot tell you that the other which followed within a few days did not exceedingly surprise and even astonish me. Nor in truth am I yet recovered out of that trance, nor can I imagine how from being thought a pretty wise fellow I became suddenly to have no understanding and to be of no use. It fell upon me in an ill time, and how I shall shift I know not, being under a vast debt, and possessed of a very small estate; and so like to be in streights enough: nor do I know what is more intended. I thank God I fear nothing that my enemies can bring against me: though the number of them is great and that of my friends fewer than I could imagine.

. . . I am not conscious of having done or said anything in discharge of my publick trust, which I would not have done or said if I had been that minute to expire. I am accused of insolence and sawciness in debates, of which, it is said, you had long direction to advertise me. In truth I think I have been frequently bold enough, in which I am sure my intention was always full of duty, and I am confident you will swear for me that duty shall never decline. If I know myself I shall never be less warm in all the King's concernments than I have ever been: and it is not impossible that I

[13] Carte MS 48 f.473. [14] *ibid* 35 f.706.
[15] *ibid* 215 f.389 Cooke to Ormonde on September 21, 1667. I have used the modernised text of this letter printed in the Appendix to Carte's *Ormond*. The original is Carte MS 35 f.733.

289

may yet do him more service under his displeasure that I have been able to do in his favour.

. . . I am pretty well composed in my mind, and if I am suffered, shall be glad to spend this winter here, and at the spring shall retire into some corner of the country, where I may be able to get bread. I must not omit to tell you that the Duke of York hath been and is as gracious to me, and as much concerned for me as is possible. I have not many other friends to brag of. I confess I have so much mortification upon the humours of men that the very ridiculousness thereof is some allay to the melancholick . . .

. . . If there be not an absolute necessity of Allan Broderick's being with you, and I am verily persuaded there is not, his presence here is of great use to me.

Broderick's fidelity and affection together with that of his own children rewarded Clarendon's own generosity of spirit when support was most needed. He did not expect the conspicuous deviation of the Duke of York from the line taken by the King and his court. James coldly accepted the resignation of Sir William Coventry as his own secretary and appointed Clarendon's secretary, Matthew Wren, as his successor. Henry Brouncker, once a boon companion, was dismissed from his household for saying that it would not become the King 'to be hectored out of his resolution by his brother'. The phrase used by Clarendon in his autobiography is identical to that reported in a contemporary letter of Anglesey's to Ormonde.[16]

The enormous expenditure on Clarendon House had made this the worst possible moment at which to lose office. The schedule of his debts drawn up for him at the beginning of the year had amounted to £34,527. 18s. 7d.[17] — about three and a half million in our money. This was his most pressing preoccupation. What could he have meant by getting bread in some obscure corner of the country? He could hardly, as an ex-Lord Chancellor, resume the successful career at the bar that he had had to abandon in 1642. The writing of his memoirs which, no question, he must have been turning over in his mind was not in the seventeenth century the magic resolution of the retired statesman's embarrassments that it has since become. Perhaps he meant that he was thinking of selling Clarendon House and going to ground at Cornbury among his books and pictures.

But on October 10 Parliament met and it was soon plain that the House of Commons would not content itself with returning thanks to the King for his gracious message promising never to employ the fallen minister again. The move to impeach him brought him out, predictably, ready and anxious to do battle with his enemies. No more knifework behind the arras but a fair fight in front of the highest tribunal in

[16] *ibid* 217 f.405 August 31, 1667.   [17] Lister iii 535–6.

the land. Clarendon's right hand had forgot her cunning before he could decline such a challenge. Of course it was the last thing the King wanted. And, in less time than it takes to tell, both Houses of Parliament were locked in an alarming jurisdictional quarrel, the Lords throwing out the impeachment as not good in law, the Commons, or some of them '. . . saying openly what could they doe next but vote ye Lords uselesse and dangerous, as the rump had done'.[18]*

Ready as Clarendon was (and remained) to face every accusation that could be brought against him, he yielded in the end to the command, backed by threats, from his royal master. The threats took two forms. The first, that of arrest and indefinite imprisonment without legal process, he tells us in his autobiography: '. . . the thought and apprehension whereof was more grievous to him than of death itself.'[19] The second, a subtler but no less deadly manifestation of the King's treachery to his most faithful servant, is spelt out in the letter that Cornbury wrote to Ormonde on December 8 explaining his father's flight: '. . . a designe to prorogue the Parliament on purpose to try him by a jury of Peeres (by which meanes he might fall into the hands of the protesting Lords).' Since there was no chance of bringing home a charge of treason before the House of Lords itself, the King was preparing to pack a jury that would oblige. The Duke of Buckingham, now restored to favour and to all his offices, was tipped to preside as Lord High Steward over the trial.

Parliament met on October 10. Clarendon embarked for France on the night of November 30. During those seven intervening weeks his fate was the central issue of politics. Although he wrote his own account of that nightmare period some five years later only two contemporary letters of his are known. The first, written to Ormonde on October 15, deals almost exclusively with the dispute with the Duke of York already referred to. Clarendon, whose obsession with the subject Ormonde had already remarked, was sending over a legal expert, Dr Gorges, to advise him on that and other Irish questions. 'He understands all the affayres of Ireland so well and the many proiectes that are now on foote with reference to that Kingdome, and to shake that settlement, that he may in many respectes be of use to you . . . I will say nothinge to you of myselfe, but that I am in a strange country, where I know nobody, and where are very few who do remember they ever knew me.'[20] The main attack was not opened in the Commons for another ten days but it was already plain that plans were being laid for

---

* The story is told well and clearly in D. T. Witcombe's book and in Ronald Hutton's more recent work.

[18] Carte MS 217 ff.425–6 Anglesey to Ormonde, December 3, 1667: misdated but otherwise correctly printed in Lister iii 477.

[19] *Cont.* 1178–9. [20] Carte MS 35 f.762.

it. The King was bringing heavy pressure to bear. Sir Hugh Cholmley told Pepys on November 4 that those who went to see the fallen minister 'ventured their fortunes' and Sir George Carteret, Clarendon's kind host in Jersey, a week later 'did tell me how the King doth all he can in the world to overthrow my Lord Chancellor and that notice is taken of every man about the King that is not seene to promote the ruine of the Chancellor'.

It was to the King that Clarendon wrote his second letter, dated November 16:

May it please your majesty,

I am so broken under the daily insupportable instances of your majesty's terrible displeasure, that I know not what to do, hardly what to wish. The crimes which are objected against me, how passionately soever pursued, and with circumstances very unusual, do not in the least degree fright me. God knows I am innocent in every particular as I ought to be; and I hope your majesty knows enough of me to believe that I had never a violent appetite for money, that could corrupt me. But, alas! your majesty's declared anger and indignation deprives me of the comfort and support even of my own innocence, and exposes me to the rage and fury of those who have some excuse for being my enemies; whom I have sometimes displeased, when (and only then) your majesty believed them not to be your friends. I hope they may be changed; I am sure I am not, but have the same duty, passion and affection for you, that I had when you thought it most unquestionable, and which was and is as great as ever man had for any mortal creature. I should die in peace, (and truly I do heartily wish that God Almighty would free you from further trouble, by taking me to himself,) if I could know or guess at the ground of your displeasure which I am sure must proceed from your believing, that I have said or done somewhat I have neither said [nor] done.

If it be for anything my lord Berkley hath reported, which I know he hath said to many, though being charged with it by me he did as positively disclaim it; I am innocent in that whole affair [*sc.* the marriage of Frances Stuart to the Duke of Richmond], and gave no more advice or counsel or countenance in it, than the child that is [not] born: which your majesty seemed once to believe, when I took notice to you of the report, and when you considered how totally I was a stranger to the persons mentioned, to either of whom I never spake word or received message from either in my life. And this I protest to your majesty is true, as I have hope in heaven: and that I have never wilfully offended your majesty in my life, and do upon my knees beg your pardon for any overbold or saucy expressions I have ever used to you; which, being a natural disease in old servants who have received too much countenance, I am sure hath always proceeded from the zeal and warmth of the most sincere affection and duty.

I hope your majesty believes that the sharp chastisement I have received from the best-natured and most bountiful master in the world, and whose kindness alone made my condition these many years supportable, hath enough mortified me as to this world; and that I have not the presumption or the madness to imagine or desire ever to be admitted to any employment or trust again. But I do most humbly beseech your majesty, by the memory of your father, who recommended me to you with some testimony, and by your own gracious reflection upon some one service I may have performed in my life, that hath been acceptable to you; that you will by your royal power and interposition put a stop to this severe prosecution against me, and that my concernment may give no longer interruption to the great affairs of the Kingdom; but that I may spend the small remainder of my life, which cannot hold long, in some parts beyond the seas, never to return; where I will pray for your majesty, and never suffer the least diminution in the duty and obedience of,

   May it please your majesty,
    Your majesty's
     Most humble and most
      Obedient subject and servant
       Clarendon[21]

The recipient of this remarkable letter read it through and then burned it in the flame of a candle standing on his table, 'and only said "that there was somewhat in it that he did not understand, but that he wondered that the chancellor did not withdraw himself."' It seems a characteristic response.

The turmoil of Clarendon's emotions can be clearly seen though the lucid and vigorous argument. What chief minister, what private secretary to the sovereign, could have written to his master in terms of such passionate devotion? When Burnet, who could not have seen this letter, talked of Clarendon 'doating on the King', the expression was surely accurate. Two particular stimuli were acting on a man of passionate temperament already in great distress. One was the return of the Duke of Buckingham, 'that vile man' as Ormonde called him, to the King's favour: and the other was the crowning stroke of misfortune, the incapacitation of Clarendon's most powerful champion the Duke of York by an attack of small pox, reported by Pepys in his entry for November 10. That Jack Berkeley, once a beloved friend, should take the opportunity of revenging himself for Clarendon's having advised Lady Morton against accepting his overtures years ago in Paris was probable enough. But whether it was wise to repeat the categorical denial of involvement in the Richmond marriage was doubtful. Candour antagonises the devious.

As William Coventry, to Clarendon from first to last the villain of the piece, was in the process of finding out. In the debates in the House

---

[21] *Cont.* 1181. Clarendon kept file copies of personal as well as official letters.

of Commons he had defended Clarendon from an accusation he knew to be untrue and had produced a letter from Monck proving that he, not Clarendon, had advised the government that the Medway defences were sure. His own words to Pepys, spoken in private, are explicit: 'I have done my do, in helping to get him out of the administracion of things for which he is not fit; but for his life and estate, I will have nothing to say to it; besides that, my duty to my maister, the Duke of York is such that I will perish before I do anything to displease or disoblige him where the very necessity of the Kingdom doth not in my judgment call me.'[22] Such straightforwardness was uncongenial to Charles II.

But if some whom Clarendon reckoned enemies were ready to stand up for fair play some of the bitterest attacks on him were launched by those who had once been his friends. In the Lords, predictably, Bristol supported Buckingham at every move. In the Commons two friends of his young manhood, John Vaughan and Edmund Waller, were hot for his impeachment. Neither had played, to put it mildly, a hero's part in the Civil War or during the lean years that had followed for the cause of constitutional Royalism that Hyde had kept alive and which he was now accused of betraying. Waller, the old pupil of George Morley, by whom he had been introduced to the Great Tew circle, was never forgiven by Clarendon for saving his own skin in the detected plot for a rising in the City in 1643. Clarendon had blocked his appointment to the Provostship of Eton in 1665. His hostility could hardly have come as a surprise, whereas, to judge from the *Life*, Vaughan's did. That Ossory, the son of his greatest friend, should speak and vote against him must have been more painful. But Ossory and Arlington, married to sisters, were close friends politically and personally. Clarendon passes over Ossory's role in his autobiography. That two ultra-Royalist bishops, Cosin of Durham and Croft of Hereford, should have voted against him in the Lords was disgusting. But what was, by far, the most wounding feature of the whole business was the coldness and duplicity of the King. For Clarendon, in spite of his romantic adoration so passionately expressed, was under no illusion or misapprehension as to what Charles was saying and doing. He records his two-faced behaviour with the circumstantiality of the historian.[23] Perhaps it was this knowledge that led him to volunteer in his letter to go into perpetual exile.

Against this was his attachment, deeper than any personal affection, to the ideas of Justice and of Law. As he said of himself he 'had been bred of the gown'.[24] To take flight was not only to leave the field to wicked men. It was by implication and inference to admit guilt of

[22] *Diary* viii, 560.   [23] *Cont.* 1163–4.   [24] *ibid* 1170.

charges for which as his increasingly desperate and unscrupulous
enemies well knew there was not evidence to hang a cat. Politically too
it was to undermine the principles of oblivion and reconcilation on
which the Restoration settlement was based. Sir Thomas Osborne who,
according to Clarendon, 'had told many persons in the country before
parliament met , "that . . . if [the Chancellor] were not hanged, he
would be hanged himself"²⁵ attacked him for his arraignment of the
Court of York of which the Earle of Strafford was President', quoting
liberally from the speech he had made on July 6, 1641.²⁶ Osborne's
father had been Strafford's Vice-President. This was raking up old
scores with a vengeance. There were many closer at hand.

The anxiety of the time was felt by all who were charged with the
conduct of affairs. The administration was at its wits' end for money:
the war had piled up a mountain of public debt: and the income from
customs and every other form of taxation had plunged to disaster. In
the height of danger with the Dutch in the river and Parliament in
recess Clarendon had proposed the raising of an immediate loan
through the Lords Lieutenant. The unwisdom of inviting the Crown to
investigate methods of extra-parliamentry taxation was a gift to his
enemies. But the King's embarrassments now that Parliament had re-
assembled became daily more pressing. He had thought that the
dismissal of his great minister would clear the way for supply. But it
had not. The traffic of public business had ground to a halt in a quarrel
between the two houses that threatened yet worse danger if it were not
settled quickly.

Clarendon certainly needed no telling that everything he had
worked for was in jeopardy. And he was told, repeatedly, that the King
wanted him to resolve the crisis by flight. But though he has been
criticised, perhaps justly, by modern historians for blundering and
tardy reaction to the difficulties that confronted him in his years of
power he has never been accused of being frightened into easy evasive
action at the expense of long-term objectives. Strategy came much
more naturally to him than tactics. So, even after the King's reception
of his letter of November 16, he held on. Law, Justice, the Constitution, above all the power and reputation of the Crown as their
guarantor, were at stake, as well as his own honour and the future of his
family and of his friends. The last quarter of a century had shewn that
politics was a rough business. The tolerance and good nature for which
he had pleaded so eloquently in his first address to the Convention

²⁵ *ibid* 1164.
²⁶ BL Add. MS 28045 f.11.
This document does not, as Dr Clayton Roberts in his valuable article appears to suggest, state
that Clarendon promoted Strafford's impeachment though it is perfectly possible that he did
so and even more possible that Danby (as Osborne is better known) said that he did.

Parliament were aspirations shared by too few. If he went down, as he warned Ormonde, matters would not end there.

The King redoubled his pressure. The threat of a packed jury of peers, an expedient that, to quote Dr Hutton, 'violated every principle of natural justice',[27] was in fact technically legal and, if applied, unanswerable. Would the King have the nerve to face the outcry at so shocking a manoeuvre? But would not the putting of that to the test be to take too terrible a risk with everything Clarendon had spent his life in upholding? It was Heads I win Tails you lose.

The Stuart style was inimitably demonstrated in the King's dealing with his old servant in the fortnight that elapsed between Clarendon's letter of November 16 and his flight on the 30th.[28] Croft, the Bishop of Hereford, 'who had been very much obliged to the chancellor, and throughout this whole affair had behaved himself with very signal ingratitude to him, and thereby got much credit in the court,' went to see Clarendon's 'fast and unshaken friend' Morley, the Bishop of Winchester, intimating that it was the King's wish that he should accompany him to induce Clarendon to listen to an unofficial proposition. Morley complied, but Clarendon refused to have anything to do with Croft 'who had carried himself so unworthily towards him, and might probably misreport any thing he should say'. Morley, however, persuaded him to relent. Croft then embarked on a recital made the more complicated by the fact that he simultaneously claimed and yet explicitly disavowed royal authority for what he had to offer. 'The sum of all was, "that if the chancellor would withdraw himself into any parts beyond the seas, to prevent the mischiefs that must befall the Kingdom by the division and difference between the two houses: he [i.e. Croft speaking with the unacknowledged authority of Charles II] would undertake upon his salvation" which was the expression he used more than once, "that he should not be interrupted in his journey; and that after he should be gone, he should not be in any degree prosecuted, or suffer in his honour or fortune by his absence."'

The echo of Charles I's promise to Strafford would not have been lost on Clarendon. He replied crisply that he well understood what the implications and consequences of such a withdrawal would be for him but that if he had a clear command from the King to do so he would obey. Otherwise there was nothing doing. The Bishop parried and pleaded. Clarendon receded from his original condition, accepting that the Bishop was in fact the King's ventriloquial dummy, but insisted that in view of his state of health — he was already in pain, could not walk unassisted and might at that season be at any moment totally

[27] *op. cit.* 284.
[28] This account is based on, and unacknowledged quotations are taken from *Cont.* 1184–8.

prostrated by gout — he must be given a pass from the King which he could produce if struck down while still within the dominions of the Crown. Croft agreed but next day sent word that the King dared not go even that far in case the existence of such a pass should become known to Parliament. The Chancellor however could go in as perfect a security, relying on the word of the King. Clarendon declined.

At this point two further weights were thrown into the scale. The French ambassador, Ruvigny, a Huguenot nobleman of the same family as Southampton's first wife, called on Clarendon with whom he had done business over a number of years and assured him that he would be very welcome in France, should he choose to retire there. Within a few days the Duke of York, now out of quarantine for small-pox was visited by the King who, in an ugly mood at the rejection of the terms offered through the Bishop of Hereford, 'bade him "advise the chancellor to be gone"'. James at once sent Morley for the last time to Clarendon House to tell him that he must leave at once and that he personally confirmed the King's promise as conveyed by the Bishop of Hereford. Morley's visit, according to Clarendon, took place towards the end of Saturday morning, November 30.[29] His friend Sir John Wolstenholme, a Commissioner of the Customs, at whose house, Nostell Priory, he had taken refuge when he had last fled from London in 1642, arranged to delay the sailing of the customs cutter from Erith that very night. He climbed into his coach after dark accompanied by two servants. At about eleven he said good-bye to his two sons and two or three other friends who had ridden down with him, and went on board. The vessel cast off and the wind carried him downstream. An hour later it fell light and died, so that the rising tide carried him back to an anchorage close to his point of departure. It was three days before he landed in Calais and at least as long before his flight, a well-kept secret, became generally known. Even Pepys did not hear about it till December 3.

John Evelyn who had called on the Chancellor several times since his fall and had even attended what was probably the last of the sadly few dinner parties given at Clarendon House appears to have been his last visitor:

'I found him in his Garden at his new built Palace sitting in his Gowt wheele chayre, & seeing the Gates towards the North & fields setting up: he looked & spake very disconsolately, after some while deploring his condition to me. I tooke my leave, & the next morning heard he was

---

[29] He says Saturday, November 29; but the 29th was a Friday: and he repeats that this all took place on a Saturday. In his *Vindication* dated July 24, 1668 he says that the Duke commission-ed the Duchess to send word to her father: but there is no necessary inconsistency; Morley would have been the obvious choice to carry her message.

gon: though I am perswaded had he gon sooner, though but to Corn-
bery & there lay quiet, it would have satisfied the Parliament: That
which exasperated them was his presuming to stay, & contest the Accusation as long as twas possible, & that they were upon the point of
sending him to the Tower &c.'[30]

Several people agreed with Evelyn's criticism. Ormonde wrote on
December 12: 'By all I yet understand of that matter (which is but
little, and that confusedly enough) I incline to wish he had gone sooner
or staid out that trial.'[31] Clarendon himself continued to be racked by
similar doubts. Anglesey, on the spot and in office, reported to
Ormonde on December 3: '. . . The wisest I meet with blame his withdrawing and that he would leave so long a discourse [the letter
addressed to the Lords, presented by his son] to beare every man's
descant where none can make a faire exposition. Some fancy his goeing
hath a rise not appearing, many are amazed, his enemyes not
reioycing . . .'[32]

Perhaps, complete though their victory appeared, they were wise
not to rejoice. Clarendon's intuition that he might yet do more service
under the King's displeasure than he had been able to do in his favour
was to prove a sure one. The spirit was to triumph over the world and
the flesh.

[30] *Diary* iii 502.
[31] Carte. *Ormond* (1735) iii Appendix p. 50. To Conway.
[32] Carte MS 217 ff.425–6.

XXIII

The Second Exile

CLARENDON'S unflinching insistence on looking to the long term in history and on judging actions by the criteria of morals and law, not of immediate effects, was never more searchingly tried than in Charles II's treatment of him in the closing months of 1667. It was evident to a large number of contemporaries and has been generally agreed by historians that it was high time the old man went. It could not be seen by contemporaries but has been discerned by at least some historians that the Stuart monarchy never recovered from abandoning him. The Dutch War that he had steadily opposed had, as Dr Paul Seaward has convincingly argued, 'halted and indeed reversed' the recovery of the Crown's authority for which Clarendon had laboured:

'The need for large grants of extraordinary taxation meant that Parliament's influence again expanded. The revival of court faction in 1666 added to the government's problems. The combination of discontented courtier and "country" MP had posed problems enough in 1663; but when such a combination occurred again, in 1666 and 1667, with Parliament furious at the misconduct of the war, it was to wreck the stability which ministers had worked hard to achieve. The consequent crisis destroyed the consensus of the early 1660s, and Clarendon with it.'[1]

The despatches of Ruvigny, the French ambassador in London, vividly confirm this. On September 19 he reported to his master that Arlington and Coventry were frightened that Buckingham and his followers might join forces with Clarendon's friends to secure his own ascendancy and the return of his places. On the 26th he heard that Buckingham had achieved his aim without the assistance of the

[1] 'Court and Parliament: The Making of Government Policy, 1661–1665'. I am much indebted to Dr Seaward for his kindness in allowing me to make use of this D.Phil Thesis submitted at Oxford in December 1985.

Clarendonians, and on the 30th that Parliament was not only going
to attack Clarendon (here styled 'M. le Chancelier Hyde'), but also
Arlington and Coventry who were losing their nerve and, it was said,
beginning to regret their part in the Chancellor's overthrow. On
November 9 it was Buckingham who, fearing betrayal, had resolved
to destroy Hyde's sons and everyone who had endeavoured to keep
him in office. On December 12, six days after he had heard of Clarendon's landing in Calais, Ruvigny depicted the political scene in terms
of a great natural disaster, dwarfing the gang warfare that had
preceded it:

'L'entrée du comte de Clarendon en France avait tellement
echauffé les humeurs que pendant trois jours il a paru un emporte-
ment si violent qu'on pourrait plus tot le nommer un ouragan
capable de tout renverser qu'une bourasque qui n'est pas tant à
craindre.'[2]

The address to the House of Peers that Clarendon composed, apparently while the customs vessel was becalmed off Erith since he tells
us that 'the packet boat [which bore it back to England] was ready to
depart when the chancellor landed at Calais', is a dignified and lucid
refutation of the main charges against him, notably those of corruption, arbitrary use of power and interference in the conduct of the
war. The Lords at first ordered it to be entered in their journals: but
that was the last glimmer of fair play. Without any examination of
evidence, let alone any sort of trial, an Act was passed for banishing
him unless he surrendered himself to the Lieutenant of the Tower or
one of the Secretaries of State by February 1; his address was to be expunged from the Lords' Journals and burnt by the common
hangman. The act was presented to the King for his signature on
December 19 when the Houses rose for Christmas. Anglesey giving
the news to Ormonde reported 'much discourse and wagering
whether he will come or not. The most generall and probable opinion
is that he will returne by the day.' This hypothesis was supported by
the news of his moving to Dieppe when ordered by the King of
France* to leave his dominions.[3] The political climate was graphically
described by the same writer in two letters at the turn of the year: '. . .
we have here a very dolefull christmasse: the worke of this time was
wont to be love and friendly converse, now there is nothing but practice to undermine and supplant one another . . . my Lord Barkley is a
great intriguer.'[4] With the coming of the new year he exclaimed:

---

* See p. 301.
[2] 'The Earl of Clarendon's arrival in France has raised such violent feelings that for three days it
seemed that, rather than just a passing squall, a hurricane was bursting on us that might
sweep everything away'. CP 90 ff.21, 35, 55, 148, 151. I have altered the dates to Old Style.
[3] Carte MS 217 f.435 December 24, 1667.   [4] *ibid* f.431.

'. . . in what a sad and declining state affaires are and all confidence among men so broken by late intrigues and caballs that there are scarce any two that dare trust one the other.'[5] The words might have been Clarendon's own.

Was he, after all, going to come back and face what would now, surely, have to be regular impeachment and not a hole-and-corner trial rigged by his enemies with the collusion of the King? When he left England with the royal promise of 'salvation' underwritten by the Duke of York he clearly did not imagine that he was consenting to a decree of perpetual banishment. On his arrival at Calais he was, he tells us, 'unresolved how to dispose of himself, only that he would not go to Paris, against which he was able to make many objections'.[6] He might want to stay in France or if that proved awkward to take refuge in the papal enclave of Avignon. He might move to the Low Countries. Or he might well return to England. In this uncertainty Rouen seemed a good base with excellent communications. He therefore wrote to his old enemy St Albans at Paris with whom he had been corresponding as the envoy charged with negotiating a treaty with France 'from whose very late professions he had reason to expect civility, and that was all he did expect',[7] to ask whether there would be any objection to his going there and, if not, that a coach might be hired to meet him at Abbeville. The French authorities had naturally informed the court of his arrival. By the same post that he received 'a very dry letter from the earl of St Albans' grudgingly allowing his request, he had a most courteous letter from no less a person than Louis XIV's secretary of state, welcoming his proposal and arranging the provision not only of a coach but of an escort and instructing the governors of the towns on his route 'to treat him as a person of whom the King had esteem'.[8]

Clarendon lost no time. It was within a few days of Christmas. Winter was coming on; at any moment he might be immobilised by the visitation of his seasonal malady. The governors were hospitable. The coach was waiting for him at Abbeville. But even with everything made smooth it was an exhausting journey for a man in his condition.

'It was Christmas-eve when he came to Dieppe, and it was a long journey the next day to Roan [his invariable, and misleading, spelling of Rouen]; which made him send to the governor to desire that the ports might be open much sooner than their hour, which was granted: so that he came to a very ill inn, well known at Tostes, near the middle way to Roan, about noon. And when he was within view of that place, a gentleman, passing by in a good gallop with a couple of servants, asked, "whether the chancellor of England was in that coach." Presenting a letter of accreditation from the King he told him "that the king

[5] *ibid* f.433.   [6] *Cont.* 1202.   [7] *ibid.*   [8] *ibid.*

had lately received advertisement from his envoy in England that the parliament there was so much incensed against him, the chancellor, that if he should be suffered to stay in France it would be so prejudicial to the affairs of his Christian majesty . . . that it might make a breach between the two crowns; and therefore he desired him to make what speed he could out of his dominions; and that he might want no accommodation for his journey that gentleman was to accompany him till he saw him out of France."'9

So began a relationship that, with some stormy passages, was to be characterised by goodwill, perhaps even affection, on both sides. M. de Lafont (or le Fonde as Clarendon calls him) was a gentleman in ordinary belonging to Louis XIV's household. He reported to the French foreign secretary, Lionne, and acted as a kind of personal envoy to Clarendon.

The immediate question that Christmas Day was what on earth to do next. He was left at perfect liberty to choose what exit he preferred: Italy or Switzerland to the south, the Low Countries, the Rhine: but go he must. On the other hand he had made arrangements for money and such papers as he might be allowed from England to be sent to Rouen. Lafont 'seemed to think that it would be better to return to Dieppe, and so to Calais, as the shortest way out of France: but he had no commission to urge that, and so condescended to go that night to Roan; with a declaration "that it was necessary for him to be the next day very early in the coach, which way soever he intended to make his journey."'10

Lafont prudently remounted his horse for the journey to Rouen which was only reached late that night. The unfortunate Clarendon suffered no less than three overturnings in his coach so that he 'was really hurt and bruised, and scarce able to set his foot to the ground'. He told Lafont that travelling next day was out of the question and that he himself would write to friends in Paris (he probably had the abbé Mountagu in mind) to make his excuses to the King and to ask permission for a recuperative pause. Lafont tried to argue but when he saw that he would get nowhere he also wrote supporting letters to the court, the English ambassador and others.[11]

Once Clarendon had taken to his bed the gout fell upon him with its expected ferocity. Lafont, a gentle and humane man, was not the less terrified of incurring his master's displeasure by seeming too indulgent. On January 2 he wrote to ask for guidance since his instructions were to show his distinguished charge every consideration. Yet, though Clarendon had clearly been in terrible pain, Lafont knew that he was expecting one of his sons from England 'avec tout son train. je

9 *ibid* 1204.   10 *ibid* 1205.   11 *ibid* 1206.

croy que c'est la cause de son retardement, n'ayant mille comodités, s'estant sauvé de Londres avec un seul valet.'* The Earl talked constantly of withdrawing to Italy but Lafont did not believe he would get further than Avignon because of his illness. His valet had confirmed that for the last seven years his master had suffered attacks of similar severity.[12]

It must have been at this time that Clarendon heard of the act requiring his presence in England by February 1, for on the same date Ruvigny was reporting from London 'that all Clarendon's family except the Duchess of York were against this project of returning to face his accusers'. She had told the ambassador that she was much distressed [fort touchée] by the King's ordering her father out of France. On the other hand Arlington had warned him that there was a general feeling in the country that Louis was simply play-acting. France would gain by getting tough with the old man. Already the royal order for him to leave the country had had a great effect. At one stroke it had destroyed the idea of secret collusion between Charles II and his exiled Chancellor. Ruvigny supported Arlington's recommendation.[13]

On January 7 Clarendon dictated letters to Lionne and to the King, signing the last in a shaking hand. He thanked the King for 'his great bounty and charity in permitting him to repose himself here [at Rouen] till it please God to give him strength to undergo so great a journey' and drily expressed the wish that 'His Majesty's service in England may be promoted by the Earle's withdrawing himself out of France proportionably to His Majesty's expectation . . .' To Lionne he promised to give notice of his movements and expressed his intention of returning to Calais and transporting himself to London as soon as his health permitted. 'The Earl of Clarendon looks upon it as a great addition to his misfortune that he hath not language himself, nor hath any servant about him skillful enough in it, by which he might express his sense of the civilities extended to him.'[14] In fact as he indicates in his autobiography these thanks were ironic. He considered Lionne's hustling and harrying behaviour unworthy of a statesman. The language barrier was no affectation. All his conversation with Lafont was conducted in Latin. When shortly after this he was joined by his secretary William Shaw the case was no better for Shaw had no French either.[15]

Lafont felt himself sinking deeper and deeper into his master's black books. On January 19, the day on which Clarendon was at last supposed to leave, another postponement was requested. Finally on the 24th, a

---

* '. . . with his full retinue. I think this is why he won't move on as he hasn't much in that way, having fled from London with a single servant.'
[12] CP 91 ff.10–11.   [13] *ibid* f.6.   [14] *ibid* ff.23, 24.
[15] This is clear from the *procès-verbal* that followed the affair at Evreux — see below, p. 307.

month after they had arrived in Rouen, he wrote that the Earl was at that very moment leaving the town with the intention of going to Dunkirk and from there to the Low Countries.[16] No doubt Clarendon did not wish to show his hand unnecessarily. His real intention was, as he had first indicated to Louis XIV, to go to Calais and, once there, decide on the basis of advice from his friends in England whether to return or to make for Holland or Flanders. On the 31st he arrived in Calais 'so broken with the fatigue of the journey and the defluxion of the gout, that he could not move but as he was carried, and was so put into a bed; and the next morning the physicians found him in a fever, and thought it necessary to open a vein, which they presently did.' He was in such agony that he could not even turn over in bed, much less sleep. He could not read the 'many letters he found there from England . . . nor in truth could speak and discourse with anybody. Monsieur le Fonde, out of pure compassion, suffered him to remain some days without vexation, until he received fresh orders from Paris . . .'[17]

There could be no question of his returning to London by the day appointed, no doubt to the relief of Charles II and his ministers. The act for his perpetual banishment was double-shotted against a royal pardon by requiring a vote of both Houses for its repeal. Anglesey, reasonably and courageously, argued that this was an unconstitutional infringement of the royal prerogative, but seems to have had no support from its life tenant. English political life could now proceed on the assumption that its greatest living figure had been safely eliminated. Clarendon's friends and supporters made the necessary adjustments. Ormonde lost no time in instructing his son Ossory to indicate his readiness to co-operate with the new ministry. Sheldon, resentful of his old friend's religious latitudinarianism, wrote that 'for these divers years I have had little reason to be fond of him'.[18] Clarendon's two elder sons never failed to defend their father in Parliament but both were anxious to keep their places. Cornbury wrote to Ormonde asking his protection with the King. Ormonde promised his good offices but was himself displaced a year later. The crucial support that maintained Cornbury in his post in the Queen's household was that of his sister. As early as the end of December Ruvigny was reporting that she was beginning to favour a reconciliation between her husband and Buckingham.[19] Long afterwards, in January 1669, Lionne told Ruvigny's successor Colbert that it was the reconciliation between Anne herself and Lady Castlemaine that had been decisive.[20] No doubt it flattered Castlemaine's self-importance to feel that she had with one hand

---

[16] CP ff.53, 60.
[18] Quot. Hutton *op. cit.* 277.
[20] *ibid* 96 f.228.

[17] *Cont.* 1215.
[19] CP 91 f.17 January 5, 1668 NS.

thrown down the great minister and with the other raised his son from the ruins. The spirit of the masque was not yet forgotten.

But what, meanwhile, of the sufferer in Calais? He had arrived, by his own account, on January 31, by that of Lafont on the 28th.[21] On February 6 he dictated a letter to Lionne explaining that he had re- solved to make his way to Holland or even to England if his friends advised it but 'une furieuse goutte' prevented his leaving his bed. How 'furieuse' it was may be gauged from the agonized signature here reproduced.

On the same day Lafont asked whether Lionne still wanted him to attend on the bedridden exile and reported that the Duke of York and his friends had advised against Holland and were urging a retreat to Avignon. The French government, adamantine, sent a stream of orders for Clarendon's instant departure. By the second half of February Lafont had reached the end of his tether. The Duke of York had told his father-in-law that Ruvigny was responsible for the harsh- ness shewn to him: 'depuis ce temps le comte de Clarendon atribue à nous seuls la cause de son despart quoi'que je l'aie fort assuré du con- traire . . .'[22] In fact Ruvigny was going about on the other tack. On February 2 he had been shocked when Cornbury had shewn him a letter from his father, written in Rouen, which made him break down in tears as he read it because of his father's miseries and the brutality with which he was being treated in so unhappy a condition. Cornbury too was advising his father to give up the idea of the Low Countries and to make for Avignon. As a result Ruvigny urged moderation. The present severity was beginning to have repercussions among his friends in England. Why not let him make for Avignon by easy stages?[23]

March came, and with it uglier threats from Paris. Lafont was at his wits' end. On the 3rd he visited his charge and suggested that he should obey the King's order and cross the frontier to the nearest town in Flanders where he might recover full health at his leisure. Claren- don, whose own account of the interview confirms Lafont's, exploded. Not only could he not leave the kingdom, he could not leave his bed. He had heard from the abbé Mountagu in Paris that the French

---

[21] *Cont.* 1215 CP 91 f.85. Both dates NS which will be used henceforth unless otherwise stated.

[22] '. . . from this moment the Earl of Clarendon has held us solely responsible for his having to leave, although I have categorically assured him that this is not the case . . .' *ibid* ff.83–4, 85, 104, 109.

[23] *ibid* f.80v.

government had authorised no such order and that Charles II's special envoy to the French court, Sir John Trevor, had assured him that the English king was making no request for his expulsion from France. Clarendon's own account of this and another similar interview which followed shortly after show that he did not mince his words either to Lafont 'who was well bred, and in his nature very civil' or to the government that instructed him. 'He told him "that though the king was a very great and powerful prince, he was not yet so omnipotent, as to make a dying man strong enough to undertake a journey . . ." And in this passion he added some words of reproach to le Fonde, which were more due to Monsieur de Lionne, who in truth had not behaved himself with any civility.'[24]

Lafont had to admit defeat. The doctors told him that the patient no longer had fever and that the swelling of his feet would not prevent his travelling by litter or by canal to St Omer. But Clarendon refused to move. Was he to use force?

As the month dragged on tension eased. Clarendon's health slowly began to mend. The fall in pressure from London was felt in Paris. 'No one talks of the Earl of Clarendon here any more and I believe, as I have already indicated, that a less rigorous treatment of him will do no harm to French interests,' wrote Ruvigny on March 15.[25] Most important of all, news of the Triple Alliance concluded at the end of January between England, Holland and Sweden to check the rise of French power reversed Louis XIV's attitude towards his English cousin. There was no longer any motive for seeking to please him by bullying his exiled chancellor. Clarendon's request that he might be allowed to pause at Bourbon to take the waters on his way to Avignon was granted with a cordial *politesse* that was, happily, to characterise French treatment of him for the future. On March 31 Lafont wrote to report that Clarendon was to leave Calais in two days' time and would be in Rouen on April 7.[26] During the fortnight he spent there he was visited by a young Englishman setting out on the Grand Tour to Naples and Leghorn. 'My Lord received me . . . very civilly entertaining us in discourse near an hour's tyme. He is a fayre, ruddy, fatt, middle staturd handsome person & in age 60 years old: mighty affable . . . he seemed much troubled with ye Gout.' Interestingly in view of what was immediately to follow this traveller heard that the captain of an English ship in the port who had promised Clarendon a piece of salt beef had been told by his crew that they would throw him overboard if he did any such thing.[27]

The route south from Rouen lay through Evreux. About five o'clock

[24] *ibid* ff.136–7. *Cont.* 1216–18.   [25] CP 91 f.168v. Author's translation.
[26] *ibid* f.200.   [27] Rawl. MS C.782 ff.6–7.

in the afternoon of April 23 Clarendon, still enfeebled, halted to spend the night there at the Auberge de la Madeleine. Because of what followed[28] we have an unusually detailed description of the style in which, now that the Sun King smiled on him, he was travelling. His coach was drawn by six horses, followed by a waggon and four and attended by six horsemen. Of these three were English gentlemen of his household; two French-speaking servants, one a Parisian, the other, his butler, from Brussels, and, most important of all, his secretary William Shaw. Rooms were engaged, dinner ordered, and the Chancellor was helped from his coach to his suite on the ground floor. News of so distinguished a visitor flew round the little town and all too soon came to the ears of a company of English naval gunners who had taken service with the French crown and were, at that moment, on garrison duty at Evreux. Their English pay was months or even years in arrear: their French pay the same. Bored, aggrieved, hopeless, without family or friends, they had no resource but drink. Already by early evening several of them were pretty far gone. Hearing that Clarendon, the hated minister who had bilked them of their pay, sold Dunkirk to the French and spent his ill-gotten fortune on a vast palace in London, was actually only a couple of streets away, they rushed shouting towards the Madeleine, gathering companions from the inns on their way. At first they seem to have had some fuddled notion of making him pay up what was due to them. But the situation rapidly got out of hand. Their officer, an Irishman called Edward Howard, seems to have tried at first to calm them down. But he himself had been plying the bottle with some old shipmates recently arrived from Dieppe and was not sober enough to be in charge of men who were soon baying for blood. According to Clarendon's own account Howard was at the head of the men who broke into his room, knocked him down and then dragged him, screaming with pain, into the court-yard to finish him off. At that moment the forces of law and order im-probably but opportunely arrived. The changed policy of the French Court towards Clarendon had brought the Lieutenant-Governor of Rouen and the Chief Magistrate of Upper Normandy to Evreux to wait on him. Hearing the disturbance at the centre of the town they quickly supplemented their own small escort by calling out the citizens to their support. It was this large makeshift force that turned the scale.

Clarendon's own attendants, who were not military men (one was only a boy of sixteen), had been easily overpowered. Lafont, wounded in the head and body, and covered with blood, had put up a stout resistance and had sent a boy to ring the tocsin just as relief arrived.

---

[28] For this affair see Claude Lannette *Deux affaires politiques à Evreux sous Louis XIV* Con-naissance de L'Eure. no 22 (Evreux 1976), to which I am much indebted.

Several of the rioters were taken prisoner on the spot: the rest ran away but were easily rounded up. Clarendon himself more dead than alive was carried in a kind of bo'sun's chair to the château of the Duc de Bouillon, judged more secure than the Madeleine. It is hardly surprising that such an experience left him far from confident in any measures taken by the authorities at Evreux. He demanded, and obtained, a guard of ten men. Next morning he and his attendants received proper medical attention and were found to have escaped with bruises and flesh wounds. Lafont was not so fortunate. One of the bullets was still lodged in a head wound and might have hurt the skull. Trepanning might be necessary. Lafont therefore decided to have himself taken to Paris where better surgeons were to be found. Luckily for him he made a complete recovery without their ministrations.

Clarendon was anxious not to stay a moment longer than he had to in so dangerous a town as is evident from his letter to his old friend the abbé Mountagu written from Evreux at nine o'clock in the evening of April 26, three days after the events described.[29]

'I am now out of my depth, and have an affliction befaln me, though God's wonderfull mercy to me in preserving my life miraculously by his owne arme is some comfortable evidence to me that he will not abandon me to ye rage of my enemies . . . I had left Rouen (intending for Bourbon) on Sunday morning shortly after 7, and yet ye leagues were so longe and ye wayes so ill yt it was upon ye pointe of 8 . . . when we got hither, where your desire of finding me a ground chamber because I was not well able to goe up stayres brought us to ye worst Inne in ye towne . . .

'. . . an English company consisting wholy of seamen . . . who were to serve in ye Ordnance as Gunners were even then gathered about ye doores with such expressions as made theyr intentions very justly to be suspected. Ye little company we had, got to ye doore and defended it as well as they could by ye conduct and example of Mr le Fond who behaved himself with exemplary courage: but ye gate of ye house being broken down they were forced to retire into my chamber, where by barrocadoeing ye doores we hoped to defend ourselves till some assistance could come to us from ye towne; but theyr numbers were so great and they quickly made theyr entrance, both at ye doores and ye windows, and having first fired some pistolls and received some hurt themselves they entred at both places. M. Le Fond at ye window having hurt severall of them received himselfe a shot from a pistol in his head and some hurts with swords.

'When ye Rabble were in ye chamber they gave me all the ill language you can imagine, told me I had received all theyr pay, yt they

---

[29] A transcript, forwarded by the English ambassador in Paris, is in the PRO SP 29/238 f.180 I.

were 3 yeares in arreare, yt I was a Papist and yt I had betrayed ye King to ye King of France.

'One Ensigne Edward Howard was theyr principall Conductor & after a very few ill words clapped his pistoll to my face and twice endeavoured to shoot it of, but it pleased God that both times it missed fireing & another fellow with a great broadsworde strucke me with all his force upon my head, which without doubt had cleft my head asunder, if it had not fallen upon ye flatt, which only amazed me that I knew little more what they did. Then they began to have some difference among themselves whether they should kill me in ye chamber or take me out into ye Court, some of them cryinge out that they would carry me to London and have me hanged there, which in-clination I did all I could to cherish, & some there were, 3 or 4, that had more tenderness to me than ye rest, yet I am confident yt when they dragged me out of ye chamber, beinge neither able to goe or stande, they resolved to have killed me in ye Courte, but it pleased God some of ye company fell to pillageing and to takeing up my trunkes and boxes, & in ye instant that they had dragged me into ye Court, ye Lieutenant of ye Company, a very civill gent., one Captain Swayne, draweing his sword, by threats and blows rescued me from them, many goeing away with ye booty they had got. [Swayne took him back into his chamber: the 'Provost of ye Countrey and Magistrates' arrived] and upon conference with M. la Fond brought me into ye Castle of ye Duke of Bologne . . . & thus Munday night was spent. M. la Fond haveing, notwithstanding all his hurts, before he would sleep dispatched two expresses, one to ye Court and another to Rouen.'

On Tuesday morning the physicians and surgeons examined the party and pronounced that no one was seriously hurt. Clarendon's own wounds 'would prove but a contusion and in a short time would be wrought away . . . & 2 or 3 of my servants, who are most hurt, beinge all with swords would be in a condition to travell in 2 or 3 dayes. And to that purpose M. la Fond, who thought himself in ye best condition, contracted with ye Surgeons to accompany us as far as Orleans within a day or two: but to my infinite grief and astonish-ment I find his woundes much worse than he tooke them to be . . . soe yt to my unspeakable discomforte we are separated, he being neyther able to come to me, or I to him . . . God knowes when he will be able to remove and in what condition. I shall be without him whose conversation hath been full of delight to me, nor doe I thinke with what security to stay or to goe, nor am I in a house that hath any convenience in it, though ye magistrates of ye towne are all very civill to me . . . I hope there is no danger from my head and then I have only yt humour to contend with which I brought with me, which is yet greater than it was, soe I cannot tell how I gott up hither to ye top of a house, soe I cannot imagine how I shall be able to get downe.'

Until he heard from the Court Clarendon knew that he could not move or even plan his onward journey, 'which for many respects I should be impatient to doe if my gratitude to M. la Fond did not obliege me to be very unwilling to part with him . . . you must know the state I am in as well as I doe and therefore I beseech you continue your protection to me in that court & send me counsel what I am to doe, beinge destitute of any friend to advise me having but one servant beside Mr Canell who can speake a word of French, and though they be both honest men yet you will not believe them competent counsell in my condicion.' The only good news he has to tell is the immediate and complete recovery of all his papers and possessions except for trifling sums of money taken out of his pockets.

Once again, and for the last time, Lafont came to his rescue. A post-script written on the morning of Thursday the 27th reports his imminent departure for Paris in a litter to have wounds attended to '. . . & does warmly advise me at the same time to leave this towne in order to which he will provide me a guard to Chartres which advice I yet thinke necessary to follow . . . I shall be at Dreux to-morrow night & at Chartres on Saturday & at Orleans on Monday where I doe promise myselfe to hear from you . . . I am very unfortunate to be without a good Companion.' His ultimate objective is still Bourbon, in what is now the departement of the Allier.

His attackers were kept close prisoners while an energetic inquiry was conducted. On May 4 they were brought to trial and next day convicted and sentenced. Six of them went to the galleys (to serve as gunners) and three were hanged, Edward Howard being hanged and strangled under a wheel, not broken on it as Clarendon asserts. Still, the punishment was savage enough, perhaps, to satisfy Charles II's wishes as expressed to the French ambassador.[30]

The journey to Bourbon was long but apparently uneventful. At the spa itself his treatment, medical, social and political, won his unstinted praise. He resumed his journey much restored in body and spirit, spent a week at Lyon and arrived at Avignon about the middle of June 'by the pleasant passage of the Rhone'.[31]

Here he was received with every possible civility. The Vice-Legate and the Archbishop, both Genoese, called on him immediately, offering him every privilege should he choose to settle there. The town authorities followed suit in a Latin speech. All this 'together with the cheapness and convenience of living, and the pleasantness of the country round about it, might have inclined him to reside there. Yet

[30] CP 91. f.249 May 7, 1668.   [31] *Cont.* 1235.

the ill savour of the streets by the multitude of dyers and of the silk manufactures, and the worse smell of the *sewers*,* made him doubt that it could be a pleasant place to make an abode in during the heat of summer'.[32]

It is easy to understand his subsequent decision to settle in Montpellier. There is a cheerfulness, an air of good manners and ease about the place that not even the formidable vulgarization of our age has impaired. The University and the botanic garden were as celebrated as those of Oxford. But the immediate motive for his going there was the presence of Lady Mordaunt, wife to the daring Royalist agent of ten years earlier, who was now like Clarendon himself disgraced and dismissed though with better reason and on fairer terms. The youngest daughter of an Elizabethan dandy who had shewn much enterprise and little scruple in making his way at court, she was a notable beauty and a woman of profound religion, the close friend of John Evelyn and Margaret Godolphin. She knew Clarendon's world and belonged to his favourite part of it. She was also well established in the society of Montpellier, where she had been living for some nine months to recover her health, and introduced Clarendon to it. The Governor of the town, the principal law officers, the civic authorities came at once to pay their respects. The Duc de Verneuil, Governor of the province of Languedoc, never failed to call on Clarendon when he came each year to open the meeting of the estates. All this Clarendon attributes to Lady Mordaunt. The warmth with which he writes of her 'and the consolation he received from her during the time of her stay there' suggests that it was the spiritual comfort of her friendship that he valued beyond the entrée to the salons of Montpellier. His deepest friendships were founded on his religion.

Whether it was owing to the ministrations of Lady Mordaunt or to the inner resources that Ormonde had invoked in his letter on Frances's death, it would be dullness of soul not to admire the strength and completeness of Clarendon's recovery from distresses that call to mind the Book of Job. His own account of this reconstitution demands quotation:

'When he found himself at this ease . . . he began to think of composing his mind to his fortune, and of regulating and governing his

---

* The word 'sewers' is here italicised because in the original transcript made for the printer it was misread as 'Jews' and has so appeared in every subsequent edition. That a man of so liberal and humane a temper, a man moreover so exceptionally well versed in the religious literature and the history of the Jews (his last benefaction to his old university was to be a manuscript of Josephus), should express a vulgar anti-semitism seemed out of character. Dr Robert Latham brilliantly guessed a reading of 'stews'. This prompted recourse to Clarendon's holograph which immediately cleared him of the imputation.

[32] *ibid* 1236: but see Clar. MS 123 f.853.

own thoughts and affections towards such a tranquillity as the sickness of mind and body, and the continued sharp fatigue in the six or seven precedent months had not suffered to enter into any formed deliberation. And it pleased God in a short time, after some recollections, and upon his entire confidence in him, to restore him to that serenity of mind and resignation of himself to the disposal and good pleasure of God, that they who conversed most with him could not discover the least murmur or impatience in him or any unevenness in his conversations. He resolved to improve his understanding of the French language, not towards speaking it, the defect of which he found many conveniences in, but for the reading any books; and to learn the Italian; towards both which he made a competent progress, and had opportunity to buy or borrow any good books he desired to peruse.

'But in the first place he thought he was indebted to his own reputation, and [obliged] for the information of his children and other friends, to vindicate himself . . .'[33]

Here is marked out the ground he proposed to cultivate for the rest of his life: resignation to the will of God, acceptance of his situation and determination to put it to good use, both in developing his intellectual life and in composing his *apologia pro vita sua*. It is characteristic that the French language was to be so studied as to make him free of its literature but not to expose him to social importunity. The vindication he had in mind was not simply the rebuttal of the absurd charges brought against him in Parliament (though those would be dealt with first and faithfully), but the defence of the principles he had stood for and of the friends who, like himself, had been ready to sacrifice everything for them. The forms employed would include autobiography, history, essays, works of controversy both political and theological, dialogues on the Platonic model, even religious meditation. They would be composed during the three years that he was to spend at Montpellier and the three years he was to pass at Moulins after the visit of his son Laurence had raised his hopes that he might at last after so many wanderings be allowed home to die.

In the next chapter the riches of this late harvest must be considered. But now that so long and so various a life can be seen to be drawing to its close it may be convenient to sketch what is known of its circumstances. At Montpellier Lady Mordaunt was joined by her husband, 'coming . . . thither when he received information from England of a design to assassinate him [Clarendon] by some Irish'.[34] This was a half-baked plot instigated by some private family grievance apparently arising out of the Irish land settlement. The agent was a native of Lyme in Dorset who gave up partly because his money ran out and partly

[33] *ibid* 1242–3.   [34] *ibid* 1239.

because he was advised against it by Sir Richard Temple 'then residing in Montpillier'.[35] According to Clarendon Temple was the only Englishman that came to Montpellier who failed to pay his respects to him 'and dissuaded others from doing it as a matter the parliament would punish them for'.[36] This ploy was ineffective, indeed counter-productive. Temple was humiliated and 'left the town sooner than he intended'. Since he had been one of Clarendon's bitterest enemies in the Commons his conduct can hardly have come as a surprise.

A sidelight on Clarendon at Montpellier at the end of 1669 and the beginning of 1670 is shed by two brief references in the letters of Dr Aglionby who was bear-leading a particularly odious young man on the Grand Tour. 'I goe often to my Lord Chancellors: hee is kind to mee, and does mee more honour than I could hope for . . . if you . . . may afford us some newes it will bee gratefull to my Lord Chancellor heere from whom I gett some from England . . .'[37] Direct correspon-dence with Clarendon was expressly forbidden by Parliament except to his family who had to submit their letters to the Secretary of State. No doubt one of the attractions of Montpellier was the constant coming and going of well-informed English travellers.

For all the resignation and serenity towards which Clarendon disci-plined himself he was too rational to be without fears and misgivings, and too convinced a Christian to be without hope. His fears that the abominable treatment to which he had been subjected might at any moment be resumed at the whim of his enemies in England were he tells us soothed by the abbé Mountagu whose knowledge of and in-fluence with the French court were a great consolation. But he was, as he says, in effect a prisoner at Montpellier. When he asked the French authorities if he might move to Orleans to be nearer his children should they be allowed to visit him he was refused, but eventually granted permission to move to Moulins. As to hope, his confidence in Divine Justice would not let him dismiss the possibility of his own rehabilitation and the punishment of the wicked men who had con-spired against him. Even as he reproached himself with the extra-vagance and imprudence of building Clarendon House, he could not bear to give his sons permission to sell it in case he should be allowed to return.[38]

The disorder in which he had left his finances and the danger that supplies might be maliciously obstructed or even cut off added to his uneasiness. His health imposed an expensive style of life. Even when

---

[35] Clar. MS 87 ff.53, 56: February 26, April 9, 1669.   [36] *Cont.* 1240.
[37] Cambridge University Library MS Dd.11.57 ff.42, 45v. I am grateful to Dr Edward Chaney for drawing these letters to my attention.
[38] *Cont.* 1353–9.

free from the gout 'his knees, legs and feet [were] so weak that he could not walk, especially up or down stairs, without the help of two men'.[39] When ill he needed additional nursing 'so that to the English servants he had brought with him which with a cook and a maid to wash his linen amounted to six or seven he was compelled to take four or five French servants for the market and other offices of the house; and his lodgings cost him above two hundred pistoles'.

To these troubles were added anxieties about family and friends who might suffer for their assocation with him. One of his first acts on being driven into exile had been to write from Calais resigning the Chancellorship of the University of Oxford. It is a noble letter.

Good Mr Vicechancellor,

Having found it necessary to transport myself out of England, and not knowing when it will please god that I shall returne againe, it becomes me to take care that the University be not without the service of a person better able to be of use to them than I am like to be, and I doe therfore hereby surrender the office of chancellour into the hands of the said University to the end that they may make choice of some other person better qualified to assist and protect them than I am; I am sure he can never be more affectionate to it. I desire you as the last suit I am like to make to you, to believe that I do not fly my country for guilt, and how passionatly soever I am pursued, that I have not done any thing to make the University ashamed of me, or to repent the good opinion they had once of me; and though I must have no further mention in your public devotions (which I have always exceedingly valued) I hope I shall alwayes be remembred in your private prayers as
                    Your affectionate servant
                        Clarendon.

The University immediately proceeded to elect Sheldon, whose magnificent benefaction had been the glory of Clarendon's chancellorship. But the Archbishop for all his Oxonian antecedents and all his munificence could not spare the time to go there (it is said that he never saw the theatre that bears his name), and himself resigned a year later to be succeeded by Ormonde. In this at least the Chancellor over the water must have felt that what he held sacred had not been profaned.

There was no general proscription of the Clarendonians. Ormonde lost the Lord Lieutenancy of Ireland in the spring of 1669 but retained his important offices at Court and elsewhere. Morley was dismissed in a conspicuously insulting manner from his Deanery of the Chapel Royal, as was Dolben, Bishop of Rochester, from his Clerkship of the Closet.[40]

39 *ibid* 1352.
40 Clar. MS 87 ff.84–5. Morley to Clarendon. Pepys *Diary* ix, 53.

What was more grievous to Morley, as it was to his old friend in exile, was the defection of the Duchess of York to the Church of Rome. As an old family friend and her sometime spiritual director, he wrote, as her father did from Montpellier, pressing her not to take any such step before she had listened to what might be said on the other side of the particular arguments that were influencing her. He reminded her of her promise, made during a long visit to him at Farnham Castle, 'that if any Romish priest entred into discourse of Religion, she would command them to give it in writing so that she could forward it either to him or to Dr Blandford . . . For though God hath given you an extraordinary good understanding yet I am sure you have not so high an opinion of it as to conclude that what you cannot answer is therefore unanswerable in itself or that it cannot be answered by others.'[41] That letter was written on January 24, 1670. In August she was secretly received into the Church of Rome and died in that communion in March 1671.

Contemporary gossip attributed this alteration in one who was agreed to have been an unusually devout and serious Christian to her friendship with Lady Castlemaine and, more convincingly, to her anxiety to retain her husband's wandering affections. She herself has provided reasons that show her in this, as in so much else, her father's daughter. The political manoeuvres of the House of Tudor did not seem to her a credible instrument for the operations of the Holy Spirit.[42] It had, by her account, been the reading of the Laudian Peter Heylyn's *History of the Reformation* that had prompted this train of thought.

Her father's letter is not only an intensely moving document but perhaps the pithiest statement of a lifetime's reading, argument and meditation on the question that, in one form or another, had made such havoc of the world he knew. His mind, like Morley's, had been formed in the *convivium theologicum* of Great Tew. Young Mr Hyde's politics might need some literary art, perhaps even a certain economy of truth, to square with the sentiments of Lord Chancellor Clarendon. But in religion the line ran straight:

'The common argument that there is no salvation out of the Church, and that the Church of Rome is that only true Church, is both irrational and untrue; there are many Churches in which salvation may be attained as well as in any one of them; and were many even in the Apostles time, otherwise they would not have directed their Epistles to so many several Churches, in which there were different opinions received, and very different doctrines taught . . . If the Apostles taught

[41] G. Morley *A Letter to her Royal Highness*, pp. 13–14 in *Several Treatises . . .* (1683).
[42] Clar. MS 87 ff.62–3.

true doctrine, the reception and retention of many errors does not destroy the essence of a Church; if it did the Church of Rome would be in as ill, if not in a worse condition than most other Christian Churches, because its errors are of a greater magnitude and more destructive to religion. Let not the canting discourse of the Universality and extent of that Church, which has as little of truth as the rest, prevail over you. They who will imitate the greatest part of the world, must turn heathens . . . and God knows in that very communion there is as great a discord in opinion, and in matters of as great moment, as is between other Christians.'

He was writing in generalities because he was fighting in the dark: 'I presume you do not intangle yourself in the particular controversies between the Romanists and us, or think yourself a competent judge of all difficulties which occur therein; and therefore it must be some fallacious argument of Antiquity and Universality . . .'

When Clarendon wrote this letter,[43] which bears no date, he did not know whether Anne had taken the step which, he leaves her in no doubt, 'would break his heart; you condemn your father and your mother (whose incomparable virtue and piety, and devotion, hath placed her in Heaven) for having impiously educated you; and you declare the Church and State, to both which you owe reverence and subjection, to be in your judgment Antichristian . . .' Bishop Burnet, citing Morley as his authority, says that the letter only arrived after the Duchess's death.[44] This is not improbable. There had been rumours, which the letter makes clear had reached Clarendon earlier in his exile, of her conversion: but the fact was a closely guarded secret as was that of her husband, of which her father was evidently ignorant, for he clinches his appeal by underscoring the disgrace that she would bring on the Duke. The agony of mind and heart was the crueller for not being able to talk to her. 'It is to me the saddest circumstance of my banishment, that I may not be admitted, in such a season as this, to confer with you.' She had been his first and favourite child and it was through her that his grandchildren would succeed to the throne he had re-established.

From the handful of letters that survive from the years of his second exile it seems that he lived up to the principles he had set himself of 'composing his mind to his fortune'. Reading and writing, always congenial occupations, became the business of his life. The affability and good humour that had won him so many friends did not turn sour. An enchanting letter to his latest daughter-in-law, Henry's second wife whom he married in 1670, written from Moulins in March 1672

---

[43] Printed in several authorities. I have here followed *Clar. SP* iii Appendix xxxviii–xl.
[44] Burnet, i, 556.

complains humorously of his sons' failure to maintain a regular correspondence 'which I know not how to draw more naturally than from my other children; and therefore I must exspecte that from thee and thy two sisters [his own daughter Frances and Laurence's wife Harriet], which brothers will not performe, and that one of you will every weeke lett me know that you are all well, which will keepe me quyett and without grumblinge, and if thou givest them this order, I doubte not but they will observe it, and take ther turnes. It may be ther may be that civillity payde to Ladyes, that this letter may finde the way to thee without beinge opened, of which if I am assured, I will hereafter sende thee all the newes that Molins affordes, wher ther dyed this weeke a good woman, that had lyved a widdow full threeskore and tenn yeares since her husband's death, and the good capuchinn in whose arms she dyed, assured me that he did believe in his conscience that if she had lyved so much longer, shee would never have married.

'. . . Lett thy next tell me that thy husbande is resolved to bringe thee in May to Bourbon, which for many reasons will be very wellcome newes, and in the meane tyme send me word what English Ladyes are like to come thither. Speake to thy husbande, that when he findes the opportunity of any friends comminge this way, that he will send me Gerard's Herball, if he can in coulours, and since he intendes guardninge so much I will inable myselfe to conferr with him in his owne dialecte, and I would be gladd of any booke of husbandry that Mr Evelin hath sett out . . .'[45]

Moulins is only sixteen miles from Bourbon l'Archambault whose waters enjoyed such a reputation in the seventeenth century. Clarendon moved there in the spring of 1671. The handsome Palais de Justice, symbol of the royal authority then in plenitude of power, had only recently been built. Even apter to Clarendon's historical concerns is the magnificent Mausoleum of the Duc de Montmorency who had incited the estates of Languedoc to challenge the monarchy and had been publicly executed at Toulouse in 1632. His adoring widow, a member of the Orsini family, had commissioned the great artists, including Pietro da Cortona, whose patronage they boasted. History has a less visible but more splendid shrine in Moulins, for it was here that Laurence Hyde brought his father the manuscript of the first books of his *History of the Rebellion*, taking the story up to the beginning of 1644, which he had written in his first exile between 1646 and 1648. For two years Clarendon had been at work on his autobiography. It was at Moulins that he conceived the idea of incorporating the later work in the earlier and confining the *Life* and

45 *HMC Bath MSS* ii, 154.

Continuation of the Life to a personal record that began earlier and continued later than the quarter century that ended with the Restoration.

Laurence's visit renewed the hope, expressed in a letter to the King, that 'your Majesty's compassion towards an old man, who hath served the Crown above thirty years, in some trust, and with some acceptation, will permit me to end my days, which cannot be many, in my own country and in the company of my own children'.[46] In any case the fact of direct contact permitted the hope of its being repeated. 'I do assure you,' he wrote to his daughter-in-law Lady Cornbury in January 1673, 'your husband shall deny me very impudently, if he doth not bringe you to me, which is one of the greatest happinesse I pray to injoy in this worlde, which if my enimyes could depryve me of, I should not exspecte, but since it is in my frendes power to grante, I cannot imagyne it will be denyed [Henry Coventry had become Secretary of State in 1672]. God knowes the company of my wife and children was alwayes my greatest delight, when I injoyed many other blessings, and if I coulde still possesse what is left of those, I shoulde feele all other losses very little. I have had some hopes of gettinge neerer to Englande, that wee might not be at such a huge distance from each other, but whether that may be done you will know before I shall do.'

Laurence was allowed to visit him a second time in March 1673 and bore back with him Clarendon's critique of Hobbes's *Leviathan*, an astonishingly powerful piece of controversial writing not inferior in acuteness of criticism or strength of reasoning to the productions of his prime. In a covering letter commending it to the King he explains that it is only his concern for his service that has prevailed with him 'to expose my exploded name to the reproaches it shall be sure to undergo'. Charles II was, in Clarendon's view, hardly likely to have read *Leviathan*. 'But if you will please to call to Lory [the intimate form of his son's name is in this context oddly touching] for a short extract of his [i.e. Hobbes'] desperate conclusions as well in Policy as Religion, which I believe have never been presented to you, nor, it may be, taken notice of by many who have read his book, I am confident your Majesty will think it very requisite that they receive some confutation . . .'[47] He makes no request to be allowed to return and writes 'without any other suit than that you will believe me to be an honest man, who always served you with great fidelity, and whose affection and duty can never suffer any diminution . . .'

In his solitudes and his sufferings there is never a note of self-pity. A letter written to his other daughter-in-law, dated October 29 and belonging from internal evidence either to 1672 or 1673, radiates

---

[46] *Clar. SP* iii, Supplement xl.   [47] *ibid* xlii.

cheerfulness. He is in good health '. . . and want only good company in the better reception whereof I have taken 2 or 3 chambers in the next house: you complayne of weather and wee have not had a fowle day these six months: and it is yett so warme that there is no fyre but in the kitchen.'[48]

The first edition of *Paradise Lost* had been published in the year of Clarendon's fall and its 1,300 copies had sold out by the year of his death. It is in the highest degree unlikely that he was a purchaser. Yet no contemporary more fully exemplified the lines

> The mind is its own place, and in it self
> Can make a Heav'n of Hell, a Hell of Heav'n.

[48] Clar. MS 129 f.31. A reference in the letter to the birth of his grandson (ultimately to succeed as fourth and last Earl of Clarendon of this creation) rules out an earlier date than 1672.

XXIV

Late Harvest

THE FLOWERING of Clarendon's exile had its roots in two motives; to vindicate himself from his traducers and to bring himself to accept God's judgment on him. From this flowed the great stream of historical, autobiographical, controversial and devotional writing, the vast bulk of which was still unpublished at his death. As a lawyer he knew himself to be innocent: as a Christian he knew himself a sinner. He was not inhibited by good breeding, false modesty or the fear of ridicule from asserting either of these positions or from facing the rational consequences that derived from them. To compose his mind to his fortune the first essential was to rid himself of the self-destructive passions of anger and resentment. As a man who had to put his ideas into a form that other men could understand before he could be sure that he understood them himself his pen was the necessary instrument of his purgation.

The first, and least interesting, of these productions was *A discourse by way of Vindication of myself from the charge of High Treason*.[1] The charges were in the main so foolish or so trivial that their rebuttal yields little of value. That Clarendon was corrupt, that he was responsible for dividing the fleet or for treacherously selling Dunkirk to the French no student of the period can possibly believe. Indeed as he remarks '. . . the Treatment I have received since my coming into France is an unquestionable Evidence that that King did never take himself to be beholden to me for that, or any other service, as in Truth he never was'.[2] Dated Montpellier July 24, 1668, this must have been begun within two or three weeks of his arrival. Its concluding pages thus offer an earlier version of Clarendon's last interview with Charles II than that given in *The Continuation of the Life*. The chief difference is that in the *Vindication* the King specifically promises the Minister

---

[1] *Tracts* 1–88.   [2] *ibid* 36.

that if he will resign the seals and retire into the country he will be protected from any further proceedings. Exile is not mandatory. Whether
this guarantee would have been more strictly honoured than that
which Clarendon, on his obedience, ultimately accepted may be
questioned.

The pattern of the Chancellor's reading and writing in the first
months at Montpellier is best set out in the dedication *To My
Children*[3] written in February 1671 as a kind of foreword to his *Contemplations and Reflections upon the Psalms of David*. 'With what
hard and uncomfortable Circumstances I entred into this my Second
Banishment; the Severe Treatment I receiv'd when I thought myself in
a Place of Security and Repose; the sharp Sickness of Body and Mind I
was to contend with, while I was not suffered to rest, when I was not
able to stir, is all well known to you; and I do not enlarge upon,
because writing this to you in a perfect Serenity of Mind, I would not
give you or my self the disturbance of any melancholick or uncharitable
Animadversions. When under this rigorous Visitation I began to
discern some hope of Health and Repose, I thought of preparing some
Diet for my Mind, that might recover it to the Sobriety and Method of
Thinking, which after any notable Distraction is a Preparative not
easily made: And in order thereunto I writ to one of you, to transmit to
me a Case of Papers, in which there was some rough Draughts and
imperfect Conceptions, upon several Arguments, which I had a purpose to polish, when I should find myself in such a Place as I might
confidently reside in; and I was in no such Place till I came hither to
Montpelier . . .'

Lady Mordaunt's civilities are particularly noticed. 'Now I begun to
find my self vacant to my own Recollections, God having restored me
to a good Degree of Health, and thought to examine those Papers
which I had sent to you for . . .' But when he opened the trunk he
found it was not the one he expected 'but another which contained
many loose Papers, which I wondered how they were ever got together,
nor can to this Day ever call to mind that I did ever put them there . . .'
He might, he thought, have swept them all off his desk 'into that
porte-feuille . . . being suddenly called away or some Persons coming
suddenly in upon me'. Anyway among them were 'Six Sheets of Paper
not half written, which as far as it was written contained the Continuance of those Reflections I had made upon the *Psalms* . . . the last
Psalm there being the Seventieth . . . which by the Date it bore
appeared to have passed my Hand at Antwerp, shortly after my return
from Spain [i.e. in the middle of 1651] . . .'

Clarendon at once decided that his literary priorities had been

3 *ibid* 369–77.

ordered for him. 'I felt within my self a Reprehension from my own Conscience; and looked upon this Accident as an Animadversion of Providence, to renew and continue a Course of Devotion I had so long intermitted.' He resolved 'to set aside some direct time to revolve that part of Scripture which is comprehended in the *Psalms* of *David*, and to fix my Mind upon the Contemplation of them; and then to begin again where I left, and to prosecute the same Method of Meditation to the End of the whole Hundred and Fifty'. The object of this undertaking was to bring his mind in frame. 'What is it necessary to know,' asks Hooker, perhaps his most admired model, 'that the Psalms do not teach?' It is the combination of universality with direct heart-searching personal application, expressed in images of astounding beauty, that give them their unique place in scripture. As Clarendon points out they are more frequently quoted in the New Testament than any other part of the Bible: '. . . in all Times, somewhat extraordinary hath been thought to be contain'd therein, for the Instruction, Encouragement, and Reformation of Mankind, and for the rendring our Lives more acceptable to God Almighty.'

Since the work was not intended as a technical piece of scholarship he did not feel himself obliged to consider questions of authorship or chronology. One great difficulty, however, presented itself to the author of a subjective meditation. Part of the power of the Psalms derives from the recurrence of two or three fundamental themes. How is tautology to be avoided? Clarendon characteristically made a virtue of necessity. 'It is very hard to avoid those Reflexions which are very near the same . . . which I do not conceive ought to be industriously avoided; and therefore I observed a contrary Course, by never reading what I had said upon the like Subject, and so not affecting any variation, left my self at liberty to entertain those Notions and Expressions which flow'd upon the Disquisition . . .'

It is thus the most intimate, least highly wrought, of all his formal writings. The self-examination it demanded chimed naturally with the composition of his autobiography, the *Life*, which proceeded simultaneously.[4] He began the *Life* on July 25, 1668, the day after he had started the Vindication, and by August 1670 had brought the story down to the Restoration. No page in it contains such profound self-revelation as the address to his children with which he introduces the *Reflections on the Psalms*. Although he had begun the book at Christmas 1647 when he was in Jersey it was not until he was ambassador in Madrid in 1650 that it came into its own. In Jersey he had

---

[4] The fullest and most careful inquiry into the dates at which the different parts of the *History* and the *Life* and *Continuation* were written is to be found in Sir Charles Firth's three articles in the *EHR* vol 19 (1904) which I have followed.

had rational grounds for hope, small and remote though they might be. In Madrid he had none. It is to men in this condition that the Psalms ring out like the trumpet call in Beethoven's *Fidelio*.

'. . . The Publick Calamities . . . my forced Absence for so many years from your Dear Mother, and from you; the Nature of the Employment I had from the King, and the Scene upon which that Employment was to be acted, added very much to the Melancholique of the Condition I was in; being then an Ambassador in a proud Court, (as that of *Spain* will always be) to sollicit the Cause of all Kings, when no other King could be prevailed with to think himself concerned in what as great a Monarch as any of themselves . . . had so lately suffered before their Eyes; in a Court where very few men knew, or cared, what was done three Leagues out of the narrow little Town, where they spent, and desired to spend, the whole Term of their Lives; and where all (some very few excepted) believed that no Protestants could be used worse than they deserved to be . . . in a Court which at that very Time maintained an Ambassador with those very Regicides . . . and in this court I was to sollicit for Aid and Assistance, in the Behalf of a young Protestant Prince, driven out of his Kingdoms by the Power of bloody Rebels, who were hated, and feared, and courted at once.

'Every Day administered such Matter of Mortification to me (though towards my own Person they were civil enough) that I quickly discerned that what I laboured and longed for, could not come to pass by any Hand that held a Scepter upon Earth; that he only who could pull down all other Kings, and bring Desolation upon all other Nations, could raise the low and miserable Estate of my King and Country; and I must confess the frequent reading of the *Psalms* of *David*, gave me great hopes he would do it. The more I read and revolved the Subject Matter of those *Psalms*, the inevitable Judgments pronounced upon prosperous Wickedness, Pride and Oppression; and the Protection and Exaltation promised to those who suffer unjustly, and are not weary of their Innocence, nor depart from it upon any Temptation, I found Cause enough to believe that both the one and the other might possibly fall out and come to pass in this World, as it must unavoidably do in the next. Methought I found so many lively Descriptions of our selves, and our Condition, and so many lively Promises of Comfort and Assistance, as if some of them had been Prophecies concerning us, and intended to raise and preserve our Souls from Despair: and upon this Ground I proposed to make some Reflection upon every *Psalm* in Order . . .'

This passage has been quoted at some (though not at full) length because it expresses in the author's own words the essence of his theory and his practice, both as a statesman and as a historian, and identifies its source. The policy that led to the Restoration; the understanding of the life and the world he was, in 1671, engaged in describing; the hope that even yet he might be allowed, like Odysseus, to see his own country again, are all rooted here. The sensation he describes of the particular aptness of the Psalms must have been fortified when he turned to the very first with which he had to deal: 'Cast me not away in the time of age. Forsake me not when my strength faileth me.'

The medicine he had prescribed for himself not only affected a complete cure. It restored him to the intellectual health and vigour of his prime. It also went far to supply what was to him a grave deficiency 'which accompanies this my Second Banishment, which I did not sustain in my former, when I was never without the daily Exercise of my Religion, in a Congregation of the same Faith, performed by some very learned Divine of the Church of England . . . whereas to my unspeakable Discomfort during the whole Time of this my Second Banishment, I have been without a Chaplain, and consequently without any Exercise of that Religion which I have always embraced with my Soul, and in which I resolve to die, how destitute soever I may be of the Exercise of it at my Death . . .' The contemplation of the Psalms had become a regular observance 'except want of Health or intolerable Pain restrained me'. He admits to being pleased with the result and commends the reading of them to his children with some confidence, stipulating 'that if by the Advice of your learned and pious Friends, you shall think fit to publish them to the World, which I neither command nor forbid, I wish they may come into the Light with this Dedication to you, that all Men may know the Joy and Comfort I take in you: And that amongst the infinite Blessings which God hath vouchsafed to confer upon me, from my Cradle to this Time, I look upon it as the greatest that he hath given me such Children.'

The sentence which follows seems to be addressed, from its sense, to the Duchess of York and from its plural pronouns to include her husband. 'You, whom God hath raised to a State and Condition so much above me, and your Father's House, that by it he hath inverted the Course of Nature, and made my Duty a Debt to you, have yet behaved your selves towards me with the same Kindness, the same Tenderness and even with the same Duty, as if you were still under the Discipline and Dependance of my own Family. And you Two [Henry and Laurence], who are in a Condition, by God's Blessing, to be able to do me more Good than I can to you, have prosecuted and relieved me with the same Piety, as if all you have were mine.' The two youngest, James and Frances, 'who are not yet arrived at Years to govern your selves . . . are already what I can wish, so you will be what the others are. And I were very unworthy of you all, if I did not look upon you as a peculiar, a very extraordinary Evidence of God's Favour towards me, above all the Titles of Honour, and all the Fortune I am or have been possessed of . . .' Since this affectionate dedication is dated February 28, 1671 and the Duchess of York died a month later professing the Roman Catholicism her father abhorred, it supports Burnet's view that he had only heard rumours of her inclination and that his anxious letter* arrived after her death.

Clarendon had started writing the *Vindication* and the *Life* in the last week of July 1668. The date on which he resumed work on the *Reflections* was December 13. A political apologia, an autobiography and a work of religious meditation might seem a somewhat egocentric literary programme. Yet none of these writings answer that description. The *Vindication* deals with charges that others had brought against him, not with proclaiming his own merits (though, on principle, he does not hesitate to do so: 'It is not Modesty, but stupidity to conceal, or not to acknowledge, and with some Joy to magnify any Invention of our own, by which ourselves or the Publick, have received any notable Advantage . . .'[5]). The *Life* tells us much more about the times and, above all, the leading figures of the day than it does about its author. And the *Reflections* is the masterwork that seizes on the great questions that so many prefer to evade: what is the meaning of life and how should we try to live it? What are the political and general implications of our answers? Obviously the *Life* and the *Reflections*, composed, one gathers, at separate times of day over a long period, influenced each other profoundly.

The *Reflections* express, often epigrammatically, ideas which were to be crucial to later works, other than the *Life* and the *History*, or to be elaborated in the *Essays* that were thrown off at this time. The central notion of his last work *Religion and Policy* is to be found, for instance, in a passage inspired by Psalm 78: 'Christ . . . and his Apostles . . . made so short and plain a Scheme of all that we are obliged to believe or to do, that wee need have no Recourse to Tradition to guide us into the necessary Paths of our Salvation . . . this Rope of Sand, which Tradition is . . .'[6] His fundamental criticism of Hobbes that he would never expose his ideas to the bracing winds of conversation can perhaps be discerned in '. . . he who informs others, often teaches himself; it being a Blessing upon Communication, that new and useful thoughts occur in the Acts of Communication'.[7] Even beyond his own productions, may not Dr Johnson's memorable phrase in his *Life of Savage* have taken its origin from Clarendon's '. . . to sleep out our Time to our own lazy Desire'[8]?

Especially pertinent to the *Life* are the passsages that reprehend open criticism of monarchs. '. . . the Dignity and Reputation of a

---

* See p. 314.
5 *Tracts* 459.   6 *ibid* 582–3.   7 *ibid* 593, Ps. 81.   8 *ibid* 723, Ps. 121.

325

Prince is of such inestimable Importance to his own Security, and to the Peace and Happiness of the People, that all his Defects and Infirmities are to be covered and concealed, with the same Care that *Shem* and *Japhet* covered their Father's Nakedness, without beholding it. Speaking Truth in those Cases hath more Malice in it than Lying . . .'[9] And, in the commentary on an earlier Psalm, 'They who are too inquisitive into the Weakness and Infirmities of Princes' are compared to Noah's other son Cham who unhappily lacked his brothers' sense of propriety.[10] Indeed in his Address to his Children that precedes the work unswerving reverence and duty to the King are enjoined, '. . . and that no Sense of the hard Measure I have undergone, do make you less sollicitous and zealous to advance his Service'.[11]

The point was one he was acutely aware of in writing his own recollections. The *History* that he had embarked on twenty years earlier had been intended as a State Paper for the benefit of Charles I. But as Sir Charles Firth pointed out:

'In 1669 the situation had altered. As Clarendon was no longer writing for the king's eye, his former reticence was unnecessary. He could be outspoken without fear of giving offence. Moreover experience and his own treatment had opened his eyes to the faults of the masters he had served. In the character which he gives of Charles I he concludes by saying that "he was without some parts and qualities which have made some kings great and happy", and blames him as being "more irresolute than the conjuncture of his affairs would admit."'[12] He was later to amplify that judgment to include James I and Charles II: '. . . that unfixedness and irresolution of judgment that was natural to all his family of the male line'.[13]

Why did he write the *Life*? Certainly, emphatically, not for publication in his own time. Partly, as he himself says in its concluding paragraphs, because intellectual activity was the necessary condition to peace of mind. Partly he wished to leave a record to his children that would show his own innocence: it was surely no coincidence that he embarked on it at the same time as the *Vindication*. Partly it was a religious self-examination which gained force from the chance arrival of his earlier manuscript on the Psalms: it was 'a strict review and recollection into all the actions, all the faults and follies, committed by himself and others in his last continued fatigue of seventeen or eighteen years'.[14] But there was surely, though unavowed, perhaps unconscious, the instinct of the artist to make sense of experience; to put it into some form; to render it intelligible.

Fortunately for us Clarendon's deepest apprehensions were

[9] *ibid* 716, Ps. 119. [10] *ibid* 555 Ps. 72. [11] *ibid* 376.
[12] *EHR* 19 (1904), p. 249. [13] *Cont.* 928. [14] *ibid* 1391.

personal. As he went on with his history the men he had known rose before him in the fresh tints of life. It was at this period that he discovered the full range of his powers as a portraitist. Sir Charles Firth's comparison of the original *History* written in 1646–8 with the *Life* is particularly illuminating in this respect.[15] People who were barely mentioned in the *History* are drawn at full length in the later work. Indeed as Firth points out 'he wrote several independent pieces of the kind, which are not included in either the *History* or the *Life*. At Montpellier in April 1669, just after he had completed the first part of his own autobiography, he suspended the progress of that work in order to put together three biographical sketches of the Earl of Bristol, Lord Berkeley, and Lord Arlington. All three were his enemies.' Graham Roebuck has recently pointed out that there are in fact four characters. The first two paragraphs of what is printed in the Clarendon State Papers as a character of Arlington clearly form a sketch of someone else.[16] Roebuck suggests the second Duke of Buckingham.[17] But some of the circumstances seem to fit rather better Henry Jermyn, first Earl of St Albans.[18] He was, like Buckingham, one of the men whom Clarendon particularly despised and disliked.

The portraits of Jack Berkeley, once a close friend, and Henry Bennet, never a friend but once, arguably, a protégé, are etched in acid. That of Bristol is a masterpiece, comparable in subtlety, depth and finish to that of Falkland, though tragedy inspires the one and comedy the other. Part of it was eventually incorporated in the conflated *History of the Rebellion* which Clarendon put together two years later by tearing material out of the *Life* and stitching it into his earlier, abandoned *History* brought out to him in France by his son Laurence in 1671.

Fascinated himself, the author fascinates his readers. Nearing the end of thirty folio pages in which there is not a dull line or an inert phrase, he reins himself in:

'I did not intend to have reflected upon so many particulars, much less to have taken any survey of the active life of this very considerable person; but it was hardly possible to give any lively description of his nature and humour, or any character even of his person and composition, without representing some instances of particular actions; which, being so contradictory to themselves, and so different from the same effects which the same causes naturally produce in other men, can only qualify a man to make a conjecture what his true constitution and

[15] *EHR op. cit.* 255–6.   [16] *op. cit.* iii, supplement lxxxi–ii.
[17] 'A "New" Portrait by Clarendon' *Notes & Queries* 20 (1973), 168–70.
[18] e.g. in the allusion to his passion for gambling and to his having lived 'above forty years at the expense of the Crown'. Buckingham had inherited vast wealth: and he was only just turned forty-one in 1669.

nature was; and at best it will be but a conjecture, since it is not possible to make a positive conclusion or deduction from the whole or any part of it, but that another conclusion may be as reasonably made from some other action and discovery. It is pity that his whole life should not be exactly and carefully written, and it would be as much pity that any body else should do it but himself, who could only do it to the life, and make the truest description of all his faculties, and passions, and appetites, and the full operation of them; and he would do it with as much ingenuity and integrity as any man would do, and expose himself as much to the censure and reproach of other men, as the malice of his greatest enemy could do; for in truth he does believe many of those particular actions which severe and rigid men do look upon as disfigurings of the other beautiful part of his life, to be great lustre and ornament to it; and would rather expose it nakedly to have the indiscretion and unwarrantable part of it censured, than that the fancy and high projection should be concealed, it being an infirmity that he would not part with, to believe that a very ill thing subtilly and warily designed, and well and bravely executed, is much worthier of a great spirit, than a faint acquiescence under any infelicity, merely to contain himself within the bounds of innocence; and yet if any man concludes from hence that he is of a fierce and impetuous disposition, and prepared to undertake the worst enterprise, he will find cause enough to believe himself mistaken, and that he hath softness and tenderness enough about him to restrain him, not only from ill, but even from unkind and ill-natured actions . . . No man can judge, hardly guess, by what he hath done formerly, what he will do in the time to come, whether his virtues will have the better and triumph over his vanities, or whether the strength and vigour of his ambition and other exorbitances will be able to suppress, and even extinguish his better disposed inclinations and resolutions, the success of which will always depend upon circumstances and contingencies, and from somewhat without, and not within himself.'[19]

It is a measure of Clarendon's magnanimity no less than of his mastery that this was written after Bristol's attempt to have him impeached, botched in 1663, had in effect been crowned with success. Not all his portraits are so shiningly clear of rancour. The character of Arundel is an instance to the contrary. The friend and patron of Rubens,[20] the greatest connoisseur in the age that saw the flowering of English connoisseurship, the traveller who chose Inigo Jones for his companion in Italy (a country whose language and manners he knew

---

[19] *Clar. SP* iii supplement lxxiii.
[20] For a true estimate of Arundel's importance in the history of taste see David Howarth *Lord Arundel and his circle* (1985).

better than any Englishman of his time) and Hollar for his journey up the Rhine and the Danube, is thus dismissed by Clarendon, in the character of collector: 'whereas in truth he was only able to buy them [*sc.* statues and medals: his pictures are not even mentioned], never to understand them; and as to all parts of learning he was most illiterate, and thought no other part of history considerable but what related to his own family.' Clarendon, so far as we know, never looked at pictures except for those which showed him what a man or a woman looked like. He was certainly without any shred of qualification to pass such a judgment. But Arundel was not only an aesthete of European reputation. He was also a great nobleman who was employed from time to time on the most important diplomatic missions, as Clarendon derisively points out 'being sent ambassador extraordinary into Germany for the treaty of that general peace, for which he had great appointments, and in which he did nothing of the least importance'.[21]

Here we are on ground where Clarendon was in a position to know. Not only was the conduct of foreign affairs for long the chief business of his life but he actually possessed the dispatches that Arundel wrote on this mission, of which a number are printed in the first volume of the Clarendon State Papers. To read them is to be left with the impression of a capable, thorough and forceful head of mission who had been dealt the weakest of hands. There is, indeed, truth enough in some of Clarendon's other criticisms. Arundel was notoriously proud and haughty. His command of the army in the First Bishops War was ludicrous. Yet the author has weakened our belief in his own integrity of judgment by the absurdity of his assertions.

Why was he so unfair? Three reasons suggest themselves. Arundel was unsound on the Church of England to which he nominally conformed. A scion of the premier Roman Catholic family, he was suspected by some, and evidently by Clarendon, of having no religion at all. Again the Hydes were all clients of the first Duke of Buckingham, Arundel's deadly, and successful, rival. That this rivalry extended to the world of artistic patronage and connoisseurship may well explain the crude partisanship with which Arundel's reputation is denounced. Lastly he held the office of Earl Marshal and in that capacity had presided over the Earl Marshal's Court, an institution that excited the young Mr Hyde's especial scorn and which in the Long Parliament he had taken the lead in overthrowing. Might it be that the young barrister had appeared before the arrogant grandee and been snubbed into the ground?

Macray's edition of the *History* and Firth's articles in the *English Historical Review* have settled every question of chronology and

21 *Hist.* I, 119.

method that arises from the composition of both the *History* and *Life* in the form in which they were eventually published. Dr Brian Wormald has, in a brilliant book, traced the trucking shots that Clarendon's historical camera has taken as it moved silently across the landscape of events, changing its angles as it did so. Any man who writes the history of affairs in which he himself has played no small part cannot help trying to justify himself. 'Memory, which is nothing but thinking and Reflection, is the natural Result of a rational Soul.'[22] A more candid description of Clarendon's approach could hardly be asked for. Both Dr Wormald and Professor Trevor-Roper have argued strongly for Clarendon's profound understanding of the historical forces that moved his world, as against S. R. Gardiner and Sir Charles Firth who appear to derive his merits as a historian from his defects as a thinker. 'It is scarcely a paradox to say that his vivid presentment of the actors sprang in part from his imperfect comprehension of the drama itself.'[23]

'I take it to be no less the true end of history, to derive the eminency and virtue of those persons, who lived and acted in the times of which he writes, faithfully to posterity, than the counsels which were taken, or the actions which were done.'[24] This ringing declaration of faith in the importance of historical biography belongs to the first period of the *History*'s composition. As Firth pointed out, the writing of the *Life* gave this objective even ampler scope. Clarendon (using the name as the collective literary term for the *History* and the *Life*) is a classic. It is one of the marks of a classic that every reader finds there some reflection of himself. What he brings to it will colour what he takes away.

The reader who has made some study of Clarendon's friendships and circumstances, his ideas, his beliefs, his tastes, will find much to deepen his understanding and not a little to baffle or perplex. Whatever else the *History* in its curious multiple gestation may or may not have been intended to be, it is intensely personal. The style is the man with a vengeance. The charm and intimacy of some of the portraiture, the irony or sharpness of others, the brilliant epigrams that lay open with a Johnsonian clarity some labyrinthine issue, the interminable parentheses, the double and sometimes treble qualifications, the enthusiastic digressions, the legal mufflings and clearings of the throat when the ground shows signs of giving way under the argument, are in the highest degree characteristic. They are found as readily in his private, unstudied correspondence as in his formal compositions. Even at its most objective, the *History* does not make for the shelter of impersonal verbs, passive voices, the distilled water, as it were, with which modern scholarship seeks to purify its conclusions from the taint

[22] *Tracts* 687. Ps. 119.   [23] Firth, *EHR* 19, p. 253.   [24] *Clar. SP* ii 328.

of humanity. The historical process which Clarendon, like most of his contemporaries, identified with the Divine Will, is indeed often invoked: but the reader is left in no doubt that there is a person, a mind, invoking it.

Take for instance the opening paragraphs of the ninth book written at Moulins on August 12, 1671 about the events of 1645:

'1.   We are now entering upon a time the representation and description whereof must be the most unpleasant and ingrateful to the reader, in respect of the subject matter of it; which must consist of no less weakness and folly on the one side than of malice and wickedness on the other; and as unagreeable and difficult to the writer, in regard that he shall please very few who acted then upon the stage of business, but that he must give as severe a character of the persons, and as severely censure the actions of many who wished very well, and had not the least thought of disloyalty or infidelity, as of those who, with the most deliberate impiety, prosecuted their design to ruin and destroy the Crown: a time in which the whole stock of affection, loyalty and courage, which at first alone engaged men in the quarrel, seemed to be quite spent, and to be succeeded by negligence, laziness, inadvertency and dejection of spirit, contrary to the natural temper, vivacity, and constancy of the nation, and in which they who pretended most public-heartedness, and did really wish the King all the greatness he desired to preserve for himself, did sacrifice the public peace and the security of their master to their own passions and appetites, to their ambition and animosities against each other, without the least design of treachery or damage towards his majesty: a time in which want of discretion and mere folly produced as much mischieve as the most barefaced villainy could have done, and in which the King suffered as much by the irresolution and unsteadiness of his own counsels, and by the ill-humour and faction of his counsellors, by their not foreseeing what was evident to most other men, and by their jealousies of what was not like to fall out, sometimes by deliberating too long without resolving, and as often resolving without any deliberation, and, most of all, not executing vigorously what was well deliberated and resolved, as by the indefatigable industry and the irresistible power and strength of his enemies.

'2.   All these things must be very particularly enlarged upon, and exposed to the naked view, in the relation of what fell out in this year [1645] in which we are engaged, except we will swerve from that precise rule of ingenuity and integrity which we profess to observe, and thereby leave the reader more perplexed to see the most prodigious accidents fall out without discerning the no less prodigious causes which produced them; which would lead him into as wrong an estimate of things, and persuade him to believe that a universal corruption of the hearts of the whole nation had brought forth those lamentable effects; which proceeded only from the folly and the frowardness, from the weakness and the wilfulness, the pride and the passion, of particular persons, whose memories ought to be charged with their own evil actions, rather than they should be preserved as the infamous charge of the age in which they lived; which did produce as many eminent for their loyalty and incorrupted fidelity to the Crown as any that had preceded it. Nor is it possible to discourse all these particulars with that clearness that must subject them to common understandings, without opening a door for such reflections upon the King himself as shall seem to call both his wisdom and his courage into question, as if he had wanted the one to apprehend and discover, and the other to prevent, the mischieves which threatened him. All which considerations might very well discourage, and even terrify, me from prosecuting this part of the work with that freedom and openness as must call many things to memory which are forgotten, or were never understood, and rather persuade me to satisfy myself with a bare relation of what was done, and with the known event of that miserable year, (which in truth produced all that followed in the next), without prying too strictly into the causes of those effects, which might rather seem to be the production of Providence, and the instances of divine displeasure, than to proceed from the weakness and inadvertency of any men, not totally abandoned by God Almighty to the most unruly lust of their own appetite and inventions.

'3.   But I am far too embarked in this sea already, and have proceeded with too much simplicity and sincerity with reference to things and persons, and in the examination of the grounds and oversights of counsels, to be frighted now with the prospect of those materials which must be comprehended within the relation of this year's transactions. I know myself to be very free from any of those passions which naturally transport men with prejudice towards the persons whom they are obliged to mention, and whose actions they are at liberty to censure. There is not a man who acted the worst part in this ensuing year with whom I had ever the least difference or personal unkindness, or towards whom I had not much inclination of kindness, or from whom I did not receive all invitations of further endearments. There were many who were not free from very great faults and oversights in the counsels of this year with whom I had great friendship, and which I did not discontinue upon those unhappy oversights, nor did flatter them, when they were past, by excusing what they had done. I knew most of the things myself which I mention, and therefore can answer for the truth of them; and the most important particulars which were transacted in places very distant from me were transmitted to me by the King's immediate direction . . . And as he was always severe to himself in censuring his own oversights, so he could not but well foresee that many of the misfortunes of this ensuing year would reflect upon some want of resolution in himself, as well as upon the gross errors and over-sights (to call them no worse) of those who were trusted by him.

'And therefore as I first undertook this difficult work with his appro-bation and by his encouragement, and for his vindication, so I enter upon this part of it principally that the world may see (at least if ever there be a fit season for such a communication, which is not like to be in this present age) how difficult it was for a prince, so unworthily reduced to those straits his majesty was in, to find ministers and instru-ments equal to the great work that was to be done; and how impossible it was for him to have better success under their conduct whom it was very natural for him to trust with it; and then, without being over solicitous to absolve him from those mistakes and weaknesses to which he was in truth liable, he will be found not only a prince of admirable virtue and piety, but of great parts, of knowledge, wisdom, and judg-ment; and that the most signal parts of his misfortunes proceeded most from the modesty of his nature, which kept him from trusting himself enough, and made him believe that others discerned better who were much inferior to him in those faculties, and so to depart often from his own reason, to follow the opinions of more unskilful men, whose affections he believed to be unquestionable to his service.'

Perhaps no passage in the whole work brings the author more im-mediately before us both in what it discloses and in what it conceals. What is most striking is the impression of a working head. Clarendon, that supposed pillar of stolid conservatism, never stands still. In his attitude to the monarch we see that he has moved from the position of Shem and Japhet nearer to that of Cham, as defined only six months earlier in his Address to his Children. Reverent averting of the gaze will not do for the historian. What is also clear is how much it cost him emotionally to relive the years of defeat and of demoralisation. The writing hurts him and he expects it to hurt the reader. This personal declaration precedes the claim to truthfulness and to freedom both from prejudice and from vindictiveness. Clarendon sets out to be just. Twenty-five years earlier he had written to his old friend John Earles that he was 'careful to do justice to every man who hath fallen in the quarrel, on which side soever, as you will find by what I have said of Mr Hambden himself'.[25] But he can hardly claim to be impartial. And the assertion that he always was, and had subsequently remained, in a state not only of Christian charity but of uninterrupted friendship with the persons whose conduct he is about to censure leaves the reader dumbfounded. The personal asperities in his text can hardly be

---

[25] *ibid* 386 December 14, 1647.

reconciled with such a statement: and they are nothing to what is to be found in his correspondence. He hated and deplored Sir Richard Grenville. He deplored, and evidently distrusted, George Goring though they were both too well mannered to be incivil on social occasions. Indeed they dined together in Madrid when Clarendon was ambassador there. And as for Prince Rupert — well, as the Duke of Wellington said, if you can believe that, you can believe anything.

Was Clarendon a man of integrity, a man who did not consciously misrepresent persons and things? Such a question might be more profitably answered by drawing attention once again to the legalism that is so marked a characteristic of his mind. Is it extravagant to note that in his letter to Earles he makes it a point of honour to do justice to those who had fallen in the quarrel, and that those military men to whom he is, to say the least, unfair, Goring, Wilmot, Rupert *et al.* had in fact survived it? To feel humbled by the voluntary sacrifice of life is natural to anyone whose humanity is not depraved. Clarendon no doubt felt freer to criticise whose who had not paid it. His legalism, moreover, penetrates his understanding of his own most fundamental beliefs. It has been offered as a criticism of *Paradise Lost* that Milton makes God Almighty argue like a lawyer. But could not the same be said of Clarendon when he told Charles II that God who had done such great things for him 'expected some proportionable return'[26]?

The idea of the divine purpose is central to Clarendon's understanding of the events through which he lived, to the policy that, in 1660, had been crowned with success, and to the hope that sustained his declining years of a royal change of heart. Its dominance is recognised by Firth as a final acknowledgment that it is not individuals who determine the course of history but rather that great and inscrutable forces carry men they know not whither. The account of the Restoration which Clarendon wrote at Moulins, in the spring of 1672, 'contrasts curiously with his account of its [the Rebellions's] beginning'[27] where personal influences and characteristics are identified as the roots of historical causation. Clarendon might have found this dichotomy perplexing. Was it not his argument that God acted upon, and through, individuals? But he would surely have agreed that his mind, like all properly constituted rational minds, was in constant motion. 'Memory, which is but thinking and Reflection . . .' His acute perception was a function of his moral and intellectual awareness.

The wholeness of life is the underlying theme of all his writings during the seven-year scrutiny to which he subjected his own experience. A horror of fragmentation, of divorcing thought from action, of prayer from practice, runs through them all. He had always despised people

[26] *Cont.* 920.   [27] *EHR* 19, 483.

who only knew about and cared for one part of life, whether it was an aristocrat like the Earl of Pembroke and Montgomery who 'pretend to no other qualifications than to understand horses and dogs very well' or the monks, the object of his especial scorn, who retired from the world to devote themselves to the life of religion. Man, he wrote, 'is sent upon an Errand and to do the Business of Life: he hath Faculties given him to judge between Good and Evil . . . he hath not acted his Part in doing no Harm: his duty is not only to do Good and to be Innocent himself, but to propagate virtue, and to make others better than they would otherwise be.' Asceticism is deprecated as a rejection of life: 'To be without Wishes, or without Appetite, is the Property of a Carcase, not of a Man; who is not more a reasonable than an active Creature; whose first Testimony that he hath a Soul is the Noise he makes: and there cannot be a worse Omen in the Birth of any Child than its Silence.'[28] The Franciscans he had seen on the Continent excite his particular disgust: 'Why those antique, uneasie, unhandsome and un-wholesome Cloaths? Why no Linnen, no Shoes? . . . Why to this un-comely and uncleanly Wardrobe, so little Meat as cannot satisfy Nature and less Sleep than it requires? . . . He who affects Poverty, and prefers sickness before Health that he may be devout, may as well pray for the Plague that he may have good Company.'[29]

The burden of his objection is not a no-nonsense impatience at allowing religion priority over the serious affairs of life such as making money or eating and drinking. On the contrary: 'Repentance is the greatest Business we have to do in this World . . . It is almost the only Point of Faith upon which there is no Controversy . . . Repentance is as necessary to living as to dying well . . . and the World receives more Benefit by our living well than by our dying well.'[30]

The mistake, Clarendon insists, is to simplify our problems by ignoring the difficult parts. Treating the world as if it wasn't there will not do. 'It is very difficult, if not impossible, whilst we are in this World, totally to restrain our Affections from it . . . though we are to be content with Poverty, and with Sickness, as that which God thinks fit for us, we are not forbid to prefer Health and Plenty before either, it is enough if we do not murmur to part with them, though we would be glad to keep them.' Even more concisely: 'We may warrantably love Life, so we do not love it too well, prefer it before him who gave it to us, and look upon it as the End, and not the beginning of a Journey.'[31] There is no making sense of our necessarily finite experience on purely finite terms. To some extent this insight might be held to run counter to the comfort that Clarendon derived from his reading of the Psalms.

---

[28] *Tracts* 190, 191. *Essay on an Active and on a Contemplative Life.*
[29] *ibid* 173–4.   [30] *ibid* 148–50 *of Repentance.*   [31] *ibid* 684, Ps. 118, 622, Ps. 90.

But in insisting on the acceptance of life in its totality, not leaving out the bits one might not like or understand, Clarendon accepts discontinuity and obscurity, as St Paul did. He does not offer, and is not in the market for, explanations of the human situation that are coherent, rational and complete. He knows that he does not know: that for a large part of experience, and that part the most important to him, religious, moral, political, he has to make up his mind as best he can on the information he can obtain and the faith he can muster. The symmetry and comprehensiveness of post-Tridentine Catholicism or of the political theories advanced by his old friend Thomas Hobbes are dangerous, even pernicious, because they can only have achieved their elegant appearance by cutting corners or suppressing awkward truths. Hence his most important controversial works, the critique of *Leviathan* and the polemic against another old friend and fellow-member of the Great Tew circle, Hugh Cressy, who had become a Benedictine and had written several books against the Church of England, in one of which he had alleged that Falkland was a Socinian.[32] Both these works assert the intellectual pluralism of Great Tew against its renegades.

For this, when all is said and done, is the heart of Clarendon's saying and doing. Good temper, good nature, limited claims for limited ends, may not sound a rousing or ambitious manifesto. Yet it is the source of all that is most admirable in the English political tradition and the European civilisation of which it is part. Its champions, Clarendon and his friends, Selden, Falkland, Morley, Earles, Ormonde and the rest, will always appear in their own age and to its later students as somewhat humdrum, middle-of-the-road figures. They lack the dash and unpredictability of Cromwell, the pathos and the allure of Charles I, the lightness and ease of Charles II. In an earlier century and a different conflict Luther and Loyola have commanded wider and more enthusiastic admiration than Erasmus. And it is, as Professor Trevor-Roper has emphasised, from Erasmus and Hooker that Great Tew traces its descent.

Towards the end of his refutation of Cressy Clarendon recalls him to the spirit of that place engendered by 'that unparallel'd Lord'. 'It is an ungenerous thing to fall from streight embraces to publick revilings . . . and Mr Cressy should for his own sake allow some beauty to have been in the Church that did for so long detain him . . . This I expected from his natural genius and from the conversation he frequented,

---

[32] Clarendon's reply, published in November 1673, was *Animadversions upon a Book Intituled Fanaticism Fanatically Imputed to the Catholick Church by Dr Stillingfleet And the Imputation Refuted and Retorted by S.C.* [S.C. is Serenus Cressy, the name taken in religion at Hugh Cressy's profession as a Benedictine]. Clarendon's name did not appear on the title page which styles the author 'a Person of Honour'.

where bitterness of words was never allowable towards men whose opinions were very different . . .'[33]

Hobbes too is reprimanded for his want of controversial decency in kicking the Church of England when she was down: 'And therefore it was below the education of Mr Hobbes, and a very ungenerous and vile thing, to publish his *Leviathan* with so much malice and acrimony against the Church of England when it was scarce struggling in its own ruines . . .'[34] Clarendon has no difficulty in exposing weak links in the argument where Hobbes has ventured into the fields of history and of law. 'Mr Hobbes consulted too few Authors and made use of too few Books; the benefit of which my present condition has also deprived me of . . .' Indeed it is this lack that has further prevented him from criticising 'gross errors and grosser over-sights in those parts of science in which Mr Hobbes would be thought to excel which are likely to put him out of countenance than any thing I can urge him by how much he values himself more upon being thought a good Philosopher and a good Geometrician than a modest Man or a good Christian'.[35] Nonetheless as an ex-Chancellor of Oxford University he seizes the opportunity of Hobbes's attack on it to cite 'the Rev Dr Ward, the present Lord Bishop of Salisbury, and Dr Wallis, the worthy Professor of Geometry in Oxford' as instances of men who have convicted Hobbes of mistakes in that study.[36]

But, formidable as the purely intellectual side of Clarendon's critique is, the most telling assault, and the most characteristic, is moral. He ridicules Hobbes's fundamental premise that the fear of death is the universal passion on which society is founded. This Hobbes has projected 'from looking into himself'. In a phrase once again suggestive of Johnson, Clarendon counters that another man 'could no more by looking into himself know Mr Hobbes's present thoughts and the extent of his fear, then he could by looking into his face, know what he hath in his Pocket'.[37] What is wicked in this is that Hobbes here strikes at the true and fruitful first principle of society: 'He deprives man of the greatest happiness and glory that can be attributed to him, who divests him of that gentleness and benevolence towards other men, by which he delights in the good fortune and tranquillity that they enjoy.'[38] Disinterested good nature is a better title to humanity than dexterity in argument.

That Clarendon's own love for his fellow men was not unspotted from the world in which he lived is evident from the closing paragraphs of the book. He reminds Hobbes that he was originally enabled to publish his pernicious work by a legacy from Sidney Godolphin 'whose

[33] *op. cit.* 238.   [34] *A Brief View and Survey . . .* (Oxford, 2nd ed. 1676) 305.
[35] *ibid* 4.   [36] *ibid* 298.   [37] *ibid* 13.   [38] *ibid* 28.

untimely Loss in the beginning of the War was too lively an instance of the inequality of the contention, when such inestimable Treasure was ventured against dirty people of no name'.[39] This and similar if less contemptuous expressions have been fairly cited by Christopher Hill to demonstrate that Clarendon saw the Civil War in terms of a class struggle and, incidentally, to diminish Great Tew to a mutual admiration society of the well-to-do who shared a taste for empty professions of highmindedness. That Clarendon never lost an opportunity of asserting the Royalist superiority in breeding and education, in civilization and in taste, is undeniable. That he wished to convey that impression is not so much an index of its truth as of its importance in his view of the world of his day. His cousin Lucy Hutchinson would have denied it with equal passion and sharpness. The modern literature on the subject is vast and it is far outside the scope of this book to determine the question between them. But that Great Tew is rooted in privilege, that its social assumptions were aristocratic, is inescapable. Clarendon, like the rest of us, was a child of his time.

His recognition of its aristocratic structure is reflected in the *Dialogue . . . concerning Education.*[40] 'I must confine myself,' begins the principal speaker, 'only to the Education of noble and generous Persons; I mean to the children of Persons of Quality, who can be at the Charge, for good Education is chargeable, and leave the rest to those common Ways which their Fortunes as well as their Inclinations lead them unto.' The aim of the piece is to persuade the aristocracy to send their sons to the universities rather than to France where they learn to laugh at everything they do not understand 'which understanding so little, makes their laughter very immoderate'. Very likely they will turn Papist into the bargain. In order to attract these sprigs of nobility, the Bishop (who is one of the speakers) proposes 'a Royal Commission . . . for the Visitation of the Universities and Inspection into the Manners thereof and of the Discipline of the several Colleges and Halls'. The Colonel (himself a graduate of the University of Oxford and of all the speakers perhaps the most entirely Clarendonian) puts in a word for the polite accomplishments of riding, dancing and fencing, but would not abate the habit (often disused) of speaking in Latin.

Clarendon was here advancing for the universities the same strategy that Pepys was pursuing for the Navy, that of involving the aristocracy, who formed by far the richest, most powerful, most closely-knit social group, in maintaining and promoting those institutions on which the future of the country depended. Without aristocratic patronage the universities would remain in the suburbs of national life. If the country were to be more civilised and intelligent they should be near its centre.

---

[39] *ibid* 319.   [40] *Tracts* 313–48.

To achieve this a reformation of manners and discipline was the first essential.

Clarendon had argued in the spring of 1666 the merits of a university training to Orrery for a young man in whom they were both interested. Orrery bowed to his recommendation but stated his own objections in language which must have lingered in his friend's mind when he wrote his *Dialogue*:

'I have chosen to undergo the charge of giving my two sons their education separated from crowds of yonge students, rather than hazard their acquiring of ill habbits, by learninge their Studdies at Promiscuous scooles at Universities. I know many Persons Eminent for virtue as well as letters, have had their education only ther; but I must say I have knowne very Few yonge lords and gentelmen born to great Fortunes which have returned from thence eminent for knowledge. Possibly 'tis ye Fate of great Estates to be without great learninge: or ye Fault of Universitie Tutors to please rather than Instruct ye children of ye nobility . . . Besides such of those Tutors which are studious have no time to Instruct & supervise ye manners of their scollers, and such as are not studious are more likely to give them bad than good examples.'[41]

To urge scholars to be gentlemen and gentlemen to be scholars was not, in that age, socially divisive, still less snobbish. Rather it was an attempt to mitigate the boorishness of the one and the overbearingness of the other. Restricted in its social origins Great Tew inevitably was: but in a world of self-righteousness, of arrogance, of Pharisaism, of intolerance, it stood for the free exchange of ideas, for learned inquiry, for respect for the personality if not for the opinions of others, in a word, for good manners and good nature. 'Good nature, a virtue so appropriated by God Almighty to this nation, that it can be translated into no other language, hardly practised by any other people . . .' In the most famous speech of his life this most famous phrase epitomises Clarendon's vision of his country.

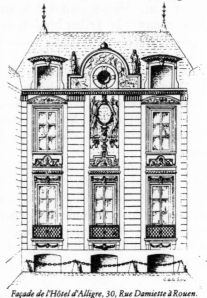

Façade de l'Hôtel d'Alligre, 30, Rue Damiette à Rouen.

---

41 Clar. MS 84 ff.171–4. May 18, 1666.

XXV

Closing Scene

IN THE spring of 1674 Clarendon determined to leave Moulins. A crack or two had appeared in the ice of royal disdain that hemmed him in. Not only had Laurence been granted permission for a visit of several weeks duration but Henry had also been to see him.[1] Furthermore the King had indicated to the Duke of York that he would not oppose Clarendon's removal to Rouen.[2] He arranged for the renting of a suitable house there, a handsome hôtel *entre cour et jardin* built in the late sixteenth century. The French Court went out of its way to show him respect. He was told that he could live wherever he liked and the great minister Le Tellier himself wrote to the Parliament of Rouen to urge the reconnection of the water supply to a fountain in the garden.[3] This was an adornment of life that he had learnt from Cottington.

What he hoped for, yearned for, was the final relenting of the King that would allow him to die in his own country and among his own family and would at last still the contention in his heart between his two lifelong passions, loyalty and justice. In the last letter that he was to write to the King, dated from Rouen on August 29, he does not cringe:

'I can never repent any of the confidence I have reposed in your Majesty; I do confess the opinion I had, that I knew your Majesty very well, and the assurance I had, that you knew me better than any other man could do, was, under my dependance upon God's Providence, all my security, which made me neglect all other arts, and possibly some necessary wariness, which might have preserved me. How successful soever that confidence hath proved, I will never depart from it, nor

---

[1] *Clar. SP* iii, supp. xliii. This letter from Clarendon to Cornbury dated from Moulins March 17, 1674 contains the phrase 'when you went from hence'.
[2] *ibid.*
[3] *Bulletin de la Commission des Antiquités de la Seine-Inférieure* (Rouen 1889) vii, 146–52. This is the source of the drawing reproduced on p. 339.

practise any other artifices or devices towards my restoration, but by all humble supplication to yourself . . . The wound was inflicted only by your own hand, and no other can cure it.'[4]

The word 'restoration', used in that context by that writer, has a unique force. Had not the Civil War itself been caused, in his view, by making it impossible to reconcile the duty of a subject with the maintenance of justice and of law? It could never be right to buy the one at the expense of the other. That was the proposition to which Clarendon had given a lifetime's service. He was not going to unsay it because he was lonely and ill and could see death coming closer. He had made the same point from a different angle in the letter to Henry written shortly before he left Moulins. He there cautions both him and his brother against being 'esteemed a better courtier than a Son'. Their loyalty to the King must be absolute, but it need not make them appear insensible to 'the foul arts' they saw practised against their father.[5]

The letter to the King was accompanied by two shorter ones to the Queen and to the Duke of York. His son-in-law is thanked for past support and asked to use his good offices with his brother: '. . . since it will be in no-body's power long to keep me from dying, methinks the desiring a place to die in should not be thought a great presumption . . .' That to the Queen is warmer and more touching. She had, it seems, moved the King to allow his son's visit. 'It hath been an incredible refreshment to me in my deepest mortification, to hear that your Majesty still retains, with some compassion, a gracious memory of my desire to serve you, of which you have given a gracious testimony, in granting your permission to my Son to come to me, which hath exceedingly obliged me, and if he hath, after so long absence, transgressed your commands by staying longer than your bounty warranted him, I most humbly beseech your Majesty to pardon it, and to excuse an old man, who having nothing left to delight in but his children is overjoyed when he gets the company of any of them.'[6] The portrait she had given him for his Gallery charmingly conveys that tenderness of nature from which he now drew comfort.

All three letters were entrusted to Henry to deliver or not as he saw fit. From the last of his many letters to survive it seems that his son thought that no useful purpose would be served by his doing so. This letter, written firmly and clearly in his own hand, is dated September 24 and endorsed by its recipient 'L[d] Clar. to L[d] Cornbury'. As an account of its writer's state of mind and body as he stood upon the threshold of the next world it may bear a complete transcription.

---

[4] *Clar. SP* iii, supp. xliv.   [5] *ibid* xlii.   [6] *ibid* xlv.

I have yours of the 7 and wounder that in all the tyme you had spent you gave me no accounte of all the letters you were charged with, which makes me believe that you thought not fitt to deliver any of them. I am content. Your hare is newly come to the kay, but* will not deliver his small marchandise in two or three dayes. I shall more longe for the arryvall of the Beere and Ale which is much more gratefull to me, which I never thought it would be: it will alwayes come much better in bottles than in vessells in many respects, because I can then keepe it for my selfe.

Your well consideringe and deliberatinge upon your domestique affayres will best determyne what you are to do. I am gladd you have writt to my Lord Ormonde, and that expedient which his rent† may supply may probably bringe all our ends to passe: if ther can be enough to keepe me in my necessary expense, which I will lessen by all the wayes I can, I am well content that the reste be applyed to assiste your house keepinge, but I am sure that nothinge that can be saved, or nothinge that can be gott, is worth the mischieve that must unavoidably fall out, by any jealosy or unkindnesse that may attende your separacion, and therefore for gods sake avoyd and praevent that. You will give me a larger account of Cittie and country, when you returne from your longe progresse, and I see you depende upon my creditt with Mr Wilkins,‡ of which indeede I shall have use within five days.

Yesterday was a greate rayne all the day, and cold, but this day wee have agayne very fayre weather, which promises a good end to our vintage. None of us have cause of beinge in a worse condicion of health than you left us. Ned hath bledd and purged, and my turne will be next for prevencion. I have had a better Sept. heare then I had the last yeare at Molins, and for October the Towne promises fayrely, and that wee make no fyre but in the kitchin till Novemb: and then I shall not begrutch the keepinge good fyres. In the meane tyme you cannot imagyne how warme wee have made all this syde of the house with [? skesses], and stoppinge all holes. Looke that my Cheshire frend be seasonably putt in minde of the cheese, upon which housekeepinge much depends. God blesse you all: I must not forgett to tell you that never was better venison eaten.[7]

Here is the whole man: the Stoic, the Christian, the Epicurean: above all one who, in Evelyn's happy phrase, 'was of a jolly temper, after the Old English fashion'.[8] In the high place of Norman gastronomy it is to English beer, Cheshire cheese, game from Wychwood Forest that he turns. The robustness of the victuals matches the cheerfulness of the writer, ready to make the best of things.

* Perhaps a word or a name signifying the shipping agent has dropped out here: there is no lacuna in the MS.
† Ormonde rented Clarendon House certainly from 1670–3 (Evelyn *Diary* ed. de Beer iii 629 n.2) and may, as this suggests, have extended his tenancy.
‡ Clarendon's banker at Rouen who had obtained his house for him (*Clar. SP* iii supp, xliii).
[7] Kent CRO Darnley MSS U565 f.38.   [8] *Diary* iv. 339.

There is too that refusal, so rare among the well-to-do, to allow lack of money and a louring financial outlook to colour the scene. All through the second exile this had been a present anxiety. In the letter to the King that Henry had kept back he had adverted to '. . . impossible stories of my corruptions, which are sufficiently confuted by my undeniable poverty, which is so great and pressing, that I am no longer able to subsist, and to pay my debts, without the sale of most of the Records of your Royal bounty, which I hoped might have descended to my posterity, as a testimony both of your blessed Father's and your own gracious acceptation of my poor service'.[9]

Above all there is the manliness, the stoicism, with which he accepts his son's implicit verdict in the cause he had most at heart. 'I am content.' His discipline of prayer and meditation, achieved against a turbulent and proud nature in the bustle of politics and business, underpins those three words.

Clarendon died at seven o'clock in the morning of December 11[10] (December 21 NS). A full clinical account of the last weeks of his life is given in Latin lightly dusted with Greek, by one of Charles II's physicians who had been brought over to attend him.[11] On Saturday, November 28 William Shaw, the secretary who had shared his exile wrote to Laurence: 'He would never consent till this moment that either my Lord Cornbury or you should be sent for to him, although he was very sensible of his condition, but in this very instant he gives order to write for one of you. Pray god you come tyme enough. Be pleased to consider whether it will not be fitt to bring some Eminent Physician with you. I have this morning by his direction removed most of his Papers into good hands as I will the rest before night . . .'[12] Both brothers hurried over, bringing with them the doctor, John Poore, whose account of Clarendon's terminal illness and post mortem examination is in the British Library. Its Latinity gives it an oddly modern look, using the word 'arthritis' where the patient would have written 'gowte' and finding the root cause of his ailments in the sedentary habits of his earlier life. The immediate cause of his trouble was overindulgence in an unhealthy diet. He suffered a stroke in the early stages of his illness. The will which he made on December 1 simply

---

9 *Clar. SP* iii supp. xliv.
10 BL Add. MS 4619 f.44v. Wood's assertion in *Ath. Ox.* iii 1024 that he died on the 9th, though based apparently on somebody else's marginal note to an early obituary, has been followed by every subsequent writer, including Lister and Firth. It is supported by Laurence Hyde's meditations on the first anniversary of his father's death (*The Correspondence of Henry Hyde, Earl of Clarendon and of his brother Laurence Hyde, Earl of Rochester* ed. Singer 1828, i, 645–7). But the specific evidence of a professional writing within days of the event seems to me preferable. If the son were anything like his father, accuracy of dating would not have mattered much to him.
11 MS *cit*.   12 Clar. MS 87 ff.237–8.

343

appoints his two elder sons his executors and makes no dispositions except for the careful arrangements for his papers and writings about which Henry and Laurence are to take the advice of Sheldon and Morley.[13]

In view of Clarendon's previous lament that he was without the ministrations of a chaplain it might seem strange that neither he nor his secretary, William Shaw, appear to have asked for one. Had this need already been supplied, under the kindlier régime of Henry Coventry? In the State Papers Domestic for 1672 there is a licence to William Levett, Rector of Husbands Bosworth, to receive the revenues of that rectory '. . . during his absence . . . to remaine in the service of the Earle of Clarendon as tutor to his children . . .'[14] James, the youngest of the Hyde children, would only have been twelve in 1672, Frances perhaps eighteen. There is no evidence that either of them visited their father in France. But there is the clearest evidence that Levett did.

'I did think,' wrote Clarendon to his eldest son on March 17, 1674, 'that . . . you would have informed me whether the Bishop of Winchester, and some others, who have been my friends, do think that the Dean of Christ Church [Dr Fell] deals well with me, and whether his gravity intends to proceed as speedily with Mr Levett as he threatens, that I may send him over to try whether he can shift better for himself.'[15]

It is not hard to guess the cause of Clarendon's anxiety. Levett, a pluralist who already held another rectory besides Husbands Bosworth,[16] was also a student (i.e. a Fellow) of Christ Church.[17] Doubtless Dr Fell, that formidable disciplinarian, was seeking to deprive him of his studentship for failing to keep the University terms. Levett's whole career suggests close involvement with the Hyde family. After matriculating at Magdalen Hall in 1659 he migrated first to Corpus Christi and then to Christ Church, from which he took his B.A. on February 20, 1664. The Chancellor's son Edward was then a student there. In 1681 Levett succeeded Clarendon's cousin, James Hyde, the Regius Professor of Medicine, as Principal of Magdalen Hall. After Levett's death in 1694 Anthony à Wood resentfully recalled that he had been employed by Henry, second Earl of Clarendon 'to rake and scrape up witnesses' in order 'to ruin the author and his cause'.[18] That he was Clarendon's chaplain at Moulins on the eve of the move to

---

[13] Printed in Lister ii 489–90.   [14] S.P. 44/35[B].

[15] *Clar. SP* iii, supp. xlii.   [16] Foster *Alumni Oxonienses*.

[17] Nichols *History . . . of Leicester* ii (1798) part ii, p. 498 n.10.
    Wood *Life* (ed. Bliss), xci. The inscription on his monument, now huddled away in the northwest corner of the Cathedral, confirms the fact.

[18] *ibid*, cxxi.

Rouen is virtually certain. It seems a probable inference from Shaw's silence eight months later that Dr Fell had been, for once, headed off, and that the ex-Chancellor of the University was allowed the last rites of the Church he had so stoutly defended.

Clarendon had continued the reading and writing that for years now had been the real business of his life until the paralysis that followed the stroke prevented him from holding a pen. *Religion and Policy* — that vigorous, witty and learned assault on the pretensions of the Papacy both spiritual and temporal — had been finished at Moulins in February. The upheaval of moving to Rouen disrupted his intellectual life during the spring and summer. But during the autumn he had resumed his learned correspondence. A few days before his final illness his old adversary Stephen Goffe had written to him from the Oratory in Paris: '. . . Mons. Herman is esteemed and learned but his stile seems too diffuse for an Historian: We have had his St Athanasius in our Refectory and could have bin glad of quicker sauce to our meat . . . It is very true that he is sufficiently severe to Eusebius who even by his best friend is termed δίγλωττορ [double-tongued, deceitful] and without doubt continued a semi-Arian to his dying day; though he hath had ye good luck to be a canonized saint here in France, where they have an office for him and 3 peculiar lessons.'[19]

At sunset in Rouen as in the clear noon of Great Tew there is the unmistakable sound of civilised discourse: 'where men, holding perhaps strong opinions, can coolly compare notes, and help each other to understand a question without arguing.'[20] Goffe, on his record, was exactly the sort of man whom Clarendon might be counted on to deplore. The son of a Puritan clergyman, he had, after serving Charles I and Henrietta Maria in diplomatic ventures that made Clarendon shudder, become, like Cressy, a Roman Catholic priest. Besides that he had a distinguished regicide brother who had escaped to America at the Restoration and was never caught. Years before, his lunatic scheme for attacking Guernsey with a motley rabble of mercenaries had brought him into collision with Clarendon at a moment when the Royalist cause was already desperate. Yet from this unpromising source came perhaps the first letter of condolence that Henry received at Rouen, containing an epitaph both eloquent and convincing:

'. . . He hath ended his course with extraordinary glory both in his prosperitie and adversity, this latter having rendred his most excellent endowments so much known abroad that where ever he hath passed He hath left a character of a great person behind him, as I have bin assured myself by some of those eminent Bishops and others of quality who have given themselves the honour to visite him . . . Of late He was

[19] Clar. MS 87 f.249.   [20] *Letters and Journals of William Cory* (1897), 154.

pleased to entertaine a particular and kind commerce with me by ample letters in literary matters; and I persuade myselfe one of mine was one of the last which He read before his falling sicke, which I am certaine by His Lordship's delight in subjects of that nature would have produced a large and learned reply if it had pleased God to have lett him and his bookes together a little longer . . .'[21]

His body was brought back for burial in the vault in Westminster Abbey where his mother and Frances lay. No public countenance was given to the event, still less any royal gesture of affection, of gratitude or of shame. Henry Coventry's letter to Sir John Nicholas, Edward's son, the 'my tutour' of the 1640s and '50s, closes the story with his unfailingly felicitous touch:

> Deare Sir,
>
> Your old friend is to be buryed this night & though we doe it very privately yett I have given notice of it to two or three of his friends, who I am sure loved him & amongst them I venture to give you notice that about six of the clock in the evening we shall be in ye Old Pallace Yard at ye little brick house at ye foote of ye staires going up to the House of Lords wch is all the trouble shall be given you at present, deare Sir
>
>   Monday noone, January 4 1674.[22]

One of the pall-bearers was Sir Ralph Verney, son of the Knight Marshal whose conversation with Clarendon at the time of the raising of the Standard at Nottingham states with simplicity and beauty a position not so far from Clarendon's own, and one that was, substantially, that of Lord Falkland. The coffin 'was met by the Dean (in his episcopal habit) & Chapter, who sang him to his grave'.[23] The Dean was John Dolben, Bishop of Rochester, who after gallant service in the war had been ordained secretly in the Interregnum and had helped Sheldon to keep up the forbidden Prayer Book services. Like Morley he had lost his place at court on Clarendon's fall. In the darkness of the Abbey nothing could be seen but the faces of friends.

[21] Clar. MS 87 f.247 December 24, 1674.   [22] BL Egerton MS 2540 f.22.
[23] *Verney Memoirs* (1892 repr. 1970) iv, 195.

Appendix I

Clarendon's Will of January 1666

The following is a partial transcript of the will drawn up by Clarendon, witnessed and signed at Cornbury on January 20, 1666. The original, a five-page holograph, written in a firm, clear hand and paragraphed with uncharacteristic lucidity, is in the Bodleian Library Clarendon MS 84 ff.35–42. A good summary is printed in volume V of the *Calendar of Clarendon State Papers* ed. F. J. Routledge pp. 526–7.
Where I have summarised the wording I have printed the passage between square brackets.

. . . beinge in as a good a state of health as my age and disposition to the gowte will suffer me, which I thanke god is not very grievous, do make this my laste will and Testament.
[Asks for God's mercy and acceptance of his soul] and that he will accepte . . . my weake endeavours by his grace to please him and according to my weaknesse to lyve according to the rules he hath prescribed in the religion of the church of Englande which without any faction or worldly ends and contrary to many worldly temptacions I have longe and do from my soule imbrace and beleeve to be a religion very acceptable to him, and in which (without the presumpcyon of accusinge or reproovinge those Churches which in many particulars doe differr from it) a man cannot fayle of salvacion, if he lyves accordinge to that religion, and therefore I do very earnestly recommende it to my wife and children and to that posterity which it shall please god to give me in this world, that they may never swarve from that religion, and I do heartily and humbly aske god and that his Church of Englande pardon and forgivenesse if in the course of my life (by the corruption of my owne will and affections, or by the occacions and distraction of businesse, to which I have beene designed, and in which I have exercised myselfe longer and in more difficultyes than have beene proportionable to my weake understandinge) I have behaved myselfe

in thoughts, wordes or deedes, as a man, not worthy of a sunn of the Church of Englande, in whose communion I dy with greate assurance of a happy resurrection.

. . . unto my deerly beloved wife (who hath accompanyed and assisted me in all my distresses with greater resignacion and courage, and in all respectes deserved much more from me than I can returne to her) for her supporte in the quality god hath pleased to rayse her to [lands rented at £640 p.a. in Blunsden, Co. Wilts. lands rented at £500 p.a. in Leics. and Rutland and likewise £500 p.a.] to be payd to her out of my lands and leases at Clarendon, Co. Wilts. provided she release the Pirton lands settled on her by her jointure to the eldest sunn. . . which I know well she will manage for the good of her children, and assiste them out of it, as well as she can: having always beene as good and discreete a mother as ever I knew.

to my sunn Henry Lord Cornebury my house and parke at Cornebury with all my lands which I have purchased thereabouts, togither with the command of the Forest of Wychwood, my manors of Langley, Rumsden and Leefield, which I purchased of the Duke of York together with all my other lands in County of Oxforde . . . my manor and farm of Witney which I holde by lease from the Bishop of Winchester . . all my lands, tenements and hereditaments in Pirton, the manor of Cricklade and lands in and about Clarendon and all my other lands in the said County of Wiltshire . . . [to his heirs male, failing them to Laurence and his, then to James and his] hopinge that they and their posterity will long injoy the estate I leave to them, and the same having beene very honestly obtained and gotten by me, which I looke upon as the greatest blessinge I leave to them.

[To Laurence the reversion, after Lady Clarendon's decease, of the Whichcott estate (plus £10,000 in money to be paid within 3 months of Clarendon's death) and] my landes and house at Twitnam Co. Middlesex . . . which is god knowes as much as my present state will beare, without too much hurtinge my other children, but if it please god to blesse me with many more yeares of life I hope to inlarge his fortune to which I holde myself obliged not only by his very dutifull carriage and behaviour towards mee, but likewise for his wife's sake, and her father and mother, who very generously gave her to my sunn, with a very noble and greate porcion, and who in her selfe deserves as much from me, as can be imagined, and whom I looke upon with the hearty kindnesse of a father, and as a singular honour vouchsafed by god Almighty to my family.

[. . . to my daughter the Lady Frances Hyde £5000 plus all unassigned goldplate if its value exceeds £5000:: if not the sum to be made up to her by Executors.]

. . and I charge her always to be ruled and governed by her mother and never to marry without her consent [or if she be dead, Cornebury] I beinge most assured and exceedingly comforted in that assurance that her mother and all her brothers will be very kinde to her, and willinge to assist her all they can

. . . to my youngest sunn James Hyde the yeerly sum of £200 for his life . . . and is as much as I am able to leave to him, except God shall give me a longer life.

[begs the King] my most gracious and bountiful master to accept a gold cup of £200 valew . . . in memory of his true and faythfull servant, who served him (how weakely soever) with as much fidelity and zeal as I was able to doe and since it appeares by this my will, that in so few years after his Majesty's happy returne I am able to make such a competent provisyon for my wife and children, whiche even I myselfe do wounder at, and consequently others may be apt to charge as a reproch upon my memory, I do beseech his Majesty to believe that I have never since my beinge admitted into the service of his Royall father or himselfe taken the least summ of mony corruptly from any man, nor indeede receaved any benefitt any way but from his owne Royall bounty and from the just and lawfull perquisites of the office I hold under him, and which upon all the enquiry I could make have been ever receaved and avowed by all my predecessors for above one hundred yeares and the new yeares presents I have receaved, I could not refuse without some affectacion, and I am confident I never receaved any, upon the least contracte beforehande (which I thanke god very few men have ever attempted to make with me) or rewarde for any thinge done which justice and civillity alone did not obliege me to doe, and in truth I do not believe that all the fortune I now dy worth and leave to my wife and children doth in any considerable degree exceede the valew of what I have receaved from his Majesty's owne immediate bounty in England and out of Irelande, the yeerely profits of the office not beinge a competent supporte for the dignity of so greate an office: and I do hope that this unusuall excursion in a will, consideringe the calumnyes I have been exposed to without any cause on my parte, will not be lyable to reproch, and I do most humbly begg my royall Master the King, to continue his grace and goodnesse to my wife and children, who I doubte not will never fayle from ther duty towards him, and are like to stande in neede of his royall bounty and protection.

[a gold cup each of £100 value to] the two Queenes, his Majesty's mother and consorte as a small testimony of my duty and devocion to ther Majesties my most gratious mistresses.

[same to Duke of York] as a poore remembrance of his servant who god knowes hath alwayes and in all tymes out of the conscience of my duty borne the highest devocon to his person, and as I have received many evidences of his princely favour, so I dy with prayers for him and for his prosperity.

[same] to my daughter the Dutchesse of York . . . conceavinge it not decent in many respects to present her with a greater legacy [prayers for divine support and protection] in this high condicion to which he hath pleased (sic) to exalt her.

. . . [Arrangements about the payment of the £10,000] to my sunn Laurence Hyde . . . which summ . . I stande obliged by the Articles upon his marriage to pay to him and for which I have paid him the interest quarterly from the tyme of his marriage. [If the purchase of Christchurch is not begun by the time of Clarendon's death there will be money enough: but if he dies in mediis rebus the money will have to be raised some other way. He suggests the sale] of my lease of the houses in Long Acre Co. Middlesex which I holde of the company of Mercers for 98 yeeres yett to come or thereabouts . . . the sayd lease havinge cost me so much money yeeres since, and therefore I believe is much more worth now . . .

I do likewise give and bequeath unto my sunn Cornebury my new house in the fields called Clarendon house, he payinge such monyes as are owinge by me for the buildinge thereof, which if it please god to give me a little longer life I hope to pay, and fully to finish the sayd house, which hath cost me much more money than in common dis-crecion a man of so meane a fortune should lay out in buildinge, yett I had some reason for it, . . . it beinge always understoode and declared that my deere wife shall have and injoy during her naturall life what appartiments and lodgings she shall chuse to make use of in the said house, which she shall injoy as her owne, which I charge shee may likewise have at Cornbury when she shall chuse to resyde ther, all which I am sure my sunn Cornebury will be well content with, and as it was one of the principle ends I proposed to myselfe in all my buildings, that I might injoy the company of my wife and children, upon whom I have always looked as the greatest blessings god Almyghty hath bestowed upon me, so when I am deade I heartily wish that they will lyve togither as much as ther severall occasyons will permitt, and I doubt not but that they will always be a singular com-forte to each other, and because so greate a house is much more than is proportionable to the estate I leave to my sunn, I do intirely referr it to his discrecion to sell it if he findes it convenient, presuming he will lay out the money for the improvement of his fortune, and that he will settle the lands he shall purchase upon the sale thereof upon his family as I have done the rest, and in that case he is to provyde such a house in London for his mother during her naturall life as she shall be well pleased with: as I make not the least doubte that he will be always desyrous to please her in all thinges, and that she will be as kinde to him and the rest of her children as she hath alwayes bene.

. . . to my sunn Cornbury all my library of bookes and papers which are in my house at Worcester house, which I desyre he will keepe togither (for which I have builte a particular roome in Clarendon house) and suffer to descende to the heyre of the family, descended from me, and because the good will or curiosity of many of my friends who have to good an opinion of me, may possibly desyre that some of my papers may be published, which I have not for many yeeres perused, and which were writt in my retirement and when I was without those conveniences of bookes and other helpes, which in such exercises are necessary, I do entirely leave the publishing or not publishing all or any of them of what sorte soever, to the discrecion and will of my sunn Cornebury wishing him that he first take the advice of my very worthy frends the Lord Archbishop of Canterbury [Sheldon], the Lord Bishop of Winchester [Morley], L. C. J. Bridgeman, Sir Jeffrey Palmer, H.M. Attorney generall and Sir Heneage Finch, H.M. sollicitour generall, or as many of them as he can prevayle with to peruse and correct the same, which beinge done lett him publish or not publish what he thinkes fitt.

[Last paragraph appointment of Executors, Overseers, legacies to servants (not named) etc. see *Cal. Clar. SP,* v.527.]

. . at Cornbury on Saturday the 20 of January in the yeere 1665 [O.S.]

Appendix II

The Hyde Children

Name	Date of birth or baptism	Remarks
Anne	b. March 12, 1637	subsequently Duchess of York
Henry	b. June 2, 1638	succeeded as second Earl
Edward I	christened April 9, 1640[1]	died July/August 1642
Laurence	christened March 15, 1642[1]	created Earl of Rochester
Edward II	christened April 1, 1645	student of Christ Church d. January 10, 1665 buried Westminster Abbey January 13[2]
Frances	? 1655[3]	married Thomas Keightley July 9, 1675
Charles	March 1658	On March 22, 1658 a secret letter from a Royalist in Holland to his contact in London, written in lemon juice but intercepted by Thurloe's agents and still legible: 'Sir Edward Hyde . . . his Lady is lately brought to bed of a son wh. the K: christens and the D. of Glo. stands for him . . . the Lady lyes in at Breda.' Mentioned by Sir Charles Cottrell in a letter to Hyde January 17, 1659: 'Mr Charles is a very grave gentleman'. Died March/April 1660[4]
James	March 1660	drowned 1682

Notes

All the children were by Frances, his second wife. The first daughter Anne was presumably named after the first wife who died of smallpox, having been prematurely delivered of a still-born child.

Henry was presumably named after Clarendon's father and the two Edwards after himself. Laurence was a common name in the family and had been borne by Clarendon's elder brother. Frances was, one imagines, named after her mother and Charles and James after the King and the Duke of York.

But who was 'your young soone Mince' who blotted his mother's letter on October 17, 1658?[5] Perhaps he came between Frances and Charles. Edward would have been beyond such infantile delinquencies.

Sources

1. *Parish Registers of St Margaret's Westminster* ed. Burke (1914).
2. *Westminster Abbey Registers* ed. J. L. Chester (1876).
3. Clar. MS f.32 'Frank asks her papa's blessing' September 29, 1658, described as 'borne at Breda' in a petition for naturalization (n.d. but c. December 1660) SP 29/23 f.109.
4. Rawl. A 63 f.251 (printed in *Thurloe State Papers* vi, 869);
   Cal. Clar. SP iv, 129, 610. *Clar. SP* iii 735.
5. Clar. MS 129 f.34.

Sources

1 *MSS Collections*

Bodleian Library
Clarendon MSS
Carte MSS
Tanner MSS
Sheldon MSS
Dolben Papers
Miscellaneous   Collections
identified in references.

British Library
Additional MSS
Althorp Papers
  [Spencer MSS]
Egerton MSS
Lansdowne MSS
Sloane MSS
Stowe MSS

Guildford Muniment Room
Broderick MSS

Kent CRO
Darnley MSS

Longleat
Bath MSS
Coventry MSS

Paris, Quai d'Orsay
Archives   des   affaires
  étrangères   (Angleterre)

Public Record Office
State Papers Domestic

2 *Printed*
Most of these will be found in the
Select Bibliography but the follow-
ing have primary status.

Clarendon State Papers 3 vols
  (1767–1786)
*Calendar of the Clarendon State
  Papers* 5 vols (1872–1970)
Commons Journals
Lords Journals
Cobbett's *Parliamentary History*
  vol iv
*Historical Manuscripts
  Commission*
Bath MSS
Finch MSS
Heathcote MSS
Ormonde MSS
Verulam MSS

A *Catalogue of the MSS . . . of
the great Earl of Clarendon*
Auction sale catalogue April
9–10, 1764. Samuel Baker,
bookseller.

T. H. LISTER. Life and administration of Lord Chancellor
Clarendon. 3 vols (1838)
Earliest and best of the
biographies. Prints a great
number of original docu-
ments, not always accurately

transcribed or dated. Lister was the first husband of Lady Theresa Lewis (see below).

WOOD. *Athenae Oxonienses* ed. Bliss 4 vols (1813).

The Correspondence of Henry Hyde, Earl of Clarendon and his brother Laurence Hyde, Earl of Rochester ed. Singer 2 vols (1828).

I have not listed the works of S. R. Gardiner and Sir Charles Firth to which reference is constantly made. But two works indispensable to any student of Clarendon and his world are the definitive editions of the two greatest diarists of the period.

The Diary of John Evelyn ed. E. S. de Beer 6 vols (1955).

The Diary of Samuel Pepys ed. R. C. Latham and W. Matthews 11 vols (1970–83)

Finally of Clarendon's own works the editions I have used are:

History of the Rebellion ed. Macray 6 vols (1888).

The Life and *Continuation of the Life* 2 vols (1857).

History of the Rebellion and Civil Wars in Ireland 1719–20 (see p. 272 n. 19) repr. 1849.

Religion and Policy and the countenance and assistance each should give to the other. With a survey of the power and jurisdiction of the Pope in the dominions of other princes. 2 vols (1811)

A Brief View & Survey of the Dangerous & Pernicious Errors to CHURCH and STATE in Mr Hobbes's Book entitled LEVIATHAN 2nd ed. (1676).

Animadversions upon a Book, Intituled Fanaticism Fanatically Imputed to the Catholick Church by Dr Stillingfleet, And the Imputation Refuted and Retorted by S[erenus] C[ressy]. By a person of Honour [i.e. Clarendon]. (1673)

A Collection of several Tracts of the Rt. Hon. Earl of Clarendon (1727)

Reliquiae Wottonianae 3rd ed. (1672)
pp. 184–202 'The Difference and Disparity between the Estate & Conditions of George, Duke of Buckingham, and Robert, Earl of Essex written by the Earl of Clarendon in his younger dayes' (see p. 24 n. 8).

Select Bibliography

The following is by no means a complete list of the works I have consulted in writing this book. In compiling it I had in mind two considerations: first, to supplement the list of sources: second, as a brief suggestion of further reading to any one who wanted more information on particular points. To this end I have sometimes indicated my opinion of the scope and quality of the work in question.

Dr Wormald's *Clarendon: Politics, History and Religion* is the starting-point of all scholarly study of the subject. Professor Trevor-Roper's two lectures on Clarendon, one delivered at Los Angeles in 1964 and the second before the University of Oxford ten years later, are superlative. This book would have gained much if it had not gone to press before the appearance in *Catholics, Anglicans, Puritans* of his essay on the Great Tew circle.

ABERNATHY, G. R., 'English Presbyterians and the Stuart Restoration 1648–1663' in *Trans. American Phil. Soc.* 55 part 2 (1965).
   'Clarendon and the Declaration of Indulgence' in *Journal of Eccles. History* II, pp. 55–75, marshals the arguments for Clarendon against charges of religious bigotry.
ASHLEY, Maurice, *General Monck* (1977).
BARBOUR, Violet, *Henry Bennet, earl of Arlington* (1914).
BARWICK, P., *The life of . . . John Barwick . . .* (1724).
BERKELEY, Sir John (Lord Berkeley of Stratton), 'Memoirs of Sir John Berkeley (1699)' reprinted as Appendix vi to vol 2 of *A Narrative by John Ashburnham* ed. Ashburnham (1830).
BINDOFF, S. T., 'The Parliamentary History of Wiltshire 1529–1688' in *VCH Wilts.* V (1957).
BROWNLEY, Martine Watson, *Clarendon and the Rhetoric of Historical Form* (Philadelphia, 1985), contains some interesting perceptions based on observant reading of the Clarendon MSS.
BURNET, Gilbert, *A History of My Own Time* part I, 2 vols ed. O. Airy (1897).
   A Supplement to [the above] ed. H. C. Foxcroft (1902).

CARTE, Thomas, *Original Letters* 2 vols (1739).
  Life of James, Duke of Ormond, 3 vols (1735–6).
CHESTER, J. L., *Westminster Abbey Registers* (1876).
COATE, Mary, *Cornwall in the Great Civil War and Interregnum* (1933), particularly valuable on Clarendon's relations with Sir John Grenville and Sir Robert Long.
  Letter Book of John, Viscount Mordaunt (ed.) (1945).
COOPER, J. P., 'The Fall of the Stuart Monarchy' in the *New Cambridge Modern History* vol iv.
COSIN, John, *Correspondence* ed. G. Ornsby 2 vols. Surtees Society (1869–1872).
DONNE, John, *Pseudomartyr* (1610). The source of a good deal of Clarendon's favourite quotations from Baronius and other ecclesiastical historians and controversialists.
FANSHAW, Sir Richard, *Original Letters and Negotiations* . . . (1724).
FEILING, Sir Keith, *British Foreign Policy 1660–72* (1925).
  A History of the Tory Party 1640–1714 (1924).
FRASER, Lady Antonia, *King Charles II* (1979), for a different view of the relations between Clarendon and his master.
GREEN, I. M., *The Re-establishment of the Church of England 1660–1663* (1978).
HARDACRE, P. H., 'Clarendon and the University of Oxford 1660–1667' in *British Journal of Educational Studies* ix (1960–1) pp. 117–131. A valuable account of Clarendon's Chancellorship.
HAVRAN, M. J., *Caroline Courtier: The Life of Lord Cottington* (1973).
HOLDSWORTH, W. S., *History of English Law* vol vi 2nd ea. (1937).
HOSKINS, S. E., *Charles II in the Channel Islands* 2 vols (1854), some interesting correspondence and first-hand evidence of Hyde's state of mind and style of life in 1647.
HUTTON, Ronald, *The Restoration: a Political and Religious History of England and Wales 1658–67* (1985), a modern account, by no means friendly to Clarendon, based on wide archival research which deserved a fuller apparatus and a proper index.
  'Clarendon's History of the Rebellion' *EHR* XCVII, no 382 pp. 70–88. A powerful and detailed criticism of Clarendon's use of evidence.
LEWIS, Lady Theresa, *Lives of the Friends and Contemporaries of Lord Chancellor Clarendon*. 3 vols. (1852), equally valuable for its information and its intelligence. The author was the widow of T. H. Lister, Clarendon's biographer, and the sister of Queen Victoria's Foreign Secretary, the fourth Earl of the second creation.
MARRIOTT, J. A. R., *The Life and Times of Lucius Cary, Viscount Falkland* (1907).
MAY, Thomas, *A Breviary of the History of the Parliament of England*. Imprimatur 10 June 1650. (1680)
  The History of the Parliament of England which began November 3rd 1640 . . . (1647).
MIDDLE TEMPLE RECORDS, Minutes of Parliament, ii 1603–49 ed. C. H. Hopwood (1904). p. 933 locates Hyde's chambers: 'A whole chamber

on the second floor in the new buildings in Pumpe Court on the north side, on the west side of the buildings.'

[MORLEY] George, Lord Bishop of Winton, *Several Treatises* . . . (1683).

NICHOLAS PAPERS ed. Warner 4 vols Camden Society. (1886–1920).

OGG, David, *England in the Reign of Charles II*. 2 vols 2nd ed. (1956).

RAMSEY, R. W., *Studies in Cromwell's Family Circle* (1930), good account of Clarendon's unfortunate cousin, Sir Henry Hyde.

ROBERTS, Clayton, 'The Impeachment of the Earl Of Clarendon' in *Cambridge Historical Journal* XIII (1957) pp. 1–18.

ROEBUCK, Graham, *Clarendon and Cultural Continuity: A Bibliographical Study* (1981), the only modern bibliography.

SPALDING, Ruth, *The Improbable Puritan: a Life of Bulstrode Whitelocke 1605–75* (1975).

STEMMATA SHIRLEIANA 2nd ed. (1873), contains interesting information on the connexions of Sir Robert Shirley.

STOYE, J. W., *English Travellers Abroad 1604–1667* (1952 repr. New York 1968), has a fascinating chapter on Clarendon's scapegrace brother-in-law, William Aylesbury.

THEOLOGIAN AND ECCLESIASTIC vol vi (1848) vol vii (1849) vol ix (1850) vols xi and xii (1851) vol xiii (1852) vol xv (1853), prints much valuable correspondence of Clarendon's Great Tew friends during the Interregnum.

TREVOR-ROPER, H. R., 'Clarendon and the Practice of History' in *Milton and Clarendon* (Los Angeles 1965).

Edward Hyde, Earl of Clarendon (Oxford 1975).

TULLOCH, J., *Rational Theology and Christian Philosophy in Seventeenth Century England* 2 vols. (1872 2nd ed. 1874).

UNDERDOWN, David, *Royalist Conspiracy in England 1649–60* (Yale 1960).

VALE, V., 'Clarendon, Coventry and the sale of naval offices 1660–8' in *Cambridge Historical Journal* XII (1956) pp. 107–125.

WALKER, Sir Edward, *Historical Discourses* ed. Hugh Clopton (1705).

WEBER, Kurt, *Lucius Cary, 2nd Viscount Falkland* (N.Y. 1940), gives a good account of the Great Tew circle.

WHITELOCKE, Bulstrode, *Memorials* . . . n. e. (1732).

WHITEMAN, Anne, 'The Church of England Restored' in *From Uniformity to Unity* ed. G. F. Nuttall and O. Chadwick (1962).

WILTSHIRE ARCHAEOLOGICAL AND NATURAL HISTORY MAGAZINE vols xiii and xxiv, much valuable topographical and family material.

WORMALD, B. H. G., *Clarendon: Politics, History and Religion, 1640–1660* (Cambridge 1951: repr. Chicago 1976).

Index

Note:

In these entries I have tried not to repeat what is stated in, or easily deducible from, the table of contents. The omission of some names or topics and the inclusion of others is determined by the necessities of signposting, not by their relative importance. And the treatment of some figures who play a great part — Charles II for instance — is on the same principle eclectic.

The abbreviation 'C' stands for Clarendon.